SECOND EDITION

The Prentice Hall Reader

GEORGE MILLER
University of Delaware

PRENTICE HALL
Englewood Cliffs, New Jersey

Library of Congress Cataloging-in-Publication Data

The Prentice-Hall reader / [compiled by] George Miller. — 2nd ed.
p. cm.
ISBN 0-13-706103-X
1. College readers. 2. English language—Rhetoric. I. Miller.
George. II. Prentice-Hall, Inc.
PE1417.P74 1989 88-28283
808′.0427—dc19 CIP

For Lisa, her book

Editorial/production supervision and interior design: Virginia Rubens
Development editor: Irwin L. Zucker
Cover design: Lundgren Graphics, Ltd.
Manufacturing buyer: Laura Crossland

On the cover:

Edward Hopper, *The Lighthouse at Two Lights* (1929).
The Metropolitan Museum of Art, Hugo Kastor Fund, 1962.

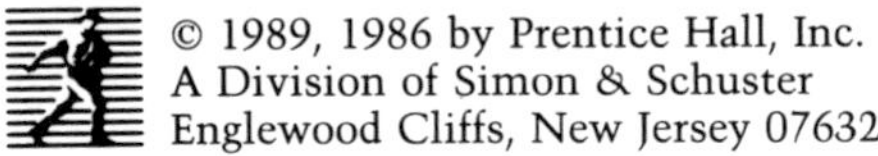

Printed in the United States of America
10 9 8 7 6 5 4 3

ISBN 0-13-706103-X 01

Prentice-Hall International (UK) Limited, *London*
Prentice-Hall of Australia Pty. Limited, *Sydney*
Prentice-Hall Canada Inc., *Toronto*
Prentice-Hall Hispanoamericana, S.A., *Mexico*
Prentice-Hall of India Private Limited, *New Delhi*
Prentice-Hall of Japan, Inc., *Tokyo*
Simon & Schuster Asia Pte. Ltd., *Singapore*
Editora Prentice-Hall do Brasil, Ltda., *Rio de Janeiro*

Contents

2
Narration 61

3
Description 101

5
Comparision and Contrast 197

6
Process 251

9
Argumentation and Persuasion 413

10
Revision 489

Preface

The Prentice Hall Reader is predicated on two premises: that reading plays a vital role in learning how to write and that writing and reading can best be organized around the traditional division of discourse into a number of structural patterns. Such a division is not the only way that the forms of writing can be classified, but it does have several advantages.

First, practice in these structural patterns encourages students to organize knowledge and to see the ways in which information can be conveyed. How else does the mind know except by classifying, comparing, defining, or seeking cause and effect relationships? Second, the most common use of these patterns occurs in writing done in academic courses. There students are asked to narrate a chain of events, to describe an artistic style, to classify plant forms, to compare two political systems, to tell how a laboratory experiment was performed, to analyze why famine occurs in Africa, to define a philosophical concept, or to argue for or against a nuclear freeze. Learning how to structure papers using these patterns is an exercise that has immediate application in students' other academic work. Finally, because the readings use these patterns as structural devices, they offer an excellent way in which to integrate reading into a writing course. Students can see the patterns at work and learn how to use them to become more effective writers and better, more efficient readers.

To these ends, the second edition of *The Prentice Hall Reader* includes 62 selections, ranging from classic to contemporary essays. Some of the selections and nearly all of the writers are old friends, but some fresh selections by young writers are included as well. Each reading was chosen to demonstrate the pattern under discussion and to be accessible to the college freshman.

What Is Different About This Book?

Even though rhetorically organized readers have similar tables of contents, they are not all alike. The second edition of *The Prentice Hall Reader* contains a number of unique or substantially different features that make it easier for students to use in learning how to write.

Prose in Revision

As every writing instructor knows, getting students to revise is never an easy matter. Having written a paper, most students do not even want to see it again, let alone revise it. Furthermore, for many students revising means making word substitutions and correcting grammatical and mechanical errors—changes that instructors rightfully regard as proofreading, not revising. To help make the need for revision more vivid and to show how writers revise, the second edition of *The Prentice Hall Reader* includes four features.

1. The final chapter, "Revision," presents seven selections by professional writers showing a final draft and an earlier version. These selections were *not* commissioned for this reader; they are actual drafts of previously published works. Each example is accompanied by discussion questions that focus attention on *how* the writer revised. The writers who graciously agreed to share their revisions include Andrew Ward, Nora Ephron, Chuck Stone, James Villas, Susan Allen Toth, William Ouchi, and Joseph Epstein.
2. The introduction to each chapter of readings includes a first draft of a student essay, a comment on the draft's strengths and weaknesses, and a final, revised version. These essays, realistic examples of student writing, model the student revision process.
3. The introduction to the final chapter includes advice to students on how to revise a paper. This section, intended to

supplement classroom activities, is written to the student and provides some simple tips on what to do when revising.

4. The second writing suggestion after each selection, which asks students to write an essay, is accompanied by prewriting and rewriting activities. In all, the text provides about 180 specific rewriting activities. These activities are designed to help students to organize ideas and to revise what they have written.

Selections

The second edition of *The Prentice Hall Reader* includes a large number of selections to offer the instructor maximum flexibility in choosing readings. No chapter has fewer than five selections and most have six or more. The readings are scaled in terms of length and sophistication. Each chapter begins with at least one brief example of the pattern under discussion, includes two or more relatively short selections, and concludes with at least one longer, more complex example.

Writing Suggestions

Each selection is followed by three writing suggestions: the first calls for a paragraph-length response; the second, an essay; and the third, an essay involving research. Each of the three suggestions is related to the content of the reading to which it is attached, and each calls for a response in the particular pattern being studied. In the second edition, the emphasis on the writing process is increased through the addition of prewriting and rewriting activities after the second writing suggestion for each selection.

Introductions

The introduction to each chapter offers clear and succinct advice to the student on how to write that particular type of paragraph or essay. The introductions anticipate students' questions, provide answers, and end with a checklist, titled "Some Things to Remember," to remind students of the major concerns they should have when writing in a particular pattern.

Annotated Instructor's Edition

An annotated edition of the second edition of *The Prentice Hall Reader* is available to instructors. Each of the selections in the text is annotated with teaching suggestions, additional classroom activities, important background information, and sample responses to the discussion questions. The marginal annotations emphasize how to teach each selection and how to develop class discussions, focusing on how each essay works as a piece of writing.

The Structure of This Book

After an introductory chapter on writing and reading and the writing process, the next nine chapters follow a similar approach. Each chapter begins with an introduction to the pattern, which includes two drafts of a student essay and ends with a checklist.

The writing selections begin with example because example is essential in any type of effective writing. Narration and description are treated next, with a special emphasis on how each is used in expository writing. The key patterns of expository development—division, comparison and contrast, process, and cause and effect—follow. Definition, because it can include all of the other patterns, is placed at the end of the expository section. Argumentation and persuasion is the penultimate and largest chapter. A final chapter offers seven examples of revised prose by professional writers. An appendix—"How to Read an Essay"—further discusses critical reading and includes a sample analyzed essay.

Each selection has three groups of questions: a set on subject and purpose, directing the student to what was written about and why; a set on strategy and audience, asking the student to analyze how the essay is structured and how it is influenced by its intended audience; and a set on vocabulary and style, focusing attention on how style and language contribute to purpose. The apparatus after each reading also includes three writing suggestions. For the second of these three, specific prewriting and rewriting activities are given.

A glossary of terms can be found at the back of the text. For those intructors who wish to use the readings in a way other than the rhetorical organization, two additional tables of contents are included: one arranged by subject and a second by intended audience (this one is found in the Annotated Instructor's Edition). Sample syllabi keyed to the text and additional classroom activities are also found in the Annotated Instructor's Edition.

What Is New in the Second Edition

The second edition of *The Prentice Hall Reader* features 62 selections (there were 60 in the first edition), 18 of which are new. As in the first edition, the readings are chosen on the basis of how well they demonstrate a particular pattern of organization, appeal to a freshman audience, and promote interesting and appropriate discussion and writing activities. An appendix, "How to Read an Essay," which includes a sample analyzed essay, has been added. Some of the discussion questions have been changed; others have been reworded to be more precise. New writing suggestions have been added, as have prewriting and rewriting activities. In all, the second edition of *The Prentice Hall Reader* provides about 180 writing suggestions and about 360 prewriting and rewriting activities. An Annotated Instructor's Edition with marginal notes—the first ever for a college reader—does away with the awkwardness of a separate Teacher's Manual.

ACKNOWLEDGMENTS

Although writing is a solitary activity, no one can write without the assistance of others. This text owes much to many people: To the staff at Prentice Hall who played a large role in planning and developing this reader, especially Philip Miller, as sympathetic and supportive an executive editor as an author could find; Lynne Rosenfeld, the editor for the second edition, who has promoted the project in every way; Jane Baumann, editorial assistant; Cecil Yarbrough, the development editor on the first edition; Irwin Zucker, the development editor on this edition, who worried with me and for me over every word in the book; Hilda Tauber and Virginia Rubens, the production editors; and Carol Carter, Prentice Hall's tireless marketing manager.

To my reviewers, who wrote extensive critiques of the manuscript and saved me from many embarrassments: Mary M. Blackburn, University of South Alabama, Mobile; Janet Eber, County College of Morris, Randolph, N.J.; Evelyn A. Elder, Montgomery College, Rockville, Md.; Edward H. Garcia, Cedar Valley College, Lancaster, Texas; John Hagaman, Western Kentucky University, Bowling Green; Jay Jernigan, Eastern Michigan University, Ypsilanti, Mich.; Peggy Jolly, University of Alabama at Birmingham; Don Nemanich, West Virginia Northern Community College, Wheeling, W.Va.; Suzanne C. Padgett, Shelby State Community College, Memphis, Tenn.; Carole M. Sherman, College of DuPage, Glen Ellyn, Ill.; John T. Smith, North Texas State University, Denton, Texas; Haskell Springer, University of Kansas, Lawrence; Josephine Koster Tarvers, Rutgers University, New Brunswick, N.J., and Karen W. Willingham, Pensacola Junior College, Pensacola, Fla.

To my editorial assistants on the first edition—Susan Kubica Howard, Jan Thompson, Allison Foote, and Anthony Bernardo. To Meoghan Byrne, my editorial assistant on the second edition, without whose help and energy no deadlines would have been met. To the writing staff at the University of Delaware and the students in my own writing classes who tested materials, offered suggestions, and contributed essays to the introductions. To my secretary, Deborah Lyall, who for thirteen years has made the chore of writing and rewriting easier. And finally to my wife, Rachel, who always understands and encourages, and my children, Lisa, Jon, Craig, Valerie, and Eric, who have learned over the years to live with a father who writes.

Introduction

How Does Reading Help You Write?

You read in a writing course for three purposes. First, readings are a source of information: you learn by reading and what you learn can then, in turn, be used in your writing. Any paper that involves research requires selective, critical reading on your part as you search for and evaluate sources. Second, readings offer a perspective on a particular subject, one with which you might agree or disagree. In this sense readings can serve as catalysts or stimuli to provoke writing. Many of the writing suggestions in this text are outgrowths of the readings. You are asked to explore some aspect of the subject more fully, to employ the same type of strategy with a different subject, to reply to a writer's position, or to expand on or refine that position. And finally, readings offer models to a writer; they show you how another writer dealt with a particular subject.

The first two purposes—readings as a source of information or as a stimulus to writing—are fairly obvious, but the third might seem confusing. Exactly how are you as a writer to use an example of professional writing as a model? Are you supposed to sound like E. B. White or Joan Didion or Maya Angelou? Are you to mimic their styles or their approaches to a subject? To model in the sense that it is being used here does not mean to produce a slavish imitation. You are not expected to construct your papers in exactly the same ways that these writers do, nor are you expected to imitate their style, tone, or approach. Rather, what you can learn from these writers is how to handle information; how to adapt writing to a particular audience; how to structure the body of an essay; how to begin, make transitions, and end; how to achieve effective paragraphs and sentence variety. In short, the readings are examples of writing techniques.

You learn to write effectively in the same way that you learn to do any other activity. You study the rules or advice on how it is done; you practice, especially under the watchful eye of an instructor or a coach; and you study how others have mastered similar problems and techniques. A young musician learns how to read music and play an instrument, practices daily, studies with a teacher, and listens to and watches how other musicians play. A baseball player learns the proper offensive and defensive techniques, practices daily, is supervised by a coach, and listens to the advice and watches the performance of other players. As a writer in a writing class, you do the same thing: follow the advice offered by your instructor and textbooks, practice by writing and revising, listen to the advice and suggestions of your fellow students, and study the work of other writers.

How Does Writing Help You Read?

The interaction between reading and writing works in both ways: by becoming a good writer you will also become a more effective reader. As a writer you learn how to put an essay together, how to use examples to support a thesis, how to structure an argument, how to make an effective transition from one point to another. You learn how to write beginnings, middles, and ends, and most especially you learn how essays can be organized. For example, you know that a comparison and contrast paper can be organized either by the subject-by-subject or the point-by-point pattern. You know that narratives are structured in time and that cause and effect analyses are linear and sequential. As a result, when you read an essay you look for structure and pattern, realizing that such devices are not only creative tools you use in writing but also analytic ones you can use in reading. They help you understand what the essay says by revealing to you an underlying organizational pattern. In order to become an efficient reader, however, you need to exercise the same care and attention that you do when you write. You do that by becoming an active rather than a passive reader.

Active Rather Than Passive Reading

Every reader first reads a piece of writing for plot or subject matter. On that level, the reader wants to know what happens, what is the subject, whether it is new or interesting. Generally that first reading is done quickly, even, in a sense, superficially. The reader is a spectator waiting passively to be entertained or informed. Only after the reader's curiosity about plot or subjects has been satisfied does the next stage of active reading begin. On this level, the reader asks questions, seeks answers, looks for organizational structures, and concentrates on the thesis and the quality of evidence presented. Careful reading requires this active participation of the reader.

For this reason you should never read any piece of writing just once. It is easy to assume that if you have read the essay assigned for tomorrow's class once, you are prepared. But after that first reading you should return to the selection for a slower, more careful, more active reading. Now that you know in a general sense what the essay is about, you can look at it critically or analytically. As a guide to this rereading, ask yourself these questions:

1. What is the writer's thesis? What particular point is the writer trying to make about the subject? How do the examples of evidence contribute to defining or developing that thesis?
2. To whom is the writer writing? Where did the selection first appear? How does the intended audience help shape the essay or control the language used?
3. How is the essay structured? How are the individual parts—the paragraphs or groups of paragraphs—integrated into a whole?
4. Do I understand what is being said in each sentence?
5. Do I know the meaning of every word the author uses?

Your rereading should also involve answering, at least to yourself, the specific questions that follow each selection in this anthology. Only when you have actively involved yourself with the selection will you clearly understand what the writer was trying to do. The process of actively reading prose is really no different from what you do when you read a poem. With a poem you expect to have to reread and to study what is being said.

Learning to read actively and critically is an important skill—one crucial not just in English courses but in every academic course and even in every job situation. In a piece of writing some things are always more important than others. As an efficient reader, you need to isolate those important points and concentrate on them. If you are studying for an examination and find that you have underlined most of your text or have copied out large sections from the assigned readings, you have not spent enough time looking critically at what you have read. You have not actively involved yourself in the reading process. Active reading promotes understanding and also saves time.

A Writer's Purpose

A writer writes to fulfill three fundamental purposes: to entertain, to inform, or to persuade. Obviously, though, the purposes are not necessarily separate or discrete. All three can be found together: an interesting, maybe even humorous, essay that documents the health hazards caused by cigarettes can, at the same time, attempt to persuade readers to give up smoking. In this case the main purpose is still persuasion; entertainment and information play subordinate roles in catching the reader's interest and in documenting with appropriate evidence the argument being advanced.

These three purposes are generally associated with the traditional division of writing into four forms—narration, description, exposition (including division, comparison and contrast, process, cause and effect, and definition), and argumentation. A narrative or descriptive essay typically tells a story or describes a person, object, or place in order to entertain a reader and recreate the experience. Maya Angelou in "Sister Monroe" and Langston Hughes in "Salvation" artfully narrate events from their past. William Allen White in "Mary White" and William Least Heat Moon in "Nameless, Tennessee" recreate for their readers through descriptive detail a person and a place. Expository essays primarily provide information for a reader. Bernard Berelson in "The Value of Children" dispassionately analyzes the reasons why people want to have children; Bruce Catton in "Grant and Lee" explains how these two Civil War generals were symbols of two forces at work in America; Peter Elbow in "Quick Revising" tells how to revise (quickly) a piece of writing; Andrew Revkin in "Hard Facts About Nuclear Winter" describes a controversial possible effect of a nuclear war; and Marie Winn in "TV Addiction" defines what it means to be "hooked" on television. Argumentative or persuasive essays, on the other hand, seek to move a reader, to gain support, to advocate a particular type of action. Jesse Jackson in "Why Blacks Need Affirmative Action" and Marya Mannes in "Wasteland" both seek to arouse a response in a reader—one works with logic and factual evidence, the other with emotional appeal.

As you read each selection, try to determine which of the purposes are exhibited and which seems to be primary.

A Writer's Subject and Thesis

A subject is what a piece of writing is about; a thesis is a particular idea or assertion about that subject. Bruce Catton's subject in "Grant and Lee" is the two generals; his thesis is that the two represented or symbolized "two diametrically opposed elements in American life." Lewis Thomas in "On Medicine and the Bomb" writes about what medicine can and cannot do in saving victims of cancer, burns, and trauma. His thesis is that medicine has "nothing whatever to offer, not even a token benefit, in the event of thermonuclear war." A thesis is not always clearly or even explicitly stated. Susan Allen Toth in "Cinematypes" classifies the men who take her to the movies and compares them and her experiences with the fun that she has alone, watching films in which "the men and women always like each other." Toth leaves the reader to infer that solitariness can be fun and is certainly preferable to neurotic relationships. Judy Syfers in "I Want a Wife" catalogs the stereotypical male demands in marriage but never explicitly states a thesis or argues for a course of action. Are her readers to avoid marriage, divorce their husbands, insist on a premaritial contract specifying joint responsibilities?

When you read, watch for an explicit or implicit statement of thesis: try to find or create a single sentence that defines the thesis. Remember that a thesis is a central and controlling idea, the thread that holds the essay together.

A Writer's Audience

Audience is a key factor in every writing situation, although it is one that may not have played a significant role in your writing in the past. Most of the writing that you have done in academic courses has been intended only for the instructor. Such writing essentially involves an audience of one. However, outside of college, a piece of writing always has many possible readers. An effective writer learns to adjust to an audience and to write for that audience; for a writer, like a performer, needs and wants an audience. The awareness of audience shapes every aspect of the written product from choosing a subject to creating an appropriate style.

In "Cut," for example, Bob Greene writes about being cut from a junior high school basketball team, narrating his own experience and that of four other men. Greene's essay originally appeared in *Esquire*, a magazine intended for and read by young successful men, an audience likely to be interested in such a subject. That audience, moreover, would also probably accept Greene's thesis—that being cut made each man a superachiever later in life—without proper statistical evidence. Greene's subject and approach would have been inappropriate for a general circulation magazine, or a sports magazine, or even a magazine that would have an audience more critical of his evidence (such as *Psychology Today*). On the other hand, Judith Viorst in "How Books Helped Shape My Life" traces the influence of fictional heroines on her own personality, showing how they served "as ideals, as models, as possibilities." Her essay originally appeared in *Redbook*, a magazine targeted at an audience of women between the ages of 18 and 34.

Writers adjust their style and tone on a spectrum ranging from informal to formal. Bob Greene and Judith Viorst adopt a language and a style that is almost conversational. They write in the first person, use contractions, favor popular and colloquial words, write relatively short sentences and paragraphs, and sometimes use sentence fragments. At the opposite end of the spectrum, Bernard Berelson in "The Value of Children" and William Ouchi in "Why We Need to Learn" use a more formal style that involves an objective and serious tone, a more learned vocabulary, and longer and more complicated sentence and paragraph constructions. In the informal style the writer injects his or her personality into the prose; in the formal style the writer remains detached and impersonal. A writer adopts whatever style seems appropriate for a particular audience or context. An effective writer does not have just one style or voice, but many.

When you read, try to characterize the audience being addressed. Where was the selection originally published? What do you know or what might you guess about the composition of that intended audience? Its age? Its values? Its prejudices? Its interests? How does the writer's choice of subject reflect that audience? How are the language, the tone, the sentence structures, and the paragraphing influenced by that audience?

A Final Word on the Writing Process

Writing a paper, no matter how long it is, always involves a series of activities or a process that you follow. That process is normally divided into three stages: prewriting or planning, writing, and rewriting or revising. Although the stages are sequential, that does not mean that writers necessarily complete each one before moving on to the others. More often, writers move back and forth—planning, jotting down ideas, drafting sentences or paragraphs, rejecting those sentences and paragraphs, and moving back to planning again. In short, the writing process is recursive—it turns back upon itself rather than moving only forward.

Even though the three stages do blend into one another, it is still important to recognize that each stage is a necessary part of the writing process. If you try to save time by skipping a stage or by compressing it into as little time as possible, you are inviting problems. It is in this area of allotting time that professional and student writers differ most markedly. A professional writer knows that before he or she can write, information must be gathered. A newspaper reporter interviews sources, reads previously published background articles, gathers new information, and only then begins to write. Even an autobiographer spends time sifting experiences, recalling events, ordering details before writing. That prewriting or information-gathering stage can last for days, weeks, even months. As a student you can rarely afford to devote that much time to planning an essay, especially if writing assignments are made weekly or biweekly. On the other hand, if you do not spend time gathering your information first, if you try to plunge immediately into writing, you will discover that writing becomes much more difficult. Instead of trying to select and organize information, you are forced to do the gathering, organizing, and writing at the same time.

The same problem occurs in the rewriting or revising stage. Revising does not mean just substituting words or making grammatical and mechanical corrections. Instead, revision should take place on every level, from the choice of a subject and thesis, to the organizational pattern used, to the structure of paragraphs and sentences, and even to the selection of individual words. In order to revise effectively, you need to get some distance from what you have written, and distance comes in part with elapsed time. Ideally, you should allow at least a day to pass before you return to a piece of writing. Even more time is preferable. If you are forced to compress the writing and revising stages together, you will not be revising, you will just be proofreading.

CHAPTER 1

Example

Effective writing in any form depends upon examples. Without them you are forced to rely on generalizations. Examples make writing vivid; they represent particular instances that illustrate the points you are trying to make. That general statement needs an example.

Life magazine asked writer Malcolm Cowley for an essay on what it was like to turn 80. The result was "The View from 80." Since nearly all of his readers would be less than 80, Cowley needed to show his readers what it was like to be "old." He does so through a series of examples, including at one point a simple list that begins like this:

> The body and its surroundings have their messages for him, or only one message: "You are old." Here are some of the occasions on which he receives the message:
> —when it becomes an achievement to do thoughtfully, step by step, what he once did instinctively
> —when his bones ache
> —when there are more and more little bottles in the medicine cabinet, with instructions for taking four times a day
> —when he fumbles and drops his toothbrush (butterfingers)
> —when his face has bumps and wrinkles, so that he cuts himself while shaving (blood on the towel)
> —when year by year his feet seem farther from his hands
> —when he can't stand on one leg and has trouble pulling on his pants
> —when he hesitates on the landing before walking down a flight of stairs

—when he spends more time looking for things misplaced than he spends using them after he (or more often his wife) has found them
—when he falls asleep in the afternoon
—when it becomes harder to bear in mind two things at once
—when a pretty girl passes him in the street and he doesn't turn his head*

Cowley's list of examples is atypical. Most writing tasks do not involve quite so many illustrations, and most demand that the examples be worked into the paragraphs rather than set apart in a list.

How Important Are Examples?

Examples are very important because failing to provide examples or illustrations almost inevitably leads to ineffective writing. When you write without having enough information, you are forced to rely on generalizations or commonplace observations. Joan Didion could have stated her thesis in several sentences devoid of examples: "It is absurd and somehow appropriate to have twenty-four-hour wedding 'chapels' in such a gaudy and bizarre city as Las Vegas." Instead, she includes a series of details and examples: the legal requirements for marriage in Nevada, the hours during which licenses can be obtained, the marriage marathon of 1965, the advertisements of the nineteen wedding chapels, the typical wedding, and even two particular brides. The examples capture for the reader the absurdity and the tackiness of turning marriage into something analogous to a fast-food operation.

How Many Examples Are Enough?

It would make every writer's job much easier if there were a single, simple answer to the question of how many examples to use. Instead, the answer is "enough to do the job,"

*From *The View from 80* by Malcolm Cowley. Copyright © 1980 by Malcolm Cowley. Reprinted by permission of Viking Penguin Inc.

"enough to persuade the reader," "enough to convince the reader that you know what you are talking about." Sometimes one fully developed example might be enough. The advertisements for organizations such as Save the Children often tell the story of a specific child in need of food and shelter. The single example, accompanied with a photograph, is enough to persuade many people to sponsor a child. Tom Wolfe in the opening paragraphs of his essay "A Sunday Kind of Love" focuses on one example: two teenagers lost in a kiss at 8:45 A.M. in a New York City subway station on a weekday. That example of "love at rush hour" set against the swirl of hurrying people with "no time" for such behavior represents the type of experience normally set apart for Sundays in New York.

Other times you might need to use many examples. In "Cut," for instance, Bob Greene writes about how being "cut" from the junior high school basketball team changed his life. To support his thesis and extend it beyond his own personal experience, Greene includes the stories of four other men who had similar experiences. But why four examples? Why not three or five or seven? There is nothing magical about the number four—Greene might have used four because he had space for four—but the four give authority to Greene's assertion, or at least they create the illusion of authority. To prove the validity of Greene's thesis would require a proper statistical sample. Only then could it be said with certainty that the experience of being "cut" makes men superachievers later in life. In most writing situations, however, such thoroughness is not needed. If the examples are well chosen and relevant, the reader is likely to accept your assertions.

Where Can You Find Examples?

Unfortunately, finding examples to use is generally not an easy matter. Even when you are narrating an experience that happened to you or describing something that you saw or presenting a personal opinion, you will have to spend some time remembering the events, sorting out the details of the experience, or deciding just exactly what it is that you believe. If you are presenting information about a subject outside of yourself, your problems are even greater. No matter how much you once knew about a subject, you forget specific details. Remember all the studying you did for a history course—all the dates, names, theories, and interpretations that you had on instant recall the day of the examination? A semester or a year later, how much can you remember? If the subject is totally new, you will have to gather examples from sources outside of yourself.

Before she began writing "Marrying Absurd," Joan Didion probably did not know any more about her subject than anyone else. Yet her essay depends upon a series of details and examples. Such information could only be gathered through extensive research. In the process Didion surely uncovered more information than she could possibly have used. Probably she made her final selection of examples only after she began to write. Nevertheless, without that research, she could never have written the essay.

You do not necessarily have to go to a library in search of examples, for they can also be found in a number of other places. Your memories, your experiences, and your observations can be good places to begin. In writing "Computer Fallout," Russell Baker found a ready source of examples in his own experience with word processors. Other people can also be excellent sources. The examples of college slang in William Safire's "Words for Nerds" come from students at a number of eastern colleges and universities. Given the short-lived nature of such words, the library would probably not be a good place to look for examples of similar expressions used at your school. Surely most of the examples in Robin Lakoff's "You Are What You Say" were the result of a careful study and analysis of what people say.

Using Examples: A Student Paragraph

Charles Jenkins chose to write a paragraph that added to the examples of campus slang William Safire had compiled in "Words for Nerds." His first draft appears below:

Some Examples of Campus Slang

> "How'd ya do on the exam?" "I *aced* it. How about you?" "I *bombed* it, *big time.* I think I'll just *bag* my class and go *crash.*" Confused? Does it sound like a foreign language? No, it is still English, but with frequent interjections of college slang found on many campuses such as here at the University of Delaware. Campus slang, in itself, is nothing new, but is a constantly changing phenomenon. Old expressions fade away and new ones rise to take their places just as new students replace old students. Now it is time for some translations. "Acing" an exam or "getting an ace" is a reference to getting an A on that exam. On the other hand, "bombing" or "bombing, big time" evokes images of a disaster or failure, and that is precisely what it means, to fail or fail miserably. Slang on campus, however, is not limited to exams. "Bagging" class is today's form of yesterday's practice of "cutting" class. After a student has "bagged" or "cut" his class, he is likely to go "crash." To "crash" is to go back to the dorm and sleep. "Crashing" could be a reference to the sound made when a tired student flops into bed after a tough day; it is unclear. The surface has been barely scratched in campus slang; a full exposition would take much longer, but at least you won't be totally in the dark.

When Charles came to revise his paragraph, he had his instructor's comments and the reactions of several classmates. Everyone had agreed that he had chosen good examples and, by using them in an imagined dialogue, had caught his readers' attention. Charles was troubled by his final sentence, but was not sure how else to conclude. After the class had discussed slang and how quickly it changes, he found an idea for a new concluding sentence— one that was more in keeping with the tone he had established. Charles changed several sentences to avoid empty generalizations and clichés—phrases such as "old expressions fade away," "surface barely scratched," and "won't be totally in the dark." In the time between drafts, Charles found another example to add as well. The revision follows:

Example

Some Strange New Words on Campus

"How'd ya do on the exam?"

"I *aced* it. How about you?"

"I *bombed* it, *big time*. I think I'll just *bag* my classes and go *crash*."

Confused? Does it sound like a foreign language? No, it is still English, but with frequent interjections of college slang found on many campuses such as here at the University of Delaware. Campus slang, in itself, is nothing new, but it is a constantly changing phenomenon. Now it is time for a translation. The phrase "acing an exam" or "getting an ace" is today's campus terminology for getting an A. On the other hand, "bombing" or "bombing, big time" evokes images of a disaster or a failure, and that is precisely what it means, to fail or fail miserably. Campus slang, however, is not limited to exams. "Bagging" class is today's term for yesterday's practice of "cutting" class. After a student has "bagged" his classes, he is likely to go "crash." To "crash" is to go back to the dorm and sleep. "Crashing" might be a reference to the sound made when a tired student flops into bed after a tough day. Even the social life on campus is not immune to the use of slang. Consider the word "scope," a shortened form of "telescope." "Scope" can be used as either a noun or a verb. To "scope" is to spend time gazing longingly at members of the opposite sex. As a noun, it is most often used to refer to the one person, who after many hours of "scoping," you find especially enchanting. If you don't understand all these strange new words, don't worry—they will soon be as obsolete as "cool" and "peachy keen."

Some Things to Remember

1. Use examples—effective writing depends upon them.
2. The number of examples necessarily varies. Sometimes one will do; sometimes you will need many. If you want your readers to do or to believe something, you will need to supply some evidence to gain their support or confidence.
3. Since you can never remember everything you once knew, you need to go outside of your own memory to

gather examples and illustrations. In short, finding examples often requires some type of research.

4. Choose examples that are relevant and accurate. Quality is more important than quantity. Make sure your examples support your argument or illustrate the points you are trying to make. If you use an outside authority—either an oral or a printed source—make sure that the source is knowledgeable and reliable.

A Sunday Kind of Love

TOM WOLFE

Tom Wolfe was born in Richmond, Virginia, in 1931 and received a Ph.D. in American Studies from Yale in 1957. He worked for the Washington Post *before joining the staff of the* New York Herald Tribune's *Sunday magazine,* New York, *in 1962, where he developed the flamboyant style and interest in new trends in popular culture that have become his trademark. His books include* The Kandy-Kolored Tangerine-Flake Streamline Baby *(1965),* The Electric Kool-Aid Acid Test *(1968),* Mauve Gloves & Madmen, Clutter & Vine *(1976),* From Bauhaus to Our House *(1981), and* The Purple Decades *(1983). In 1987 he published his first novel,* The Bonfire of the Vanities, *a work that was originally serialized in* Rolling Stone, *beginning in 1984.* The Right Stuff *(1979), a history of the early space program, won the American Book Award. Much of Wolfe's writing has appeared in* Esquire, Harper's *and* Rolling Stone, *where he cheerfully deflates contemporary society's vanities. In these paragraphs from the beginning of his essay "A Sunday Kind of Love," Wolfe describes two kids lost in a kiss at 8:45 on a weekday morning during the subway rush hour. What could be more improbable in a city where real love has to wait until Sunday?*

Love! Attar of libido in the air! It is 8:45 A.M. Thursday 1
morning in the IRT subway station at 50th Street and Broadway and already two kids are hung up in a kind of herringbone weave of arms and legs, which proves, one has to admit, that love is not *confined* to Sunday in New York. Still, the odds! All the faces come popping in clots out of the Seventh Avenue local, past the King Size Ice Cream machine, and the turnstiles start whacking away as if the world were breaking up on the reefs. Four steps past the turnstiles everybody is already backed up haunch to paunch for the climb up the ramp and the stairs to the surface, a great funnel of flesh, wool, felt, leather, rubber and steam-

ing alumicron, with the blood squeezing through everybody's old sclerotic arteries in hopped-up spurts from too much coffee and the effort of surfacing from the subway at the rush hour. Yet there on the landing are a boy and a girl, both about eighteen, in one of those utter, My Sin, backbreaking embraces.

He envelops her not only with his arms but with his chest, which has the American teen-ager concave shape to it. She has her head cocked at a 90-degree angle and they both have their eyes pressed shut for all they are worth and some incredibly feverish action going with each other's mouths. All round them, tens, scores, it seems like hundreds, of faces and bodies are perspiring, trooping and bellying up the stairs with arteriosclerotic grimaces past a showcase full of such novel items as Joy Buzzers, Squirting Nickels, Finger Rats, Scary Tarantulas and spoons with realistic dead flies on them, past Fred's barbershop, which is just off the landing and has glossy photographs of young men with the kind of baroque haircuts one can get in there, and up onto 50th Street into a madhouse of traffic and shops with weird lingerie and gray hair-dyeing displays in the windows, signs for free teacup readings and a pool-playing match between the Playboy Bunnies and Downey's Showgirls, and then everybody pounds on toward the Time-Life Building, the Brill Building or NBC. 2

The boy and the girl just keep on writhing in their embroilment. Her hand is sliding up the back of his neck, which he turns when her fingers wander into the intricate formal gardens of his Chicago Boxcar hairdo at the base of the skull. The turn causes his face to start to mash in the ciliated hull of her beehive hairdo, and so she rolls her head 180 degrees to the other side, using their mouths for the pivot. But aside from good hair grooming, they are oblivious to everything but each other. Everybody gives them a once-over. Disgusting! Amusing! How touching! A few kids pass by and say things like "Swing it, baby." But the great majority in that heaving funnel up the stairs seem to be as much astounded as anything else. The vision of love at rush hour cannot strike anyone exactly as romance. It is a feat, like a 3 fat man crossing the English Channel in a barrel. It is an earnest accomplishment against the tide. It is a piece of slightly gross heroics, after the manner of those knobby, varicose old men who come out from some place in baggy shorts every year and run through the streets of Boston in the Marathon race. And somehow that is the gaffe against love all week long in New York, for everybody, not just two kids writhing under their coiffures in the 50th Street subway station; too hurried, too crowded, too hard, and no time for dalliance. Which explains why the real thing in New York is, as it says in the song, a Sunday kind of love.

QUESTIONS ON SUBJECT AND PURPOSE

1. What is so unusual about the kiss that Wolfe witnesses? Why write about such a seemingly ordinary event?
2. How does the setting influence Wolfe's reaction to the kiss?
3. Characterize Wolfe's attitude or tone in the selection. For example, does he seem to be offended by such a public display of affection? Does he seem to be amused?

QUESTIONS ON STRATEGY AND AUDIENCE

1. What type of detail does Wolfe notice? In the scene? In the crowd? In the two teenagers?
2. Speculate on how Wolfe gathered all the details. Did he remember everything he saw? Did he stop to take notes?
3. What expectations does Wolfe seem to have about his audience? What evidence (setting, detail, subject, language) can you cite to support your argument?

QUESTIONS ON VOCABULARY AND STYLE

1. How is the selection both formal and informal at the same time? Why mix informal language with such unusual word choices (e.g., "attar of libido" in paragraph 1)?

2. Wolfe has a fondness for the exclamation mark. How often does he use it in this passage? What is the effect of such a device?
3. Find some examples of parallelism in the selection. Why does Wolfe use parallelism?
4. Be able to define the following words: *attar* (paragraph 1), *libido* (1), *sclerotic* (1), *embroilment* (3), *ciliated* (3), *gaffe* (3), *coiffures* (3), *dalliance* (3).

WRITING SUGGESTIONS

1. Sit somewhere public and people-watch. You might try a cafeteria or a street or even a part of your campus. Watch for typical behavior that seems unusual in its context. Describe what you see in a paragraph. Remember to focus on a single example. Watch for other people's reactions to what you see.
2. Are you ever offended by what people do in public? Write an essay explaining why a certain activity or behavior is inappropriate in a public place. Be sure to use specific examples.

   Prewriting:
   a. Select a public place where you can observe people. Make a list of unusual activities and behavior that you observe.
   b. Ask friends and relatives for examples of public behavior to which they object.
   c. Check to see if your college prohibits any particular types of public behavior.

   Rewriting:
   a. Ask friends or classmates to read your essay. How do they react to your examples? Use their reactions to rethink your choice of examples.
   b. Remember that several important, developed examples are more effective than a series of silly or unrealistic examples. Did you adequately develop your examples? Are they realistic or true?

3. Can two young (and unmarried) people kiss in public anywhere in the world? Are such displays of public affection acceptable? Select several cultures or countries and research the problem. In an essay complete with examples, present your findings to an audience of American college students.

Computer Fallout

RUSSELL BAKER

Born in Loudoun County, Virginia, in 1925, Russell Baker received a B.A. from Johns Hopkins University in 1947. He began his journalistic career with the Baltimore Sun, *then in 1954 joined the* New York Times *Washington bureau. In 1962 be began his "Observer" column for the* Times, *and received the Pulitzer Prize in 1979 for distinguished commentary. Baker's most recent collections of essays are* Poor Russell's Almanac *(1972),* So This Is Depravity *(1980), and* The Rescue of Miss Yaskell and Other Pipe Dreams *(1983), all of which demonstrate his ability to use humor to puncture the solemnities of politicians, social theorists, and abusers of the English language. His autobiography,* Growing Up *(1982), won Baker a second Pulitzer. In 1987 he discussed the writing of* Growing Up *in an essay published in William Zinsser's* Inventing the Truth: The Art and Craft of Memoir. *In "Computer Fallout," published in* The New York Times Magazine, *Baker makes vivid the temptations of revising prose on a word processor.*

The wonderful thing about writing with a computer instead of a typewriter or a lead pencil is that it's so easy to rewrite that you can make each sentence almost perfect before moving on to the next sentence. 1

An impressive aspect of using a computer to write with 2

One of the plusses about a computer on which to write 3

Happily, the computer is a marked improvement over both the typewriter and the lead pencil for purposes of literary composition, due to the ease with which rewriting can be effectuated, thus enabling 4

What a marked improvement the computer is for the writer over the typewriter and lead pencil 5

6 The typewriter and lead pencil were good enough in their day, but if Shakespeare had been able to access a computer with a good writing program

7 If writing friends scoff when you sit down at the computer and say, "The lead pencil was good enough for Shakespeare

8 One of the drawbacks of having a computer on which to write is the ease and rapidity with which the writing can be done, thus leading to the inclusion of many superfluous terms like "lead pencil," when the single word "pencil" would be completely, entirely and utterly adequate.

9 The ease with which one can rewrite on a computer gives it an advantage over such writing instruments as the pencil and typewriter by enabling the writer to turn an awkward and graceless sentence into one that is practically perfect, although it

10 The writer's eternal quest for the practically perfect sentence may be ending at last, thanks to the computer's gift of editing ease and swiftness to those confronting awkward, formless, nasty, illiterate sentences such as

11 Man's quest is eternal, but what specifically is it that he quests, and why does he

12 Mankind's quest is

13 Man's and woman's quest

14 Mankind's and womankind's quest

15 Humanity's quest for the perfect writing device

16 Eternal has been humanity's quest

17 Eternal have been many of humanity's quests

18 From the earliest cave writing, eternal has been the quest for a device that will forever prevent writers from using the word "quest," particularly when modified by such adjectives as "eternal," "endless," "tireless" and

19 Many people are amazed at the ease

20 Many persons are amazed by the ease

21 Lots of people are astounded when they see the nearly perfect sentences I write since upgrading my writing instrumentation from pencil and typewriter to

22 Listen, folks, there's nothing to writing almost perfect sentences with ease and rapidity provided you've given up

the old horse-and-buggy writing mentality that says Shakespeare couldn't have written those great plays if he had enjoyed the convenience of electronic compositional instrumentation.

23 Folks, have you ever realized that there's nothing to writing almost

24 Have you ever stopped to think, folks, that maybe Shakespeare could have written even better if

25 To be or not to be, that is the central focus of the inquiry.

26 In the intrapersonal relationships played out within the mind as to the relative merits of continuing to exist as opposed to not continuing to exist

27 Live or die, a choice as ancient as humanities' eternal quest, is a tough choice which has confounded mankind as well as womankind ever since the option of dreaming was first perceived as a potentially negating effect of the quiescence assumed to be obtainable through the latter course of action.

28 I'm sick and tired of Luddites saying pencils and typewriters are just as good as computers for writing nearly perfect sentences when they—the Luddites, that is—have never experienced the swiftness and ease of computer writing which makes it possible to compose almost perfect sentences in practically no time at

29 Folks, are you sick and tired of

30 Are you, dear reader

31 Good reader, are you

32 A lot of you nice folks out there are probably just as sick and tired as I am of hearing people say they are sick and tired of this and that and

33 Listen, people, I'm just as sick and tired as you are of having writers and TV commercial performers who oil me in cornpone politician prose addressed to "you nice folks out

34 A curious feature of computers, as opposed to pencils and typewriters, is that when you ought to be writing something more interesting than a nearly perfect sentence

35 Since it is easier to revise and edit with a computer than

with a typewriter or pencil, this amazing machine makes it very hard to stop editing and revising long enough to write a readable sentence, much less an entire newspaper column.

QUESTIONS ON SUBJECT AND PURPOSE

1. What is the subject of Baker's essay? In what way is the essay itself an example of "computer fallout"?
2. Why does Baker cast his message in this particular form? Why not write a more conventional essay?
3. What exactly do the examples that form the body of the essay prove?

QUESTIONS ON STRATEGY AND AUDIENCE

1. What structure, if any, is there to Baker's essay? Is the structure effective?
2. Does Baker attempt to make transitions from one example to another? If so, how are transitions made?
3. Does this essay seem to follow the rules for good writing that you have learned? Explain why or why not.
4. Who is Baker's audience? How might he want you to respond to the essay? Is he warning against using a word processor?

QUESTIONS ON VOCABULARY AND STYLE

1. Try to characterize his tone in the essay. Is he serious? humorous? How exactly do you know?
2. What allusions or clichés appear in Baker's essay? Check the Glossary at the back of this book for definitions of both terms.
3. Be able to define each of the following words or terms: *effectuated* (paragraph 4), *superfluous* (8), *quiescence* (27), *Luddites* (28).

WRITING SUGGESTIONS

1. Write a paragraph discussing the purpose of revision. Using Baker's essay as an example, you can address the issues of how much revision is necessary, what the goals of revision are, or

what can happen if you allow too much time for revising. For some additional information you might also read Peter Elbow's "Quick Revising" (Chapter 6) or the introductory material to Chapter 10. Obviously you can draw upon your own experience in revising as well.

2. Choose an item that is intended to make life easier, more efficient, or more interesting. The item should be either totally worthless or absolutely indispensable. In an essay support your position about the value of this item by using examples. Do not try, however, to imitate the structure of Baker's essay.

Prewriting:

a. When you are watching television or reading magazines, look for advertisements of products intended to make your life easier (a vegetable slicer, a sweater vacuum, a paring knife that can cut nails). Make a list of such devices.
b. Spend some time thinking about an object that is absolutely indispensable to daily life. What things do you use every day?
c. Once you have chosen your subject, do the following: make a list of instances when the item either failed or worked brilliantly; decide why you bought the item in the first place; think about what your audience already knows about this object (if it is widely advertised or commonly owned, your audience will understand your essay more easily).

Rewriting:

a. Choosing a structure can be tricky, especially since you probably do not want to imitate Baker's. Remember to introduce the device early in the essay—this is not a mystery the reader is supposed to solve. You might begin by quoting some of the advertising phrases associated with a particularly popular item.
b. Notice that Baker does not describe a computer or a word processor. He focuses instead on the results of using one. Depending upon what you are writing about, you might also be able to concentrate on results only, without actually describing the item and how it works. Rethink your descriptive strategies in the essay.
c. Find some friends who are willing to read your essay. Ask them if the paper is clear. What do they think your purpose was? Does their understanding agree with your original intention? If not, change your essay.

3. Some simple, everyday inventions/devices have become so essential in our lives that it is difficult to imagine what life was like without them. Select such an object, and research its invention/discovery/origin and subsequent success. You might consider writing either a traditional college research paper or a feature article for a popular magazine.

   As a way of stimulating your thinking, you might consider the following possible subjects:

   a. Nylon stockings or panty hose
   b. Ball point pens
   c. Athletic shoes
   d. Portable radios
   e. Digital watches
   f. Hand-held calculators

Cut

BOB GREENE

Bob Greene was born in Columbus, Ohio, in 1947 and received a B.J. from Northwestern University in 1969. He was a reporter and later a columnist for the Chicago Sun-Times *from 1969 to 1978, then began a syndicated column for the* Chicago Tribune *which appears in more than 150 newspapers. Greene has been a contributing editor for* Esquire *with his column "American Beat" and a contributing correspondent for "ABC News Nightline." His books include* We Didn't Have None of Them Fat Funky Angels on the Wall of Heartbreak Hotel, and Other Reports from America *(1971),* Running: A Nixon-McGovern Campaign Journal *(1973),* Billion Dollar Baby *(1974),* Johnny Deadline, Reporter: The Best of Bob Greene *(1976),* American Beat *(1983),* Good Morning, Merry Sunshine: A Father's Journal of His Child's First Year *(1984), and* Cheeseburger: The Best of Bob Greene *(1985). In this essay from* Esquire, *Greene relates the stories of five successful men who shared the experience of being "cut from the team." Does being "cut," Greene wonders, make you a superachiever later in life?*

I remember vividly the last time I cried. I was twelve years old, in the seventh grade, and I had tried out for the junior high school basketball team. I walked into the gymnasium; there was a piece of paper tacked to the bulletin board. 1

It was a cut list. The seventh-grade coach had put it up on the board. The boys whose names were on the list were still on the team; they were welcome to keep coming to practices. The boys whose names were not on the list had been cut; their presence was no longer desired. My name was not on the list. 2

I had not known the cut was coming that day. I stood and stared at the list. The coach had not composed it with a great deal of subtlety; the names of the very best athletes were at the top of the sheet of paper, and the other members 3 of the squad were listed in what appeared to be a descending order of talent. I kept looking at the bottom of the list, hoping against hope that my name would miraculously appear there if I looked hard enough.

I held myself together as I walked out of the gym and 4
out of the school, but when I got home I began to sob. I couldn't stop. For the first time in my life, I had been told officially that I wasn't good enough. Athletics meant everything to boys that age; if you were on the team, even a substitute, it put you in the desirable group. If you weren't on the team, you might as well not be alive.

I had tried desperately in practice, but the coach never 5
seemed to notice. It didn't matter how hard I was willing to work; he didn't want me there. I knew that when I went to school the next morning I would have to face the boys who had not been cut—the boys whose names were on the list, who were still on the team, who had been judged worthy while I had been judged unworthy.

All these years later, I remember it as if I were still 6
standing right there in the gym. And a curious thing has happened: in traveling around the country, I have found that an inordinately large proportion of successful men share that same memory—the memory of being cut from a sports team as a boy.

I don't know how the mind works in matters like this; I 7
don't know what went on in my head following that day when I was cut. But I know that my ambition has been enormous ever since then; I know that for all of my life since that day, I have done more work than I had to be doing, taken more assignments than I had to be taking, put in more hours than I had to be spending. I don't know if all of that came from a determination never to allow myself to be cut again—never to allow someone to tell me that I'm not good enough again—but I know it's there. And apparently it's there in a lot of other men, too.

Bob Graham, thirty-six, is a partner with the Jenner & 8
Block law firm in Chicago. "When I was sixteen, baseball was my whole life," he said. "I had gone to a relatively

small high school, and I had been on the team. But then my family moved, and I was going to a much bigger high school. All during the winter months I told everyone that I was a ballplayer. When spring came, of course I went out for the team.

"The cut list went up. I did not make the team. Reading 9
that cut list is one of the clearest things I have in my memory. I wanted not to believe it, but there it was.

"I went home and told my father about it. He suggested 10
that maybe I should talk to the coach. So I did. I pleaded to be put back on the team. He said there was nothing he could do; he said he didn't have enough room.

"I know for a fact that it altered my perception of myself. 11
My view of myself was knocked down; my self-esteem was lowered. I felt so embarrassed; my whole life up to that point had revolved around sports, and particularly around playing baseball. That was the group I wanted to be in—the guys on the baseball team. And I was told that I wasn't good enough to be one of them.

"I know now that it changed me. I found out, even 12
though I couldn't articulate it at the time, that there would be times in my life when certain people would be in a position to say 'You're not good enough' to me. I did not want that to happen ever again.

"It seems obvious to me now that being cut was what 13
started me in determining that my success would always be based on my own abilities, and not on someone else's perceptions. Since then I've always been something of an overachiever; when I came to the law firm I was very aggressive in trying to run my own cases right away, to be the lead lawyer in the cases with which I was involved. I made partner at thirty-one; I never wanted to be left behind.

"Looking back, maybe it shouldn't have been that 14
important. It was only baseball. You pass that by. Here I am. That coach is probably still there, still a high school baseball coach, still cutting boys off the baseball team every year. I wonder how many hundreds of boys he's cut in his life?"

15 Maurice McGrath is senior vice-president of Genstar Mortgage Corporation, a mortgage banking firm in Glendale, California. "I'm forty-seven years old, and I was fourteen when it happened to me, and I still feel something when I think about it," he said.

16 "I was in the eighth grade. I went to St. Philip's School in Pasadena. I went out for the baseball team, and one day at practice the coach came over to me. He was an Occidental College student who had been hired as the eighth-grade coach.

17 "He said, 'You're no good.' Those were his words. I asked him why he was saying that. He said, 'You can't hit the ball. I don't want you here.' I didn't know what to do, so I went over and sat off to the side, watching the others practice. The coach said I should leave the practice field. He said that I wasn't on the team, and that I didn't belong there anymore.

18 "I was outwardly stoic about it. I didn't want anyone to see how I felt. I didn't want to show that it hurt. But oh, did it hurt. All my friends played baseball after school every day. My best friend was the pitcher on the team. After I got whittled down by the coach, I would hear the other boys talking in class about what they were going to do at practice after school. I knew that I'd just have to go home.

19 "I guess you make your mind up never to allow yourself to be hurt like that again. In some way I must have been saying to myself, 'I'll play the game better.' Not the sports game, but anything I tried. I must have been saying, 'If I have to, I'll sit on the bench, but I'll be part of the team.'

20 "I try to make my own kids believe that, too. I try to tell them that they should show that they're a little bit better than the rest. I tell them to think of themselves as better. Who cares what anyone else thinks? You know, I can almost hear that coach saying the words. 'You're no good.' "

21 Author Malcolm MacPherson (*The Blood of His Servants*), forty, lives in New York. "It happened to me in the ninth grade, at the Yalesville School in Yalesville, Connect-

icut," he said. "Both of my parents had just been killed in a car crash, and as you can imagine, it was a very difficult time in my life. I went out for the baseball team, and I did pretty well in practice.

"But in the first game I clutched. I was playing second 22
base; the batter hit a pop-up, and I moved back to catch it. I can see it now. I felt dizzy as I looked up at the ball. It was like I was moving in slow motion, but the ball was going at regular speed. I couldn't get out of the way of my own feet. The ball dropped to the ground. I didn't catch it.

"The next day at practice, the coach read off the lineup. 23
I wasn't on it. I was off the squad.

"I remember what I did: I walked. It was a cold spring 24
afternoon, and the ground was wet, and I just walked. I was living with an aunt and uncle, and I didn't want to go home. I just wanted to walk forever.

"It drove my opinion of myself right into a tunnel. Right 25
into a cave. And when I came out of that cave, something inside of me wanted to make sure in one manner or another that I would never again be told I wasn't good enough.

"I will confess that my ambition, to this day, is out of 26
control. It's like a fire. I think the fire would have pretty much stayed in control if I hadn't been cut from that team. But that got it going. You don't slice ambition two ways; it's either there or it isn't. Those of us who went through something like that always know that we have to catch the ball. We'd rather die than have the ball fall at our feet.

"Once that fire is started in us, it never gets ex- 27
tinguished, until we die or have heart attacks or something. Sometimes I wonder about the home-run hitters; the guys who never even had to worry about being cut. They may have gotten the applause and the attention back then, but I wonder if they ever got the fire. I doubt it. I think maybe you have to get kicked in the teeth to get the fire started.

"You can tell the effect of something like that by exam- 28
ining the trail you've left in your life, and tracing it backward. It's almost like being a junkie with a need for success. You get attention and applause and you like it, but you never quite trust it. Because you know that back then you

were good enough if only they would have given you a chance. You don't trust what you achieve, because you're afraid that someone will take it away from you. You know that it can happen; it already did.

"So you try to show people how good you are. Maybe you don't go out and become Dan Rather; maybe you just end up owning the Pontiac dealership in your town. But it's your dealership, and you're the top man, and every day you're showing people that you're good enough." 29

DAN RATHER, fifty-two, is anchor of the CBS *Evening News*. "When I was thirteen, I had rheumatic fever," he said. "I became extremely skinny and extremely weak, but I still went out for the seventh-grade baseball team at Alexander Hamilton Junior High School in Houston. 30

"The school was small enough that there was no cut as such; you were supposed to figure out that you weren't good enough, and quit. Game after game I sat at the end of the bench, hoping that maybe this was the time I would get in. The coach never even looked at me; I might as well have been invisible. 31

"I told my mother about it. Her advice was not to quit. So I went to practice every day, and I tried to do well so that the coach would be impressed. He never never even knew I was there. At home in my room I would fantasize that there was a big game, and the three guys in front of me would all get hurt, and the coach would turn to me and put me in, and I would make the winning hit. But then there'd be another game, and the late innings would come, and if we were way ahead I'd keep hoping that this was the game when the coach would put me in. He never did. 32

"When you're that age, you're looking for someone to tell you you're okay. Your sense of self-esteem is just being formed. And what that experience that baseball season did was make me think that perhaps I wasn't okay. 33

"In the last game of the season something terrible happened. It was the last of the ninth inning, there were two outs, and there were two strikes on the batter. And the coach turned to me and told me to go out to right field. 34

"It was a totally humiliating thing for him to do. For him to put me in for one pitch, the last pitch of the season, in front of all the other boys on the team . . . I stood out there for that one pitch, and I just wanted to sink into the ground and disappear. Looking back on it, it was an extremely unkind thing for him to have done. That was nearly forty years ago, and I don't know why the memory should be so vivid now; I've never known if the coach was purposely making fun of me—and if he was, why a grown man would do that to a thirteen-year-old boy. 35

"I'm not a psychologist. I don't know if a man can point to one event in his life and say that that's the thing that made him the way he is. But when you're that age, and you're searching for your own identity, and all you want is to be told that you're all right . . . I wish I understood it better, but I know the feeling is still there." 36

QUESTIONS ON SUBJECT AND PURPOSE

1. Greene's "cuts" all refer to not making an athletic team. What other kinds of "cuts" can you experience?
2. It is always risky to speculate on an author's purpose, but why would Greene write about this? Why reveal to everyone something that hurt so much?
3. How might Greene have gone about gathering examples of other men's similar experiences? Why would they be willing to contribute? Would everyone who has been cut be so candid?
4. What can be said in the coaches' defense? Should everyone who tries out be automatically guaranteed a place on the team?

QUESTIONS ON STRATEGY AND AUDIENCE

1. Greene structures his essay in an unusual way. How can the essay be divided? Why give a series of examples of other men how were "cut"?
2. How many examples are enough? What if Greene had used two examples? Eight examples? How would either extreme have influenced your reaction as a reader?

3. Greene does not provide a final concluding paragraph. Why?
4. Are you skeptical after you have finished the essay? Does everyone react to being cut in the same way? What would it take to convince you that these reactions are typical?

QUESTIONS ON VOCABULARY AND STYLE

1. How would you characterize the tone of Greene's essay? How is it achieved? Through language? Sentence structure? Paragraphing?
2. Why does Greene allow each man to tell his own story? Why not just summarize their experiences? Each story is enclosed in quotation marks. Do you think that these were the exact words of each man? Why?
3. What do *inordinately* (paragraph 6) and *stoic* (18) mean?

WRITING SUGGESTIONS

1. What is it like to "make the team"? Remember a time when you were chosen and others were not. How did it feel? What are the benefits of "making it"? In a paragraph describe a similar experience when you were a part of a team, an organization, a fraternity or sorority—or when you won a prize or were elected to an office.
2. Describe a similar experience you have had. It might have happened in an academic course during your school years, in a school or community activity, in athletics, in music or dance lessons. We can be "cut" from almost anything. Remember to make your narrative vivid through the use of detail. Try to show the reader what happened and how you felt.

   Prewriting:

   a. Make a list of some possible events about which to write.
   b. Select one of those events and brainstorm. Jot down whatever you remember about the event and your reactions to it. Do not worry about writing complete sentences.
   c. Use the details generated from your brainstorm in your essay. Do not try to include every detail, but select those that seem the most revealing. Always ask yourself, how important is this detail?

Rewriting:

a. Remember that in writing about yourself it is especially important to keep your readers interested. They need to feel how significant this experience was. Do not just *tell* them; *show* them. One way to do this is to dramatize the experience. Did you?

b. Look carefully at your introduction. Do you begin in a vivid way? Does it make your reader want to keep reading? Test it by asking friends or relatives to read just the opening paragraphs.

c. How effective is your conclusion? Do you just stop? Do you just repeat in slightly altered words what you said in your introduction? Try to find another possible ending.

3. Check the validity of Greene's argument. What can you find in your library about the psychological effects of such vivid rejections? A reference librarian can help you start your search for information. Use that research in an essay about the positive or negative effects of such an experience. You might write your paper in one of the following forms (each of which has a slightly different audience):
   a. A conventional research paper for a college course.
   b. An article for a popular magazine (e.g., *Esquire, Ms., Cosmopolitan, Psychology Today*).
   c. A feature article for your school's newspaper.

Words for Nerds

WILLIAM SAFIRE

William Safire was born in New York City in 1929 and attended Syracuse University for two years before becoming a war correspondent for WNBC and the Armed Forces Radio Network. Safire wrote speeches for Richard Nixon and in 1968 was appointed special assistant to the president. In 1974 Safire began a political column for The New York Times *and later the column "On Language" for the* Times *magazine. His investigation of Bert Lance (an assistant to President Carter) won him a Pulitzer Prize in 1978. His works include the political thriller* Full Disclosure *(1977), a collection of political writings (*Safire's Washington, *1980), three collections from his language columns,* On Language *(1980),* What's the Good Word? *(1982), and* Take My Word for It *(1986). In 1987 he published* Freedom, *a historical novel about Abraham Lincoln and the Civil War. For a* Times *magazine column on campus slang, Safire uses a wide range of college informants, whom he refers to in the article as "The Lexicographic Irregulars." Not only is "campusese" always changing, but, as Safire's examples show, it varies widely from one campus to another.*

"Collegians now register for 'guts,'" writes Faith Heisler of the University of Pennsylvania, ". . . to lessen the necessity to become 'throats.'" 1

This prime example of campusese, instantly understandable to any college student, was submitted in response to a query in this space for a current review of the slang that has replaced the hip expressions of yesteryear. 2

Remember "snap course," the subject you took for a breather? That is called a "gut course" today, presumably because you know the answers in your intestines, and has been growing in use since the early fifties. Variations 3 include the middle western "cake course" (from "a piece of cake," or "easy") and the Californian "mick course" (not an ethnic slur, but a derivation of "Mickey Mouse," or "inconsequential").

Examples of gut courses—where "gut gunners" get an 4
"easy Ace" (A) as opposed to a "Hook" (C) or "Flag" (F)—are on the analogy of "Rocks for Jocks," a generation-old putdown of a geology course attended by athletes. More recent examples are astronomy's "Stars for Studs," art's "Nudes for Dudes," psychology's "Nuts and Sluts," European civilization's "Plato to NATO," anthropology's "Monkeys to Junkies," and comparative religion's "Gods for Clods." Students of linguistics engage in "Blabs in Labs." Courses on the art of film are referred to as "Monday Night at the Movies," music appreciation is "Clapping for Credit," and any science course aimed at liberal arts students includes a technocrat's derogation of the generalist as "Physics for Poets."

Students take these courses to avoid becoming 5
"throats," which is the term for what used to be called "grinds," which in turn replaced "bookworms." "The term 'throat,'" explains Mitchel A. Baum of the University of Pennsylvania, "is short for 'cutthroat' and refers to a person who wants an A at any cost and who would dilute your standardized solution of hydrochloric acid if given half a chance. At Penn, these students are often called 'premeds,' regardless of their postcollege plans."

Other replacements of "grind" are "squid" (an ink 6
squirter), "pencil geek," "spider," "cereb," and "grub." "'Grub' is often used as a verb as well," writes Philip Frayne of Columbia University, "as in 'He's in the library grubbing for a history exam.'" At Yale, the grind is a "weenie"—not "wienie," as spelled here not long ago—and at Harvard, the excessively studious student is derided as a "wonk," which Amy Berman, Harvard '79, fancifully suggests may be "know" spelled backward. (In British slang, "wonky" means "unsteady.") At some southern colleges, such people are "gomes," which Sean Finnell describes as

"those who carry a calculator hooked onto their pants belt or, off campus, wear black socks with loafers and shorts (sorry, Dad). The derivation of this word undoubtedly comes from 'Gomer,' as in 'Gomer Pyle.'"

"Here at MIT," observes Robert van der Heide, "we refer to someone who studies too much as a 'tool.' At MIT, 'nerd' is spelled 'gnurd.' There is a distinction between gnurds and tools. Tools study all the time, perhaps to get into med school. Gnurds study all the time because they like to. Gnurds are a subset of tools." (Not so at Colgate, reports Mathi Fuchs, where a tool is one who exploits others.) 7

"Nerd," no matter how spelled, is a big word with the youthful set. 8

Its origin is probably in a forties variation of "nuts"—as in "nerts to you"—and a "nert" became a "nerd," probably influenced by a rhyming scatological word. Like so many campusisms, the noun is turned into a verb with the addition of "out." "At Brown," writes Alison Kane, "the sons and daughters of the previous generation of 'bookworms' are called 'nerds' instead of 'grinds.' Rather than 'grind away' at their books, they prefer to 'nerd out.'" 9

What about "cramming"? That word is still used a lot ("alot," on campus, is one word), though a variation exists. "Staying awake the whole night through to 'cram' is called 'pulling an all-nighter,'" writes Susan Chumsky of Penn, noting: "An 'all-nighter' is never 'spent,' never 'had,' but only 'pulled.'" 10

New terms for "cramming" are "shedding" (from "woodshed"), "speeding," and "heavy booking" or "megabooking." At schools of architecture, "charretting" is used. "'Charretting' (to describe pulling an all-nighter)," write Carey Reilly and Peter Fein of Yale, "comes from the French word for cart. A cart was used to collect the architectural drawings of a student in any atelier of the Ecole des Beaux-Arts in Paris, mostly between 1860 and 1930. The word has come to mean the harried period in which a student's drawings are completed, or simply working all night to complete 11 the next day's assignment." (Professor Susan Fiske of Carnegie-Mellon spells it "charette," which is the spelling *Webster's Third New International Dictionary* prefers, but ascribes it to a drawing tool.)

In the event that the all-night pullers do not succeed in passing the exam, their reaction is vividly described in an "out" verb used at Cornell, situated high above Cayuga's waters. "One threatens to 'gorge out,'" testifies Michele Cusack, "which does not refer to eating three banana splits (that's 'pigging out'), but to jumping off one of the many scenic bridges on campus." Other schools prefer "veg out," soft *g*, or to turn into a vegetable after one "blows off," or fails. 12

A traditional, generation-spanning campus activity is vomiting. Accordingly, students have their own terms for the habit. In my college days, "upchuck" was the preferred euphemism, and since then the alliterative "losing your lunch" and the debonair "tossing your cookies" have been in use. Today the activity—usually from an introduction to overindulgence in alcohol by a "pin," or an innocent with a weak stomach—has upchucked the verb "to boot". The origin of "booting" may be to use your shoe as a receptacle, but that is speculative. Mathew Shapiro of Columbia submits the most descriptive: "Praying to the Great White Porcelain God (kneeling required)." 13

"'Power' is a common prefix at Dartmouth," reports Rick Jones, "e.g., 'power book' or 'power boot.'" A "tool" or "grind" is sometimes called a "power tool" or an "auger"—a boring tool. The "Power Tower" at many schools is the administration building. 14

Whatever happened to "Big Man on Campus"? He's gone—sometimes remembered only in acronym form, as "bee-moc"—though Anne Griffin says he is called a "politico" at the University of Virginia, and J. Barrett Hickman recalls a Hamilton College usage of "Young God." Nobody remembers what a "co-ed" is, though the term is sometimes used now to refer to men who attend colleges that formerly catered to women. A "stud"—the horse-breeding 15 term used recently to admire sexual prowess—is now a derogation of BMOC.

Remember the pleasures of cutting classes? "'Cutting' 16
is practically never used anymore," says Audrey Ziss at Skidmore. "The new terminology is 'bucking.'" This newly favored verb is not to be confused with the sixties favorite, "to bust"—to arrest. Today, with sit-ins and other demonstrations only dimly remembered, a "bust" is no longer a police raid and "busting" is not a dreaded activity. "One is busted on the basketball court when one's shot is blocked," explains Bob Torres of New Brunswick, illustrating "busted's" new meaning of being bested. "One is busted in conversation by snappy rejoinder. 'Busting GQ' means to dress in high fashion. . . . GQ refers to *Gentlemen's Quarterly*, the men's fashion magazine. Hence one has outdressed the exemplar when one 'busts GQ.'"

The term for "farewell," which was the inane "bye 17
now" a generation ago, is "later," from "see you later," but pronounced "lay-tah." Parents are "rents," reflecting a tendency to clip a syllable rather than any gratitude for payments of upkeep. Pizza has been shortened to "tza," pronounced "za". Nancy Pines of Mount Holyoke reports: "You guys want to go in on a za?" Reply: "Intense!" For years, the most common intensifying adjective was "terrific" or "cosmic"; it is somehow fitting that the leading intensifier has become "intense." Its only competition at the moment is "flaming," as in "flaming youth."

A word that kept cropping up in this rewarding response 18
by the Lexicographic Irregulars was "random." My happiest days at Syracuse U. were spent just strolling about, determined to be aimless, and that wandering wonderment now has a verb: to random. The word, normally an adjective meaning "haphazard," is also a college noun that Edward Fitzgerald of MIT interprets as "a person who does not belong on our dormitory floor," or, by extension, a welcome foreigner.

We'd better conclude this megabooking before some 19
Young God gorges out. Lay-tah.

QUESTIONS ON SUBJECT AND PURPOSE

1. What is slang? Check a dictionary for a definition. In what way are these examples of slang?
2. How does slang get invented? Why is it used so much?
3. What subjects or activities lend themselves best to slang?
4. Why would a reader—especially someone not currently at college—be interested in reading an article such as this?

QUESTIONS ON STRATEGY AND AUDIENCE

1. How does Safire structure his essay? Is there a distinct transition from section to section?
2. How effective is Safire's introduction? His conclusion? Why does he begin and end the way he does?
3. What assumptions does Safire seem to make about his audience? Can you point to specific remarks or passages that support your conclusion?

QUESTIONS ON VOCABULARY AND STYLE

1. How would you characterize the tone of Safire's essay? What is the result of mixing formal works—such as those listed in question 3, below—with campus slang?
2. Safire's essay was originally written for a newspaper. How does that seem to have influenced the essay's structure or style?
3. Be able to define the following words: *technocrat* (paragraph 4), *derogation* (4), *scatological* (9), *atelier* (11), *harried* (11), *euphemism* (13), *alliterative* (13), *debonair* (13), *acronym* (15).

WRITING SUGGESTIONS

1. Compile some examples of campus slang used at your school. Ask your friends and classmates for examples. Spend some time listening and talking to people. Once you have gathered a range of examples, select the best—maybe three or four words—and write a paragraph explaining them.
2. If you have gathered a particularly good range of examples, write an essay guide to your school's slang. You might write for one of the following audiences:

a. Your fellow students. Such a guide might appear in your campus newspaper or magazine.
b. Parents. The school administration has decided to send home a brochure to help parents understand their children's new vocabulary.
c. Local residents. The editor of the town newspaper is interested in an article on the new campus slang. Remember that the majority of the newspaper's readers are neither students nor parents of students.

Prewriting:
a. Use the two strategies described in Writing Suggestions 1 to gather examples.
b. Once you have 8 or 10 possible words or phrases, ask your friends to review the list and to contribute additional usages.
c. Your essay will be more effective if your examples are fresh. No one wants to read about words that have been used for years. Test your words by checking them in dictionaries of slang available in your library. If they are listed, they probably are too old to be valuable.

Rewriting:
a. Have you adequately defined each word and phrase? Have you given sample sentences showing how each is used?
b. If possible, ask several older people to read your essay to see if they are familiar with any of these expressions.
c. Many readers might feel that Safire's ending is too "cute." Do not just imitate what he has done. Try to find another way of ending your essay.

3. Select a particular period in time—the 1950's, the 1960's, or the 1970's for example—and compile examples of slang then common. You might ask your older brothers or sisters, your parents, or your grandparents for contributions. Magazines and books published during those years are also helpful. Write an essay guide for those words.

Marrying Absurd

JOAN DIDION

Joan Didion was born in Sacramento in 1934 and received a B.A. degree from the University of California at Berkeley in 1956. Didion is as famous for her novels Run River *(1963),* Play It As It Lays *(1970),* A Book of Common Prayer *(1977), and* Democracy *(1984) as for her essay collections* Slouching Towards Bethlehem *(1968) and* The White Album *(1979). In both genres, she vividly portrays the personal chaos of modern American life. She has written of a visit to El Salvador in* Salvador *(1983) and has produced a number of screenplays in collaboration with her husband John Gregory Dunne, including* A Star Is Born *(1976) and* True Confessions *(1981). Her latest book,* Miami *(1987), examines Washington's mistreatment of Miami's Cuban population. In "Marrying Absurd" Didion examines the Las Vegas wedding business—a round-the-clock, seven-days-a-week, no-waiting convenience industry.*

To be married in Las Vegas, Clark County, Nevada, a bride must swear that she is eighteen or has parental permission and a bridegroom that he is twenty-one or has parental permission. Someone must put up five dollars for the license. (On Sundays and holidays, fifteen dollars. The Clark County Courthouse issues marriage licenses at any time of the day or night except between noon and one in the afternoon, between eight and nine in the evening, and between four and five in the morning.) Nothing else is required. The State of Nevada, alone among these United States, demands neither a premarital blood test nor a waiting period before or after the issuance of a marriage license. Driving in across the Mojave from Los Angeles, one sees the signs way out on the desert, looming up from that moonscape of rattlesnakes and mesquite, even before the Las Vegas lights appear like a mirage on the horizon: "GETTING MARRIED? Free 1

License Information First Strip Exit." Perhaps the Las Vegas wedding industry achieved its peak operational efficiency between 9:00 p.m. and midnight of August 26, 1965, an otherwise unremarkable Thursday which happened to be, by Presidential order, the last day on which anyone could improve his draft status merely by getting married. One hundred and seventy-one couples were pronounced man and wife in the name of Clark County and the State of Nevada that night, sixty-seven of them by a single justice of the peace, Mr. James A. Brennan. Mr. Brennan did one wedding at the Dunes and the other sixty-six in his office, and charged each couple eight dollars. One bride lent her veil to six others. "I got it down from five to three minutes," Mr. Brennan said later of his feat. "I could've married them *en masse*, but they're people, not cattle. People expect more when they get married."

What people who get married in Las Vegas actually do 2
expect—what, in the largest sense, their "expectations" are—strikes one as a curious and self-contradictory business. Las Vegas is the most extreme and allegorical of American settlements, bizzare and beautiful in its venality and in its devotion to immediate gratification, a place the tone of which is set by mobsters and call girls and ladies' room attendants with amyl nitrate poppers in their uniform pockets. Almost everyone notes that there is no "time" in Las Vegas, no night and no day and no past and no future (no Las Vegas Casino, however, has taken the obliteration of the ordinary time sense quite so far as Harold's Club in Reno, which for a while issued, at odd intervals in the day and night, mimeographed "bulletins" carrying news from the world outside); neither is there any logical sense of where one is. One is standing on a highway in the middle of a vast hostile desert looking at an eighty-foot sign which blinks "STARDUST" or "CAESAR'S PALACE." Yes, but what does that explain? This geographical implausibility reinforces the sense that what happens there has no connection with "real" life; Nevada cities like Reno and Carson are ranch towns, Western towns, places behind which there is some historical imperative. But Las Vegas seems to exist

only in the eye of the beholder. All of which makes it an extraordinarily stimulating and interesting place, but an odd one in which to want to wear a candlelight satin Priscilla of Boston wedding dress with Chantilly lace inserts, tapered sleeves and a detachable modified train.

And yet the Las Vegas wedding business seems to appeal to precisely that impulse. "Sincere and Dignified Since 1954," one wedding chapel advertises. There are nineteen such wedding chapels in Las Vegas, intensely competitive, each offering better, faster, and, by implication, more sincere services than the next: Our Photos Best Anywhere, Your Wedding on a Phonograph Record, Candlelight with Your Ceremony, Honeymoon Accommodations, Free Transportation from Your Motel to Courthouse to Chapel and Return to Motel, Religious or Civil Cermonies, Dressing Rooms, Flowers, Rings, Announcements, Witnesses Available, and Ample Parking. All of these services, like most others in Las Vegas (sauna baths, payroll-check cashing, chinchilla coats for sale or rent) are offered twenty-four hours a day, seven days a week, presumably on the premise that marriage, like craps, is a game to be played when the table seems hot. 3

But what strikes one most about the Strip chapels, with their wishing wells and stained-glass paper windows and their artificial bouvardia, is that so much of their business is by no means a matter of simple convenience, of late-night liaisons between show girls and baby Crosbys. Of course there is some of that. (One night about eleven o'clock in Las Vegas I watched a bride in an orange minidress and masses of flame-colored hair stumble from a Strip chapel on the arm of her bridegroom, who looked the part of the expendable nephew in movies like *Miami Syndicate*. "I gotta get the kids," the bride whimpered. "I gotta pick up the sitter, I gotta get to the midnight show." "What you gotta get," the bridegroom said, opening the door of a Cadillac Coupe de Ville and watching her crumble on the seat, "is sober.") But Las Vegas seems to offer something other than "convenience"; it is merchandising "niceness," the facsimile of proper ritual, to children who do not know how else to find 4 it, how to make the arrangements, how to do it "right." All day and evening long on the Strip, one sees actual wedding parties, waiting under the harsh lights at a crosswalk, standing uneasily in the parking lot of the Frontier while the photographer hired by The Little Church of the West ("Wedding Place of the Stars") certifies the occassion, takes the picture: the bride in a veil and white satin pumps, the bridegroom usually in a white dinner jacket, and even an attendant or two, a sister or a best friend in hot-pink *peau de soie*, a flirtation veil, a carnation nosegay. "When I Fall in Love It Will Be Forever," the organist plays, and then a few bars of Lohengrin. The mother cries; the stepfather, awkward in his role, invites the chapel hostess to join them for a drink at the Sands. The hostess declines with a professional smile; she has already transferred her interest to the group waiting outside. One bride out, another in, and again the sign goes up on the chapel door: "One moment please—Wedding."

I sat next to one such wedding party in a Strip restaurant 5
the last time I was In Las Vegas. The marriage had just taken place; the bride still wore her dress, the mother her corsage. A bored waiter poured out a few swallows of pink champagne ("on the house") for everyone but the bride, who was too young to be served. "You'll need something with more kick than that," the bride's father said with heavy jocularity to his new son-in-law; the ritual jokes about the wedding night had a certain Panglossian character, since the bride was clearly several months pregnant. Another round of pink champagne, this time not on the house, and the bride began to cry. "It was just as nice," she sobbed, "as I hoped and dreamed it would be."

QUESTIONS ON SUBJECT AND PURPOSE

1. What does *absurd* mean? Why is this "marrying absurd"? What is it about the whole situation that strikes Didion as absurd?
2. What is particularly appropriate about the wedding "business" being in Las Vegas?

3. What seems to be Didion's attitude toward such a phenomenon? How does Didion convey this attitude?
4. What is your attitude toward such a phenomenon? Would you want to be married in Las Vegas?

QUESTIONS ON STRATEGY AND AUDIENCE

1. How does Didion use examples to make her narrative vivid? Make a list of examples and be prepared to tell how they contribute to the narrative.
2. How effective is the openning? The conclusion?
3. How does Didion organize the narrative? Outline the narrative.
4. What expectations does Didion seem to have of her audience? How do you know that?

QUESTIONS ON VOCABULARY AND STYLE

1. How much dialogue does Didion use in the narrative? How does that dialogue contribute to the narrative?
2. Why does Didion enclose three sentences in parentheses (paragraphs 1,2, and 4)? What is the effect of doing this?
3. Didion frequently encloses words within quotation marks (e.g., "time," "bulletins," "real," "convenience," "niceness," "right"). What effect does that create?
4. Be able to define the following words: *mesquite* (paragraph 1), *venality* (2), *bouvardia* (4), *peau de soie* (4), *jocularity* (5), *Panglossian character* (5).

WRITING SUGGESTIONS

1. America has a growing fascination with 24-hour availability. Businesses have 24-hour 800 numbers, banks offer automated tellers, convenience stores and even supermarkets never close. Select a particular 24-hour service and describe for a reader how and why it works. Be sure to use examples to make your narrative vivid.
2. What we choose to make popular can offer interesting insight into the values of our society. Choose something—an object, an activity, a person, or a group—that is enjoying popular attention. Try to explain why it is popular. What does it reveal about

our society? Use your "something" as an example to reveal current values.

Prewriting:

a. Remember that whatever you choose should not only be popular, but should also offer an insight into our society's values. Make a list of possible subjects, and note beside each item some remark about its significance.
b. Once you have a subject that seems promising, brainstorm for an hour. Write your subject in the center of a sheet of paper. In the surrounding space jot down reasons for its popularity.
c. Do a "group think." Ask some friends to brainstorm with you about your particular subject. If possible, tape record the session and take notes later.

Rewriting:

a. Look back to Didion's essay. Instead of telling the reader that Las Vegas weddings are absurd, she shows examples that reveal her attitude. Showing is more effective than telling. How much showing and how much telling did you do?
b. Check over your introduction and conclusion. Do you grab your reader's attention? Will the reader want to keep reading? Did you end forcefully? Did you avoid a boring ending that says, in effect, "in conclusion it is obvious that ——— is popular because it reflects the following societal values: . . ."?

3. "——— Absurd." Find another American absurdity, and research and analyze it for the reader. Some possibilities might be divorcing, dying, suntanning, drinking, smoking, fast-fooding.

You Are What You Say

ROBIN LAKOFF

Robin Lakoff was born in Brooklyn, New York, in 1942, received her B.A. from Radcliffe, and, in 1967, earned a Ph.D. from Harvard. She has taught linguistics at the University of Michigan and classics and linguistics at the University of Illinois; since 1976, she has been a professor of linguistics at the University of California at Berkeley. Lakoff is recognized for her work both in generative semantics and in sociolinguistics. Her books include Abstract Syntax and Latin Complementation *(1968) and* Language and Woman's Place *(1975). In 1984 she co-authored* Face Value: The Politics of Beauty *with Raquel Scherr. Her essay "You Are What You Say," first published in* Ms. *magazine, concerns the particular language spoken by women. By identifying certain speech pattens and word choices found exclusively in the linguistic behavior of women, Lakoff reveals how language reinforces society's attitude about women.*

"Women's language" is that pleasant (dainty?), euphemistic, never-aggressive way of talking we learned as little girls. Cultural bias was built into the language we were allowed to speak, the subjects we were allowed to speak about, and the ways we were spoken of. Having learned our linguistic lesson well, we go out in the world, only to discover that we are communicative cripples—damned if we do, and damned if we don't. 1

If we refuse to talk "like a lady," we are ridiculed and criticized for being unfeminine. ("She thinks like a man" is, at best, a left-handed compliment.) If we do learn all the fuzzy-headed, unassertive language of our sex, we are ridiculed for being unable to think clearly, unable to take part in a serious discussion, and therefore unfit to hold a position of power. 2

It doesn't take much of this for a woman to begin feeling she deserves such treatment because of inadequacies in her own intelligence and education. 3

"Women's language" shows up in all levels of English. For example, women are encouraged and allowed to make far more precise discriminations in naming colors than men do. Words like *mauve, beige, ecru, aquamarine, lavender,* and so on, are unremarkable in a woman's active vocabulary, but largely absent from that of most men. I know of no evidence suggesting that women actually *see* a wider range of colors than men do. It is simply that fine discriminations of this sort are relevant to women's vocabularies, but not to men's; to men, who control most of the interesting affairs of the world, such distinctions are trivial—irrelevant. 4

In the area of syntax, we find similar gender-related peculiarities of speech. There is one construction, in particular, that women use conversationally far more than men: the tag question. A tag is midway between an outright statement and a yes–no question; it is less assertive than the former, but more confident than the latter. 5

A *flat statement* indicates confidence in the speaker's knowledge and is fairly certain to be believed; a *question* indicates a lack of knowledge on some point and implies that the gap in the speaker's knowledge can and will be remedied by an answer. For example, if, at a Little League game, I have had my glasses off, I can legitimately ask someone else: "Was the player out at third?" A *tag question,* being intermediate between statement and question, is used when the speaker is stating a claim, but lacks full confidence in the truth of that claim. So if I say, "Is Joan here?" I will probably not be surprised if my respondent answers "no"; but if I say, "Joan is here, isn't she?" instead, chances are I am already biased in favor of a positive answer, wanting only confirmation. I still want a response, but I have enough knowledge (or think I have) to predict that response. A tag question, then, might be thought of as a statement that doesn't demand to be believed by anyone but the speaker, a way of giving leeway, of not forcing the addressee to go along with the views of the speaker. 6

Another common use of the tag question is in small talk when the speaker is trying to elicit conversation: "Sure is hot here, isn't it?" 7

But in discussing personal feelings or opinions, only the speaker normally has any way of knowing the correct answer. Sentences such as "I have a headache, don't I?" are clearly ridiculous. But there are other examples where it is the speaker's opinions, rather than perceptions, for which corroboration is sought, as in "The situation in Southeast Asia is terrible, isn't it?" 8

While there are, of course, other possible interpretations of a sentence like this, one possibility is that the speaker has a particular answer in mind—"yes" or "no"—but is reluctant to state it baldly. This sort of tag question is much more apt to be used by women than by men in conversation. Why is this the case? 9

The tag question allows a speaker to avoid commitment, and thereby avoid conflict with the addressee. The problem is that, by so doing, speakers may also give the impression of not really being sure of themselves, or looking to the addressee for confirmation of their views. This uncertainty is reinforced in more subliminal ways, too. There is a peculiar sentence intonation-pattern, used almost exclusively by women, as far as I know, which changes a declarative answer into a question. The effect of using the rising inflection typical of a yes–no question is to imply that the speaker is seeking confirmation, even though the speaker is clearly the only one who has the requisite information, which is why the question was put to her in the first place: 10

(Q) When will dinner be ready?

(A) Oh . . . around six o'clock . . .?

It is as though the second speaker were saying, "Six o'clock—if that's okay with you, if you agree." The person being addressed is put in the position of having to provide confirmation. One likely consequence of this sort of speech-pattern in a woman is that, often unbeknownst to herself, the speaker builds a reputation of tentativeness, and others will refrain from taking her seriously or trusting her with any real responsibilities, since she "can't make up her mind," and "isn't sure of herself."

Such idiosyncrasies may explain why women's language sounds much more "polite" than men's. It is polite to leave a decision open, not impose your mind, or views, or claims, on anyone else. So a tag question is a kind of polite statement, in that it does not force agreement or belief on the addressee. In the same way a request is a polite command, in that it does not force obedience on the addressee, but rather suggests something be done as a favor to the speaker. A clearly stated order implies a threat of certain consequences if it is not followed, and—even more impolite—implies that the speaker is in a superior position and able to enforce the order. By couching wishes in the form of a request, on the other hand, a speaker implies that if the request is not carried out, only the speaker will suffer; noncompliance cannot harm the addressee. So the decision is really left up to the addressee. The distinction becomes clear in these examples: 11

Close the door.
Please close the door.
Will you close the door?
Will you please close the door?
Won't you close the door?

In the same ways as words and speech patterns used by women undermine her image, those used *to describe* women make matters even worse. Often a word may be used of both men and women (and perhaps of things as well); but when it is applied to women, it assumes a special meaning that, by implication rather than outright assertion, is derogatory to women as a group. 12

The use of euphemisms has this effect. A euphemism is a substitute for a word that has acquired a bad connotation by association with something unpleasant or embarrassing. But almost as soon as the new word comes into common usage, it takes on the same old bad connotations, since feelings about the things or people referred to are not altered by a change of name; thus new euphemisms must be constantly found. 13

There is one euphemism for *woman* still very much 14
alive. The word, of course, is *lady. Lady* has a masculine counterpart, namely *gentleman,* occasionally shortened to *gent.* But for some reason *lady* is very much commoner than *gent(leman).*

The decision to use *lady* rather than *woman* or vice 15
versa, may considerably alter the sense of a sentence, as the following examples show:

(a) A woman (lady) I know is a dean at Berkeley.

(b) A woman (lady) I know makes amazing things out of shoelaces and old boxes.

The use of *lady* in (a) imparts frivolous, or nonserious, 16
tone to the sentence: the matter under discussion is not one of great moment. Similarly, in (b), using *lady* here would suggest that the speaker considered the "amazing things" not to be serious art, but merely a hobby or an aberration. If *woman* is used, she might be a serious sculptor. To say *lady doctor* is very condescending, since no one ever says *gentleman doctor* or even *man doctor.* For example, mention in the San Francisco *Chronicle* of January 31, 1972, of Madalyn Murray O'Hair as the *lady atheist* reduces her position to that of scatterbrained eccentric. Even *woman atheist* is scarcely defensible: sex is irrelevant to her philosophical position.

Many women argue that, on the other hand, *lady* carries 17
with it overtones recalling the age of chivalry: conferring exalted stature on the person so referred to. This makes the term seem polite at first, but we must also remember that these implications are perilous: they suggest that a "lady" is helpless, and cannot do things by herself.

Lady can also be used to infer frivolousness, as in titles 18
of organizations. Those that have a serious purpose (not merely that of enabling "the ladies" to spend time with one another) cannot use the word *lady* in their titles, but less serious ones may. Compare the *Ladies' Auxiliary* of a men's group, or the *Thursday Evening Ladies' Browning and Garden Society* with *Ladies' Liberation* or *Ladies' Strike for Peace.*

What is curious about this split is that *lady* is in origin a 19 euphemism—a substitute that puts a better face on something people find uncomfortable—for *woman*. What kind of euphemism is it that subtly denigrates the people to whom it refers? Perhaps *lady* functions as a euphemism for *woman* because it does not contain the sexual implications present in *woman*: it is not "embarrassing" in that way. If this is so, we may expect that, in the future, *lady* will replace woman as the primary word for the human female, since *woman* will have become too blatantly sexual. That this distinction is already made in some contexts at least is shown in the following examples, where you can try replacing *woman* with *lady*:

(a) She's only twelve, but she's already a woman.

(b) After ten years in jail, Harry wanted to find a woman.

(c) She's my woman, see, so don't mess around with her.

20 Another common substitute for *woman* is *girl*. One seldom hears a man past the age of adolescence referred to as a boy, save in expressions like "going out with the boys," which are meant to suggest an air of adolescent frivolity and irresponsibility. But women of all ages are "girls": one can have a man—not a boy—Friday, but only a girl—never a woman or even a lady—Friday; women have girlfriends, but men do not—in a nonsexual sense—have boyfriends. It may be that this use of *girl* is euphemistic in the same way the use of *lady* is: in stressing the idea of immaturity, it removes the sexual connotation lurking in *woman*. *Girl* brings to mind irresponsibility: you don't send a girl to do a woman's errand (or even, for that matter, a boy's errand). She is a person who is both too immature and too far from real life to be entrusted with responsibilities or with decisions of any serious or important nature.

21 Now let's take a pair of words which, in terms of the possible relationships in an earlier society, were simple male–female equivalents, analogous to *bull* : *cow*. Suppose we find that, for independent reasons, society has changed in such a way that the original meanings now are irrelevant. Yet the words have not been discarded, but have acquired new meanings, metaphorically related to their original senses. But suppose these new metaphorical uses are no

longer parallel to each other. By seeing where the parallelism breaks down, we discover something about the different roles played by men and women in this culture. One good example of such a divergence through time is found in the pair, *master* : *mistress*. Once used with reference to one's power over servants, these words have become unusable today in their original master-servant sense as the relationship has become less prevalent in our society. But the words are still common.

Unless used with reference to animals, *master* now gen- 22
erally refers to a man who has acquired consummate ability in some field, normally nonsexual. But its feminine counterpart cannot be used this way. It is practically restricted to its sexual sense of "paramour." We start out with two terms, both roughly paraphrasable as "one who has power over another." But the masculine form, once one person is no longer able to have absolute power over another, becomes usable metaphorically in the sense of "having power over *something*." *Master* requires as its object only the name of some activity, something inanimate and abstract. But *mistress* requires a masculine noun in the possessive to precede it. One cannot say: "Rhonda is a mistress." One must be *someone's* mistress. A man is defined by what he does, a woman by her sexuality, that is, in terms of one particular aspect of her relationship to men. It is one thing to be an *old master* like Hans Holbein, and another to be an *old mistress*.

The same is true of the words *spinster* and *bachelor*— 23
gender words for "one who is not married." The resemblance ends with the definition. While *bachelor* is a neuter term, often used as a compliment, *spinster* normally is used pejoratively, with connotations of prissiness, fussiness, and so on. To be a bachelor implies that one has the choice of marrying or not, and this is what makes the idea of a bachelor existence attractive, in the popular literature. He has been pursued and has successfully eluded his pursuers. But a spinster is one who has not been pursued, or at least not seriously. She is old, unwanted goods. The metaphorical

connotations of *bachelor* generally suggest sexual freedom; of *spinster*, puritanism or celibacy.

These examples could be multiplied. It is generally con- 24
sidered a *faux pas*, in society, to congratulate a woman on her engagement, while it is correct to congratulate her fiancé. Why is this? The reason seems to be that it is impolite to remind people of things that may be uncomfortable to them. To congratulate a woman on her engagement is really to say, "Thank goodness! You had a close call!" For the man, on the other hand, there was no such danger. His choosing to marry is viewed as a good thing, but not something essential.

The linguistic double standard holds throughout the life 25
of the relationship. After marriage, bachelor and spinster become man and wife, not man and woman. The woman whose husband dies remains "John's widow"; John, however, is never "Mary's widower."

Finally, why is it that salesclerks and others are so quick 26
to call women customers "dear," "honey," and other terms of endearment they really have no business using? A male customer would never put up with it. But women, like children, are supposed to enjoy these endearments, rather than being offended by them.

In more ways than one, it's time to speak up. 27

QUESTIONS ON SUBJECT AND PURPOSE

1. According to Lakoff, how does our language define us? How does it reveal our cultural biases?
2. Define, either from the essay or from a dictionary, each of the following terms:
   a. syntax
   b. connotation
   c. denotation
   d. tag question
   e. euphemism
3. What does Lakoff mean by her final sentence? What purpose does she appear to have? What does she want her readers to do?

QUESTIONS ON STRATEGY AND AUDIENCE

1. How is Lakoff's essay organized? Make a simple outline of her essay.
2. How does she mark the transition from one topic or subdivision to another?
3. What assumptions does Lakoff make about her audience? Point to specific evidence to support your conclusion.

QUESTIONS ON VOCABULARY AND STYLE

1. At the start of her essay Lakoff calls women "communicative cripples." Does she literally mean this? Why make such a statement?
2. Characterize Lakoff's tone in the essay. Is she angry? Is she indignant? Is she just objectively reporting what she notices? Support your characterization with specific evidence.
3. Be able to define the following words: *euphemistic* (paragraph 1), *leeway* (6), *subliminal* (10), *derogatory* (12), *chivalry* (17), *denigrate* (19), *blatantly* (19), *consummate* (22), *pejoratively* (23), *celibacy* (23), *faux pas* (24).

WRITING SUGGESTIONS

1. We are also defined by how we behave. Society has certain expectations of what a woman or a man can or cannot do. In a paragraph define an aspect of "women's behavior" or "men's behavior."
2. In an essay, explore how our society defines masculinity or femininity. Remember that your definition will involve examples.

   Prewriting:

   a. Spend some time thinking about how you behave in society as a man or a woman. What things are you expected to do? What things must you avoid? Make a list using your own experiences.
   b. Television commercials and programs as well as print advertisements and magazines are good sources of gender stereotypes. Broaden your list by using examples drawn from television and magazines.

c. Make a brief outline, choosing examples from your list and placing them in a logical order.

Rewriting:

a. Remember that your generalizations must be supported with specific, relevant examples. Check to make sure that you provide adequate evidence for every assertion.
b. On the other hand, remember that your paper should not be just a collection of randomly organized examples. Once your draft is complete, check your outline to be sure you have followed your plan.
c. Check back to see if your transitions from one section to another are carefully made. An essay should always be a coherent whole and not a series of unconnected pieces.

3. How has the definition of a man or a woman changed during this century? Research how either term was defined in 1900. What did a man or a woman do? What expectations did society have? How was either sex portrayed in advertisements, in fiction, or in art? Using your research, define the term *man* or *woman* as it would have been defined in 1900. Remember to support generalizations with specific details.

CHAPTER 2

Narration

When a friend asks, "What did you do last night?" you reply with a narrative: "After the chemistry midterm was over at 8:30, we went to Shakey's for pizza. Then we stopped at the bowling alley for a couple of games, and about 11 we split up and I went back to the dorm for some serious sleeping." A narrative is a story, and all stories, whether they are personal narratives, or novels, or histories, have the same essential ingredients: a series of events arranged in an order and told by a narrator for some particular purpose. Your reply, for example, exhibits all four elements: a series of events (the four things you did last evening) arranged in an order (chronological) and told by a narrator ("I," a first-person narrator) for some particular purpose (to answer your friend's question).

Any type of writing can and does use narration; it is not something found only in personal experience essays or fiction. Historian Samuel Eliot Morison in "Victory in the Pacific" tells his story in the same way that autobiographers Langston Hughes and Maya Angelou do. Narration can also be used to provide evidence in an argument. Bob Greene in "Cut" (Chapter 1) groups five personal narrative examples to support his assertion that being cut from an athletic team can make you a superachiever in life. Narration can also be found mixed with description in William Least Heat Moon's "Nameless, Tennessee" (Chapter 3) or underlying a persuasive essay in Richard Rodriguez's "None of This Is

Fair" (Chapter 9). In fact, there are examples of narration in the readings found in every chapter of this text.

What Do You Include in a Narrative?

No one, probably not even your mother, wants to hear everything you did today. Readers, like listeners, want you to exercise selection, for some things are more important or interesting than others. Historians have to select out of a mass of data what they will include and emphasize. They cannot tell the whole story, for if they did, the reader would get entangled in trivia, and the significant shape and meaning of the narrative would be lost. Samuel Eliot Morison's few paragraphs about the end of the war with Japan could have been expanded into subject matter for a whole book. Even in personal experiences you condense and select. Generally you need to pare away, to cut out the unnecessary and the uninteresting. What you include depends, of course, on what happened and, more important, upon the purpose or meaning that you are trying to convey. Morison felt that the use of the atomic bomb on Hiroshima and Nagasaki was justified, that in the end it saved lives. Therefore he did not include, for example, descriptions of the suffering of the civilian victims of those blasts.

How Do You Structure a Narrative?

Time structures all narratives, although events do not always need to be arranged in chronological order. A narrative can begin at one point in time and then "flash back" to an earlier action or event. Langston Hughes's "Salvation" is told by a narrator looking back at an experience that occurred when he was thirteen, although the story itself is told in the order in which it happened. The most typical inversion is to begin at the end of the narrative and then to move backward in time to explain how that end was reached. Two cautions are obvious: first, do not switch time too frequently, especially in short papers; second, make sure that the switches are clearly marked for your reader.

Remember as well that you control where your narrative begins and ends. For example, the experience that E. B. White narrates in "Once More to the Lake" began when he and his son arrived at the lake and ended with their departure. The essay, however, begins with a flashback to his first summer at the lake thirty-seven years earlier. It ends as he watches his son pull on his cold, soggy bathing suit. The essay builds to that single moment of insight, and so that scene serves as the appropriate end of the narrative. It would have been anticlimactic for White to have added another paragraph detailing their final departure from the lake. Do not feel the need to "finish" the story if, in fact, you have achieved your purpose. Try to build to a climactic moment and end there.

Writers frequently change or modify an actual personal experience in order to tell the story more effectively, heighten the tension, or make their purpose clearer. In her essay "On Keeping a Notebook" (Chapter 6), Joan Didion remarks:

> I tell what some would call lies. "That's simply not true," the members of my family frequently tell me when they come up against my memory of a shared event. "The party was *not* for you, the spider was *not* a black widow, *it wasn't that way at all.*" Very likely they are right, for not only have I always had trouble distinguishing between what happened and what merely might have happened, but I remain unconvinced that the distinction, for my purposes, matters.

Whenever you recall an experience, even if it just happened last week, you do not necessarily remember it exactly as it happened. The value of a personal narrative does not rest in accuracy to the original experience. It does not matter, for example, whether the scene with Sister Monroe in the Christian Methodist Episcopal Church occurred exactly as Maya Angelou describes it years later. What does matter is that it could have happened and that it is faithful to the purpose Angelou intends.

How Are Narratives Told?

Two things are especially important in relating your narrative. First, you need to choose a point of view from which to tell the story. Personal experience narratives, such as those by Hughes, Angelou, and White, are generally told in the first person: the narrator is an actor in the story. Historical narratives and narratives used as illustrations in a larger piece of writing are generally told in the third person. Morison, for example, is outside his narrative and provides an objective view of the actions he is describing. Point of view can vary in one other way. The narrator can reveal only his or her own thoughts (and so use what is known as the limited point of view), or the narrator can reveal what anyone else in the narrative thinks or feels (and so use the omniscient, or all-knowing, point of view).

Second, you need to decide whether you are going to "show" or "tell" or mix the two. You "show" in a narrative by dramatizing a scene and creating dialogue. Hughes recreates his experience for the reader by showing what happened and by recording some of the conversation that took place the night he was "saved from sin." The other option is "telling," that is, summarizing what happened. E. B. White tells the reader what he experienced and how he felt. He never dramatizes a particular scene and he never uses dialogue. Showing makes a narrative more vivid, for it allows the reader to experience the scene directly. Telling, on the other hand, allows you to include a greater number of events and details. Either way, selectivity is necessary. Hughes does not dramatize all of the events that happened; White does not summarize day-to-day activities. Each writer selects those moments which best give shape and significance to the experience.

What Do You Write About If Nothing Ever Happened to You?

It is easy to assume that the only things worth writing about are once-in-a-lifetime experiences—a heroic or death-defying act, a personal tragedy, an Olympic medal-winning performance. But a good personal experience narrative does not need to be based on an extraordinary experience. In fact, ordinary experiences, because they are about things familiar to every reader, are the best sources for personal narratives. There is nothing extraordinary, for example, about the events related in Langston Hughes's "Salvation," even though Hughes's experience was a turning point in his life. Sister Monroe's unintentionally comic performance in Maya Angelou's narrative was actually only one of several similar performances that Angelou relates in the first part of her autobiography *I Know Why the Caged Bird Sings.* E. B. White's return to the lake where he summered as a child, and even his feelings as he watches his son, are ordinary experiences shared and understood by every parent revisiting the past.

The secret to writing a good personal experience narrative lies in two areas. First, you must tell your story artfully. Following the advice outlined in this introduction is a good way to ensure that your narrative will be constructed as effectively as possible. Just telling what happened is not enough, though, for you must do a second, equally important thing: you must reveal a purpose in your tale. Purposes can be many. You might offer insight into human behavior or motivation; you might mark a significant moment in your life; you might reveal an awareness of what it is to be young and to have dreams; you might reflect on the precariousness of life and inevitability of change and decay. What is important is that your narrative have a point, a reason for being, and that you make the reason clear to your reader.

Writing a Narrative: A Student Example

Lisa Nagy decided to write about a minor automobile accident she had had, unfortunately a fairly common experience today. Even though no one was hurt, it was obvious that the experience was one that Lisa would remember. Her first draft begins with an explicit reference to that fact:

My Automobile Accident

On July 21, 1984, I experienced something I will never forget. I was in a car accident which was all my fault. It was raining and the roads were slippery. I was on my way to see my boyfriend when I decided to stop at a Burger King to get something to eat. Leaving the parking lot, I had to wait until the traffic was clear. A car in the first lane heading northbound had stopped and signaled that it was clear to go. As I started to turn onto the southbound lane, I never saw the stationwagon speeding towards me. The car's backend hooked my car's front and pulled my car around. The stationwagon then proceeded down the road and hit a third car.

I just sat in my car and started shaking. It took a few seconds before I realized what had just occurred. I got out of my car and headed towards the front of the car. I couldn't believe what I saw. The car's whole front fender was lying on the ground. The police arrived and wrote up an accident report. The officer lectured me about listening to other people. I should never have pulled out just because the other driver signaled for me to go.

I still think of so many "ifs": if I hadn't stopped to eat, if I had only looked. I let so many people down that day. I learned you shouldn't be in a hurry when you're driving and you shouldn't trust other people's advice.

When Lisa went back to revise her paper, she started by writing out a statement of her purpose: "To tell how I let everyone down, especially my parents." Since her accident had been minor, she realized that there was no reason to narrate the event in great detail. As a result, she decided to include her parents in the narrative. She tried also revealing her feelings rather than just summarizing what she had learned from the accident. Lisa's revision begins with an entirely new opening that shifts the reader's attention to her father and provides some suspense as well.

If Only . . .

My father was enjoying his usual Saturday round of golf. As he was about to tee off on the tenth hole, he saw Ted Hammond, the golf pro, approaching in a golf cart. "Bob," he shouted, "I'm going to have to take you in. Your daughter

Lisa's been in a car accident." When my father dropped his club in shock, Ted quickly added that Lisa wasn't hurt.

I'll never forget that day. It was raining, the roads were slippery, and I was in a hurry to see my boyfriend. I stopped at a Burger King for some lunch, and things were fine until I started to leave the parking lot. Waiting at the exit, I noticed that a car in the northbound lane had stopped and was signaling for me to go. Without thinking or looking, I turned into the southbound lane. I never saw the stationwagon until it struck my car, spun me around, and slammed into a third car.

I just sat there and started to shake. It was several seconds before I realized what had happened. All these thoughts and fears ran through my mind. The only thing I really wanted was my daddy. The hardest part was calling home. Mom called the country club and got dad off the course. They were there within half an hour.

To this day, I still think about all the "ifs": if I had not stopped to eat; if I had only looked. I let so many people down that afternoon.

Some Things to Remember

1. Decide first why you are telling the reader *this* story. You must have a purpose clearly in mind.
2. Choose an illustration, event, or experience that can be covered adequately within the space limitations you face. Do not try to narrate the whole of World War II in an essay!
3. Decide on which point of view you will use. Do you want to be a part of the narrative or an objective observer? Which is more appropriate for your purpose?
4. Keeping your purpose in mind, select those details or events which seem the most important or the most revealing.
5. Arrange those details in an order—either a strict chronological one or one that employs a flashback. Remember to keep your verb tenses consistent and to signal any switches in time.
6. Remember the differences between showing and telling. Which method will be better for your narrative?

Victory in the Pacific

SAMUEL ELIOT MORISON

Samuel Eliot Morison (1887-1976) was born into a prominent Boston family and in 1912 received a Ph.D. from Harvard, where he taught for forty years. A sense of his family's history and a love of the sea turned Morison toward American nautical history, to which he brought literacy and a concern for individuals rather than trends. He won the Pulitzer Prize for Admiral of the Ocean Sea *(1942) and* John Paul Jones: A Sailor's Biography *(1959). His other books include the fifteen-volume* History of United States Naval Operations in World War II *(1947-1962) and* The Oxford History of the American People *(1965). Morison was the recipient of numerous awards and honors, including the Balzan Foundation Award for History in 1963 and the Presidential Medal of Freedom in 1964. In this selection from* The Oxford History, *Morison narrates the events leading up to the bombing of Hiroshima and Nagasaki. "It is difficult to see how the Pacific war could otherwise have been concluded," Morison comments, "except by a long and bitter invasion of Japan."*

1 The Combined Chiefs of Staff, meeting at Quebec in September 1944, figured that it would take eighteen months after the surrender of Germany to defeat Japan. Actually, the war in the Pacific ended with a terrific bang only three months after V-E Day. President Truman and Winston Churchill, meeting with the C.C.S. at Potsdam, presented Japan with an ultimatum on 26 July 1945. The surrender must be complete, and include Allied occupation of Japan, and the return of all Japanese conquests since 1895 to their former owners. But the Japanese people were assured that the occupation would end as soon as "a peacefully inclined and responsible government" was established, and that they would neither "be enslaved as a race or destroyed as a nation." The alternative was "prompt and utter destruc-

tion." If Suzuki, the Japanese premier, had made up his
mind promptly to accept the Potsdam declaration as a basis
for peace, there would have been no atomic bomb explosion
over Japan. But Suzuki was more afraid of the Japanese mili-
tarists than he was of American power.

The fearful consequences were the result of prolonged 2
experiment and development in atomic fission. In 1939
Albert Einstein, Enrico Fermi, Leo Szilard, and other phys-
icists who had sought refuge in the United States from tyranny in their native countries, warned President Roosevelt
of the danger of Germany's obtaining a lead in uranium
fission. The President entrusted a project of that nature to
the Office of Scientific Research and Development, set up
in May 1941. On 2 December 1942 Fermi and others
achieved the first self-sustaining nuclear chain reaction,
halfway mark to the atomic bomb. Army engineers under
General W.S. Groves then took over and built a small city at
Oak Ridge, Tennessee, for producing the atomic bomb. By
1944 research had so progressed that a special physics laboratory was erected at Los Alamos, New Mexico, for which
J. R. Oppenheimer was responsible; and on 16 July 1945 the
first atomic bomb was exploded there.

President Truman conveyed the news at Potsdam to 3
Winston Churchill, who remarked, "This is the Second
Coming, in wrath." That indeed it was for Japan.

We had it, but whether or not to use it was another 4
question. President Truman's committee of high officials
and top atomic scientists recommended that atomic bombs
be exploded over Japan at once, and without warning. On 25
July the President issued the necessary order to the XX
Army Air Force at Saipan, whither the first two bombs had
been sent, to prepare to drop them at the first favorable
moment after 3 August, if Japan had not by then accepted
surrender. He and Secretary of State Byrnes waited in vain
for word from Japan. All they got was a silly statement from
Suzuki that the Potsdam declaration was unworthy of
notice. So the fateful order stood.

"Enola Gay," as the chosen B-29 was called, was com- 5
manded by Colonel Paul W. Tibbets. At 9:15 a.m., 6 August,

the bomb was toggled out at an altitude of 31,600 feet over Hiroshima. This city had been given the tragic target assignment as the second most important military center in Japan. The bomb wiped out the Second Japanese Army to a man, razed four square miles of the city, and killed 60,175 people, including the soldiers. Around noon 9 August, a few hours after Russia had declared war on Japan, the second atomic bomb exploded over Nagasaki, killing 36,000 more.

Although many Americans have expressed contrition 6
over exploding the first atomic bombs, it is difficult to see how the Pacific war could otherwise have been concluded, except by a long and bitter invasion of Japan; or what difference it would have made after the war if the secret had temporarily been withheld. The explosion over Hiroshima caused fewer civilian casualties than the repeated B-29 bombings of Tokyo, and those big bombers would have had to wipe out one city after another if the war had not ended in August. Japan had enough military capability—more than 5000 planes with kamikaze-trained pilots and at least 2 million ground troops—to have made our planned invasion of the Japanese home islands in the fall of 1945 an exceedingly bloody affair for both sides. And that would have been followed by a series of bitterly protracted battles on Japanese soil, the effects of which even time could hardly have healed. Moreover, as Russia would have been a full partner in these campaigns, the end result would have been partition of Japan, as happened to Germany.

Even after the two atomic bombs had been dropped, and 7
the Potsdam declaration had been clarified to assure Japan that she could keep her emperor, the surrender was a very near thing. Hirohito had to override his two chief military advisers and take the responsibility of accepting the Potsdam terms. That he did on 14 August, but even after that a military coup d'etat to sequester the emperor, kill his cabinet, and continue the war was narrowly averted. Hirohito showed great moral courage; and the promise to retain him in power despite the wishes of Russia (which wanted the war prolonged and Japan given over to anarchy) was a very wise decision.

After preliminary arrangements had been made at Manila with General MacArthur's and Admiral Nimitz's staffs, an advance party was flown into Atsugi airfield near Tokyo on 28 August. Scores of ships of the United States Pacific Fleet, and of the British Far Eastern Fleet, then entered Tokyo Bay. On 2 September 1945 General MacArthur, General Umezu, the Japanese foreign minister, and representatives of Great Britain, China, Russia, Australia, Canada, New Zealand, the Netherlands, and France, signed the surrender documents on the deck of battleship *Missouri*, a few miles from the spot where Commodore Perry's treaty had been signed ninety-two years before. 8

QUESTIONS ON SUBJECT AND PURPOSE

1. What is the subject of this passage? Does it differ in any way from what you might expect to find in a textbook?
2. How does Morison feel about the bombing of Hiroshima and Nagasaki? How and where does that come through?
3. What should be the task of the historian? Can you ever record history without also interpreting or shaping it?

QUESTIONS ON STRATEGY AND AUDIENCE

1. Within the space of eight paragraphs, Morison narrates a very complex series of events. He obviously cannot tell the whole story; he must select what he feels are the most important details. Look at Morison's selection. What does he include? What does he leave out?
2. What assumptions does Morison make about his audience? Can you point to specific passages or remarks that reveal those assumptions?
3. Why does Morison allude at the end of this selection to Commodore Perry's treaty? What was that? What does the allusion suggest?

QUESTIONS ON VOCABULARY AND STYLE

1. Why does Morison set paragraph 3 apart? What is the effect of putting this quotation in a separate paragraph?

2. Why does paragraph 5 contain so many precise details? Does Morison include any details in the paragraph that support his attitude toward the use of the bomb?
3. Be able to define or identify the following: *V-E Day* (paragraph 1), *the Second Coming* (3), *toggled out* (5), *contrition* (6), *coup d'etat* (7), *Commodore Perry's treaty* (8).

WRITING SUGGESTIONS

1. Select an event—local, state, national, or international. Using newspaper, radio and television, and newsmagazine articles, contruct a paragraph narrative of what happened. Avoid interpreting or evaluating the event. Stick to the facts.
2. Select a local or campus event that has occurred within the past two weeks. In an essay, narrate what happened, but do so in a way that interprets or evaluates the event. In other words, you want the reader to be aware of your "reading" of this incident; you are not just being totally objective. You have a thesis.

   Prewriting:

   a. Visit your college library and look through the most recent issues of the school newspaper. Look for an event that interests you, but one also that lends itself to illustrating a particular point you want to make. Make a list of possibilities.
   b. Remember that significance can be found in many events. For example, an athletic event might lead you to opinions on recruitment, on the funding of women's athletic teams, on academic eligibility, on student apathy (or overzealousness). From your list, select one event that seems particularly significant.
   c. Do some freewriting about the event you have selected. Write for 15 minutes without stopping, trying to keep your focus on the event's significance. You are just trying to generate more ideas, so do not worry about writing complete, correct sentences. At the end of the time, stop, reread, and then write for another 15 minutes.

   Rewriting:

   a. Once you have a draft of your essay, look back through to see if you have interpreted, not just summarized. Do not try to tell the reader exactly how to feel; try to shape reader reaction through your choice of detail and language.

b. Test your essay by having a classmate read it. Does your reader agree or disagree with your interpretation? Get a specific response from your reader. Use that response to reexamine what you have written.

3. How widely shared is the view Morison expresses in paragraph 6? Sample the research available in your library. Using the interpretations and analyses of other historians, write an essay either supporting or criticizing the use of the bomb. Limit the focus of your argument to the bombings of Hiroshima and Nagasaki. Do not try to include every possible consequence that has emerged since 1945 (e.g., nuclear winter).

Salvation

LANGSTON HUGHES

Langston Hughes (1902-1967) was born in Joplin, Missouri, and spent most of his childhood in Lawrence, Kansas, with his grandmother after the separation of his parents. He attended high school in Cleveland, Ohio, where he first began to read and to write poetry. In 1921, he enrolled in Columbia University, where he studied for one year and published many of his first poems, the most significant being "The Negro Speaks of Rivers." Hughes then abandoned his studies to work at various odd jobs in New York and to travel abroad. When he returned to the States, he continued to work on poems he had begun while at school and, in 1926, published his first volume, entitled The Weary Blues *(1926). This book won him critical acclaim and launched his successful career as a poet. Hughes was granted a scholarship to Lincoln University in Pennsylvania, where he graduated in 1929. By 1930, he had won several awards for his poetry and become an important member of the literary circle that helped form the Harlem Renaissance. Among his writings are* Not Without Laughter *(1930),* The Ways of White Folks *(1940),* Simple Speaks His Mind *(1950), and* Selected Poems *(1959). Hughes stands as one of the most eminent black poets of the twentieth century. His poems tell of the trials and tribulations of a black people in America and celebrate their quest for freedom and social justice. Hughes was also a gifted prose writer, as this famous selection about his experience at a revival reveals: "I was saved from sin when I was going on thirteen."*

I was saved from sin when I was going on thirteen. But not really saved. It happened like this. There was a big revival at my Auntie Reed's church. Every night for weeks there had been much preaching, singing, praying, and shouting, and some very hardened sinners had been brought to Christ, and the membership of the church had grown by leaps and bounds. Then just before the revival ended, they held a spe- 1 cial meeting for children, "to bring the young lambs to the fold." My aunt spoke of it for days ahead. That night I was escorted to the front row and placed on the mourners' bench with all the other young sinners, who had not yet been brought to Jesus.

My aunt told me that when you were saved you saw a 2
light, and something happened to you inside! And Jesus came into your life! And God was with you from then on! She said you could see and hear and feel Jesus in your soul. I believed her. I had heard a great many old people say the same thing and it seemed to me they ought to know. So I sat there calmly in the hot, crowded church, waiting for Jesus to come to me.

The preacher preached a wonderful rhythmical sermon, 3
all moans and shouts and lonely cries and dire pictures of hell, and then he sang a song about the ninety and nine safe in the fold, but one little lamb was left out in the cold. Then he said: "Won't you come? Won't you come to Jesus? Young lambs, won't you come?" And he held out his arms to all us young sinners there on the mourners' bench. And the little girls cried. And some of them jumped up and went to Jesus right away. But most of us just sat there.

A great many old people came and knelt around us and 4
prayed, old women with jet-black faces and braided hair, old men with work-gnarled hands. And the church sang a song about the lower lights are burning, some poor sinners to be saved. And the whole building rocked with prayer and song.

Still I kept waiting to *see* Jesus. 5

Finally all the young people had gone to the altar and 6
were saved, but one boy and me. He was a rounder's son named Westley. Westley and I were surrounded by sisters and deacons praying. It was very hot in the church, and getting late now. Finally Westley said to me in a whisper: "God damn! I'm tired o' sitting here. Let's get up and be saved." So he got up and was saved.

Then I was left all alone on the mourner's bench. My 7
aunt came and knelt at my knees and cried, while prayers and song swirled all around me in the little church. The whole congregation prayed for me alone, in a mighty wail of

moans and voices. And I kept waiting serenely for Jesus, waiting, waiting—but he didn't come. I wanted to see him, but nothing happened to me. Nothing! I wanted something to happen to me, but nothing happened.

I hear the songs and the minister saying: "Why don't you come? My dear child, why don't you come to Jesus? Jesus is waiting for you. He wants you. Why don't you come? Sister Reed, what is this child's name?" 8

"Langston," my aunt sobbed. 9

"Langston, why don't you come? Why don't you come and be saved? Oh, Lamb of God! Why don't you come?" 10

Now it was really getting late. I began to be ashamed of myself, holding everything up so long. I began to wonder what God thought about Westley, who certainly hadn't seen Jesus either, but who was now sitting proudly on the platform, swinging his knickerbockered legs and grinning down at me, surrounded by deacons and old women on their knees praying. God had not struck Westley dead for taking his name in vain or for lying in the temple. So I decided that maybe to save further trouble, I'd better lie, too, and say that Jesus had come, and get up and be saved. 11

So I got up. 12

Suddenly the whole room broke into a sea of shouting, as they saw me rise. Waves of rejoicing swept the place. Women leaped in the air. My aunt threw her arms around me. The minister took me by the hand and led me to the platform. 13

When things quieted down, in a hushed silence, punctuated by a few ecstatic "Amens," all the new young lambs were blessed in the name of God. Then joyous singing filled the room. 14

That night, for the last time in my life but one—for I was a big boy twelve years old—I cried. I cried, in bed alone, and couldn't stop. I buried my head under the quilts, but my aunt heard me. She woke up and told my uncle I was crying because the Holy Ghost had come into my life, and because I had seen Jesus. But I was really crying because I couldn't bear to tell her that I had lied, that I had deceived everybody in the church, that I hadn't seen Jesus, and that now I didn't 15 believe there was a Jesus any more, since he didn't come to help me.

QUESTIONS ON SUBJECT AND PURPOSE

1. Who narrates the story? From what point in time is it told?
2. What does the narrator expect to happen when he is to be saved? What does happen?
3. Why does the narrator cry at the end of the story?
4. What was Hughes's attitude toward his experience when it first happened? At the time he originally wrote this selection? How does the opening sentence reflect that change in attitude?

QUESTIONS ON STRATEGY AND AUDIENCE

1. Why not tell the story in the present tense? How would that change the story?
2. How much dialogue is used in the narration? Why not use more?
3. Why does Hughes blend telling with showing in the story?
4. How much time is represented by the events in the story? Where does Hughes compress the time in his narrative? Why does he do so?

QUESTIONS ON VOCABULARY AND STYLE

1. What is the effect of the short paragraphs (5, 9, and 12)? How does Hughes use paragraphing to help shape his story?
2. How much description does Hughes include in his narrative? What types of details does he single out?
3. What is the effect of the exclamation marks used in paragraph 2?
4. Try to identify or explain the following phrases: *the ninety and nine safe in the fold* (paragraph 3), *the lower lights are burning* (4), *a rounder's son* (6), *knickerbockered legs* (11).

WRITING SUGGESTIONS

1. We have all been disappointed by something or someone in our life. Single out a particular event from your life. Spend some time trying to remember what happened and exactly how you

felt. In a paragraph or an essay, narrate that experience. Remember that you need to make your reader understand how you felt and what it all meant to you. Try using some dialogue.

2. Have you ever experienced anything that changed your life? It does not need to be a dramatic change—just a conviction that you will never do *that* again or that you will *always* do that again. In a paragraph or an essay, narrate your experience.

   Prewriting:
   a. Divide your prewriting sessions for this paper into a series of activities done on different days. On day one, concentrate just on making a list of possible vivid experiences—a near miss, a careless moment, a time you were caught, a stupid choice.
   b. On day two, spend a half an hour freewriting about two of the events from your list. Try to do one writing in the morning and one in the afternoon. Do not worry about writing complete, correct sentences. Do not stop during the writing.
   c. On day three, spend an hour thinking about one of the two events. Jot down as much detail as you can remember.
   d. On day four, write a draft of the essay, using the details gathered from the activities above.

   Rewriting:
   a. A successful narrative has a shape and a purpose. You do not need to include everything that happened, just those events relevant to the experience and its effect on you. Look again at the narratives included in this chapter. Notice what they include and exclude. Does your narrative show the same economy?
   b. Did you use any dialogue? Sparing use will probably make your narrative more vivid—that is, it will show rather than tell.
   c. Is the order of events clear to the reader? Is the story told in a strict chronological order? Did you use flashbacks? Think about other possible arrangements for your narrative.

3. Two recent U.S. presidents have described themselves as "born-again" Christians. Exactly what does that phrase mean? Research the origins of the term and the growth of such belief in America today. Write an essay relating your findings.

Sister Monroe

MAYA ANGELOU

Maya Angelou was born Marguerita Johnson in St. Louis, Missouri, in 1928. She was raised, along with her brother, by their grandmother in rural Stamps, Arkansas. She served as a coordinator for the Southern Christian Leadership Conference at the request of Martin Luther King, Jr. Her most significant writings have been her series of five autobiographical works: I Know Why the Caged Bird Sings *(1970),* Gather Together in My Name *(1974),* Singin' and Swingin' and Gettin' Merry like Christmas *(1976),* The Heart of a Woman *(1981), and her most recent volume,* All God's Children Need Travelin' Shoes *(1987), a record of her visit to Ghana from 1962 to 1964. In this passage from the first of her memoirs, Angelou recalls how Sister Monroe "got the spirit" one Sunday morning at the Christian Methodist Episcopal Church.*

In the Christian Methodist Episcopal Church the children's section was on the right, cater-cornered from the pew that held those ominous women called the Mothers of the Church. In the young people's section the benches were placed close together, and when a child's legs no longer comfortably fitted in the narrow space, it was an indication to the elders that that person could now move into the intermediate area (center church). Baily and I were allowed to sit with the other children only when there were informal meetings, church socials or the like. But on the Sundays when Reverend Thomas preached, it was ordained that we occupy the first row, called the mourners' bench. I thought we were placed in front because Momma was proud of us, but Bailey assured me that she just wanted to keep her grandchildren under her thumb and eye. 1

Reverend Thomas took his text from Deuteronomy. And I was stretched between loathing his voice and wanting to listen to the sermon. Deuteronomy was my favorite book 2 in the Bible. The laws were so absolute, so clearly set down, that I knew if a person truly wanted to avoid hell and brimstone, and being roasted forever in the devil's fire, all she had to do was memorize Deuteronomy and follow its teaching, word for word. I also liked the way the word rolled off the tongue.

Bailey and I sat alone on the front bench, the wooden slats pressing hard on our behinds and the backs of our thighs. I would have wriggled just a bit, but each time I looked over at Momma, she seemed to threaten, "Move and I'll tear you up," so, obedient to the unvoiced command, I sat still. The church ladies were warming up behind me with a few hallelujahs and praise the Lords and Amens, and the preacher hadn't really moved into the meat of the sermon. 3

It was going to be a hot service. 4

On my way into church, I saw Sister Monroe, her open-faced gold crown glinting when she opened her mouth to return a neighborly greeting. She lived in the country and couldn't get to church every Sunday, so she made up for her absences by shouting so hard when she did make it that she shook the whole church. As soon as she took her seat, all the ushers would move to her side of the church because it took three women and sometimes a man or two to hold her. 5

Once she hadn't been to church for a few months (she had taken off to have a child), she got the spirit and started shouting, throwing her arms around and jerking her body, so that the ushers went over to hold her down, but she tore herself away from them and ran up to the pulpit. She stood in front of the altar, shaking like a freshly caught trout. She screamed at Reverend Taylor. "Preach it. I say, preach it." Naturally he kept on preaching as if she wasn't standing there telling him what to do. Then she screamed an extremely fierce "I said, preach it" and stepped up on the altar. The Reverend kept on throwing out phrases like home-run balls and Sister Monroe made a quick break and grasped for him. For just a second, everything and everyone in the church except Reverend Taylor and Sister Monroe hung loose like stockings on a washline. Then she caught 6 the minister by the sleeve of his jacket and his coattail, then she rocked him from side to side.

I have to say this for our minister, he never stopped giving us the lesson. The usher board made its way to the pulpit, going up both aisles with a little more haste than is customarily seen in church. Truth to tell, they fairly ran to the minister's aid. Then two of the deacons, in their shiny Sunday suits, joined the ladies in white on the pulpit, and each time they pried Sister Monroe loose from the preacher he took another deep breath and kept on preaching, and Sister Monroe grabbed him in another place, and more firmly. Reverend Taylor was helping his rescuers as much as possible by jumping around when he got a chance. His voice at one point got so low it sounded like a roll of thunder, then Sister Monroe's "Preach it" cut through the roar, and we all wondered (I did, in any case) if it would ever end. Would they go on forever, or get tired out at last like a game of blindman's bluff that lasted too long, with nobody caring who was "it"? 7

I'll never know what might have happened, because magically the pandemonium spread. The spirit infused Deacon Jackson and Sister Willson, the chairman of the usher board, at the same time. Deacon Jackson, a tall, thin, quiet man, who was also a part-time Sunday school teacher, gave a scream like a falling tree, leaned back on thin air and punched Reverend Taylor on the arm. It must have hurt as much as it caught the Reverend unawares. There was a moment's break in the rolling sounds and Reverend Taylor jerked around surprised, and hauled off and punched Deacon Jackson. In the same second Sister Willson caught his tie, looped it over her fist a few times, and pressed down on him. There wasn't time to laugh or cry before all three of them were down on the floor behind the altar. Their legs spiked out like kindling wood. 8

Sister Monroe, who had been the cause of all the excitement, walked off the dais, cool and spent, and raised her flinty voice in the hymn, "I came to Jesus, as I was, worried, wound, and sad, I found in Him a resting place and He has made me glad." 9

The minister took advantage of already being on the floor and asked in a choky little voice if the church would kneel with him to offer a prayer of thanksgiving. He said we had been visited with a mighty spirit, and let the whole church say Amen. 10

On the next Sunday, he took his text from the eighteenth chapter of the Gospel according to St. Luke, and talked quietly but seriously about the Pharisees, who prayed in the streets so that the public would be impressed with their religious devotion. I doubt that anyone got the message—certainly not those to whom it was directed. The deacon board, however, did appropriate funds for him to buy a new suit. The other was a total loss. 11

QUESTIONS ON SUBJECT AND PURPOSE

1. Who is the narrator? How old does she seem to be? How do you know?
2. Why does Sister Monroe behave as she does?
3. How does the section on the narrator and Bailey act as a preface to the story of Sister Monroe? Is it relevant, for example, that the narrator's favorite book of the Bible is Deuteronomy?

QUESTIONS ON STRATEGY AND AUDIENCE

1. Part of the art of narration is knowing what events to select. Look carefully at Angelou's story of Sister Monroe (paragraphs 5 to 9). What events does she choose to include in her narrative?
2. How is Sister Monroe described? Make a list of all of the physical particulars we are given about her. How, other than direct description, is Sister Monroe revealed to the reader?
3. What shift occurs between paragraph 5 and 6? Did you notice it the first time you read the selection?

QUESTIONS ON VOCABULARY AND STYLE

1. Other than a few words uttered by Sister Monroe, Angelou uses no other dialogue in the selection. How, then, is the story told? What advantage does this method have?

2. Writing humor is never easy. Having a funny situation is essential, but, in addition, the story must be told in the right way. (Remember how people can ruin a good joke?) How does Angelou's language and style contribute to the humor in the selection?
3. How effective are the following images:
   a. "She stood in front of the altar, shaking like a freshly caught trout" (paragraph 6).
   b. "The Reverend kept on throwing out phrases like home-run balls" (6).
   c. "Everyone in the church . . . hung loose like stockings on a washline" (6).
   d. "Their legs spiked out like kindling wood" (8).

WRITING SUGGESTIONS

1. Everyone has experienced a funny, embarrassing moment—maybe it happened to you or maybe you just witnessed it. In a paragraph narrate the incident.
2. Select a "first" from your experience—your first day in junior high school, your first date, your first time driving a car, your first day at college. Recreate that first. Do not just include a chronology of everything that happened. Focus your narrative around a significant feature of that first experience, whether funny or serious.

   Prewriting:
   a. Several days before your essay is due, set aside an hour to comb your memories for some significant "firsts." Make a list of possibilities, jotting down whatever details you remember. Let the list rest for a day before looking at it again.
   b. Scan your list and select the most promising item. For another hour jot down randomly whatever you remember. Focus on re-creating the event in your memory. One detail often triggers others. Do not try to write yet; just gather details.
   c. Remember that your narrative needs to hinge on a significant feature—it can be an insight (such as in Hughes's "Salvation" or White's "Once More to the Lake") or a serious or comic pattern (as in "Sister Monroe"). Write down an explicit statement of what it is you want to reveal in your

narrative. Use that statement to decide what details to include and what to exclude.

Rewriting:

a. After a draft is completed, go back and look at the purpose statement you wrote in prewriting. Carefully test each detail you included to see if it relates to that intended purpose. Omit any irrelevant or inappropriate details.
b. Look at your conclusion. How did you end? Did you lead up to a climactic moment, or did you end with a flat conclusion ("And so you can see why this experience was important to me")? Compare how the writers in this chapter end their narratives.

3. Religious experiences are not always as physical as Sister Monroe's. Select a prominent historical or contemporary figure who has had an experience—a conversion, a miracle, a vision. Research the story, and in a narrative retell the story.

Young Hunger

M. F. K. FISHER

Born in 1908 and raised in Whittier, California, M. F. K. Fisher was educated at UCLA and the University of Dijon, France. She is well known for her years of writing a cooking column for The New York Times *and for her books on food and eating. Among her early gastronomical works are* Serve It Forth *(1937) and* How to Cook a Wolf *(1942), both of which she wrote as Mary Frances Parrish. Her first novel was* Not Now But Now *(1946). She has collected earlier works in the* The Art of Eating. *Her most recent book,* Two Towns in Provence *(1983), discusses her experiences, eating and otherwise, in post-war France. In "Young Hunger" Fisher remembers what it was to be young and to be hungry.*

It is very hard for people who have passed the age of, say, 1
fifty to remember with any charity the hunger of their own puberty and adolescence when they are dealing with the young human animals who may be frolicking about them. Too often I have seen good people helpless with exasperation and real anger upon finding in the morning that cupboards and iceboxes have been stripped of their supplies by two or three youths—or even *one*—who apparently could have eaten four times their planned share at the dinner table the night before.

Such avidity is revolting, once past. But I can recall its 2
intensity still; I am not yet too far from it to understand its ferocious demands when I see a fifteen-year-old boy wince and whiten at the prospect of waiting politely a few more hours for food, when his guts are howling for meat–bread–candy–fruit–cheese–milkmilkmilk—ANYTHING IN THE WORLD TO EAT.

I can still remember my almost insane desperation 3
when I was about eighteen and was staying overnight with

my comparatively aged godparents. I had come home alone from France in a bad continuous storm and was literally concave with solitude and hunger. The one night on the train seemed even rougher than those on board ship, and by the time I reached my godparents' home I was almost light-headed.

4 I got there just in time for lunch. It is clear as ice in my mind: a little cup of very weak chicken broth, one salted cracker, one-half piece of thinly sliced toast, and then, ah then, a whole waffle, crisp and brown and with a piece of beautiful butter melting in its middle—which the maid deftly cut into four sections! One section she put on my godmother's plate. The next *two*, after a nod of approval from her mistress, she put on mine. My godfather ate the fourth.

5 There was a tiny pot of honey, and I dutifully put a dab of it on my piggish portion, and we all nibbled away and drank one cup apiece of tea with lemon. Both my god-parents left part of their waffles.

6 It was simply that they were old and sedentary and quite out of the habit of eating amply with younger people: a good thing for them, but pure hell for me. I did not have the sense to explain to them how starved I was—which I would not hesitate to do now. Instead I prowled around my bedroom while the house slumbered through its afternoon siesta, wondering if I dared to sneak to the strange kitchen for something, anything, to eat, and knowing I would rather die than meet the silent, stern maid or my nice, gentle little hostess.

7 Later we walked slowly down to the village, and I was thinking sensuously of double malted ice-cream sodas at the corner drugstore, but there was no possibility of such heaven. When we got back to the quiet house, the maid brought my godfather a tall glass of exquisitely rich milk, with a handful of dried fruit on the saucer under it, because he had been ill; but as we sat and watched him unwillingly down it, his wife said softly that it was such a short time until dinner that she was sure I did not want to spoil my

appetite, and I agreed with her because I was young and shy.

When I dressed, I noticed that the front of my pelvic 8
basin jutted out like two bricks under my skirt: I looked like a scarecrow.

Dinner was very long, but all I can remember is that it 9
had, as *pièce de résistance,* half of the tiny chicken previously boiled for broth at luncheon, which my godmother carved carefully so that we should each have a bit of the breast and I, as guest, should have the leg, after a snippet had been sliced from it for her husband, who liked dark meat too.

There were hot biscuits, yes, the smallest I have ever 10
seen, two apiece under a napkin on a silver dish. Because of them we had no dessert: it would be too rich, my godmother said.

We drank little cups of decaffeinized coffee on the 11
screened porch in the hot Midwestern night, and when I went up to my room I saw that the maid had left a large glass of rich malted milk beside my poor godfather's bed.

My train would leave before five in the morning, and I 12
slept little and unhappily, dreaming of the breakfast I would order on it. Of course when I finally saw it all before me, twinkling on the Pullman silver dishes, I could eat very little, from too much hunger and a sense of outrage.

I felt that my hosts had been indescribably rude to me, 13
and selfish and conceited and stupid. Now I know that they were none of these things. They had simply forgotten about any but their own dwindling and cautious needs for nourishment. They had forgotten about being hungry, being young, being . . .

QUESTIONS ON SUBJECT AND PURPOSE

1. What is Fisher's subject?
2. Why doesn't she speak up when she is hungry?
3. Why does the final sentence simply trail off: "being hungry, being young, being . . ."?

QUESTIONS ON STRATEGY AND AUDIENCE

1. How does Fisher structure her essay? What does she leave out of her narrative?
2. Why does Fisher describe the meals she ate in such careful detail? What do those descriptions contribute to the essay?
3. Who is Fisher's audience? That is, does she seem to write to young people? Old people? Does the first sentence define in any way her audience?

QUESTIONS ON VOCABULARY AND STYLE

1. At times Fisher mixes relatively informal language with formal. Find several examples of that mix. Why might she do this?
2. Why might Fisher write a line such as "guts are howling for meat–bread–candy–fruit–cheese–milkmilkmilk—ANYTHING IN THE WORLD TO EAT"? What effect does it have?
3. Be able to identify the following words and phrases: *avidity* (paragraph 2), *pièce de résistance* (9), *snippet* (9), *Pullman* (12).

WRITING SUGGESTIONS

1. We have all overindulged at times. In a paragraph describe a time when you gorged yourself. What was the situation, the setting, the food? How did you feel before and after? Why did you do it?
2. Choose an area of your life that has changed as you have gotten older. It should be something that expresses a change in values, opinions, likes or dislikes, emotions, priorities. In an essay recall or describe the childhood/adolescent feeling or attitude and contrast it with your present feelings. Narrate the process of change.

   Prewriting:
   a. One possible source of material is memory/reflection. Brainstorming for an hour or more at two different times will probably help you focus your memories.
   b. Another possibility is to ask relatives about changes they remember in you.
   c. A third possibility is to observe younger children—perhaps a sister or brother. Write down things that they say or do that show how they think and feel differently from adults.

Rewriting:

a. Study Fisher's essay carefully, because it can be used as a structural model. Notice how she uses narration and description to dramatize her point. Check to see if you have managed to make your narrative vivid in the same way.

b. Remember not to tell everything that happened. Your narrative should be focused. It should support your thesis. Finish the following sentence: "The point I am trying to make in my story is———." Use that sentence as a way of testing what you include in your narrative.

3. Food and eating rituals play a significant role in every nationality and culture. Research the significance and traditions that lie behind certain foods or meals for an American ethnic or religious group. Be sure to explain both the history of those traditions and their significance. Present your findings in one of the following formats:
   a. A traditional college research paper
   b. An article for a popular magazine or a Sunday supplement to a newspaper
   c. A food magazine

Once More to the Lake

E. B. WHITE

Elwyn Brooks White (1899-1985) was born in Mount Vernon, New York, and received a B. A. from Cornell in 1921. His freshman English teacher was William Strunk, whose Elements of Style *White revised in 1959 and made into a textbook classic. In 1925 White began writing for* The New Yorker *and was one of the mainstays of that magazine, his precise, ironic, nostalgic prose style closely associated with its own. From 1937 to 1943, he also wrote the column "One Man's Meat" for* Harper's. *His books include the children's classic* Charlotte's Web *(1952),* The Second Tree From the Corner *(1954),* The Essays of E. B. White *(1977), and* The Poems and Sketches of E. B. White *(1981). White was awarded the Presidential Medal of Freedom in 1963 and a special Pulitzer Prize for his work as a whole in 1978. In "Once More to the Lake" White revisits the lake in Maine where he summered as a child. Taking his son with him, White discovers that their identities merge: "I began to sustain the illusion that he was I, and therefore, by simple transposition, that I was my father."*

One summer along about 1904, my father rented a camp on a lake in Maine and took us all there for the month of August. We all got ringworm from some kittens and had to rub Pond's Extract on our arms and legs night and morning, and my father rolled over in a canoe with all his clothes on; but outside of that the vacation was a success and from then on none of us ever thought there was any place in the world like that lake in Maine. We returned summer after summer—always on August 1st for one month. I have since become a salt-water man, but sometimes in summer there are days when the restlessness of the tides and the fearful cold of the sea water and the incessant wind that blows across the afternoon and into the evening make me wish for the placidity of a lake in the woods. A few weeks ago this 1 feeling got so strong I bought myself a couple of bass hooks and a spinner and returned to the lake where we used to go, for a week's fishing and to revisit old haunts.

I took along my son, who had never had any fresh water up his nose and who had seen lily pads only from train windows. On the journey over to the lake I began to wonder what it would be like. I wondered how time would have marred this unique, this holy spot—the coves and streams, the hills that the sun set behind, the camps and the paths behind the camps. I was sure that the tarred road would have found it out and I wondered in what other ways it would be desolated. It is strange how much you can remember about places like that once you allow your mind to return into the grooves that lead back. You remember one thing, and that suddenly reminds you of another thing. I guess I remembered clearest of all the early mornings, when the lake was cool and motionless, remembered how the bedroom smelled of the lumber it was made of and of the wet woods whose scent entered through the screen. The partitions in the camp were thin and did not extend clear to the top of the rooms, and as I was always the first up I would dress softly so as not to wake the others, and sneak out into the sweet outdoors and start out in the canoe, keeping close along the shore in the long shadows of the pines. I remembered being very careful never to rub my paddle against the gunwale for fear of disturbing the stillness of the cathedral. 2

The lake had never been what you would call a wild lake. There were cottages sprinkled around the shores, and it was in farming country although the shores of the lake were quite heavily wooded. Some of the cottages were owned by nearby farmers, and you would live at the shore and eat your meals at the farmhouse. That's what our family did. But although it wasn't wild, it was a fairly large and undisturbed lake and there were places in it which, to a child at least, seemed infinitely remote and primeval. 3

I was right about the tar: it led to within half a mile of the shore. But when I got back there, with my boy, and we settled into a camp near a farmhouse and into the kind of summertime I had known, I could tell that it was going to 4 be pretty much the same as it had been before—I knew it, lying in bed the first morning, smelling the bedroom, and hearing the boy sneak quietly out and go off along the shore in a boat. I began to sustain the illusion that he was I, and therefore, by simple transposition, that I was my father. This sensation persisted, kept cropping up all the time we were there. It was not an entirely new feeling, but in this setting it grew much stronger. I seemed to be living a dual existence. I would be in the middle of some simple act, I would be picking up a bait box or laying down a table fork, or I would be saying something, and suddenly it would be not I but my father who was saying the words or making the gesture. It gave me a creepy sensation.

5 We went fishing the first morning. I felt the same damp moss covering the worms in the bait can, and saw the dragonfly alight on the tip of my rod as it hovered a few inches from the surface of the water. It was the arrival of this fly that convinced me beyond any doubt that everything was as it always had been, that the years were a mirage and there had been no years. The small waves were the same, chucking the rowboat under the chin as we fished at anchor, and the boat was the same boat, the same color green and the ribs broken in the same places, and under the floor-boards the same fresh-water leavings and debris—the dead helgramite, the wisps of moss, the rusty discarded fishhook, the dried blood from yesterday's catch. We stared silently at the tips of our rods, at the dragonflies that came and went. I lowered the tip of mine into the water, tentatively, pensively dislodging the fly, which darted two feet away, poised, darted two feet back, and came to rest again a little farther up the rod. There had been no years between the ducking of this dragonfly and the other one—the one that was part of memory. I looked at the boy, who was silently watching his fly, and it was my hands that held his rod, my eyes watching. I felt dizzy and didn't know which rod I was at the end of.

6 We caught two bass, hauling them in briskly as though they were mackerel, pulling them over the side of the boat in a businesslike manner without any landing net, and stun-

ning them with a blow on the back of the head. When we got back for a swim before lunch, the lake was exactly where we had left it, the same number of inches from the dock, and there was only the merest suggestion of a breeze. This seemed an utterly enchanted sea, this lake you could leave to its own devices for a few hours and come back to, and find that it had not stirred, this constant and trustworthy body of water. In the shallows, the dark, water-soaked sticks and twigs, smooth and old, were undulating in clusters on the bottom against the clean ribbed sand, and the track of the mussel was plain. A school of minnows swam by, each minnow with its small individual shadow, doubling the attendance, so clear and sharp in the sunlight. Some of the other campers were in swimming, along the shore, one of them with a cake of soap, and the water felt thin and clear and unsubstantial. Over the years there had been this person with the cake of soap, this cultist, and here he was. There had been no years.

Up to the farmhouse to dinner through the teeming, 7
dusty field, the road under our sneakers was only a two-track road. The middle track was missing, the one with the marks of the hooves and splotches of dried, flaky manure. There had always been three tracks to choose from in choosing which track to walk in; now the choice was narrowed down to two. For a moment I missed terribly the middle alternative. But the way led past the tennis court, and something about the way it lay there in the sun reassured me; the tape had loosened along the backline, the alleys were green with plantains and other weeds, and the net (installed in June and removed in September) sagged in the dry noon, and the whole place steamed with midday heat and hunger and emptiness. There was a choice of pie for dessert, and one was blueberry and one was apple, and the waitresses were the same country girls, there having been no passage of time, only the illusion of it as in a dropped curtain—the waitresses were still fifteen; their hair had been washed, that was the only difference—they had been to the movies and seen the pretty girls with the clean hair.

Summertime, oh summertime, pattern of life indelible, the fadeproof lake, the woods unshatterable, the pasture with the sweetfern and the juniper forever and ever, summer without end; this was the background, and the life along the shore was the design, the cottages with their innocent and tranquil design, their tiny docks with the flagpole and the American flag floating against the white clouds in the blue sky, the little paths over the roots of the trees leading from camp to camp and the paths leading back to the outhouses and the can of lime for sprinkling, and at the souvenir counters at the store the miniature birch-bark canoes and the post cards that showed things looking a little better than they looked. This was the American family at play, escaping the city heat, wondering whether the newcomers in the camp at the head of the cove were "common" or "nice," wondering whether it was true that the people who drove up for Sunday dinner at the farmhouse were turned away because there wasn't enough chicken. 8

It seemed to me, as I kept remembering all this, that those times and those summers had been infinitely precious and worth saving. There had been jollity and peace and goodness. The arriving (at the beginning of August) had been so big a business in itself, at the railway station the farm wagon drawn up, the first smell of the pine-laden air, the first glimpse of the smiling farmer, and the great importance of the trunks and your father's enormous authority in such matters, and the feel of the wagon under you for the long ten-mile haul, and at the top of the last long hill catching the first view of the lake after eleven months of not seeing this cherished body of water. The shouts and cries of the other campers when they saw you, and the trunks to be unpacked, to give up their rich burden. (Arriving was less exciting nowadays, when you sneaked up in your car and parked it under a tree near the camp and took out the bags and in five minutes it was all over, no fuss, no loud wonderful fuss about trunks.) 9

Peace and goodness and jollity. The only thing that was wrong now, really, was the sound of the place, an unfamiliar 10 nervous sound of the outboard motors. This was the note that jarred, the one thing that would sometimes break the illusion and set the years moving. In those other summertimes all motors were inboard; and when they were at a little distance, the noise they made was a sedative, an ingredient of summer sleep. They were one-cylinder and two-cylinder engines, and some were make-and-break and some were jump-spark, but they all made a sleepy sound across the lake. The one-lungers throbbed and fluttered, and the twin-cylinder ones purred and purred, and that was a quiet sound too. But now the campers all had outboards. In the daytime, in the hot mornings, these motors made a petulant, irritable sound; at night, in the still evening when the afterglow lit the water, they whined about one's ears like mosquitoes. My boy loved our rented outboard, and his great desire was to achieve singlehanded mastery over it, and authority, and he soon learned the trick of choking it a little (but not too much), and the adjustment of the needle valve. Watching him I would remember the things you could do with the old one-cylinder engine with the heavy flywheel, how you could have it eating out of your hand if you got really close to it spiritually. Motor boats in those days didn't have clutches, and you would make a landing by shutting off the motor at the proper time and coasting in with a dead rudder. But there was a way of reversing them, if you learned the trick, by cutting the switch and putting it on again exactly on the final dying revolution of the flywheel, so that it would kick back against compression and begin reversing. Approaching a dock in a strong following breeze, it was difficult to slow up sufficiently by the ordinary coasting method, and if a boy felt he had complete mastery over his motor, he was tempted to keep it running beyond its time and then reverse it a few feet from the dock. It took a cool nerve, because if you threw the switch a twentieth of a second too soon you would catch the flywheel when it still has speed enough to go up past center, and the boat would leap ahead, charging bull-fashion at the dock.

We had a good week at the camp. The bass were biting well and the sun shone endlessly, day after day. We would be tired at night and lie down in the accumulated heat of the little bedrooms after the long hot day and the breeze would stir almost imperceptibly outside and the smell of the swamp drift in through the rusty screens. Sleep would come easily and in the morning the red squirrel would be on the roof, tapping out his gay routine. I kept remembering everything, lying in bed in the mornings—the small steamboat that had a long rounded stern like the lip of a Ubangi, and how quietly she ran on the moonlight sails, when the older boys played their mandolins and the girls sang and we ate doughnuts dipped in sugar, and how sweet the music was on the water in the shining night, and what it had felt like to think about girls then. After breakfast we would go up to the store and the things were in the same place—the minnows in a bottle, the plugs and spinners disarranged and pawed over by the youngsters from the boys' camp, the fig newtons and the Beeman's gum. Outside, the road was tarred and cars stood in front of the store. Inside, all was just as it had always been, except there was more Coca Cola and not so much Moxie and root beer and birch beer and sarsaparilla. We would walk out with a bottle of pop apiece and sometimes the pop would backfire up our noses and hurt. We explored the streams, quietly, where the turtles slid off the sunny logs and dug their way into the soft bottom; and we lay on the town wharf and fed worms to the tame bass. Everywhere we went I had trouble making out which was I, the one walking at my side, the one walking in my pants. 11

One afternoon while we were there at that lake a thunderstorm came up. It was like the revival of an old melodrama that I had seen long ago with childish awe. The second-act climax of the drama of the electrical disturbance over a lake in America had not changed in any important respect. This was the big scene, still the big scene. The whole thing was so familiar, the first feeling of oppression and heat and a general air around camp of not wanting to go very far away. In midafternoon (it was all the same) a curious darkening of the sky, and a lull in everything that had 12 made life tick; and then the way the boats suddenly swung the other way at their moorings with the coming of a breeze out of the new quarter, and the premonitory rumble. Then the kettle drum, then the snare, then the bass drum and cymbals, then crackling light against the dark, and the gods grinning and licking their chops in the hills. Afterward the calm, the rain steadily rustling in the calm lake, the return of light and hope and spirits, and the campers running out in joy and relief to go swimming in the rain, their bright cries perpetuating the deathless joke about how they were getting simply drenched, and the children screaming with delight at the new sensation of bathing in the rain, and the joke about getting drenched linking the generations in a strong indestructible chain. And the comedian who waded in carrying an umbrella.

When the others went swimming my son said he was 13
going in too. He pulled his dripping trunks from the line where they had hung all through the shower, and wrung them out. Languidly, and with no thought of going in, I watched him, his hard little body, skinny and bare, saw him wince slightly as he pulled up around his vitals the small, soggy, icy garment. As he buckled the swollen belt suddenly my groin felt the chill of death.

QUESTIONS ON SUBJECT AND PURPOSE

1. Why does White go "once more" to the lake?
2. In what ways does White's son remind him of himself as a child? Make a list of the similarities he notices.
3. What is the meaning of the final sentence? Why does he feel "the chill of death"?
4. White's essay has achieved the status of a classic. Unquestionably White is an excellent writer, but surely the popularity of the essay depends upon something more. What else might account for that popularity?

QUESTIONS ON STRATEGY AND AUDIENCE

1. How does White structure his narrative? What events does he choose to highlight?

2. No narrative can record everything, and this is certainly not an hour-by-hour account of what happened. What does White ignore? Why, for example, does he end his narrative before the end of the actual experience (i.e., leaving the lake)?
3. Why is his son never described?
4. What assumptions does White make about his audience?

QUESTIONS ON VOCABULARY AND STYLE

1. At several points White has trouble distinguishing between who is the son and who is the father. Select one of those scenes and examine how White describes the moment. How does the prose capture that confusion?
2. Can you find examples of figurative language—similes and metaphors, for example—in White's essay? Make a list.
3. Be able to define the following words: placidity (paragraph 1), gunwale (2), primeval (3), teeming (7), premonitory (12), languidly (13).

WRITING SUGGESTIONS

1. In the second paragraph, White observes: "It is strange how much you can remember about places like that once you allow your mind to return into the grooves that lead back. You remember one thing, and that suddenly reminds you of another thing." Try what he suggests. Pick a particular event you remember from your childhood. Make a list of what you remember. Then in a paragraph, narrate your experience. Do not try to make it seem significant or earthshaking. Just try to make it vivid and interesting.
2. Look for a moment or an experience in your memories that brought an insight. Suddenly you saw or you understood or you knew. Narrate the experience but build to the moment of your understanding.

   Prewriting:

   a. Make a list of your most powerful memories. Just list the events first. Later go back and make notes on each one.
   b. Select a promising event. Set aside an hour to think about what happened. Try to remember what happened just before and just after. Who else was there? What were you wearing?

c. Complete the following sentence: "The insight that I am trying to reveal is ———." Use that statement to check over your prewriting notes.
d. Study White's essay or Hughes's as possible structural models.

Rewriting:

a. Once your draft is finished, set it aside for at least a day. When you look at it again, check every detail against the purpose statement you wrote as a prewriting activity.
b. Check to make sure you have used vivid verbs and concrete nouns. Do not overuse adjectives or adverbs.
c. Just as the ending of a narrative should come to a climatic end, so its introduction ought to plunge the reader into the experience. Check to make sure you begin and end quickly and definitely.

3. What is your earliest memory? What factors control that aspect of our memories? Is it possible to remember events that took place before you could talk? What kinds of early memories are most easily recalled? In a research paper provide some answers to these questions. Since memory plays such a significant role in everyone's life, you can assume that any audience will be interested in opinions that scientists now hold of this subject. You might prepare your paper in one of the following formats:
   a. A traditional research paper for a college course
   b. A feature article for a popular magazine

CHAPTER 3

Description

You have bought a car—your first—and understandably you can hardly wait to tell your friends. "What does it look like?" they ask and you modestly reply, "A silver-gray '68 VW Beetle with red racing stripes and a sunroof." What you have done is provide a description; you have given your listeners enough information to allow them to form a mental picture of your new (and used) car. Like narration, description is an everyday activity. You describe to a friend what cooked snails really taste like, how your favorite perfume smells, how your body feels when you have a fever, how a local rock band sounded last night. Description recreates sense impressions by translating them into words.

That translation is not always easy. For one thing, when you have a first-hand experience all of your senses are working at the same time: you see, taste, smell, feel, hear. When you convey that experience to a reader or a listener, you can only record one sense impression at a time. Furthermore, sometimes it is difficult to find an adequate translation for a particular sense impression—how do you describe the smell of musk perfume or the taste of freshly squeezed orange juice? On the other hand, the translation into words offers two distinct advantages: first, ideally it isolates the most important aspects of the experience, ruling out anything else that might distract your reader's attention; second, it makes those experiences more permanent. Sensory impressions decay in seconds, but written descriptions survive indefinitely.

Consider, for example, how precisely James Agee recreates for the reader the experience of men watering their lawns on summer evenings, evoking sight, sound, and touch:

> The hoses were attached at spigots that stood out of the brick foundations of the houses. The nozzles were variously set but usually so there was a long sweet stream of spray, the nozzle wet in the hand, the water trickling the right forearm and the peeled-back cuff, and the water whishing out a long loose and low-curved cone, and so gentle a sound. First an insane noise of violence in the nozzle, then the still irregular sound of adjustment, then the smoothing into steadiness and a pitch as accurately tuned to the size and style of stream as any violin. So many qualities of sound out of one hose: so many choral differences out of those several hoses that were in earshot. Out of any one hose, the almost dead silence of the release, and the short still arch of the separate big drops, silent as a held breath, and the only noise the flattering noise on leaves and the slapped grass at the fall of each big drop. That, and the intense hiss with the intense stream; that, and that same intensity not growing less but growing more quiet and delicate with the turn of the nozzle, up to that extreme tender whisper when the water was just a wide bell of film.*

Traditionally, descriptions are divided into two categories: objective and subjective. In objective description you record details without making any personal evaluation or reaction. The first half of Roger Angell's description of a baseball is purely objective in recording weight, dimensions, colors, and materials. The ultimate in objective description is found in scientific prose such as you might find in a biology textbook.

In subjective description, you are free to interpret the details for your reader; your reactions and descriptions can be emotional and value-loaded. When Annie Dillard in "The Copperhead and the Mosquito" describes the "nerved

*James Agee, "Knoxville: Summer 1915," from *A Death in the Family* (New York: Bantam Books). First published in 1957.

rope of matter" she "sees" as the snake, the reader recognizes that this is not the type of description that would be found in a textbook. Similarly, notice how Dillard describes the body of the copperhead: "From tail to head it spread like the lines of a crescendo, widening from stillness to a turgid blast; then at the bulging jaws it began contracting again, diminuendo, till at the tip of its snout the lines met back at the infinite point that corners every angle, and that space once more ceased being a snake."

Whether objective or subjective, descriptions can serve a variety of purposes, but in every case it is important to make that purpose clear to your reader. Sometimes description is done solely to record the facts, as in Angell's description of the baseball, or to evoke an atmosphere, as in Agee's description of watering a lawn with a hose and nozzle. More often, description is used as support for other purposes. Annie Dillard, in describing the copperhead and the mosquito feeding on it, is not trying to write a precise, scientific description. Instead, she uses description to convey to the reader what she calls "a new light on the intricate texture of things in the world."

How Do You Describe an Object or a Place?

The first task in writing a description is to decide what you want to describe. As in every other writing task, making a good choice means that the act of writing will be easier and probably more successful. Before you begin, keep two things in mind: first, there is rarely any point in describing a common object or place—something every reader has seen—unless you do it in a fresh and perceptive way. Roger Angell describes a baseball, but he does so by dissecting it, giving a series of facts about its composition. All of Agee's readers had probably watered a lawn using a hose and nozzle and had seen, felt, and heard what he describes, but after reading his description what they are left with is a sense of vividness—this passage evokes or re-creates in our minds a mental picture of that activity.

Second, remember that your description needs to create

a focused impression. To do that, you need to select details which contribute to your purpose. That will give you a way of deciding which details out of the many available are relevant. Details in a description must be carefully chosen and arranged; otherwise, our reader will be overwhelmed or bored by the accumulation of detail.

How Do You Describe a Person?

Before you begin to describe a person, remember an experience that everyone has had. You have read a novel and then seen a film or a made-for-television version, and the two experiences did not mesh. The characters, you are convinced, just did not *look* like the actors and actresses: "She was thinner and blond" or "He was all wrong—not big enough, not rugged enough." Any time you read a narrative that contains a character—either real or fictional—you form a mental picture of the person, and that picture is generally not based upon any physical description that the author has provided. In fact, in many narratives, authors provide only minimal description of the people involved. For example, if you look closely at William Allen White's description of his daughter Mary, you will find only a few physical details: she was dressed in "khakis," a "little figure" with a "strong, muscular body," a "long pig-tail," and a "red hair ribbon." Of the Thurmond Watts family in William Least Heat Moon's "Nameless, Tennessee," you are told even less: Thurmond himself is "tall" and "thin"; but his wife Miss Ginny, his sister-in-law Marilyn, and his daughter Hilda are not physically described at all. In both narratives, however, you get a vivid image of the people being described.

Fictional characters or real people are created or revealed primarily through ways other than direct physical description. What a person does or says, for example, also reveals personality. The reader sees Mary in White's portrait of his daughter through what she does; the ways in which she behaves; the things, people, and values important to her. Those details re-create Mary White for the reader, and finally, they are the things most important about her. The Wattses, in Heat Moon's narrative, are revealed by how they react, what they say, how their speech sounds, what they consider to be important. These are the key factors in recreating Heat Moon's experience for the reader.

In fact, descriptions of people should not try to be verbal portraits recording physical attributes in photographic detail. Words finally are never as efficient in doing that as photographs. If the objective in describing a person is not photographic accuracy, what then is it? Go back to the advice offered earlier in this introduction: decide first what impression you want to create in your reader. Why are you describing this person? What is it about this person that is worth describing? In all likelihood the answer will be something other than physical attributes. Once you know what that something is, you can then choose those details which best reveal or display the person.

How Do You Organize a Description?

You have found a subject; you have studied it—either first-hand or in memory; you have decided upon a reason for describing this particular subject; you have selected details which contribute to that reason or purpose. Now you need to organize your paragraph or essay. Descriptions, like narratives, have principles of order, although the principles vary depending upon what sense impressions are involved. When the primary descriptive emphasis is on seeing, the most obvious organization is spatial—moving from front to back, side to side, outside to inside, top to bottom, general to specific. The description moves as a camera would. Roger Angell's description of a baseball moves outward from the cork nucleus, through the layers of rubber, wool yarn, and rubber cement, to the cowhide exterior.

Other sense experiences might be arranged in order of importance, from the most obvious to the least—the loudest noise at the concert, the most pervasive odor in the restaurant—or even in chronological order. Agee's description of the sound water makes as it surges through a nozzle follows a chronological sequence from turning on the water through adjusting the nozzle from "separate big drops" through "a wide bell of film."

Description Means Lots of Adjectives and Adverbs, Right?

Wrong. Remember that one-sentence description of your car: "A silver-gray '68 VW Beetle with red racing stripes and a sunroof." Your audience would have no trouble creating a vivid mental picture from that little bit of information, because it has seen VW Beetles before. The noun provides the primary image. The only two adjectives describe color. The point is that you can create an image without providing a mountain of detail—just as you imagine what a character looks like without being told. When Annie Dillard first sees the copperhead, she notes only that it was "twelve or thirteen inches long," that its body was "thick," and that it was marked by "the unmistakable undulating bands of brown, the hourglasses." One of the greatest dangers in writing a description lies in trying to describe too much, trying to qualify every noun with at least one adjective and every verb with an adverb. Precise, vivid nouns and verbs will do most of the work for you.

Writing a Description: A Student Example

Joy Henry wanted to describe a potter's shop she had recently visited. Its simple, timeless quality fascinated her. Her first draft was quite long partly because, like most writers, she tried to describe too much. Her first draft began with the approach to the shop:

A Potter's Shop

> The potter's shop was located in the rolling countryside of Pennsylvania. It was nestled in a small depression between two hills, one of which rose steeply to the left and formed a cliff-like wall from which the winding country road appeared to be carved. This road led us to the potter's lane. As we

> turned onto the lane, we crossed a mountain stream which was straddled by an enormous hulk of a building. This huge structure, constructed of stone and weatherboard, had been a grist mill and granary for which the stream had provided power. A footpath led us to the old, red, weathered summer kitchen turned potter's shop. The shop sat next to a charming old house of white weatherboard. The side porch of the house faced the shop. Along the back wall of the porch hung an artistically arranged collection of oriole nests. A crude circle of twisted grape vines formed a wreath on the door, and freshly cut long-needle pine boughs outlined the doorway. Bread-dough Christmas ornaments hung from a ribbon in each of the small paned windows. Upon entering the potter's shop, we were warmed by the glowing embers of an antique wood-burning cookstove.

Joy's essay was one the entire class had a chance to read. Although everyone was impressed with the detail Joy had included, most of the students commented that since so many things were described, it was hard to know what central focus Joy had in mind. When she replied that it was to convey a sense of the simplicity and beauty of the potter's shop, Joy saw what troubled her readers. It takes, for example, about 180 words until the shop itself appears in the paper. When Joy rewrote her essay, she focused on the shop. In addition she tried to sharpen her descriptions by avoiding some of the worn phrases used in the first draft—details such as "rolling countryside" and "charming old house."

> A Country Potter's Shop
>
> The potter's shop was nestled in a depression between two hills, at the end of a narrow footpath. The one-room cottage, once a summer kitchen, sat next to a two-story fieldstone farmhouse. Pushing open the weathered door, I entered a room filled with the smoky aroma of a wood fire that warmed the air just enough to take the crispness from it. Handmade wares of wood, wrought iron, and pottery filled the shop. In a corner stood hearth brooms made of sticks bound to twisted root handles, and candles hung from the ceiling in handwrought holders. Crocks, jars, and pitchers of all sizes and shapes were displayed on the sagging wooden shelves that

lined the walls. The potter chose earthy colors for his pottery and used a variety of textures: smooth and glossy contrasted with a coarse, sandlike stipple. Patterns were gouged deeply into the surfaces of many pieces—no two alike. A Christmas tree stood in the center of the room, decorated with ornaments fashioned from nature: pheasants of milkweed pod bodies and wildflower heads, woodland animals of prickly teasel, and an angel in a flowing gown of spartina grass plumes.

Some Things to Remember

1. Choose your subject carefully, making sure that you have a specific reason or purpose in mind for whatever you describe.
2. Study or observe your subject—try to see it or experience it in a fresh way. Gather details; make a list; use all your senses.
3. Use your purpose as a way of deciding which details ought to be included and which excluded.
4. Choose a pattern of organization to focus your reader's attention.
5. Use precise, vivid nouns and verbs, as well as adjectives and adverbs, to create your descriptions.

A Baseball

ROGER ANGELL

Roger Angell was born in New York in 1920 and received a B.A. from Harvard in 1942. From 1947 to 1956 he was a contributor to Holiday, *then became a fiction editor for* The New Yorker, *where his columns on baseball appear several times a year. Angell has been called "baseball's most articulate fan" and in 1980 won the George Polk Award for commentary. His books include* The Stone Arbor and Other Stories *(1966),* A Day in the Life of Roger Angell *(1970),* The Summer Game *(1972),* Five Seasons: A Baseball Companion *(1977), and* Late Innings: A New Baseball Companion *(1982).* Baseball *(1984) was a joint project combining Walter Iooss's photographs with Angell's essays. Angell's most recent book is* Season Ticket: The Baseball Companion *(1988). Angell's writing combines scientific objectivity and poetic sensitivity, qualities that can be seen in this opening paragraph from his book* Five Seasons. *Angell "sees" a baseball in two distinctly different ways.*

It weighs just five ounces and measures between 2.86 and 2.94 inches in diameter. It is made of a composition-cork nucleus encased in two thin layers of rubber, one black and one red, surrounded by 121 yards of tightly wrapped blue-gray wool yarn, 45 yards of white wool yarn, 53 more yards of blue-gray wool yarn, 150 yards of fine cotton yarn, a coat of rubber cement, and a cowhide (formerly horsehide) exterior, which is held together with 216 slightly raised red cotton stitches. Printed certifications, endorsements, and outdoor advertising spherically attest to its authenticity. Like most institutions, it is considered inferior in its present form to its ancient archetypes, and in this case the complaint is probably justified; on occasion in recent years it has actually been known to come apart under the demands of its brief but rigorous active career. Baseballs are assembled and hand-stitched in Taiwan (before this year the work was done in Haiti, and before 1973 in Chicopee, Massachusetts), and contemporary pitchers claim that there is a tangible variation in the size and feel of the balls that now come into play in a single game; a true peewee is treasured by hurlers, and its departure from the premises, by fair means or foul, is secretly mourned. But never mind: any baseball is beautiful. No other small package comes as close to the ideal in design and utility. It is a perfect object for a man's hand. Pick it up and it instantly suggests its purpose; it is meant to be thrown a considerable distance—thrown hard and with precision. Its feel and heft are the beginning of the sport's critical dimensions; if it were a fraction of an inch larger or smaller, a few centigrams heavier or lighter, the game of baseball would be utterly different.

QUESTIONS ON SUBJECT AND PURPOSE

1. Every adult has surely "seen" a baseball. Why then describe one? How does Angell's description differ from what you might expect?
2. Does it make any sense to say, as Angell does, that if a baseball were any larger or smaller the game would be "utterly different"? What might that statement mean?
3. Could you make the same claim for a football, a softball, a basketball, a soccer ball? Is there anything special about a baseball?

QUESTIONS ON STRATEGY AND AUDIENCE

1. How does Angell structure his paragraph?
2. How effective are the opening sentences? Do they catch your attention? Why or why not?
3. This selection is the first paragraph in Angell's *Five Seasons: A Baseball Companion.* Why begin a book about baseball with a description of the ball?

QUESTIONS ON VOCABULARY AND STYLE

1. What types of transitional devices does Angell use to hold his paragraph together?
2. What might Angell mean by the sentence: "Printed certifications, endorsements, and outdoor advertising spherically attest to its authenticity"?
3. Be able to define the following words: *archetype, tangible, heft.*

WRITING SUGGESTIONS

1. Generally there is no good reason to describe an everyday object in photographic detail. On the other hand, sometimes you can see the ordinary in a new and fresh way. Select something you own, something ordinary, and describe it in a paragraph. Do not try to "photograph" the object verbally; try instead to see it in a fresh way.
2. Select a drawer in your desk, dresser, or kitchen or your wallet or purse. Catalog its contents. Look at what you see. What do those things reveal about you? Using descriptive detail, write an essay about what you find—both literally and figuratively. Remember that you must also catch and hold your reader's interest.

   Prewriting:

   a. In all likelihood you cannot include everything you find in your essay. Arrange the items on a table or desk. Complete the following sentence for each item: "What is revealing/interesting about this item is ———."
   b. Once you have a list of sentences, group the items on the basis of what they reveal. Eliminate any items that do not fit into the pattern you plan to develop.
   c. Unless you have a thesis that holds the items together, your essay will probably just become a list—"Here are some things that I found." Before you begin your paper, write a thesis sentence that reflects your purpose. Eliminate any items from your list that do not fit the pattern you plan to develop.

   Rewriting:

   a. Everyone could write an essay on this topic. What makes yours particularly interesting? What might make a reader want to read it? Answer that last question in one sentence.

b. Test your essay for reader interest by asking a classmate or roommate to read it. Use this reaction as a guide to possible revision.
c. Remember that your introduction will be especially crucial. Look at what you have written. Do you start with something that will catch your reader's interest? Does your introduction provoke curiosity? Startle? Establish a common ground ("That is exactly like me!")?

3. Angell obviously researched the composition of a baseball—what it was made of, how many yards of what color yarn. Do the same for any common object. Find out how it is made; how many are made annually; how it is sold; how people who use it feel about it. In an essay describe your findings.

Mary White

WILLIAM ALLEN WHITE

William Allen White (1868-1944) was born and died in Emporia, Kansas. He is recognized as one of the most important political journalists of turn-of-the-century America. White grew up in the frontier town of El Dorado, Kansas, where his father was a doctor and storekeeper, active in Democratic politics. He attended the College of Emporia and the University of Kansas, holding various newspaper jobs. He worked on the editorial staff of the Kansas City Journal *and* The Kansas City Star. *In 1895, he bought the* Emporia Gazette *and served as its editor, writing stinging political attacks that brought him much political influence and notoriety. White was a prodigious writer who produced several collections of essays on politics and economics, political biographies, novels, and innumerable magazine articles. In 1922, he won a Pulitzer Prize for his editorial "To an Anxious Friend," a defense of American journalistic freedom. Among White's better-known works are* The Court of Boyville, *a collection of stories (1899); the novels* A Certain Rich Man *(1909) and* In the Heart of a Fool *(1918); and the Pulitzer-Prize-winning* The Autobiography of William Allen White, *published posthumously in 1946. The death of his sixteen-year-old daughter Mary in 1921 prompted his most frequently reprinted editorial, "Mary White," a loving tribute that immortalized her.*

The Associated Press reports carrying the news of Mary White's death declared that it came as the result of a fall from a horse. How she would have hooted at that! She never fell from a horse in her life. Horses have fallen on her and with her—"I'm always trying to hold 'em in my lap," she used to say. But she was proud of few things, and one was that she could ride anything that had four legs and hair. Her death resulted not from a fall, but from a blow on the head which fractured her skull, and the blow came from the limb of an overhanging tree on the parking. 1

The last hour of her life was typical of its happiness. She 2 came home from a day's work at school, topped off by a hard grind with the copy on the High School Annual, and felt that a ride would refresh her. She climbed into her khakis, chattering to her mother about the work she was doing, and hurried to get her horse and be out on the dirt roads for the country air and the radiant green fields of the spring. As she rode through the town on an easy gallop she kept waving at passers-by. She knew everyone in town. For a decade the little figure with the long pig-tail and the red hair ribbon has been familiar on the streets of Emporia, and she got in the way of speaking to those who nodded at her. She passed the Kerrs, walking the horse, in front of the Normal Library, and waved at them; passed another friend a few hundred feet further on, and waved at her. The horse was walking and as she turned into North Merchant street she took off her cowboy hat, and the horse swung into a lope. She passed the Tripletts and waved her cowboy hat at them, still moving gaily north on Merchant street. A Gazette carrier passed—a High School boy friend—and she waved at him but with her bridle hand: the horse veered quickly, plunged into the parking where the low-hanging limb faced her, and while she still looked back waving, the blow came. But she did not fall from the horse; she slipped off, dazed a bit, staggered and fell in a faint. She never quite recovered consciousness.

But she did not fall from the horse, neither was she 3
riding fast. A year or so ago she used to go like the wind. But that habit was broken, and she used the horse to get into the open to get fresh, hard exercise, and to work off a certain surplus energy that welled up in her and needed a physical outlet. That need has been in her heart for years. It was back of the impulse that kept the dauntless, little brown-clad figure on the streets and country roads of this community and built into a strong, muscular body what had been a frail and sickly frame during the first years of her life. But the riding gave her more than a body. It released a gay and hardy soul. She was the happiest thing in the world. And she was happy because she was enlarging her horizon. She came to know all sorts and conditions of men; Charley O'Brien, the

traffic cop, was one of her best friends. W. L. Holtz, the Latin teacher, was another. Tom O'Connor, farmer-politician, and Rev. J. H. J. Rice, preacher and police judge, and Frank Beach, music master, were her special friends; and all the girls, black and white, above the track and below the track, in Pepville and Stringtown, were among her acquaintances. And she brought home riotous stories of her adventures. She loved to rollick; persiflage was her natural expression at home. Her humor was a continual bubble of joy. She seemed to think in hyperbole and metaphor. She was mischievous without malice, as full of faults as an old shoe. No angel was Mary White, but an easy girl to live with, for she never nursed a grouch five minutes in her life.

With all her eagerness for the out-of-doors, she loved 4
books. On her table when she left her room were a book by Conrad, one by Galsworthy, "Creative Chemistry" by E.E. Slosson, and a Kipling book. She read Mark Twain, Dickens and Kipling before she was 10—all of their writings. Wells and Arnold Bennett particularly amused and diverted her. She was entered as a student in Wellesley in 1922; was assistant editor of the High School Annual this year, and in line for election to the editorship of the Annual next year. She was a member of the executive committee of the High School Y.W.C.A.

Within the last two years she had begun to be moved by 5
an ambition to draw. She began as most children do by scribbling in her school books, funny pictures. She bought cartoon magazines and took a course—rather casually, naturally, for she was, after all, a child with no strong purposes—and this year she tasted the first fruits of success by having her pictures accepted by the High School Annual. But the thrill of delight she got when Mr. Ecord, of the Normal Annual, asked her to do the cartooning for that book this spring, was too beautiful for words. She fell to her work with all her enthusiastic heart. Her drawings were accepted, and her pride—always repressed by a lively sense of the ridiculousness of the figure she was cutting—was a really gorgeous thing to see. No successful artist ever drank a deeper draught of satisfaction than she took from the little

fame her work was getting among her schoolfellows. In her glory, she almost forgot her horse—but never her car.

For she used the car as a jitney bus. It was her social life. 6
She never had a "party" in all her nearly seventeen years—wouldn't have one; but she never drove a block in the car in her life that she didn't begin to fill the car with pick-ups! Everybody rode with Mary White—white and black, old and young, rich and poor, men and women. She liked nothing better than to fill the car full of long-legged High School boys and an occasional girl, and parade the town. She never had a "date," nor went to a dance, except once with her brother, Bill, and the "boy proposition" didn't interest her—yet. But young people—great spring-breaking, varnish-cracking, fender-bending, door-sagging carloads of "kids"—gave her great pleasure. Her zests were keen. But the most fun she ever had in her life was acting as chairman of the committee that got up the big turkey dinner for the poor folks at the county home; scores of pies, gallons of slaw; jam, cakes, preserves, oranges and a wilderness of turkey were loaded in the car and taken to the county home. And, being of a practical turn of mind, she risked her own Christmas dinner by staying to see that the poor folks actually got it all. Not that she was a cynic; she just disliked to tempt folks. While there she found a blind colored uncle, very old, who could no nothing but make rag rugs, and she rustled up from her school friends rags enough to keep him busy for a season. The last engagement she tried to make was to take the guests at the county home out for a car ride. And the last endeavor of her life was to try to get a rest room for colored girls in the High School. She found one girl reading in the toilet, because there was no better place for a colored girl to loaf, and it inflamed her sense of injustice and she became a nagging harpie to those who, she thought, could remedy the evil. The poor she had always with her, and was glad of it. She hungered and thirsted for righteousness; and was the most impious creature in the world. She joined the Congregational Church without consulting her parents; not particularly for her soul's good. She never had a thrill of piety

in her life, and would have hooted at a "testimony." But even as a little child she felt the church was an agency for helping people to more of life's abundance, and she wanted to help. She never wanted help for herself. Clothes meant little to her. It was a fight to get a new rig on her; but eventually a harder fight to get off. She never wore a jewel and had no ring but her High School class ring, and never asked for anything but a wrist watch. She refused to have her hair up; though she was nearly 17. "Mother," she protested, "you don't know how much I get by with, in my braided pigtails that I could not, with my hair up." Above every other passion of her life was her passion not to grow up, to be a child. The tom-boy in her which was big, seemed to loath to be put away forever in skirts. She was a Peter Pan, who refused to grow up.

Her funeral yesterday at the Congregational Church was 7
as she would have wished it; no singing, no flowers save the big bunch of red roses from her Brother Bill's Harvard classmen—Heavens, how proud that would have made her! and the red roses from the Gazette force—in vases at her head and feet. A short prayer, Paul's beautiful essay on "Love" from the Thirteenth Chapter of First Corinthians, some remarks about her democratic spirit by her friend, John H. J. Rice, pastor and police judge, which she would have deprecated if she could, a prayer sent down for her by her friend, Carl Nau, and opening the service the slow, poignant movement from Beethoven's Moonlight Sonata, which she loved, and closing the service a cutting from the joyously melancholy first movement of Tschaikowski's Pathetic Symphony, which she liked to hear in certain moods on the phonograph; then the Lord's Prayer by her friends in the High School.

That was all. 8

For her pallbearers only her friends were chosen; her 9
Latin teacher—W. L. Holtz; her High School principal, Rice Brown; her doctor, Frank Foncannon; her friend, W. W. Finney; her pal at the Gazette office, Walter Hughes; and her brother Bill. It would have made her smile to know that her

friend, Charley O'Brien, the traffic cop, had been transferred from Sixth and Commercial to the corner near the church to direct her friends who came to bid her goodbye.

10 A rift in the clouds in a gray day threw a shaft of sunlight upon her coffin as her nervous, energetic little body sank to its last sleep. But the soul of her, the glowing, gorgeous, fervent soul of her, surely was flaming in eager joy upon some other dawn.

QUESTIONS ON SUBJECT AND PURPOSE

1. Why might White have chosen to write about the accidental death of his young daughter?
2. What do Mary's interests reveal about her? What kind of a person was she?
3. How does White blend telling and showing in his essay (see "How Are Narratives Told?" in the introduction to Chapter 2)? How does that help him shape his tribute?

QUESTIONS ON STRATEGY AND AUDIENCE

1. How much physical description does White give of his daughter? What physical details does he focus on? Why these?
2. What other details does White use to describe his daughter? How do you get a sense of her personality?
3. Why does White begin as he does? Why in the second paragraph does he trace her final ride in such detail?
4. How does White structure his essay?

QUESTIONS ON VOCABULARY AND STYLE

1. What is the effect of the inverted sentence at the end of paragraph 3?
2. What is the effect of the single three-word paragraph (8): "That was all"?
3. Be able to define the following words: *lope* (paragraph 2), *rollick* (3), *persiflage* (3), *hyperbole* (3), *jitney* (6), *deprecated* (7), *fervent* (10).

WRITING SUGGESTIONS

1. In a paragraph try to "capture" your best friend or your roommate or your greatest rival. Remember to select details that reveal personality; remember to keep a central focus.
2. Writing about a close friend or a relative is never easy. You know too much; you cannot be objective enough. When you have lost that person, it is even more difficult. Still, writing about the person is a way to order your experience, record your grief, and remember and memorialize your friend or relative. If you have had such an experience, try a tribute similar to White's.

   Prewriting:

   a. Spend some time thinking about possible subjects. Once you have made a choice, try freewriting for twenty minutes. Write whatever comes to mind about the person and your feelings.
   b. Finish the following sentence: "What I want the reader to know about this person is ———." Use that statement as a way of testing every detail you decide to include.
   c. Do not try to describe the person photographically. Select details that reveal personality, that reveal the qualities about the person that you wish to emphasize. Check every detail.

   Rewriting:

   a. Ask a friend or a classmate to read your essay. Once your reader has finished, ask her or him to finish the test sentence you wrote in item b above. Does your reader see the same purpose as you did?
   b. Look carefully at the structure of your essay. What type of structure did you use? Is it chronological? Would it be better to start with a flashback? Force yourself to jot down an outline of an alternate structure.

3. Select a famous young person who has died. Research the story to find details about the person's life and values. Using your research, write a sympathetic tribute.

Nameless, Tennessee

WILLIAM LEAST HEAT MOON

William Least Heat Moon is the tribal name of part-Sioux William Trogdon. Born in Missouri in 1939, he earned a Ph.D. in English from the University of Missouri in 1973. His best-selling Blue Highways: A Journey into America *(1982) is the account of his 14,000-mile journey through American backroads in a converted van called "Ghost Dancing." The book is noted for its detailed and sensitive descriptions of the lesser-known areas of America. In 1985, an 11-cassette set of Heat Moon's reading of* Blue Highways *was released. In this chapter from* Blue Highways, *he describes his experiences at a general store in Nameless, Tennessee, where he meets Thurmond and Virginia Watts, living in a world seemingly untouched by time.*

1 Nameless, Tennessee, was a town of maybe ninety people if you pushed it, a dozen houses along the road, a couple of barns, same number of churches, a general merchandise store selling Fire Chief gasoline, and a community center with a lighted volleyball court. Behind the center was an open-roof, rusting metal privy with PAINT ME on the door, in the hollow of a nearby oak lay of full pint of Jack Daniel's Black Label. From the houses, the odor of coal smoke.

2 Next to a red tobacco barn stood the general merchandise with a poster of Senator Albert Gore, Jr., smiling from the window. I knocked. The door opened partway. A tall, thin man said, "Closed up. For good," and started to shut the door.

3 "Don't want to buy anything. Just a question for Mr. Thurmond Watts."

4 The man peered through the slight opening. He looked me over. "What question would that be?"

5 "If this is Nameless, Tennessee, could he tell me how it got that name?"

The man turned back into the store and called out, "Miss Ginny! Somebody here wants to know how Nameless come to be Nameless." 6

Miss Ginny edged to the door and looked me and my truck over. Clearly, she didn't approve. She said, "You know as well as I do, Thurmond. Don't keep him on the stoop in the damp to tell him." Miss Ginny, I found out, was Mrs. Virginia Watts, Thurmond's wife. 7

I stepped in and they both began telling the story, adding a detail here, the other correcting a fact there, both smiling at the foolishness of it all. It seems the hilltop settlement went for years without a name. Then one day the Post Office Department told the people if they wanted mail up on the mountain they would have to give the place a name you could properly address a letter to. The community met; there were only a handful, but they commenced debating. Some wanted patriotic names, some names from nature, one man recommended in all seriousness his own name. They couldn't agree, and they ran out of names to argue about. Finally, a fellow tired of the talk; he didn't like the mail he received anyway. "Forget the durn Post Office," he said. "This here's a nameless place if I ever seen one, so leave it be." And that's just what they did. 8

Watts pointed out the window. "We used to have signs on the road, but the Halloween boys keep tearin' them down." 9

"You think Nameless is a funny name," Miss Ginny said. "I see it plain in your eyes. Well, you take yourself up north a piece to Difficult or Defeated or Shake Rag. Now them are silly names." 10

The old store, lighted only by three fifty-watt bulbs, smelled of coal oil and baking bread. In the middle of the rectangular room, where the oak floor sagged a little, stood an iron stove. To the right was a wooden table with an unfinished game of checkers and a stool made from an apple-tree stump. On shelves around the walls sat earthen jugs with corncob stoppers, a few canned goods, and some of the two thousand old clocks and clockworks Thurmond Watts owned. Only one was ticking, the others he just looked at. I asked how long he'd been in the store. 11

"Thirty-five years, but we closed the first day of the 12 year. We're hopin' to sell it to a churchly couple. Upright people. No athians."

"Did you build this store?" 13

"I built this one, but it's the third general store on the 14 ground. I fear it'll be the last. I take no pleasure in that. Once you could come in here for a gallon of paint, a pickle, a pair of shoes, and a can of corn."

"Or horehound candy," Miss Ginny said. "Or corsets 15 and salves. We had cough syrups and all that for the body. In season, we'd buy and sell blackberries and walnuts and chestnuts, before the blight got them. And outside, Thurmond milled corn and sharpened plows. Even shoed a horse sometimes."

"We could fix up a horse or a man or a baby," Watts said. 16

"Thurmond, tell him we had a doctor on the ridge in 17 them days."

"We had a doctor on the ridge in them days. As good as 18 any doctor alivin'. He'd cut a crooked toenail or deliver a woman. Dead these last years."

"I got some bad ham meat one day," Miss Ginny said, 19 "and took to vomitin.' All day, all night. Hangin' on the drop edge of yonder. I said to Thurmond, "Thurmond, unless you want shut of me, call the doctor.'"

"I studied on it," Watts said. 20

"You never did. You got him right now. He come over 21 and put three drops of iodeen in half a glass of well water. I drank it down and the vomitin' stopped with the last swallow. Would you think iodeen could do that?"

"He put Miss Ginny on one teaspoon of spirits of 22 ammonia in well water for her nerves. Ain't nothin' works better for her to this day."

"Calms me like the hand of the Lord." 23

Hilda, the Wattses' daughter, came out of the backroom. 24 "I remember him," she said. "I was just a baby. Y'all were talkin' to him, and he lifted me up on the counter and gave me a stick of Juicy Fruit and a piece of cheese."

"Knew the old medicines," Watts said. "Only drugstore 25 he needed was a good kitchen cabinet. None of them anteebeeotics that hit you worsen your ailment. Forgotten lore now, the old medicines, because they ain't profit in iodeen."

Miss Ginny started back to the side room where she and 26
her sister Marilyn were taking apart a duck-down mattress to make bolsters. She stopped at the window for another look at Ghost Dancing. "How do you sleep in that thing? Ain't you all cramped and cold?"

"How does the clam sleep in his shell?" Watts said in 27
my defense.

"Thurmond, get the boy a piece of buttermilk pie afore 28
he goes on."

"Hilda, get some buttermilk pie." He looked at me. 29
"You like good music?" I said I did. He cranked up an old Edison phonograph, the kind with the big morning-glory blossom for a speaker, and put on a wax cylinder. "This will be 'My Mother's Prayer,'" he said.

While I ate buttermilk pie, Watts served as disc jockey 30
of Nameless, Tennessee. "Here's 'Mountain Rose.'" It was one of those moments that you know at the time will stay with you to the grave: the sweet pie, the gaunt man playing the old music, the coals in the stove glowing orange, the scent of kerosene and hot bread. "Here's 'Evening Rhapsody.'" The music was so heavily romantic we both laughed. I thought: It is for this I have come.

Feathered over and giggling, Miss Ginny stepped from 31
the side room. She knew she was a sight. "Thurmond, give him some lunch. Still looks hungry."

Hilda pulled food off the woodstove in the backroom: 32
home-butchered and canned whole-hog sausage, home-canned June apples, turnip greens, cole slaw, potatoes, stuffing, hot cornbread. All delicious.

Watts and Hilda sat and talked while I ate. "Wish you 33
would join me."

"We've ate," Watts said. "Cain't beat a woodstove for 34
flavorful cookin'."

He told me he was raised in a one-hundred-fifty-year-old 35
cabin still standing in one of the hollows. "How many's left," he said, "that grew up in a log cabin? I ain't the last surely, but I must be climbin' on the list."

Hilda cleared the table. "You Watts ladies know how to cook." 36

"She's in nursin' school at Tennessee Tech. I went over for one of them football games last year there at Coevul." To say *Cookeville,* you let the word collapse in upon itself so that it comes out "Coevul." 37

"Do you like football?" I asked. 38

"Don't know. I was so high up in that stadium, I never opened my eyes." 39

Watts went to the back and returned with a fat spiral notebook that he set on the table. His expression had changed. "Miss Ginny's *Deathbook.*" 40

The thing startled me. Was it something I was supposed to sign? He opened it but said nothing. There were scads of names written in a tidy hand over pages incised to crinkliness by a ballpoint. Chronologically, the names had piled up: wives, grandparents, a stillborn infant, relatives, friends close and distant. Names, names. After each, the date of the unknown finally known and transcribed. The last entry bore yesterday's date. 41

"She's wrote out twenty years' worth. Ever day she listens to the hospital report on the radio and puts the names in. Folks come by to check a date. Or they just turn through the books. Read them like a scrapbook." 42

Hilda said, "Like Saint Peter at the gates inscribin' the names." 43

Watts took my arm. "Come along." He led me to the fruit cellar under the store. As we went down, he said, "Always take a newborn baby upstairs afore you take him downstairs, otherwise you'll incline him downwards." 44

The cellar was dry and full of cobwebs and jar after jar of home-canned food, the bottles organized as a shopkeeper would: sausage, pumpkin, sweet pickles, tomatoes, corn relish, blackberries, peppers, squash, jellies. He held a hand out toward the dusty bottles. "Our tomorrows." 45

Upstairs again, he said, "Hope to sell the store to the right folk. I see now, though, it'll be somebody offen the ridge. I've studied on it, and maybe it's the end of our place." He stirred the coals. "This store could give a com- 46 fortable livin', but not likely get you rich. But just gettin' by is dice rollin' to people nowadays. I never did see my day guaranteed."

When it was time to go, Watts said, "If you find anyone along your way wants a good store—on the road to Cordell Hull Lake—tell them about us." 47

I said I would. Miss Ginny and Hilda and Marilyn came out to say goodbye. It was cold and drizzling again. "Weather to give a man the weary dismals," Watts grumbled. "Where you headed from here?" 48

"I don't know." 49

"Cain't get lost then." 50

Miss Ginny looked again at my rig. It had worried her from the first as it had my mother. "I hope you don't get yourself kilt in that durn thing gallivantin' around the country." 51

"Come back when the hills dry off," Watts said. "We'll go lookin' for some of them round rocks all sparkly inside." 52

I thought a moment. "Geodes?" 53

"Them's the ones. The country's properly full of them." 54

QUESTIONS ON SUBJECT AND PURPOSE

1. At one point in the narrative (paragraph 30), Heat Moon remarks, "I thought: It is for this I have come." What does Heat Moon seem to be suggesting? What is the "this" that he finds in Nameless (paragraph 40)?
2. Why do "Miss Ginny's *Deathbook*" (paragraph 40) and the "fruit cellar" (44) seem appropriate details?
3. What might have attracted Heat Moon to this place and these people? What does he want you to sense? Is there anything in Heat Moon's description and narrative that suggests how he feels about Nameless?

QUESTIONS ON STRATEGY AND AUDIENCE

1. After you have read the selection, describe each member of the Watts family. Describe the exterior and interior of their store. Then carefully go through the selection and see how many specific descriptive details Heat Moon uses. List them.

2. What devices other than direct description does Heat Moon use to create the sense of place and personality? Make a list and be prepared to tell how those devices work.
3. How is the narrative arranged? Is the order just spatial and chronological?
4. This selection is taken from *Blue Highways: A Journey into America,* a bestseller for nearly a year. Why would a travel narrative—full of stories such as this—be so appealing to an American audience?

QUESTIONS ON VOCABULARY AND STYLE

1. Heat Moon attempts to reproduce the pronunciation of some words—e.g., *athians* (paragraph 12), *iodeen* (21), and *anteebee-otics* (25). Make a list of all such phonetic spellings. Why does Heat Moon do this? Do you think he captures all of the Wattses' accent or just some part of it? Is the device effective?
2. Examine how Heat Moon uses dialogue in his description. How are the Wattses revealed by what they say? How much of what was actually said during the visit is recorded? Can you find specific points in the story where Heat Moon obviously omits dialogue?
3. Try to define or explain the following words and phrases: *horehound candy* (paragraph 15), *bolsters* (26), *buttermilk pie* (28), *incised to crinkliness by a ballpoint* (41), *weary dismals* (48), *gallivantin' around* (51).

WRITING SUGGESTIONS

1. Choose a campus building or a location that has acquired a strange or vivid name (e.g., the cafeteria in the Student Center known as "The Scrounge"). In a paragraph describe the place to a friend who has never seen it.
2. Look for an unusual place in town (a barber shop or hair salon, a food co-op, a pool hall, a diner). In an essay describe the place for your reader. You might think of your essay as a feature article for next Sunday's local newspaper. Include descriptions of people and dialogue to help catch the right tone.

Prewriting:

a. Take a walk and make a list of possible places.
b. Visit one or more of them and take notes on what you see. Imagine yourself as a newspaper reporter. If people are present, try to write down exactly what they say.
c. Decide on a particular quality or feeling or idea that you want to convey about this place. Write a statement of purpose.
d. Do not "over-people" your description. Do not try to describe every character completely. Reveal personality through significant detail and dialogue.

Rewriting:

a. Check to make sure that you have made effective use of verbs and nouns. Do not rely on adjectives and adverbs to do the work of description.
b. Using your statement of purpose, check every detail that you included in your essay. Does it belong? Does it relate to that stated purpose?

3. Heat Moon is fascinated by unusual names, and often drives considerable distances to visit towns with names such as Dime Box, Hungry Horse, Liberty Bond, Ninety-Six, and Tuba City. Choose an unusual place name (town, river, subdivision, topographical feature) from your home state and research the origin of the name. A reference librarian can show you how to locate source materials. If possible, you could contact your local historical society or public library for help or interview some knowledgeable local residents. Using your research, write an essay about how that name was chosen.

The Inheritance of Tools

SCOTT RUSSELL SANDERS

Born in Memphis, Tennessee, in 1945, Sanders graduated from Brown University and received a Ph.D. from Cambridge University. Currently a professor of English at Indiana University, Sanders is a novelist, an essayist, a science fiction writer, and a teller of tales. His diverse accomplishments include D. H. Lawrence: The World of Five Novels *(1974);* Wilderness Plots: Tales about the Settlement of the American Land *(1983);* Fetching the Dead *(1984), a collection of stories;* Stone Country *(1985); and* Hear the Wind Blow: American Folksongs Retold *(1985). He has edited the writings of naturalist John James Audubon in* The Audubon Reader *(1986). In 1987 he wrote* The Paradise of Bombs, *an autobiographical work about his own spiritual growth and his appreciation of nature and family, despite having grown up on a weapons storage base. In this personal essay, occasioned by his father's death, Sanders explores the "inheritance" that adheres to four tools passed through four generations of his family.*

At just about the hour when my father died, soon after dawn 1
one February morning when ice coated the windows like cataracts, I banged my thumb with a hammer. Naturally I swore at the hammer, the reckless thing, and in the moment of swearing I thought of what my father would say: "If you'd try hitting the nail it would go in a whole lot faster. Don't you know your thumb's not as hard as that hammer?" We both were doing carpentry that day, but far apart. He was building cupboards at my brother's place in Oklahoma; I was at home in Indiana putting up a wall in the basement to make a bedroom for my daughter. By the time my mother called with news of his death—the long distance wires whittling her voice until it seemed too thin to bear the weight of what she had to say—my thumb was swollen. A week or so later a white scar in the shape of a crescent moon began to show above the cuticle, and month by

month it rose across the pink sky of my thumbnail. It took the better part of a year for the scar to disappear, and every time I noticed it I thought of my father.

The hammer had belonged to him, and to his father before him. The three of us have used it to build houses and barns and chicken coops, to upholster chairs and crack walnuts, to make doll furniture and book shelves and jewelry boxes. The head is scratched and pockmarked, like an old plowshare that has been working rocky fields, and it gives off the sort of dull sheen you see on fast creek water in the shade. It is a finishing hammer, about the weight of a bread loaf, too light, really, for framing walls, too heavy for cabinetwork, with a curved claw for pulling nails, a rounded head for pounding, a fluted neck for looks, and a hickory handle for strength. 2

The present handle is my third one, bought from a lumberyard in Tennessee down the road from where my brother and I were helping my father build his retirement house. I broke the previous one by trying to pull sixteen-penny nails out of floor joists—a foolish thing to do with a finishing hammer, as my father pointed out. "You ever hear of a crowbar?" he said. No telling how many handles he and my grandfather had gone through before me. My grandfather used to cut down hickory trees on his farm, saw them into slabs, cure the planks in his hayloft, and carve handles with a drawknife. The grain in hickory is crooked and knotty, and therefore rough, hard to split, like the grain in the two men who owned this hammer before me. 3

After proposing marriage to a neighbor girl, my grandfather used this hammer to build a house for his bride on a stretch of river bottom in northern Mississippi. The lumber for the place, like the hickory for the handle, was cut on his own land. By the day of the wedding he had not quite finished the house, and so right after the ceremony he took his wife home and put her to work. My grandmother had worn her Sunday dress for the wedding, with a fringe of lace tacked on around the hem in honor of the occasion. She removed this lace and folded it away before going out to help my grandfather nail siding on the house. "There she 4 was in her good dress," he told me some fifty-odd years after that wedding day, "holding up them long pieces of clapboard while I hammered, and together we got the place covered up before dark." As the family grew to four, six, eight, and eventually thirteen, my grandfather used this hammer to enlarge his house room by room, like a chambered nautilus expanding his shell.

By and by the hammer was passed along to my father. 5
One day he was up on the roof of our pony barn nailing shingles with it, when I stepped out the kitchen door to call him for supper. Before I could yell, something about the sight of him straddling the spine of that roof and swinging the hammer caught my eye and made me hold my tongue. I was five or six years old, and the world's commonplaces were still news to me. He would pull a nail from the pouch at his waist, bring the hammer down, and a moment later the *thunk* of the blow would reach my ears. And that is what had stopped me in my tracks and stilled my tongue, that momentary gap between seeing and hearing the blow. Instead of yelling from the kitchen door, I ran to the barn and climbed two rungs up the ladder—as far as I was allowed to go—and spoke quietly to my father. On our walk to the house he explained that sound takes time to make its way through air. Suddenly the world seemed larger, the air more dense, if sound could be held back like any ordinary traveler.

By the time I started using this hammer, at about the 6
age when I discovered the speed of sound, it already contained houses and mysteries for me. The smooth handle was one my grandfather had made. In those days I needed both hands to swing it. My father would start a nail in a scrap of wood, and I would pound away until I bent it over.

"Looks like you got ahold of some of those rubber 7
nails," he would tell me. "Here, let me see if I can find you some stiff ones." And he would rummage in a drawer until he came up with a fistful of more cooperative nails. "Look at the head," he would tell me. "Don't look at your hands, don't look at the hammer. Just look at the head of that nail and pretty soon you'll learn to hit it square."

Pretty soon I did learn. While he worked in the garage 8
cutting dovetail joints for a drawer or skinning a deer or tuning an engine, I would hammer nails. I made innocent blocks of wood look like porcupines. He did not talk much in the midst of his tools, but he kept up a nearly ceaseless humming, slipping in and out of a dozen tunes in an afternoon, often running back over the same stretch of melody again and again, as if searching for a way out. When the humming did cease, I knew he was faced with a task requiring great delicacy or concentration, and I took care not to distract him.

He kept scraps of wood in a cardboard box—the ends of 9
two-by-fours, slabs of shelving and plywood, odd pieces of molding—and everything in it was fair game. I nailed scraps together to fashion what I called boats or houses, but the results usually bore only faint resemblance to the visions I carried in my head. I would hold up these constructions to show my father, and he would turn them over in his hands admiringly, speculating about what they might be. My cobbled-together guitars might have been alien spaceships, my barns might have been models of Aztec temples, each wooden contraption might have been anything but what I had set out to make.

Now and again I would feel the need to have a chunk of 10
wood shaped or shortened before I riddled it with nails, and I would clamp it in a vise and scrape at it with a handsaw. My father would let me lacerate the board until my arm gave out, and then he would wrap his hand around mine and help me finish the cut, showing me how to use my thumb to guide the blade, how to pull back on the saw to keep it from binding, how to let my shoulder do the work.

"Don't force it," he would say, "just drag it easy and 11
give the teeth a chance to bite."

As the saw teeth bit down, the wood released its smell, 12
each kind with its own fragrance, oak or walnut or cherry or pine—usually pine because it was the softest, easiest for a child to work. No matter how weathered and gray the board, no matter how warped and cracked, inside there was this smell waiting, as of something freshly baked. I gathered

every smidgen of sawdust and stored it away in coffee cans, which I kept in a drawer of the workbench. When I did not feel like hammering nails I would dump my sawdust on the concrete floor of the garage and landscape it into highways and farms and towns, running miniature cars and trucks along miniature roads. Looming as huge as a colossus, my father worked over and around me, now and again bending down to inspect my work, careful not to trample my creations. It was a landscape that smelled dizzyingly of wood. Even after a bath my skin would carry the smell, and so would my father's hair, when he lifted me for a bedtime hug.

I tell these things not only from memory but also from 13
recent observation, because my own son now turns blocks of wood into nailed porcupines, dumps cans full of sawdust at my feet and sculpts highways on the floor. He learns how to swing a hammer from the elbow instead of the wrist, how to lay his thumb beside the blade to guide a saw, how to tap a chisel with a wooden mallet, how to mark a hole with an awl before starting a drill bit. My daughter did the same before him, and even now, on the brink of teenage aloofness, she will occasionally drag out my box of wood scraps and carpenter something. So I have seen my apprenticeship to wood and tools reenacted in each of my children, as my father saw his own apprenticeship renewed in me.

The saw I use belonged to him, as did my level and both 14
of my squares, and all four tools had belonged to his father. The blade of the saw is the bluish color of gun barrels, and the maple handle, dark from the sweat of hands, is inscribed with curving leaf designs. The level is a shaft of walnut two feet long, edged with brass and pierced by three round windows in which air bubbles float in oil-filled tubes of glass. The middle window serves for testing if a surface is horizontal, the others for testing if a surface is plumb or vertical. My grandfather used to carry this level on the gun-rack behind the seat in his pickup, and when I rode with him I would turn around to watch the bubbles dance. The larger of the two squares is called a framing square, a flat steel elbow, so beat up and tarnished you can barely make out the

rows of numbers that show how to figure the cuts on rafters. The smaller one is called a try square, for marking right angles, with a blued steel blade for the shank and a brass-faced block of cherry for the head.

I was taught early on that a saw is not to be used apart 15
from a square: "If you're going to cut a piece of wood," my father insisted, "you owe it to the tree to cut it straight."

Long before studying geometry, I learned there is a 16
mystical virtue in right angles. There is an unspoken morality in seeking the level and the plumb. A house will stand, a table will bear weight, the sides of a box will hold together only if the joints are square and the members upright. When the bubble is lined up between two marks etched in the glass tube of a level, you have aligned yourself with the forces that hold the universe together. When you miter the corners of a picture frame, each angle must be exactly forty-five degrees, as they are in the perfect triangles of Pythagoras, not a degree more or less. Otherwise the frame will hang crookedly, as if ashamed of itself and of its maker. No matter if the joints you are cutting do not show. Even if you are butting two pieces of wood together inside a cabinet, where not one except a wrecking crew will ever see them, you must take pains to insure that the ends are square and the studs are plumb.

I took pains over the wall I was building on the day my 17
father died. Not long after that wall was finished—paneled with tongue-and-groove boards of yellow pine, the nail holes filled with putty and the wood all stained and sealed—I came close to wrecking it one afternoon when my daughter ran howling up the stairs to announce that her gerbils had escaped from their cage and were hiding in my brand new wall. She could hear them scratching and squeaking behind her bed. Impossible! I said. How on earth could they get inside my drum-tight wall? Through the heating vent, she answered. I went downstairs, pressed my ear to the honey-colored wood, and heard the *scritch scritch* of tiny feet.

"What can we do?" my daughter wailed. "They'll starve 18
to death, they'll die of thirst, they'll suffocate."

"Hold on," I shouted, "I'll think of something." 19

While I thought and she fretted, the radio on her bedside 20
table delivered us the headlines. Several thousand people had died in a city in India from a poisonous cloud that had leaked overnight from a chemical plant. A nuclear-powered submarine had been launched. Rioting continued in South Africa. An airplane had been hijacked in the Mediterranean. Authorities calculated that several thousand homeless people slept on the streets within sight of the Washington Monument. I felt my usual helplessness in face of all these calamities. But here was my daughter weeping because her gerbils were holed up in a wall. This calamity I could handle.

"Don't worry," I told her. "We'll set food and water by 21
the heating vent and lure them out. And if that doesn't do the trick, I'll tear the wall apart until we find them."

She stopped crying and gazed at me. "You'd really tear it 22
apart? Just for my gerbils? The *wall*?" Astonishment slowed her down only for a second, however, before she ran to the workbench and began tugging at drawers, saying, "Let's see, what'll we need? Crowbar. Hammer. Chisels. I hope we don't have to use them—but just in case."

We didn't need the wrecking tools. I never had to assault 23
my handsome wall, because the gerbils eventually came out to nibble at a dish of popcorn. But for several hours I studied the tongue-and-groove skin I had nailed up on the day of my father's death, considering where to begin prying. There were no gaps in that wall, no crooked joints.

I had botched a great many pieces of wood before I mas- 24
tered the right angle with a saw, botched even more before I learned to miter a joint. The knowledge of these things resides in my hands and eyes and the webwork of muscles, not in the tools. There are machines for sale—powered miter boxes and radial-arm saws, for instance—that will enable any casual soul to cut proper angles in boards. The skill is invested in the gadget instead of the person who uses it, and this is what distinguishes a machine from a tool. If I had to earn my keep by making furniture or building houses, I suppose I would buy powered saws and pneumatic nailers; the need for speed would drive me to it. But since I carpenter only

for my own pleasure or to help neighbors or to remake the house around the ears of my family, I stick with hand tools. Most of the ones I own were given to me by my father, who also taught me how to wield them. The tools in my workbench are a double inheritance, for each hammer and level and saw is wrapped in a cloud of knowing.

All of these tools are a pleasure to look at and to hold. 25
Merchants would never paste NEW NEW NEW! signs on them in stores. Their designs are old because they work, because they serve their purpose well. Like folksongs and aphorisms and the grainy bits of language, these tools have been pared down to essentials. I look at my claw hammer, the distillation of a hundred generations of carpenters, and consider that it holds up well beside those other classics—Greek vases, Gregorian chants, *Don Quixote*, barbed fish hooks, candles, spoons. Knowledge of hammering stretches back to the earliest humans who squatted beside fires chipping flints. Anthropologists have a lovely name for those unworked rocks that served as the earliest hammers. *Dawn stones*, they are called. Their only qualification for the work, aside from hardness, is that they fit the hand. Our ancestors used them for grinding corn, tapping awls, smashing bones. From dawn stones to this claw hammer is a great leap in time, but no great distance in design or imagination.

On that iced-over February morning when I smashed my 26
thumb with the hammer, I was down in the basement framing the wall that my daughter's gerbils would later hide in. I was thinking of my father, as I always did whenever I built anything, thinking how he would have gone about the work, hearing in memory what he would have said about the wisdom of hitting the nail instead of my thumb. I had the studs and plates nailed together all square and trim, and was lifting the wall into place when the phone rang upstairs. My wife answered, and in a moment she came to the basement door and called down softly to me. The stillness in her voice made me drop the framed wall and hurry upstairs. She told me my father was dead. Then I heard the details over the phone from my mother. Building a set of

cupboards for my brother in Oklahoma, he had knocked off work early the previous afternoon because of cramps in his stomach. Early this morning, on his way into the kitchen of my brother's trailer, maybe going for a glass of water, so early that no one else was awake, he slumped down on the linoleum and his heart quit.

For several hours I paced around inside my house, upstairs and down, in and out of every room, looking for the right door to open and knowing there was no such door. My wife and children followed me and wrapped me in arms and backed away again, circling and staring as if I were on fire. Where was the door, the door, the door? I kept wondering. My smashed thumb turned purple and throbbed, making me furious. I wanted to cut it off and rush outside and scrape away the snow and hack a hold in the frozen earth and bury the shameful thing. 27

I went down into the basement, opened a drawer in my workbench, and stared at the ranks of chisels and knives. Oiled and sharp, as my father would have kept them, they gleamed at me like teeth. I took up a clasp knife, pried out the longest blade and tested the edge on the hair of my forearm. A tuft came away cleanly, and I saw my father testing the sharpness of tools on his own skin, the blades of axes and knives and gouges and hoes, saw the red hair shaved off in patches from his arms and the backs of his hands. "That will cut bear," he would say. He never cut a bear with his blades, now my blades, but he cut deer, dirt, wood. I closed the knife and put it away. Then I took up the hammer and went back to work on my daughter's wall, snugging the bottom plate against a chalkline on the floor, shimming the top plate against the joists overhead, plumbing the studs with my level, making sure before I drove the first nail that every line was square and true. 28

QUESTIONS ON SUBJECT AND PURPOSE

1. What is the subject of Sanders's essay? Is it tools? His father's death?
2. Is Sanders's father or grandfather (or his children) ever described in the story? How are they revealed to the reader?

3. What "door" (paragraph 27) is Sanders searching for?
4. What exactly has Sanders inherited from his father?

QUESTIONS ON STRATEGY AND AUDIENCE

1. How does Sanders use time to structure his essay? Is the story told in chronological order?
2. What is the function of each of the following episodes or events in the essay?
   a. The sore thumb
   b. "A mystical virtue in right angles" (paragraph 16)
   c. The wall he was building
3. What expectations does Sanders seem to have about his audience?

QUESTIONS ON VOCABULARY AND STYLE

1. How much dialogue does Sanders use in the story? What does the dialogue contribute?
2. Throughout the essay, Sanders makes use of many effective similes and metaphors. Make a list of six such devices. What does each contribute to the essay? How fresh and arresting are these images?
3. Be able to define each of the following words or phrases: *plowshare* (paragraph 2), *sixteen-penny nails* (3), *chambered nautilus* (4), *rummage* (7), *lacerate* (10), *smidgen* (12), *plumb* (14), *miter* (24), *aphorisms* (25), *shimming* (28).

WRITING SUGGESTIONS

1. Study the childhood scenes or episodes that Sanders includes in his essay—for example, calling his father to supper (paragraph 5), hammering nails (6–9), landscaping with sawdust (12). Notice how Sanders recreates sensory experiences. Then in a paragraph recreate a similar experience from your childhood. Remember to evoke sensory impressions for your reader—a sight, a sound, a smell, a touch.
2. Think about a skill, talent, or even a habit that you have learned from or share with a family member. In addition to the ability or trait, what else have you "inherited"? How does it

affect your life? In an essay describe the inheritance and its effect on you.

Prewriting:

a. Divide a piece of paper into two columns. In the left-hand column, make a list of possible subjects. Work on the list over a period of several days. In the space to the right of this list jot down the significance that you see in such an inheritance.

b. Select one of the items from your list and freewrite for 15 minutes. Concentrate on the signficance of this ability or trait in your life. How has it shaped or altered your life, your perceptions? Reread what you have just written. Then freewrite for another 15 minutes.

c. Like Sanders, you will be dealing with two "times" in the essay—your childhood and your present. Notice how Sanders manipulates time in his essay. He does not narrate the story in a strict chronological sequence. Experiment with time as an organizational strategy in your essay. Outline two or more structures for the essay.

Rewriting:

a. Check your essay to see if you have used vivid verbs and concrete nouns. Watch that you do not overwork adjectives and adverbs.

b. Did you include dialogue in your essay? If not, try adding some. Remember, though, that dialogue slows the pace of a story. Do not overuse it.

c. Look carefully at your conclusion. You want to end forcefully; you want to emphasize the significance of your inheritance. Reread your essay several times and then try freewriting a new conclusion. Try for a completely new ending. If you are using a peer reader, ask that reader to judge both conclusions.

3. The passing on of traditional crafts or skills is an important part of cultural tradition. Choose a society that interests you, and find a particular craft that is preserved from one generation to another. It might also be something that has been preserved in your family's religious or ethnic heritage. In a research paper, document the nature of the craft and the methods by which the culture ensures its transmission. What is important about this craft? What does it represent to that society? Why bother to preserve it?

The Copperhead and the Mosquito

ANNIE DILLARD

Born in Pittsburgh in 1945, Annie Dillard received an M.A. in English from Hollins College in Virginia. A poet, essayist, and literary critic, she has served as a contributing editor of Harper's *since 1973, and her work has appeared in* American Scholar, Cosmopolitan, Living Wilderness, *and* Atlantic. *Her books include the Pulitzer Prize-winning* Pilgrim at Tinker Creek *(1974),* Tickets for a Prayer Wheel *(1974),* Holy the Firm *(1977),* Teaching a Stone to Talk *(1982),* Living by Fiction *(1982), and* Encounters with Chinese Writers *(1984). In her most recent book,* An American Childhood *(1987), Dillard records her own emotional and physical growth during the 1950s. Since 1979, she has been teaching at Wesleyan University in Connecticut.* Pilgrim at Tinker Creek *displays Dillard's talent for examining spiritual questions through precise observations of the natural world. In this selection from that book, she describes how a walk is interrupted first by a copperhead and then by a mosquito which feeds upon the snake. The sight, for Dillard, sheds "new light on the intricate texture of the world."*

There was a snake at the quarry with me tonight. It lay shaded by cliffs on a flat sandstone ledge above the quarry's dark waters. I was thirty feet away, sitting on the forest path overlook, when my eye caught the dark scrawl on the rocks, the laxy sinuosity that can only mean snake. I approached for a better look, edging my way down the steep rock cutting, and saw that the snake was only twelve or thirteen inches long. Its body was thick for its length. I came closer still, and saw the unmistakable undulating bands of brown, the hourglasses: copperhead. 1

I never step a foot out of the house, even in winter, without a snakebite kit in my pocket. Mine is a small kit in rubber casing about the size of a shotgun shell; I slapped my pants instinctively to fix in my mind its location. Then I stomped hard on the ground a few times and set down beside the snake. 2

The young copperhead was motionless on its rock. Although it lay in a loose sprawl, all I saw at first was a camouflage pattern of particolored splotches confused by the rushing speckles of light in the weeds between us, and by the deep twilight dark of the quarry pond beyond the rock. Then suddenly the form of its head emerged from the confusion: burnished brown, triangular, blunt as a stone ax. Its head and the first four inches of its body rested on airy nothing an inch above the rock. I admired the snake. Its scales shone with newness, bright and buffed. Its body was perfect, whole and unblemished. I found it hard to believe it had not just been created on the spot, or hatched fresh from its mother, so unscathed and clean was its body, so unmarked by any passage. 3

Did it see me? I was only four feet away, seated on the weedy cliff behind the sandstone ledge, the snake was between me and the quarry pond. I waved an arm in its direction: nothing moved. Its low-forehead glare and lipless reptile smirk revealed nothing. How could I tell where it was looking, what it was seeing? I squinted at its head, staring at those eyes like the glass eyes of a stuffed warbler, at those scales like shields canted and lapped just so, to frame an improbable, unfathomable face. 4

Yes, it knew I was there. There was something about its eyes, some alien alertness . . . what on earth must it be like to have scales on your face? All right then, copperhead. I know you're here, you know I'm here. This is a big night. I dug my elbows into rough rock and dry soil and settled back on the hillside to begin the long business of waiting out a snake. 5

The only other poisonous snake around here is the timber rattler, *Crotalus horridus horridus*. These grow up to six 6 feet long in the mountains, and as big as your thigh. I've never seen one in the wild; I don't know how many have seen me. I see copperheads, though, sunning in the dust, disappearing into rock cliff chinks, crossing dirt roads at twilight. Copperheads have no rattle, of course, and, at least in my experience, they do not give way. You walk around a copperhead—if you see it. Copperheads are not big enough or venomous enough to kill adult humans readily, but they do account for far and away the greatest number of poisonous snakebites in North America: there are so many of them, and people, in the Eastern woodlands. It always interests me when I read about new studies being done on pit vipers; the team of herpetologists always seems to pick my neck of the woods for its fieldwork. I infer that we have got poisonous snakes as East Africa has zebras or the tropics have orchids—they are our specialty, our stock-in-trade. So I try to keep my eyes open. But I don't worry: you have to live pretty far out to be more than a day from a hospital. And worrying about getting it in the face from a timber rattler is like worrying about being struck by a meteorite: life's too short. Anyway perhaps the actual bite is painless.

One day I was talking about snakes to Mrs. Mildred 7
Sink, who operates a switchboard. A large pane separated us, and we were talking through a circular hole in the glass. She was seated in a dark room little bigger than a booth. As we talked, red lights on her desk would flash. She would glance at them, then back at me, and, finishing her point with careful calmness, she would fix on me a long, significant look to hold my attention while her hand expertly sought the button and pushed it. In this way she handled incoming calls and told me her snake story.

When she was a girl, she lived in the country just north 8
of here. She had a brother four years old. One bright summer day her brother and her mother were sitting quietly in the big room of the log cabin. Her mother had her sewing in her lap and was bent over it in concentration. The little boy was playing with wooden blocks on the floor. "Ma," he said, "I

saw a snake." "Where?" "Down by the spring." The woman stitched the hem of a cotton dress, gathering the material with her needle and drawing it smooth with her hand. The little boy piled his blocks carefully, this way and that. After a while he said, "Ma, it's too dark in here, I can't see." She looked up and the boy's leg was swollen up as big around as his body.

Mrs. Sink nodded at me emphatically and then heeded 9
the flashing light on the panel before her. She turned away; this caller was taking time. I waved and caught her eye; she waved, and I left.

The copperhead in front of me was motionless; its head 10
still hung in the air above the sandstone rock. I thought of poking at it with a weed, but rejected the notion. Still, I wished it would do something. Marston Bates tells about an English ecologist, Charles Elton, who said, with his Britishness fully unfurled, "All cold-blooded animals . . . spend an unexpectedly large proportion of their time doing nothing at all, or at any rate nothing in particular." That is precisely what this one was doing.

I noticed its tail. It tapered to nothingness. I started back 11
at the head and slid my eye down its body slowly: taper, taper, taper, scales, tiny scales, air. Suddenly the copperhead's tail seemed to be the most remarkable thing I had ever seen. I wished I tapered like that somewhere. What if I were a shaped balloon blown up through the tip of a finger?

Here was this blood-filled, alert creature, this nerved 12
rope of matter, really here instead of not here, splayed soft and solid on a rock by the slimmest of chances. It was a thickening of the air spread from a tip, a rush into being, eyeball and blood, through a pin-hole rent. Every other time I had ever seen this rock it had been a flat sandstone rock over the quarry pond; now it hosted and bore this chunk of fullness that parted the air around it like a driven wedge. I looked at it from the other direction. From tail to head it spread like the lines of crescendo, widening from stillness to a turgid blast; then at the bulging jaws it began contracting again, diminuendo, till at the tip of its snout the

lines met back at the infinite point that corners every angle, and that space once more ceased being a snake.

While this wonder engaged me, something happened that was so unusual and unexpected that I can scarcely believe I saw it. It was ridiculous. 13

Night had been rising like a ground vapor from the blackened quarry pool. I heard a mosquito sing in my ear; I waved it away. I was looking at the copperhead. The mosquito landed on my ankle; again, I idly brushed it off. To my utter disbelief, it lighted on the copperhead. It squatted on the copperhead's back near its "neck," and bent its head to its task. I was riveted. I couldn't see the mosquito in great detail, but I could make out its lowered head that seemed to bore like a well drill through surface rock to fluid. Quickly I looked around to see if I could find anyone—any hunter going to practice shooting beer cans, any boy on a motorbike—to whom I could show this remarkable sight while it lasted. 14

To the best of my knowledge, it lasted two or three full minutes; it seemed like an hour. I could imagine the snake, like the frog sucked dry by the giant water bug, collapsing to an empty bag of skin. But the snake never moved, never indicated any awareness. At last the mosquito straightened itself, fumbled with its forelegs about its head like a fly, and sluggishly took to the air, where I lost it at once. I looked at the snake; I looked beyond the snake to the ragged chomp in the hillside where years before men had quarried stone; I rose, brushed myself off, and walked home. 15

Is this what it's like, I thought then, and think now: a little blood here, a chomp there, and still we live, trampling the grass? Must everything whole be nibbled? Here was a new light on the intricate texture of things in the world, the actual plot of the present moment in time after the fall: the way we the living are nibbled and nibbling—not held aloft on a cloud in the air but bumbling pitted and scarred and broken through a frayed and beautiful land. 16

QUESTIONS ON SUBJECT AND PURPOSE

1. What is it in the scene that catches Dillard's attention? Why is she fascinated first by the copperhead and then by the mosquito biting the snake?
2. What does Dillard seem to mean by the question "Must everything whole be nibbled" (paragraph 16)?
3. How does this experience shed light on "the intricate texture of things in the world" (paragraph 16)?
4. This is the first part of a chapter taken from *Pilgrim at Tinker Creek.* In the remainder of the essay, Dillard cites examples of parasites—organisms that live on other organisms. How do parasites fit into Dillard's view of life?

QUESTIONS ON STRATEGY AND AUDIENCE

1. In the middle of her narrative why does Dillard digress for the story of Mrs. Sink and the child bitten by a snake? How does this story relate to the larger point Dillard is making?
2. Look at Dillard's descriptions of the copperhead. Is there anything unusual about them? How are they different from a description that a herpetologist (an expert on reptiles and amphibians) would give? What does Dillard see that we might not see?
3. What expectations does Dillard seem to have about her audience? What values might she and her audience share? Can you point to specific passages that support your assumptions?

QUESTIONS ON VOCABULARY AND STYLE

1. Find examples of figurative language (images, similes, and metaphors). Why does Dillard use these devices? How do they contribute to the description in the essay?
2. How many examples of unusual description can you find—phrases such as "lipless reptile smirk" (paragraph 4) or "ragged chomp in the hillside" (15). How do such phrases contribute to the effect of Dillard's essay?
3. How often does Dillard use the colon? Make a list of the occurrences. What do they have in common?
4. Define the following: *burnished* (paragraph 3), *canted* (4), *a pinhole rent* (12), *crescendo* (12), *turgid* (12), *diminuendo* (12).

WRITING SUGGESTIONS

1. Look around your room, refrigerator, apartment, house, or yard and find a living or organic object (an insect, a green bean, a leaf). In a paragraph describe what you see. Spend time "seeing" before you begin to write.
2. Write an essay on the subject of how to write a descriptive essay. You might imagine that your essay will become a handout distributed in freshman English classes this semester—advice on how to write a descriptive essay.

   Prewriting:

   a. Look back over each of the selections included in this chapter. On the basis of these examples—using them as sample texts—what principles of description do you see at work? What do these writers include? What do they exclude?
   b. Remember that you are offering advice to other writers, so it will help if you make two lists—one of do's and one of dont's. Within each list, some points will be more important than others. After you have a list, number the items in order of importance.

   Rewriting:

   a. For your essay to be effective it must offer clear, step-by-step advice to the writer. Check to make sure that each paragraph contains a single piece of advice (complete with examples). Using a colored pen, circle the key word or phrase in each paragraph. Make sure that you have only one thing to circle in each paragraph.
   b. Look carefully at how you structured your essay. Probably you either began with the most significant point or ended with it. Would the essay work any better if the order were changed? If you are writing on a word processor, shift the text around to see.

3. Locate a copy of *Pilgrim at Tinker Creek* in your library (it is also available as an inexpensive paperback). As you read the essays, notice what Dillard describes and what those descriptions reveal to her. Then in an essay explain what Dillard means by "seeing." Use appropriate examples from the book to support your conclusions.

CHAPTER

4

Division and Classification

Division breaks a subject into its parts. For example, you have learned that an essay can be divided into three sections (introduction, body, and conclusion) and that the federal government has three branches (legislative, judicial, and executive). Even this book employs division, for the structures and strategies used in writing prose have been subdivided into nine areas: example, narration, description, division and classification, comparision and contrast, process, definition, cause and effect, and argumentation and persuasion. Division begins with a single subject and then shows how it can be subdivided into smaller units. Adam Smith in "Everyday Drugs" begins with the subject "xanthines," a particular kind of chemical stimulant, and then subdivides that subject into its three most common forms: coffee, tea, and cocoa or cola. Division, in that it involves breaking or separating a whole into its constituent parts, is similar to process analysis. It differs in its purpose: process is intended to show how to do something or how something happens; division is used to show the components of a larger subject; it helps the reader understand a complex whole by considering it in smaller units.

Classification is a form of division, but instead of starting with a single subject as you do in division, in classification you begin with many items which you then group or classify into categories. Obviously a classification must have at least two categories. Laurence Perrine, for example, proposes two categories for classifying literature in his "Escape and Interpretive Literature." Depending upon how many items you start with and how different they are, you can end up having quite a few subdivisions. You probably remember in at least rough form the taxonomic classification you learned in high school biology. It begins with the broadest division into as many as five kingdoms (animals, plants, monera, fungi, and protista) and then moves downward to increasingly narrower categories (phylum or division, class, order, family, genus, species). Most classifications outside of the sciences are not as precisely and hierarchically defined. Alison Lurie in "American Regional Costume" classifies American dress into five "distinct styles" based on a geographical pattern: Old New England, Deep South, Middle American, Wild West, and Far West (or Californian). At the same time, though, Lurie acknowledges that such a scheme cannot be rigid, for some people will, for various reasons, refuse to wear the style characteristic of their section of the country.

How Do You Choose a Subject?

In choosing your subject for either division or classification, be sure to avoid the obvious approach to the obvious subject. Every teacher has read at some point a classification essay dividing teachers into three groups based solely on the grade level at which they teach: elementary school teachers teach in elementary school, middle school teachers teach in middle school, and high school teachers teach in high school. Although the division is complete and accurate, such a subject and approach are likely to lead you into writing that is boring and simply not worth either your time or your reader's. No subject is inherently bad, but if you choose to write about something common, you need to find an interesting angle from which to approach it. Before you begin to write, answer two questions: first, what is your purpose? and second, will your reader learn something or be entertained by what you plan to write?

How Do You Divide or Classify a Subject?

Since both division and classification involve separation into parts—either dividing a whole into pieces or sorting many things into related groups or categories—you have to find ways in which to divide or group. Those ways can be objective and formal, such as the classification schemes used by biologists, or subjective and informal like Susan Allen Toth's scheme in "Cinematypes." Either way, several things are particularly important.

First, you subdivide or categorize for a reason or a purpose, and your division should be made with that end in mind. Bernard R. Berelson in the "The Value of Children: A Taxonomical Essay," divides people's reasons for wanting children into six categories: biological, cultural, political, economic, familial, and personal. His purpose is to explain to the reader the various factors that motivate people to *want* children. The six categories represent the spectrum of reasons why adults *want* children. Berelson does not include, for example, a category labeled "accidental," for such a heading would lie outside of and be irrelevant to his stated purpose.

Second, your division or classification must be complete—you cannot omit pieces or leave items unclassified. How complete your classification needs to be depends upon your purpose. Given the limited purpose that Toth has, it is sufficient to offer just three types of dates. They do not represent all possible dates, but in the comic context of Toth's essay, the three are enough to establish her point. Berelson, on the other hand, sets out to be exhaustive, to isolate all of the reasons people at any time or in any place have wanted children. As a result, he has to include some categories that are essentially irrelevant for most Americans. For example, probably few if any Americans ever want children because of political reasons, that is, because their government encourages them to do so. But in some societies at certain periods of time political reasons have been important. Therefore, Berelson must include that category as well.

Third, the categories or subdivisions you establish need to be parallel in form. In mathematical terms, the categories should share a lowest common denominator. A simple and fairly effective test for parallelism is to see whether your categories are all phrased in similar grammatical terms. Perrine, for example, defines his two categories in exactly parallel form:

> Escape literature helps us pass the time agreeably.
> Interpretative literature broadens and deepens and sharpens our awareness of life.

For this reason you should not establish a catch-all category which you label something like "other." Perrine's essay establishes the two ends of a spectrum. All literature falls between these two categories. When Berelson is finished with his classification scheme, no reasons are left unaccounted for; everything fits into one of the six subdivisions.

Finally, your categories or subdivisions should be mutually exclusive; that is, items should belong in only one category. Toth's "cinematypes" cannot be mistaken for one another.

How Do You Structure a Classification Essay?

The body of a classification essay will obviously have as many parts as you have categories. Each category will probably be treated in either a single paragraph or a group of related paragraphs. That much seems simple enough. Toth, for example, organizes "Cinematypes" around the three different men with whom she has gone to the movies, treating each date in three paragraphs. The central portion of Lurie's "American Regional Costume" is also less symmetrical. The first four styles are treated in one paragraph each; however, the fifth (Far West) gets three paragraphs. Lurie orders her essay to reflect the geographical pattern: she starts in New England and moves across the United States. That is not the only order posssible, although it is a convenient one. Toth, however, could arrange her cinematypes in any order. Nothing in the material itself determines the sequence.

Not all classifications have the same flexibility in their arrangement. Some invite or imply or even demand a particular order. If you were classifying films using the ratings established by the motion pictures industry, you would essentially have to follow the G, PG, PG13, R, and X sequence. Although you could begin at either end, it would not make sense to begin with any of the three middle categories. Having an order underlying your classification can be a great help for both you and your reader. It allows you to know where to place each section, dictating the order you will follow. It gives your reader a clear sense of direction. Berelson, for example, in "The Value of Children" A Taxonomical Essay," arranges his reasons why people have children in an order that "starts with chemistry and proceeds to spirit." That is, he deals first with the biological reasons for wanting children and moves finally to the most spiritual of reasons—love.

Writing a Division: A Student Example

April Lavallee found a subject to divide in another course she was taking. Notice how the division is similar to, but not identical with, a process analysis. April's purpose is not to tell the reader how memory works—such a subject would probably be too complicated for a short paper. Instead, April uses the accepted three-part division of memory to show why we remember some things but not others.

Improving Your Memory

While attempting to memorize chapter upon chapter of unlearned material the night before a test, what college student would not want to learn more about the workings of our memory system with the hope, perhaps, of shortening the duration of time required to learn a unit of material? The first step in the process of increasing memory is to learn more about the workings and structures of our memory systems. Although controversial, the information-processing model of memory described here is a widely accepted model of our memory system and its components. This model breaks our memory down into three principal storage structures, each corresponding to a stage of processing of a stimulus. Information about a particular stimulus is entered, or registered, in the first of these structures, known as the Sensory Register, by means of one or more of the five senses. It is held here very briefly—for approximately 250 msec to 2 seconds—in raw sensory form, and eventually decays and vanishes completely. Once recognized, information can pass to the next storage structure—the Short-Term Memory (STM). Information is stored here not as raw sensory data, but as familiar recognizable patterns. By the use of rehearsal, information may be retained here for much longer than in the Sensory Register, but without the use of this, the information decays just as in the Sensory Register. Another limitation, in addition to time, on STM is the amount of material which can be stored at one time in STM, even with the help of rehearsal. The generally accepted number of items which can be held in STM is approximately seven, varying by two depending upon the individual. According to this model, increased repetition leads the information to storage in long-term memory, the third of the storage structures. This structure is relatively permanent and contains all of our knowledge about the world. Any limit on the amount of material this structure is capable of holding has not been established and is seemingly nonexistent, seeing that the amount that we can learn appears to be unlimited. Learning of material such as this can aid the diligent student in perfecting memory strategies designed to enhance his memory capabilities.

The strength of April's essay is that it has specific information to convey, information April had available because she was also taking a psychology course that semester. When her classmates had a chance to read her opening sentences on a mimeographed handout, several were anxious to read on—"anything to help with studying," remarked one student. But as soon as April heard that response, she realized a problem. Her opening sentences and her title seem to promise advice on how to improve memory. In fact, the essay analyzes the three divisions that constitute memory. As a result of the students' responses, April decided to rewrite her introduction and conclusion to reflect her real subject. In the process of revising, April decided as well to emphasize the three-part division of memory even more by introducing paragraph divisions into her paper.

The Structure of Memory

George Washington was our first President; the North defeated the South in the Civil War; the Japanese bombed Pearl Harbor during World War II; and the whale is the largest living mammal. These statements have nothing in common except that practically every American knows them. Although they are unimportant to our everyday lives, we can remember facts such as these, but we cannot remember where our keys are when we are late for work. We can recite the Pledge of Allegiance, but we cannot remember the seven digits the telephone operator just gave us. Why is this?

The information-processing model used to describe how our memories work helps explain phenomena such as these. This model defines three principal storage structures, each of which corresponds to a stage in the processing of a stimulus. Information is first entered or registered by means of one or more of the five senses in the Sensory Register. It is held here briefly—for approximately 250 msec to 2 seconds—in raw sensory form, and eventually decays and vanishes completely.

Once the information is recognized it can pass to the next storage structure—the Short-Term Memory (STM). Information is stored here as familiar, recognizable patterns. By the use of rehearsal (forced recall and repetition), information can be retained here for much longer than the Sensory Register. Without rehearsal, though, the information decays just as it does in the Sensory Register. Another limitation, in addition to time, on STM is the amount of material that can be stored here at one time, even with the help of rehearsal. The generally accepted number of items that can be held in STM is seven, plus or minus two depending on the individual.

With increased repetition, information is transferred from STM to Long-Term Memory (LTM), the third of the storage structures. This structure is relatively permanent and contains all of our knowledge about the world. Apparently LTM is unlimited in the amount of information it can hold. The secret to remembering is to get the information into LTM, so next time pay attention and rehearse that telephone number or the location of your keys and sunglasses. Then you won't forget.

Some Things to Remember

1. In choosing a subject for division or classification ask yourself: first, what is my purpose? and second, will my reader learn something or be entertained by my paper?
2. Remember that your subdivision or classification should reflect your purpose—that is, the number of categories or parts is related to what you are trying to do.
3. Make sure that your division or classification is complete. Do not omit any pieces or items. Everything should be accounted for.
4. Take care that the parts or categories be phrased in parallel form.
5. Avoid a category labeled something such as "other" or "miscellaneous."
6. Remember to make your categories or subdivisions mutually exclusive.
7. Once you have established your subdivisions, check to see whether there is an order implied or demanded by your subject.
8. As you move from one subdivision to another, provide markers for the reader so that the parts are clearly labeled.

Everyday Drugs

ADAM SMITH

Adam Smith is the pseudonym of George J. W. Goodman. He was born in 1930 in St. Louis, Missouri, and earned a B. A. from Harvard in 1952, then studied as a Rhodes Scholar at Oxford. Smith has worked as a reporter for Collier's *and* Barron's, *associate editor for* Time *and* Fortune, *editor for* Institutional Investor, *contributing editor and vice-president of* New York, *and occasional columnist for* Newsweek. *In 1969, he won the G. M. Loeb Award for his business writing. His books include* The Bubble Makers *(1955),* A Killing in the Market *(1958),* The Wheeler Dealers *(1959),* The Money Game *(1968),* Supermoney *(1972), and* Powers of Mind *(1975). Smith has a talent for making business writing lively and entertaining. He has also written the screenplays for* The Wheeler Dealers *(1963) and* The Americanization of Emily *(1964). In this selection from* Powers of Mind, *Smith points to some powerful drugs that are a part of many Americans' everyday diet. "In our society," Smith notes, "there are some drugs we think of as okay drugs, and other drugs make us gasp."*

Americans take xanthines at the rate of 100 *billion* doses per year. Xanthines are alkaloids which stimulate portions of the cerebral cortex. They give you a "more rapid and clearer flow of thought, allay drowsiness . . . motor activity is increased. There is a keener appreciation of sensory stimuli, and reaction time to them is diminished." This description, again from the pharmacology textbook, is similar to descriptions of cocaine and amphetamine. Of course, the xanthine addict pays a price. He is, says Sir Clifford Allbutt, Regius Professor of Medicine at Cambridge, "subject to fits of agitation and depression; he loses color and has a haggard appearance. The appetite falls off; the heart suffers; it palpitates, or it intermits. As with other such agents, a renewed 1 dose of the poison gives temporary relief, but at the cost of the misery."

Xanthines are generally taken orally through "aqueous extracts" of the plants that produce these alkaloids, either in seeds or leaves. In the United States the three most common methylated xanthines taken are called caffeine, theophyline, and theobromine. The seeds of *Coffea arabica* contain caffeine, the leaves of *Thea sinensis* contain caffeine and theophylline, and the seeds of *Theobroma cacao* contain caffeine and theobromine. In America the three are known as "coffee," "tea" and "cocoa," and they are consumed daily, at the rate of billions of pounds a year. They are generally drunk as hot drinks, but Americans also drink cold drinks containing caffeine from the nuts of the tree *Cola acuminata*. The original drinks ended in the word "cola," but now there are many "colas" which do not bear that name in the title. The early ads for Coca-Cola said it gave you a lift. 2

Coffee, tea, cocoa and cola drinks are all drugs. Caffeine is a central nervous system stimulant, theophylline less so, and theobromine hardly at all. All xanthines increase the production of urine. Xanthines act on smooth muscles—relaxing, for example, especially in the case of theophylline, bronchi that may have been constricted. Like the salicylates—aspirin—xanthines can cause stomach irritation. Caffeine can cause sleeplessness, and researchers have found that it causes chromosome breaks. 3

Maxwell House, meet the Regius Professor of Medicine. Is the stuff good to the last drop, or another dose of the poison? Is it a food, to be sold in supermarkets, or a stimulant to the central nervous system like the amphetamines? "The popularity of the xanthine beverages depends on their stimulant action, although most people are unaware of any stimulation," says the giant pharmacology text. 4

It is surprising to find substances we think of so cheerfully, perkin' in the pot, listed as drugs. That's the point. In our society, there are some drugs we think of as okay drugs, and other drugs make us gasp. A coffee drinker who drinks coffee all day and cannot function without it is just a heavy 5 coffee drinker, but someone using a non-okay drug is a "drug user" or an "addict."

QUESTIONS ON SUBJECT AND PURPOSE

1. What are xanthines?
2. Why does Smith wait so long to identify the three most commonly used "methylated xanthines"?
3. Is there any shift in Smith's approach to his subject? Characterize any changes you see.

QUESTIONS ON STRATEGY AND AUDIENCE

1. How does Smith structure this selection? Look at both how individual paragraphs are put together and how the group of paragraphs as a whole is structured?
2. Why does Smith have a quotation from Sir Clifford Allbutt? What does it add to his argument? Why quote from a pharmacology textbook?
3. What assumptions does Smith have about his audience? How do those assumptions help shape his remarks?

QUESTIONS ON VOCABULARY AND STYLE

1. Why does Smith use the pharmacological terminology? Why the Latin identifications?
2. What is the effect of mixing scientific terminology with such informal words as *stuff* (paragraph 4), *perkin'* (5), and *okay* (5)?
3. Be able to define the following words: *alkaloids* (paragraph 1), *cerebral cortex* (1), *amphetamine* (1), *haggard* (1), *palpitates* (1), *aqueous* (2), *bronchi* (3), *salicylates* (3).

WRITING SUGGESTIONS

1. Smith does not rigidly classify xanthines, but instead divides them into the three most commonly used forms. Select a common food or beverage and subdivide it into its constituent parts. Contents labels on packages are always a good place to start. Present your subdivision in a paragraph.

2. Americans exhibit widely differing attitudes toward the food they eat, in large part because they have the most choice of any people in the world. Some eat regularly at fast-food restaurants; other consume only health foods. In an essay, classify the American eater. Remember that you should probably have four to six categories.

   Prewriting:
   a. Establish, through observation, the range of alternatives. Visit a supermarket and a health food store. Consult the Yellow Pages for a listing of restaurants. Check food magazines at the local newsstand. Jot down your impressions. Make sure, though, that you look at food from a variety of viewpoints. Do not focus just on what appeals to you.
   b. Interview someone who has strong feelings about food or whose food habits are strikingly different from your own.
   c. Check back over the list of things to remember at the end of the introduction to this chapter. Keep that advice in mind as you plan your essay.

   Rewriting:
   a. Look at the subheads used in the essays by Lurie and Berelson. Did you use a similar strategy to organize your essay?
   b. Since classification essays involve a series of pieces, it is important to provide adequate links between those sections. Look carefully at how you made the transitions from one category to another. Compare your links to those used by Lurie and Berelson.
   c. Are your categories phrased in parallel form? On a separate sheet of paper, make a short outline of what you have written.
   d. Find a peer reader and ask for an honest reaction to your paper, its organization, and its interest.

3. Americans have become increasingly concerned about the additives put into food. Research the nature of food additives. How many are there? What do they do? Develop a classification scheme to explain the largest groups or subdivisions. Be sure to use examples.

Escape and Interpretive Literature

LAURENCE PERRINE

Laurence Perrine was born in Toronto, Ontario, and received a B.A. and M.A. from Oberlin College and a Ph.D. from Yale in 1948. From 1946 to 1981, he taught at Southern Methodist University in Dallas, eventually becoming the Fresnley Professor of English. He served as president of the South Central Modern Language Association from 1970 to 1971. Perrine has compiled the widely used anthologies Sound and Sense: An Introduction to Poetry *(1956),* Story and Structure *(1959), and* Poetry: Theory and Practice *(1962) as well as the essay collection* The Art of Total Relevance *(1978). His work has appeared in such scholarly periodicals as* Southwest Review *and* English Journal. *In this short selection from one of his textbooks, Perrine classifies fiction into two major types. Ever wonder why "best sellers" are never taught in college literature courses? Perrine suggests an answer.*

The experience of humankind through the ages is that literature may furnish . . . understanding and do so effectively—that the depiction of imagined experiences can provide authentic insights. "The truest history," said Diderot of the novels of Samuel Richardson, "is full of falsehoods, and your romance is full of truths." But the bulk of fiction does not present such insights. Only some does. Initially, therefore, fiction may be classified into two broad categories: literature of escape and literature of interpretation. 1

Escape literature is that written purely for entertainment—to help us pass the time agreeably. *Interpretive literature* is written to broaden and deepen and sharpen our awareness of life. Escape literature takes us *away* from the real world: it enables us temporarily to forget our troubles. Interpretative literature takes us, through the imagination, 2 deeper *into* the real world: it enables us to understand our troubles. Escape literature has as its only object pleasure. Interpretive literature has as its object pleasure *plus* understanding.

Having established a distinction, however, we must not 3
exaggerate or oversimplify it. Escape and interpretation are not two great bins, into one or the other of which we can toss any given story. Rather, they are opposite ends of a scale, the two poles between which the world of fiction spins. The difference between them does not lie in the absence or presence of a "moral." The story which in all of its incidents and characters is shallow may have an unimpeachable moral, while the interpretive story may have no moral at all in any conventional sense. The difference does not lie in the absence or presence of "facts." The historical romance may be full of historical information and yet be pure escape in its depiction of human behavior. The difference does not lie in the presence or absence of an element of fantasy. The escape story may have a surface appearance of everyday reality, while the tale of seeming wildest fancy may press home on us some sudden truth. The difference between the two kinds of literature is deeper and more subtle than any of these distinctions. A story becomes interpretive as it illuminates some aspect of human life or behavior. An interpretive story presents us with an insight—large or small—into the nature and conditions of our existence. it gives us a keener awareness of what it is to be a human being in a universe sometimes friendly, sometimes hostile. It helps us to understand our world, our neighbors, and ourselves.

Perhaps we can clarify the difference by suggestion. 4
Escape writers are like inventors who devise a contrivance for our diversion. When we push the button, lights flash, bells ring, and cardboard figures move jerkily across a painted horizon. Interpretive writers are discoverers: they take us out into the midst of life and say, "Look, here is the world!" Escape writers are full of tricks and surprises: they pull rabbits out of hats, saw a beautiful woman in two, and snatch brightly colored balls out of the air. Interpretive

writers take us behind the scenes, where they show us the props and mirrors and seek to make clear the illusions. This is not to say that interpretive writers are merely reporters. More surely than escape writers they shape and give form to their materials. But they shape and form them always with the intent that we may see and feel and understand them better, not for the primary purpose of furnishing entertainment.

QUESTIONS ON SUBJECT AND PURPOSE

1. What are the important ways in which escape literature differs from interpretive literature?
2. What similarities exist between the two types of literature?
3. Perrine likens the escape writer to what kind of performer? What is the effect of doing that? Does he use any similar analogy for the interpretive writer? If he does, what is the effect of the two different analogies?
4. Which kind of literature do you think Perrine feels is "better"?

QUESTIONS ON STRATEGY AND AUDIENCE

1. How does Perrine structure his classification of the two types of literature?
2. Perrine doesn't use specific examples of either kind of writing. Why not?
3. Perrine's classification is part of the first chapter of his college textbook *Literature: Structure, Sound, and Sense*, a book generally used in introduction to literature courses. How does Perrine write to that intended audience? What expectations does he have of his audience? How might that influence what he is saying?

QUESTIONS ON VOCABULARY AND STYLE

1. What does the word *escape* suggest to you? What about the word *interpretive*? Why doesn't Perrine use a word such as *serious* instead of *interpretive*?
2. Is there anything about the tone, the vocabulary, or the sen-

tence structures that signals to you that this selection is taken from a textbook?

3. Be able to define the following words: *depiction* (paragraph 1), *unimpeachable* (3), *contrivance* (4).

WRITING SUGGESTIONS

1. Using a similar two-part classification scheme, establish the ends of a spectrum for subjects such as those listed below. Present your classification in a paragraph.
   a. Commercial television/public broadcasting
   b. Metropolitan daily newspaper/*USA Today*
   c. Chain stores/independent stores
   d. Dorm or apartment dwellers/commuters
   e. Leaders/followers
2. Extend the classification suggested above to include three to five parts or subdivisions. Be sure to provide at least two examples for each subdivision.

   Prewriting:
   a. Brainstorm for a possible topic. Spend some time just making a list of possibilities. Try to add to your list over a two-day period.
   b. Rule off a sheet of paper into six equal blocks. Down the extreme left-hand margin list your possible topics. Then in the five blocks running from left to right list the various subdivisions that each topic suggests.
   c. Rule out any topics that result in stereotypes or trite and obvious subdivisions (for example, three kinds of teachers: elementary, middle, and high school).
   d. Examine your grid carefully. How many subdivisions have you established for each topic? Remember that you ought to have at least three. Check to make sure that the subdivisions are parallel in form.

   Rewriting:
   a. Look carefully at your introduction. Do you attempt to catch your reader's attention? Reread the body of your essay several times. Now freewrite a new introduction to your paper. Imagine that your article will appear in a magazine—work to grab and hold your reader's interest.
   b. Have you provided enough examples and details for each category? Remember that your paragraphs need to be

developed. No body paragraph in this type of essay should be only two or three sentences in length.

c. Look back at how you arranged the parts in your classification scheme. Is this the best order? How did you decide which parts to place first and last? The order should be a conscious decision on your part. Make a copy of your paper, cut it apart, rearrange the body paragraphs. Experiment—even if you decide to stay with your original plan.

3. The implications behind Perrine's definitions are that interpretive (serious) literature, is more significant and lasting than escape literature, but that escape literature is more popular and commercially successful. Select a popular writer, film director, artist, or musician with whose work you are familiar. Research his or her critical reputation through reviews or critical articles. Write an article about your figure that assesses the significance of his or her work. Do it as an essay that might appear in *Time* or *Newsweek*.

Cinematypes

SUSAN ALLEN TOTH

Born in Ames, Iowa, in 1940, Susan Allen Toth graduated from Smith College and Berkeley and received a Ph.D. from the University of Minnesota in 1969. She taught English at San Francisco State College from 1963 to 1964 and is currently professor at Macalester College in Minnesota. Toth has contributed articles and stories to McCall's, Harper's, Cosmopolitan, Redbook, Ms. *and* Great River Review *and written two memoirs—*Blooming: A Small Town Girlhood *(1981) and* Ivy Days: Making My Way Out East *(1984). She is currently at work on a novel and a short story collection. In "Cinematypes" Toth classifies the men who take her to movies: Aaron likes art films; Pete, films with redeeming social value; and Sam, movies that are entertaining. But her own passion, Toth confesses, is for Technicolor musicals and films in which "the men and women always like each other."*

Aaron takes me only to art films. That's what I call them, anyway: strange movies with vague poetic images I don't always understand. Long dreamy movies about a distant Technicolor past, even longer black-and-white movies about the general meaninglessness of life. We do not go unless at least one reputable critic has found the cinematography superb. We went the *The Devil's Eye,* and Aaron turned to me in the middle and said, "My God, this is *funny.*" I do not think he was pleased. 1

When Aaron and I go to the movies, we drive our cars separately and meet by the box office. Inside the theater he sits tentatively in his seat, ready to move if he can't see well, poised to leave if the film is disappointing. He leans away from me, careful not to touch the bare flesh of his arm against the bare flesh of mine. Sometimes he leans so far I am afraid he may be touching the woman on his other side. If the movie is very good, he leans forward, too, peering 2 between the heads of the couple in front of us. The light from the screen bounces off his glasses; he gleams with intensity, sitting there on the edge of his seat, watching the screen. Once I tapped him on the arm so I could whisper a comment in his ear. He jumped.

After *Belle de Jour* Aaron said he wanted to ask me if he 3
could stay overnight. "But I can't," he shook his head mournfully before I had a chance to answer, "because I know I never sleep well in strange beds." Then he apologized for asking. "It's just that after a film like that," he said, "I feel the need to assert myself."

Pete takes me only to movies that he thinks have 4
redeeming social value. He doesn't call them "films". They tend to be about poverty, war, injustice, political corruption, struggling unions in the 1930s, and the military-industrial complex. Pete doesn't like propaganda movies, though, and he doesn't like to be too depressed, either. We stayed away from *The Sorrow and the Pity*; it would be, he said, just too much. Besides, he assured me, things are never that hopeless. So most of the movies we see are made in Hollywood. Because they are always topical, these movies offer what Pete calls "food for thought." When we saw *Coming Home*, Pete's jaw set so firmly with the first half-hour that I knew we would end up at Poppin' Fresh Pies afterward.

When Pete and I go to the movies, we take turns driv- 5
ing so no one owes anyone else anything. We leave the car far from the theater so we don't have to pay for parking space. If it's raining or snowing, Pete offers to let me off at the door, but I can tell he'll feel better if I go with him while he finds a spot, so we share the walk too. Inside the theater Pete will hold my hand when I get scared if I ask him. He puts my hand firmly on his knee and covers it completely with his own hand. His knee never twitches. After a while, when the scary part is past, he loosens his hand slightly and I know that is a signal to take mine away. He sits companionably close, letting his jacket just touch my sweater, but he does not infringe. He thinks I ought to know he is there if I need him.

One night, after *The China Syndrome*, I asked Pete if he wouldn't like to stay for a second drink, even though it was past midnight. He thought a while about that, considering my offer from all possible angles, but finally he said no. Relationships today, he said, have a tendency to move too quickly. 6

Sam likes movies that are entertaining. By that he means movies that Will Jones in the *Minneapolis Tribune* loved and either *Time* or *Newsweek* rather liked; also movies that do not have sappy love stories, are not musicals, do not have subtitles, and will not force him to think. He does not go to movies to think. He liked *California Suite* and *The Seduction of Joe Tynan*, though the plots, he said, could have been zippier. He saw it all coming too far in advance, and that took the fun out. He doesn't like to know what is going to happen. "I just want my brain to be tickled," he says. It is very hard for me to pick out movies for Sam. 7

When Sam takes me to the movies, he pays for everything. He thinks that's what a man ought to do. But I buy my own popcorn, because he doesn't approve of it; the grease might smear his flannel slacks. Inside the theater, Sam makes himself comfortable. He takes off his jacket, puts one arm around me, and all during the movie he plays with my hand, stroking my palm, beating a small tattoo on my wrist. Although he watches the movie intently, his body operates on instinct. Once I inclined my head and kissed him lightly just behind his ear. He beat a faster tattoo on my wrist, quick and musical, but he didn't look away from the screen. 8

When Sam takes me home from the movies, he stands outside my door and kisses me long and hard. He would like to come in, he says regretfully, but his steady girlfriend in Duluth wouldn't like it. When the *Tribune* gives a movie four stars, he has to save it to see with her. Otherwise her feelings might be hurt. 9

I go to some movies by myself. On rainy Sunday afternoons I often sneak into a revival house or a college 10 auditorium for old Technicolor musicals, *Kiss Me Kate, Seven Brides for Seven Brothers, Calamity Jane,* even once, *The Sound of Music.* Wearing saggy jeans so I can prop my feet on the seat in front, I sit toward the rear where no one can see me. I eat large handfuls of popcorn with double butter. Once the movie starts, I feel completely at home. Howard Keel and I are old friends; I grin back at him on the screen. I know the sound tracks by heart. Sometimes when I get really carried away I hum along with Kathryn Grayson, remembering how I once thought I would fill out a formal like that. I am rather glad now I never did. Skirts whirl, feet tap, acrobatic young men perform impossible feats, and then the camera dissolves into a dream sequence I know I can comfortably follow. It is not, thank God, Bergman.

If I can't find an old musical, I settle for Hepburn and 11
Tracy, vintage Grant or Gable, on adventurous days Claudette Colbert or James Stewart. Before I buy my ticket I make sure it will all end happily. If necessary, I ask the girl at the box office. I have never seen *Stella Dallas* or *Intermezzo.* Over the years I have developed other peccadilloes: I will, for example, see anything that is redeemed by Thelma Ritter. At the end of *Daddy Long Legs* I wait happily for the scene when Fred Clark, no longer angry, at last pours Thelma a convivial drink. They smile at each other, I smile at them, I feel they are smiling at me. In the movies I go to by myself, the men and women always like each other.

QUESTIONS ON SUBJECT AND PURPOSE

1. Characterize each of Toth's cinematypes. How is each type revealed?
2. What types of movies does Toth go to alone? What common characteristics do they have?
3. Why does Toth end with the remark: "In the movies I go to by myself, the men and women always like each other"?

QUESTIONS ON STRATEGY AND AUDIENCE

1. Why does Toth begin as she does? Why not give an introductory paragraph? What would be the effect of such a paragraph?

2. Why does Toth end each of the three narrative "types" with a comment on the male-female relationship?
3. Does Toth's essay capture your interest? It is, after all, one person's experiences with three types of film-watchers. Why should we as readers be interested in the essay?

QUESTIONS ON VOCABULARY AND STYLE

1. How does Toth use parallel structures in her essay? How many different types of parallelism can you find? How does each function?
2. How would you characterize the tone of Toth's essay? How is it achieved? Be able to point to at least three different devices or techniques.
3. Be able to define the following words: *tattoo* (paragraph 8), *peccadilloes* (11), *convivial* (11).

WRITING SUGGESTIONS

1. Select a common subject and make a classification scheme. Keep it fairly simple—people who can regularly be found in the cafeteria, types of roommates, types of blind dates. In a paragraph or two present your scheme and give an example of each category.
2. Make a list of a dozen recent films. Check it against newspapers and magazines to make sure that your list is fairly representative. Then, using the list, devise a scheme of classification that accounts for the films currently being released. You could also do the same thing with books. You might consider writing for one of the following publications:
   a. local newspaper
   b. campus newspaper
   c. national newsmagagine such as *Time* or *Newsweek*

   Prewriting:
   a. Check a metropolitan newspaper. If necessary, do so in your campus library. Most Friday, Saturday, or Sunday editions include brief reviews of the new films. That will help you construct your scheme.
   b. Talk to relatives and friends about recent films as well. That will give you an additional body of information.
   c. Write the relevant pieces of information about each film on

index cards. Sort the cards into as many categories as seem appropriate. Remember, however, that you do not want twelve categories, each of which contains a single example. Try to create a scheme that contains three to six categories.

Rewriting:

a. Look again at how you organized your classification scheme. Why begin with that category? Why end with that one? Answer the following question: "The ordering principle in my essay is ———."
b. Since your reader will not have seen every one of these films, you will have to summarize each in a sentence or two. On the other hand, your essay should not consist just of summaries of the films. Make a copy of your paper and highlight in colored pen all of the sentences that summarize plot. Then look at what remains. Have you defined and analyzed the categories as well?
c. Find a peer reader and ask for some honest criticism. Did the reader find the essay interesting? Is the scheme too obvious? Are there enough examples to explain your categories?

3. Find a list of the most popular something, for example, books or films or music. *The Book of Lists* is a good source for such lists, and it can be found in almost any library. Using the list, devise a scheme of classification. Make sure that your categories are clear and separate. Use examples to make the classification vivid and interesting.

Shades of Black

MARY MEBANE

Mary Elizabeth Mebane, novelist, teacher, and civil rights activist, was born in 1933 in Durham, North Carolina. Her father was a farmer, her mother a factory laborer. She received her education at North Carolina State College and at the University of North Carolina, where she earned both her master's and doctoral degrees. Her work has been anthologized in A Galaxy of Black Writers *(1970) and* The Eloquence of Protest *(1972). A play,* Take A Sad Song, *was first produced in 1975. Her writings deal mainly with the black experience in the South and the new consciousness that was born during the years of the civil rights movement. Mebane said: "It is my belief that the black folk are the most creative, viable people that America has produced. They just don't know it." Mebane's most recent and widely acclaimed books are her autobiographies entitled* Mary *(1981) and* Mary, Wayfarer *(1983). Prejudice comes in many forms, and in this selection from* Mary, *Mebane recounts her experiences as a "dark, but not too dark" college student.*

During my first week of classes as a freshman, I was stopped one day in the hall by the chairman's wife, who was indistinguishable in color from a white woman. She wanted to see me, she said. 1

This woman had no official position on the faculty, except that she was an instructor in English; nevertheless, her summons had to be obeyed. In the segregated world there were (and remain) gross abuses of authority because those at the pinnacle, and even their spouses, felt that the people "under" them had no recourse except to submit—and they were right except that sometimes a black who got sick and tired of it would go to the whites and complain. This course of action was severely condemned by the blacks, but an interesting thing happened—such action 2 always got positive results. Power was thought of in negative terms: I can deny someone something, I can strike at someone who can't strike back, I can ride someone down; that proves I am powerful. The concept of power as a force for good, for affirmative response to people or situations, was not in evidence.

When I went to her office, she greeted me with a big smile. "You know," she said, "you made the highest mark on the verbal part of the examination." She was referring to the examination that the entire freshman class took upon entering the college. I looked at her but I didn't feel warmth, for in spite of her smile her eyes and tone of voice were saying, "How could this black-skinned girl score higher on the verbal than some of the students who've had more advantages than she? It must be some sort of fluke. Let me talk to her." I felt it, but I managed to smile my thanks and back off. For here at North Carolina College at Durham, as it had been since the beginning, social class and color were the primary criteria used in determining status on the campus. 3

First came the children of doctors, lawyers, and college teachers. Next came the children of public-school teachers, businessmen, and anybody else who had access to more money than the poor black working class. After that came the bulk of the student population, the children of the working class, most of whom were the first in their families to go beyond high school. The attitude toward them was: You're here because we need the numbers, but in all other things defer to your betters. 4

The faculty assumed that light-skinned students were more intelligent, and they were always a bit nonplussed when a dark-skinned student did well, especially if she was a girl. They had reason to be appalled when they discovered that I planned to do not only well but better than my light-skinned peers. 5

I don't know whether African men recently transported to the New World considered themselves handsome or, more important, whether they considered African women beautiful in comparison with Native American Indian 6 women or immigrant European women. It is a question that I have never heard raised or seen research on. If African men considered African women beautiful, just when their shift in interest away from black black women occurred might prove to be an interesting topic for researchers. But one thing I know for sure: by the twentieth century, really black skin on a woman was considered ugly in this country. This was particularly true among those who were exposed to college.

Hazel, who was light brown, used to say to me, "You are *dark*, but not *too* dark." The saved commiserating with the damned. I had the feeling that if nature had painted one more brushstroke on me, I'd have had to kill myself. 7

Black skin was to be disguised at all costs. Since a black face is rather hard to disguise, many women took refuge in ludicrous makeup. Mrs. Burry, one of my teachers in elementary school, used white face powder. But she neglected to powder her neck and arms, and even the black on her face gleamed through the white, giving her an eerie appearance. But she did the best she could. 8

I observed all through elementary and high school that for various entertainments the girls were placed on the stage in order of color. And very black ones didn't get into the front row. If they were past caramel-brown, to the back row they would go. And nobody questioned the justice of these decisions—neither the students nor the teachers. 9

One of the teachers at Wildwood School, who was from the Deep South and was just as black as she could be, had been a strict enforcer of these standards. That was another irony—that someone who had been judged outside the realm of beauty herself because of her skin tones should have adopted them so wholeheartedly and applied them herself without question. 10

One girl stymied that teacher, though. Ruby, a black cherry of a girl, not only got off the back row but off the front row as well, to stand alone at stage center. She could outsing, outdance, and outdeclaim everyone else, and talent proved triumphant over pigmentation. But the May Queen and her Court (and in high school, Miss Wildwood) were 11 always chosen from among the lighter ones.

When I was a freshman in high school, it became clear 12
that a light-skinned sophomore girl named Rose was going to get the "best girl scholar" prize for the next three years, and there was nothing I could do about it, even though I knew I was the better. Rose was caramel-colored and had shoulder-length hair. She was highly favored by the science and math teacher, who figured the averages. I wasn't. There was only one prize. Therefore, Rose would get it until she graduated. I was one year behind her, and I would not get it until after she graduated.

To be held in such low esteem was painful. It was diffi- 13
cult not to feel that I had been cheated out of the medal, which I felt that, in a fair competition, I perhaps would have won. Being unable to protest or do anything about it was a traumatic experience for me. From then on I instinctively tended to avoid the college-exposed dark-skinned male, knowing that when he looked at me he saw himself and, most of the time, his mother and sister as well, and since he had rejected his blackness, he had rejected theirs and mine.

Oddly enough, the lighter-skinned black male did not 14
seem to feel so much prejudice toward the black black woman. It was no accident, I felt, that Mr. Harrison, the eighth-grade teacher, who was reddish-yellow himself, once protested to the science and math teacher about the fact that he always assigned sweeping duties to Doris and Ruby Lee, two black black girls. Mr. Harrison said to them one day, right in the other teacher's presence, "You must be some bad girls. Every day I come down here ya'll are sweeping." The science and math teacher got the point and didn't ask them to sweep anymore.

Uneducated black males, too, sometimes related very 15
well to the black black woman. They had been less firmly indoctrinated by the white society around them and were more securely rooted in their own culture.

Because of the stigma attached to having dark skin, a 16
black black woman had to do many things to find a place for herself. One possibility was to attach herself to a light-skinned woman, hoping that some of the magic would rub

off on her. A second was to make herself sexually available, hoping to attract a mate. Third, she could resign herself to a more chaste life-style—either (for the professional woman) teaching and work in established churches or (for the uneducated woman) domestic work and zealous service in the Holy and Sanctified churches.

Even as a young girl, Lucy had chosen the first route. 17
Lucy was short, skinny, short-haired, and black black, and thus unacceptable. So she made her choice. She selected Patricia, the lightest-skinned girl in the school, as her friend, and followed her around. Patricia and her friends barely tolerated Lucy, but Lucy smiled and doggedly hung on, hoping that some who noticed Patricia might notice her, too. Though I felt shame for her behavior, even then I understood.

As is often the case of the victim agreeing with and 18
adopting the attitudes of oppressor, so I have seen it with black black women. I have seen them adopt the oppressor's attitude that they are nothing but "sex machines," and their supposedly superior sexual peformance becomes their sole reason for being and for esteeming themselves. Such women learn early that in order to make themselves attractive to men they have somehow to shift the emphasis from physical beauty to some other area—usually sexual performance. Their constant talk is of their desirability and their ability to gratify a man sexually.

I knew two such women well—both of them black 19
black. To hear their endless talk of sexual conquests was very sad. I have never seen the category that these women fall into described anywhere. It is not that of promiscuity or nymphomania. It is the category of total self-rejection: "Since I am black, I am ugly, I am nobody. I will perform on the level that they have assigned to me." Such women are the pitiful results of what not only white America but also, and more important, black America has done to them.

Some, not taking the sexuality route but still accepting 20
black society's view of their worthlessness, swing all the way across to intense religiosity. Some are staunch, fervent workers in the more traditional Southern churches—Baptist and Methodist—and others are leaders and ministers in the

lower status, more evangelical Holiness sects.

Another avenue open to the black black woman is excellence in a career. Since in the South the field most accessible to such women is education, a great many of them prepared to become teachers. But here, too, the black black woman had problems. Grades weren't given to her lightly in school, nor were promotions on the job. Consequently, she had to prepare especially well. She had to pass examinations with flying colors or be left behind; she knew that she would receive no special consideration. She had to be overqualified for a job because otherwise she didn't stand a chance of getting it—and she was competing only with other blacks. She had to have something to back her up: not charm, not personality—but training. 21

The black black woman's training would pay off in the 1970's. With the arrival of integration the black black woman would find, paradoxically enough, that her skin color in an integrated situation was not the handicap it had been in an all-black situation. But it wasn't until the middle and late 1960s, when the post-1945 generation of black males arrived on college campuses, that I noticed any change in the situation at all. *He* wore an afro and *she* wore an afro, and sometimes the only way you could tell them apart was when his afro was taller than hers. Black had become beautiful, and the really black girl was often selected as queen of various campus activities. It was then that the dread I felt at dealing with the college-educated black male began to ease. Even now, though, when I have occasion to engage in any type of transaction with a college-educated black man, I gauge his age. If I guess he was born after 1945, I feel confident that the transaction will turn out all right. If he probably was born before 1945, my stomach tightens, I find myself taking shallow breaths, and I try to state my business and escape as soon as possible. 22

QUESTIONS ON SUBJECT AND PURPOSE

1. What kinds of prejudice and discrimination did Mebane encounter? What were the reasons for that discrimination?

2. How does Mebane mix personal experience with commentary on human behavior? Does the mixture seem to work? What does it add to the selection?
3. What is Mebane's thesis?

QUESTIONS ON STRATEGY AND AUDIENCE

1. How is classification used in the selection? How many classifications are made?
2. How is the selection structured? Make a sketchy outline of the organization. What does it reveal?
3. How does Mebane use examples in her classification scheme? Are there examples for all of the categories? Why or why not?

QUESTIONS ON VOCABULARY AND STYLE

1. How does Mebane describe the shades of black? What types of adjectives, for example, does she use?
2. What is the difference between "established churches" and "Holy and Sanctified churches" (paragraph 16)? Why does Mebane use the capital letters?
3. Be able to define the following words: *fluke* (paragraph 3), *nonplussed* (5), *commiserate* (7), *stymied* (11) *traumatic* (13), *indoctrinated* (15), *chaste* (16), *staunch* (20).

WRITING SUGGESTIONS

1. In a paragraph classify the most obvious prejudices people have. These do not need to be based on color or race—it could be appearance, social or economic class, intelligence, social behavior. Limit your classification to two or three major topics.
2. Have you or a friend ever been classified by someone and discriminated against as a result? In an essay use your experience to show how and why that classification was made. If you have not had this experience, turn the question around. Have you ever classified someone and discriminated against that person as a result?

Prewriting:

a. If you have encountered discrimination, you will probably have a wide range of experiences from which to draw. If you have not, you will need to eamine closely your own behavior. Either way, make a list of possible experiences.

b. Remember that prejudices are based on stereotypes, which distort, reduce, ridicule. Your essay should expose the inadequacies of such ways of thinking; it should not celebrate any form of discrimination.

c. Once you have gathered examples, you must decide which ones you will include. As you saw in Chapter 1, sometimes one well-developed, appropriate example is enough; other times, a number of examples are necessary. Do not try to include every experience. Decide which ones on your list seem most promising.

d. Try freewriting about each of the examples. Set each of those freewritings aside until it is time to assemble a draft of the complete essay.

Rewriting:

a. Remember that your examples should reveal the discrimination at work. Do not just tell your readers; show them. Look carefully at your draft to see if you have made the examples dramatic and vivid enough.

b. In drawing upon your experiences in this way, your essay will probably make use of narrative as well as classification strategies. Look back through Chapter 2 to review the principles of effective narration. See how closely you followed that advice.

c. Once you have a draft of our essay, spend some time rereading and studying Mebane's essay. Notice how she tells her story, how she reveals prejudice, how she makes transitions from one aspect of the topic to another.

3. Research the problems encountered in interracial, interreligious, or intercultural marriages. What types of prejudice do people encounter? Have they changed in recent years? Classify those problems. You might write to a special audience—for example, couples planning such a marriage.

American Regional Costume

ALISON LURIE

Born in 1926 in Chicago, Alison Lurie grew up in Westchester County, New York, and was educated at Cherry Lawn School and Radcliffe. She is a professor of English at Cornell University. Primarily a fiction witer, she has written several novels including Love and Friendship *(1962),* the Nowhere City *(1965),* Imaginary Friends *(1967),* Real People *(1969),* The War between the Tates *(1974),* Only Children *(1979), and* Foreign Affairs *(1984), for which she won a Pulitzer Prize in fiction. In addition to several books for children, she has also written* The Language of Clothes *(1981), from which this selection is taken. Lurie classifies the characteristics of geographic areas of the United States on the basis of the types of clothing their residents wear.*

Even today, when the American landscape is becoming more and more homogeneous, there is really no such thing as an all-American style of dress. A shopping center in Maine may superficially resemble one in Georgia or California, but the shoppers in it will look different, because the diverse histories of these states have left their mark on costume. 1

Regional dress in the United States, as in Britain, can best be observed at large national meetings where factors such as occupation and income are held relatively constant. At these meetings regional differences stand out clearly, and can be checked by looking at the name tags Americans conventionally wear to conventions. Five distinct styles can be distinguished: (1) Old New England, (2) Deep South, (3) Middle American, (4) Wild West and (5) Far West or Californian. In border areas, outfits usually combine regional styles. 2

Americans who do not travel much within their own country often misinterpret the styles of other regions. 3

Natives of the Eastern states, for instance, may misread Far Western clothing as indicating greater casualness—or greater sexual availability—than is actually present. The laid-back-looking Los Angeles executive in his openchested sport shirt and sandals may have his eye on the main chance to an extent that will shock his Eastern colleague. The reverse error can also occur: a Southern Californian may discover with surprise that the sober-hued, buttoned-up New Englander he or she has just met is bored with business and longing to get drunk or hop into bed.

NORTHEAST AND SOUTHEAST: PURITANS AND PLANTERS

The drab, severe costumes of the Puritan settlers of New 4
England, and their suspicion of color and ornament as snares of the devil, have left their mark on the present-day clothes of New Englanders. At any large meeting people from this part of the country will be dressed in darker hues—notably black, gray and navy—often with touches of white that recall the starched collars and cuffs of Puritan costume. Fabrics will be plainer (though heavier and sometimes more expensive) and styles simpler, with less waste of material: skirts and lapels and trimmings will be narrower. More of the men will also wear suits and shoes made in England (or designed to look as if they had been made in England). The law of camouflage also operates in New England, where gray skies and dark rectangular urban landscapes are not unknown.

The distinctive dress of the Deep South is based on a 5
climate that did not demand heavy clothing and an economy that for many years exempted middle- and upper-class whites from all manual labor and made washing and ironing cheap. Today the planter's white suits and fondness for fine linen and his wife's and daughters' elaborate and fragile gowns survive in modern form. At our imaginary national meeting the male Southerners will wear lighter-colored suits—pale grays and beiges—and a certain dandyism will be apparent, expressing itself in French cuffs, more expensive ties, silkier materials and wider pin stripes. The

women's clothes will be more flowery, with a tendency toward bows, ruffles, lace and embroidery. If they are white, they will probably be as white as possible; a pale complexion is still the sign of a Southern lady, and female sun tans are unfashionable except on tourists.

MIDWEST AND WILD WEST: PIONEERS AND COWBOYS

The American Midwest and Great Plains states were settled by men and women who had to do their own work and prided themselves on it. They chose sturdy, practical clothes that did not show the dirt, washed and wore well and needed little ironing, made of gingham and linsey-woolsey and canvas. From these clothes descends the contemporary costume of Middle Americans. This style is visible to everyone on national television, where it is worn by most news announcers, politicians, talk-show hosts and actors in commercials for kitchen products. A slightly dowdier version appears in the Sears and Montgomery Ward catalogues. But even when expensive, Middle American fashion is apt to lag behind fashion as it is currently understood back East; it is also usually more sporty and casual. The pioneer regard for physical activity and exercise is still strong in this part of the country, and as a result the Midwesterners at our convention will look healthier and more athletic—and also somewhat beefier—than their colleagues from the cold, damp Northeast and the hot humid South. Their suits will tend toward the tans and browns of plowed cornfields rather than the grays of Eastern skies. More of them will wear white or white-on-white shirts, and their striped or foulard ties will be brighter and patterned on a larger scale then those purchased in sober New York and Boston. 6

The traditional Western costume, of course, was that of the cowboy on the range. Perhaps because of the isolation of those wide open spaces, this is the style which has been least influenced by those of other regions. At any national convention the Wild Westerners will be the easiest to identify. For one thing, they are apt to be taller—either gene- 7 tically or with the help of boots. Some may appear in full Western costume, the sartorial equivalent of a "he-went-thataway" drawl; but even the more conservative will betray, or rather proclaim, their regional loyalty through their dress, just as in conversation they will from time to time use a ranching metaphor, or call you "pal" or "pardner." A man in otherwise conventional business uniform will wear what look like cowboy boots, or a hat with an enlarged brim and crown. Women, too, are apt to wear boots, and their jackets and skirts may have a Western cut, especially when viewed from the rear. Some may wear red or navy-blue bandanna-print shirts or dresses, or an actual cotton-print bandanna knotted round their necks.

THE FAR WEST: ADVENTURERS AND BEACH BOYS

The men and women who settled the Far West were a mixed and rather raffish lot. Restlessness, the wish for excitement, the hope of a fortune in gold and sometimes a need to escape the law led them to undertake the long and dangerous journey over mountains and deserts, or by sea round Cape Horn. In more than one sense they were adventurers, and often desperadoes—desperate people. California was a territory where no one would ask about your past, where unconventionality of character and behavior was easily accepted. Even today when, as the country song puts it, "all the gold in California is in a bank in the middle of Beverly Hills in somebody else's name," the place has the reputation of an El Dorado. Men and women willing to risk everything on long odds in the hope of a big hit, or eager to put legal, financial and personal foul-ups behind them, often go west. 8

Present-day California styles are still in many ways those of adventurers and eccentrics. Whatever the current fashion, the California version will be more extreme, more various and—possibly because of the influence of the large Spanish-American population—much more colorful. Clothes tend to fit more tightly than is considered proper 9 elsewhere, and to expose more flesh: an inability to button the shirt above the diaphragm is common in both sexes. Virtuous working-class housewives may wear outfits that in any other part of the country would identify them as medium-priced whores; reputable business and professional men may dress in a manner which would lose them most of their clients back east and attract the attention of the Bureau of Internal Revenue if not of the police.

Southern Californians, and many other natives of what 10
is now called the Sun Belt (an imaginary strip of land stretching across the bottom of the United States from Florida to Santa Barbara, but excluding most of the Old South), can also be identified by their year-round sun tans, which by middle age have often given the skin the look of old if expensive and well-oiled leather. The men may also wear the getup known as Sun Belt Cool: a pale beige suit, open collared shirt (often in a darker shade than the suit), cream-colored loafers and aviator sunglasses. The female version of the look is similar, except that the shoes will be high-heeled sandals.

REGIONAL DISGUISE: SUNBELT PURITANS AND URBAN COWBOYS

Some long-time inhabitants of California and the other sar- 11
torially distinct regions of the United States refuse to wear the styles characteristic of that area. In this case the message is clear: they are unhappy in that locale and/or do not want anyone to attribute to them the traits associated with it. Such persons, if depressed, may adopt a vague and anonymous mode of dress; if in good spirits they may wear the costume of some other region in order to proclaim their sympathy with it. In terms of speech, what we have then is not a regional accent, but the conscious adoption of a dialect by an outsider.

In the urban centers of the West and Far West bankers 12
and financial experts of both sexes sometimes adopt an Eastern manner of speech and a Wall Street appearance in

order to suggest reliability and tradition. And today in Southern California there are professors who speak with Bostonian accents, spend their days in the library stacks, avoid the beach and dress in clothes that would occasion no comment in Harvard Yard. New arrivals to the area sometimes take these men and women for visiting Eastern lecturers, and are surprised to learn that they have lived in Southern California for thirty or forty years, or have even been born there.

The popularity of the various regional styles of Amer- 13
ican costume, like that of the various national styles, is also related to economic and political factors. Some years ago modes often originated in the Far West and the word "California" on a garment was thought to be an allurement. Today, with power and population growth shifting to the Southwestern oil-producing states, Wild West styles—particularly those of Texas—are in vogue. This fashion, of course, is not new. For many years men who have never been nearer to a cow than the local steakhouse have worn Western costume to signify that they are independent, tough and reliable. In a story by Flannery O'Connor, for instance, the sinister traveling salesman is described as wearing "a broad-brimmed stiff gray hat of the kind used by businessmen who would like to look like cowboys"—but, it is implied, seldom succeed in doing so.

The current popularity of Western costume has been 14
increased by the turn away from foreign modes that has accompanied the recent right-wing shift in United States politics. In all countries periods of isolationism and belligerently ostrichlike stance toward the rest of the world have usually been reflected in a rejection of international modes in favor of national styles, often those of the past. Today in America the cowboy look is high fashion, and even in New York City the streets are full of a variety of Wild West types. Some are dressed in old-fashioned, well-worn Western gear; others in the newer, brighter and sleeker outfits of modern ranchers; while a few wear spangled, neon-hued Electric Cowboy and Cowgirl costumes of the type most often seen on Texas country-rock musicians.

QUESTIONS ON SUBJECT AND PURPOSE

1. According to Lurie, what accounts for the differences in costume among the various geographic sections of the country?
2. Do you agree with Lurie's characterization of dress in your area?
3. What does clothing reveal about a person?

QUESTIONS ON STRATEGY AND AUDIENCE

1. How does Lurie structure her essay? Make a simple outline of the essay.
2. Lurie defines five distinct styles (paragraph 2), but then groups those styles. What larger principle of grouping does she use?
3. Lurie can be accused of stereotyping—offering conventional, rigid judgments that allow for no individuality. Most readers are rightfully wary of such an approach. Did Lurie alienate you as a reader? Why or why not?

QUESTIONS ON VOCABULARY AND STYLE

1. Look up the word *costume* in a dictionary. What are the various meanings of the word? How do those meanings relate to Lurie's essay?
2. How would you categorize her tone in this essay? Is she serious? Is her tone tongue-in-cheek? How would a reader know?
3. Be able to define the following words and phrases: *homogeneous* (paragraph 1), *dandyism* (5), *linsey-woolsey* (6), *dowdier* (6), *foulard* (6), *sartorial* (7), *raffish* (8).

WRITING SUGGESTIONS

1. Examine your own wardrobe. Make a list of your clothes and the reasons you purchased or acquired each particular item. In a paragraph classify your reasons, accounting as honestly as you can for what motivates your choice of clothes.
2. In an essay, perhaps intended for your college's newspaper, analyze and classify the dress of your fellow students. Do not try to generalize for the entire college population in the United States.

Prewriting:

a. Begin with extensive observation. Sit somewhere and watch. Take notes. Be sure to record specific details. Write the information about each subject on a separate sheet of paper or index card.
b. Once you have recorded a large variety of people, sort the cards or sheets into categories. Try to find at least three possible subdivisions.
c. Look at local stores that cater to students. How do the clothes offered there differ from those for sale in your hometown? In a large mall?
d. Remember to analyze the categories. Do not just record examples. Out of the range of possible clothing choices, why do students make these particular choices? Is it simply because this is all they can afford?

Rewriting:

a. Lurie can organize her essay geographically. That will not be possible in your essay. Once you have finished a draft, look carefully at how you organized the classification scheme. Try another arrangement.
b. Have you avoided obvious stereotypes? Or if you have stereotyped, have you provided analysis to justify that approach? Ask a peer reader for an honest appraisal of that aspect of your essay.
c. Look at your introduction. Have you tried to catch your reader's interest? Or have you written a standard thesis introduction ("On this campus, there are four distinct styles of dress")? How would *Time* or *Newsweek* begin a story on this topic?

3. Clothing styles are not the only things that vary from one geographical area to another. For example, architectural styles in home construction also show regional variations. A new home being built in the Sun Belt might look very different from a new home being built in New England. In a research essay similar to Lurie's, classify and analyze new home styles across the United States. Ask your reference librarian for advice on researching regional architecture.

The Value of Children: A Taxonomical Essay

BERNARD R. BERELSON

Bernard R. Berelson (1912-1979) was born in Spokane, Washington, educated at Whitman College and the University of Washington, and received a Ph.D. from the University of Chicago. In 1941, he joined the Foreign Broadcast Intelligence Service of the Federal Communications System. Thereafter, he divided his time between the academic world and the world of international development assistance. In 1962, he joined the Population Council, eventually serving as its president until his retirement in 1974. Berelson published extensively on population policy and the prospects for fertility declines in developing countries. Among his dozen books are Voting *(1954), a study of opinion formation in a presidential campaign;* Graduate Education in the United States *(1960); and* Human Behavior *(1964). Berelson's concern with population policy is obvious in the essay reprinted here. Using a clear scheme of classification, Berelson analyzes the reasons why people want children.*

Why do people want children? It is a simple question to ask, perhaps an impossible one to answer. 1

Throughout most of human history, the question never seemed to need a reply. These years, however, the question has a new tone. It is being asked in a nonrhetorical way because of three revolutions in thought and behavior that characterize the latter decades of the twentieth century: the vital revolution in which lower death rates have given rise to the population problem and raise new issues about human fertility; the sexual revolution from reproduction; and the women's revolution, in which childbearing and -rearing no longer are being accepted as the only or even the primary roles of half the human race. Accordingly, for about 2 the first time, the question of why people want children now can be asked, so to speak, with a straight face.

"Why" questions of this kind, with simple surfaces but 3
profound depths, are not answered or settled; they are ventilated, explicated, clarified. Anything as complex as the motives for having children can be classified in various ways, and any such taxonomy has an arbitrary character to it. This one starts with chemistry and proceeds to spirit.

THE BIOLOGICAL

Do people innately want children for some built-in reason 4
of physiology? Is there anything to maternal instinct, or parental instinct? Or is biology satisfied with the sex instinct as the way to assure continuity?

In psychoanalytic thought there is talk of the "child- 5
wish," the "instinctual drive of physiological cause," "the innate femaleness of the girl direct(ing) her development toward motherhood," and the wanting of children as "the essence of her self-realization," indicating normality. From the experimental literature, there is some evidence that man, like other animals, is innately attracted to the quality of "babyishness."

> If the young and adults of several species are compared for 6
> differences in bodily and facial features, it will be seen readily that the nature of the difference is apparently the same almost throughout the phylogenetic scale. Limbs are shorter and much heavier in proportion to the torso in babies than in adults. Also, the head is proportionately much larger in relation to the body than is the case with adults. On the face itself, the forehead is more prominent and bulbous; the eyes large and perhaps located as far down as below the middle of the face, because of the large forehead. In addition, the cheeks may be round and protruding. In many species there is also a greater degree of overall fatness in contrast to normal adult bodies. . . . In man, as in other animals, social prescriptions and customs are not the sole or even primary factors that guarantee the rearing and protection of babies. This seems to indicate that the biologically rooted releaser of babyishness may have promoted infant care in primitive man before

> societies ever were formed, just as it appears to do in many animal species. Thus this releaser may have a high survival value for the species of man.*

In the human species the question of social and personal 7
motivation distinctively arises, but that does not necessarily mean that the biology is completely obliterated. In animals the instinct to reproduce appears to be all; in humans is it something?

THE CULTURAL

Whatever the biological answer, people do not want all the 8
children they physically can have—no society, hardly any woman. Everywhere social traditions and social pressures enforce a certain conformity to the approved childbearing pattern, whether large numbers of children in Africa or small numbers in Eastern Europe. People want children because that is "the thing to do"—culturally sanctioned and institutionally supported, hence about as natural as any social behavior can be.

Such social expectations, expressed by everyone toward 9
everyone, are extremely strong in influencing behavior even on such an important element in life as childbearing and on whether the outcome is two children or six. In most human societies, the thing to do gets done, for social rewards and punishments are among the most powerful. Whether they produce lots of children or few and whether the matter is fully conscious or not, the cultural norms are all the more effective if, as often, they are rationalized as the will of God or the hand of fate.

THE POLITICAL

The cultural shades off into political considerations: repro- 10
duction for the purposes of a higher authority. In a way, the human responsibility to perpetuate the species is the grand-

*Eckhard H. Hess, "Ethology and Developmental Psychology," in Paul H. Musser, ed., *Carmichael's Manual of Child Psychology*, Vol. 1 (New York: Wiley, 1970), pp. 20-21.

est such expression—the human family pitted politically against fauna and flora—and there always might be people who partly rationalize their own childbearing as a contribution to that lofty end. Beneath that, however, there are political units for whom collective childbearing is or has been explicitly encouraged as a demographic duty—countries concerned with national glory or competitive political position; governments concerned with the supply of workers and soldiers; churches concerned with propagation of the faith or their relative strength; ethnic minorities concerned with their political power; linguistic communities competing for position; clans and tribes concerned over their relative status within a larger setting. In ancient Rome, according to the Oxford English Dictionary, the proletariat—from the root *proles*, for progeny—were "the lowest class of the community, regarded as contributing nothing to the state but offspring": and a proletaire was "one who served the state not with his property but only with his offspring." The world has changed since then, but not all the way.

THE ECONOMIC

As the "new home economics" is reminding us in its cur- 11
rent attention to the microeconomics of fertility, children are economically valuable. Not that that would come as a surprise to the poor peasant who consciously acts on the premise, but it is clear that some people want children or not for economic reasons.

Start with the obvious case of economic returns from 12
children that appears to be characteristic of the rural poor. To some extent, that accounts for their generally higher fertility than that of their urban and wealthier counterparts: labor in the fields; hunting, fishing, animal care; help in the home and with the younger children; dowry and "bridewealth"; support in later life (the individualized system of social security).

The economics of the case carries through on the nega- 13
tive side as well. It is not publicly comfortable to think of

children as another consumer durable, but sometimes that is precisely the way parents do think of them, before conception: another child or a trip to Europe; a birth deferred in favor of a new car, the *n*th child requiring more expenditure on education or housing. But observe the special characteristics of children viewed as consumer durables: they come only in whole units; they are not rentable or returnable or exchangeable or available on trial; they cannot be evaluated quickly; they do not come in several competing brands or products; their quality cannot be pretested before delivery; they usually are not available for appraisal in large numbers in one's personal experience; they themselves participate actively in the household's decisions. And in the broad view, both societies and families tend to choose standard of living over number of children when the opportunity presents itself.

THE FAMILIAL

In some societies people want children for what might be called familial reasons: to extend the family line or the family name; to propitiate the ancestors; to enable the proper functioning of religious rituals involving the family (e.g., the Hindu son needed to light the father's funeral pyre, the Jewish son needed to say Kaddish for the dead father). Such reasons may seem thin in the modern, secularized society but they have been and are powerful indeed in other places. 14

In addition, one class of family reasons shares a border with the following category, namely, having children in order to maintain or improve a marriage: to hold the husband or occupy the wife; to repair or rejuvenate their marriage; to increase the number of children on the assumption that family happiness lies that way. The point is underlined by its converse: in some societies the failure to bear children (or males) is a threat to the marriage and a ready cause for divorce. 15

Beyond all that is the profound significance of children to the very institution of the family itself. To many people, 16 husband and wife alone do not seem a proper family—they need children to enrich the circle, to validate its family character, to gather the redemptive influence of offspring. Children need the family, but the family seems also to need children, as the social institution uniquely available, at least in principle, for security, comfort, assurance, and direction in a changing, often hostile, world. To most people, such a home base, in the literal sense, needs more than one person for sustenance and in generational extension.

THE PERSONAL

Up to here the reasons for wanting children primarily refer to instrumental benefits. Now we come to a variety of reasons for wanting children that are supposed to bring direct personal benefits. 17

Personal Power. As noted, having children sometimes gives one parent power over the other. More than that, it gives the parents power over the child(ren)—in many cases, perhaps most, about as much effective power as they ever will have the opportunity of exercising on an individual basis. They are looked up to by the child(ren), literally and figuratively, and rarely does that happen otherwise. Beyond that, having children is involved in a wider circle of power: 18

> In most simple societies the lines of kinship are the lines of political power, social prestige and economic aggrandizement. The more children a man has, the more successful marriage alliances he can arrange, increasing his own power and influence by linking himself to men of greater power or to men who will be his supporters. . . . In primitive and peasant societies, the man with few children is the man of minor influence and the childless man is virtually a social nonentity* 19

Personal Competence. Becoming a parent demonstrates competence in an essential human role. Men and women 20

*Burton Benedict, "Population Regulation in Primitive Societies," in Anthony Ellison, *Population Control* (London: Penguin, 1970), pp. 176-77.

who are closed off from other demonstrations of competence, through lack of talent or educational opportunity or social status, still have this central one. For males, parenthood is thought to show virility, potency, *machismo*. For females it demonstrates fecundity, itself so critical to an acceptable life in many societies.

Personal Status. Everywhere parenthood confers status. It is an accomplishment open to all, or virtually all, and realized by the overwhelming majority of adult humankind. Indeed, achieving parenthood surely must be one of the two most significant events in one's life—that and being born in the first place. In many societies, then and only then is one considered a real man or a real woman. 21

Childbearing is one of the few ways in which the poor can compete with the rich. Life cannot make the poor man prosperous in material goods and services but it easily can make him rich with children. He cannot have as much of anything else worth having, except sex, which itself typically means children in such societies. Even so, the poor still are deprived by the arithmetic; they have only two or three times as many children as the rich whereas the rich have at least forty times the income of the poor. 22

Personal Extension. Beyond the family line, wanting children is a way to reach for personal immortality—for most people, the only way available. It is a way to extend oneself indefinitely into the future. And short of that, there is simply the physical and psychological extension of oneself in the children, here and now—a kind of narcissism: there they are and they are mine (or like me). 23

Look in thy glass and tell the face thou viewest, 24
Now is the time that face should form another;
But if thou live, remember'd not to be,
Die single, and thine image dies with thee.
—*Shakespeare's Sonnets, III*

Personal Experience. Among all the activities of life, parenthood is a unique experience. It is a part of life, or 25 personal growth, that simply cannot be experienced in any other way and hence is literally an indispensable element of the full life. The experience has many profound facets: the deep curiosity as to how the child will turn out; the renewal of self in the second chance; the reliving of one's own childhood; the redemptive opportunity; the challenge to shape another human being; the sheer creativity and self-realization involved. For a large proportion of the world's women, there was and probably still is nothing else for the grown female to do with her time and energy, as society defines her role. And for many women, it might be the most emotional and spiritual experience they ever have and perhaps the most gratifying as well.

Personal Pleasure. Last, but one hopes not least, in the 26
list of reasons for wanting children is the altruistic pleasure of having them, caring for them, watching them grow, shaping them, being with them, enjoying them. This reason comes last on the list but it is typically the first one mentioned on the casual inquiry: "because I like children." Even this reason has its dark side, as with parents who live through their children, often to the latter's distaste and disadvantage. But that should not obscure a fundamental reason for wanting children: love.

There are, in short, many reasons for wanting children. 27
Taken together, they must be among the most compelling motivations in human behavior: culturally imposed, institutionally reinforced, psychologically welcome.

QUESTIONS ON SUBJECT AND PURPOSE

1. What is "the value of children"? How many different values does Berelson cite?
2. Berelson gives positive, negative, and neutral reasons for wanting children. Is the overall effect of the essay positive, negative, or neutral?
3. Which of Berelson's reasons seem most relevant in American society today? Which seem least relevant?

QUESTIONS ON STRATEGY AND AUDIENCE

1. How does Berelson organize his classification? Can you find an explicit statement of organization?
2. Could the classification have been organized in a different way? Would that have changed the essay in any way?
3. How effective is Berelson's introduction? His conclusion? Suggest other ways in which the essay could have begun or ended.

QUESTIONS ON VOCABULARY AND STYLE

1. Berelson asks a number of rhetorical questions. Why does he ask them? Does he answer them? Does he "ventilate," "explicate," and "clarify" them (paragraph 3)?
2. Describe the tone of Berelson's essay—what does he sound like? Be prepared to support your statement with some specific illustrations from the text.
3. Be able to define the following words: *taxonomy* (paragraph 3), *physiology* (4), *phylogenetic* (6), *bulbous* (6), *sanctioned* (8), *fauna and flora* (10), *demographic* (10), *consumer durable* (13), *propitiate* (14), *sustenance* (16), *aggrandizement* (19), *nonentity* (19), *"machismo"* (20), *fecundity* (20), *narcissism* (23).

WRITING SUGGESTIONS

1. Why do you want or not want to have children? Classify your reasons in a paragraph. Focus on two or three reasons at most and be sure to have some logical order to your arrangement. You might try writing to a specific audience—for example, your fiancé or your parents.
2. Why do people in the United States go to college? In an essay classify the reasons why people make this decision. Remember that you are not just dealing with the reasons why *you* are going; you are analyzing the reasons (and values) of an entire nation.

   Prewriting:

   a. Interview twenty fellow students, asking their reasons for attending college. Try to get a broad spectrum of different ages, different social and economic backgrounds, different majors. Include some who are paying for their own education and some who have come back to school after years at home or in the job market. Do not ask just your freshman English classmates.

b. Analyze your own reasons. Make a list. Decide which seem to be the most important reasons, which the least.

c. If your instructor approves the use of outside sources, you can search for additional information from your college's library or admissions office. Studies are done each year on entering freshmen to assess, among other things, what they see as important about a college education.

Rewriting:

a. Look carefully at the organizational principle you have used in the body of your essay. How did you decide which example to put first? Which last? Try reordering the body of your paper.

b. Does each paragraph include an explicit statement of focus/topic? Make a copy of your paper and underline those statements. Using a pen of another color, mark transitions to see if they are always present.

c. Try for an interesting title. If you started with something like "The Reasons for Going to College" or "The Value of College: A Taxonomical Essay," try again.

3. Berelson gives very few specific examples to support his classification of values. Research one of his values and find an example or examples of societies that have seen children in this way. You might want to focus on the political, economic, or familial categories.

CHAPTER

5

Comparison and Contrast

Whenever you decide between two alternatives, you make a comparison and contrast. Which portable cassette player is the better value or has the more attractive set of features? Which professor's section of introductory sociology should you register for in the spring semester? In both cases you make the decision by comparing alternatives on a series of relevant points and then deciding which has the greater advantages.

In comparison and contrast, subjects are set in opposition in order to reveal their similarities and differences. Comparison involves finding similarities between two or more things, people, or ideas; contrast involves finding differences. Comparison and contrast writing tasks can involve, then, three activities: emphasizing similarities, emphasizing differences, or emphasizing both.

Like every writing task, comparison and contrast is done to achieve a particular purpose. In practical situations you use it to help make a decision. You compare cassette players or professors in order to make an intelligent choice. In academic situations comparison and contrast allows you to compare carefully and thoroughly, on a point by point basis, two or more subjects.

How Do You Choose a Subject?

Many times, especially on examinations in other academic courses, the subject for comparison and contrast is already chosen for you. On an economics examination you are asked, "What are the main differences between the public and private sectors?" In political science you are to "compare the political platforms of the Republican and Democratic parties in the last presidential election." Other times, however, you must choose the subject for comparison and contrast.

The choice of subject is crucial. It is best to limit your paragraph or essay to subjects that have obvious similarities or differences. William Zinsser compares his writing process to Dr. Brock's; John McPhee contrasts Florida and California oranges; Bruce Catton pairs Grant and Lee, the two Civil War generals. Two other cautions are also important. First, make sure that there is reason for making the comparison or contrast, that it will reveal something new or interesting or important. Second, limit your paper to important points; do not try to cover everything. You could not expect, for instance, to compare and contrast Britons and Americans in every aspect of their cultures. Like Edward Hall, you might focus on one significant difference: their attitudes toward private space.

Do You Always Find Both Similarities and Differences?

Comparison and contrast makes sense only if there is some basic similarity between the two subjects. There is no point in comparing two totally unrelated subjects. The mind could be compared to a computer since both process information, but there would be no reason to compare a computer to an orange. Remember, too, that some of the similarities which exist will be obvious and hence not worth writing about. In a paragraph from *Oranges*, John McPhee concentrates on the differences between Florida and California oranges—the similarities (both are oranges) are obvious and are omitted. This does not mean that similarities are not important or should not be mentioned. Bruce Catton, after spending most of his essay pointing out the differences between Grant and Lee, ends with the similarities these two men shared.

Once you have chosen your subject, make a list of the possible points of comparison and contrast. Be sure that those points are shared. William Zinsser, for example, organizes his comparison and contrast around six questions. To each of the six, Zinsser gives first Dr. Brock's response and then his own. The contrast depends upon the two responses to each of the six questions. If Dr. Brock had answered one group of three and Zinsser a different group of three, the contrast would not have worked.

How Do You Use Simile and Analogy?

A simile, as its name suggests, is a comparison based on a point or points of similarity. Seventeenth-century poet Robert Herrick found a witty similarity: "Fain would I kiss my Julia's dainty leg, / Which is as white and hairless as an egg." Similes are compressed analogies. Expository writing does not use many similes, but analogy can be used to make a subject more clear or to provide a new way of seeing something. J. Anthony Lukas, for example, explains his attraction to the game of pinball by an analogy:

> Pinball is a metaphor for life, pitting man's skill, nerve, persistence, and luck against the perverse machinery of human existence. The playfield is rich with rewards: targets that bring huge scores, bright lights, chiming bells, free balls, and extra games. But it is replete with perils, too: culs-de-sac, traps, gutters, and gobble holes down which the ball may disappear forever.*

The similarity Lukas establishes might well help the reader understand why arcade games—such as pinball—have a particular significance or attraction.

How Do You Structure a Comparison and Contrast?

Comparison and contrast is not only an intellectual process but also a structural pattern that can be used to organize

*J. Anthony Lukas, "The Inner Game of Pinball," *The Atlantic*, December 1979, p. 87.

paragraphs and essays. In comparing and contrasting two subjects, three organizational models are available.

1. *Subject by Subject:* you can treat all of subject A and then all of subject B (A123, B123)
2. *Point by Point:* you can organize by the points of comparison—point 1 in A then point 1 in B (A1/B1, A2/B2, A3/B3)
3. *Mixed Sequence:* you can mix the two patterns together.

The three alternatives can be seen in the essays included in this chapter.

Subject by Subject

Bruce Catton's comparison of Robert E. Lee and Ulysses S. Grant uses the subject-by-subject pattern. Paragraphs 5 and 6 of that essay are devoted to Lee; paragraphs 7, 8, and 9 to Grant; paragraph 10 to Lee; paragraph 11 to Grant. As Catton's example suggests, the subject-by-subject pattern for comparison and contrast works in paragraph units. If your comparison paper is fairly short, you could treat all of subject A in a paragraph or group of paragraphs and then all of subject B in a paragraph or group of paragraphs. If your paper is fairly long and the comparisons are fairly complicated, you might want to use either the point-by-point or mixed pattern.

Point by Point

Laurence Perrine's classification of literature into the two categories of escape and interpretive literature (see Chapter 4) uses a point-by-point pattern of contrasts. In the following paragraph, for example, Perrine alternates sentences.

> [A1] *Escape literature* is that written purely for entertainment—to help us pass the time agreeably. [B1] *Interpretive literature* is written to broaden and deepen and sharpen our awareness of life. [A2] Escape literature takes us *away* from the real world; it enables us temporarily to forget our troubles. [B2] Interpretive literature takes us, through the imagination, deeper *into* the real world: it enables us to understand our

> troubles. [A3] Escape literature has as its only object pleasure. [B3] Interpretive literature has as its object pleasure *plus* understanding.

The point-by-point, or alternating, pattern emphasizes the individual points of comparison or contrast rather than the subject as a whole. In college writing, this pattern most frequently devotes a sentence, a group of sentences, or a paragraph to each point, alternating between, subject A and subject B. If you use the alternating pattern, you must decide how to order your points—for instance, by beginning or by ending with the strongest or most significant.

Mixed Sequence

In longer pieces of writing, writers typically mix the subject-by-subject and point-by-point patterns. Such an arrangement provides variety for the reader. Edward T. Hall in his comparison of English and American concepts of space uses a mixed pattern. In the first paragraph, for example, Hall alternates sentences, in the point-by-point pattern.

> In the United States we use space as a way of classifying people and activities, whereas in England it is the social system that determines who you are. In the United States, your address is an important cue to status. . . . The Englishman, however, is born and brought up in a social system. He is still Lord—no matter where you find him. . . .

In paragraphs 2 and 3, however, Hall moves to a subject-by-subject pattern to expand upon the distinction he established in the first paragraph. Paragraph 2 is devoted to the American's need for "a room of one's own"; paragraph 3 to the Englishman's lack of a similar need.

Writing Comparison and Contrast: A Student Example

John Straumanis is a hurdler on the university's track team. For a comparison and contrast paragraph, John chose a familiar subject, and the first draft of his paragraph, which follows, began with a reference to his own experiences.

The 120 and 440 Yard Hurdles

> Many people have asked me why there are two hurdle races in track and field. Of course they are referring to the 120 yard and the 440 yard hurdles. Sure, both have ten barriers, but it's because they have almost nothing else in common is my usual reply. The 120 yard hurdle race, being the shorter of the two, is an all-out sprint where speed is of the essence. It is also a fairly simple race. Once the hurdling skill is perfected, most hurdlers run the race without even looking at the hurdles. There are always eight steps to the first hurdle, three steps in between each, then an all-out dash to the finish line. On the other hand, the 440 yard race is one of the most demanding and grueling races invented. It matches the speed of the quartermiler with the skill of a hurdler and the stamina to combine the two. The number of steps in this race varies especially towards the end, so the runner must constantly pay attention to and reanalyze the race. The 440 yard race is also more exciting. More strategy is involved, and every runner's strategy is a little bit different. The race can break open at any minute. These races are so different that many hurdlers do not compete in both, but decide to specialize.

After John had written his first draft, he stopped by the university's Writing Center to talk with a staff member. The first question his tutor asked was, "Why introduce yourself in the first three sentences?" John replied that he was a hurdler and that was why people asked him the question. After a discussion John and his tutor decided that he had two obvious options: either explain his credentials to the reader or drop the personal reference altogether. John felt that since the information he provided was factual and not open to dispute, it was not necessary for him to establish his authority. In the conference John and his tutor also talked about how he had structured his comparison/contrast. The draft paragraph first lists a similarity (each race has ten barriers) and then moves to a subject-by-subject pattern, treating first the 120 yard race and then the 440 yard race. The spacing of the hurdles in the 120 yard race is defined by the number of steps the racer takes, but not as much information is given about the spacing in the 440 yard race. John and his tutor agreed that the reader would probably wonder about that difference. In his revision, John changed his opening sentences, added some new information, and tightened his prose.

The Highs and Lows of Hurdling

Track and field competition includes two hurdle races: the 120 yard and the 440 yard. Although both races have ten barriers or hurdles, they have almost nothing else in common. The greater distance in the 440 yard race means that the hurdles must be spaced farther apart. In the 120 yard race it is 15 yards to the first hurdle and then 10 yards between each subsequent one. In the 440 yard race it is 49 1/4 yards to the first hurdle and 38 1/4 yards between each. The height of the hurdles is also different: 36 inches in the 440 yard race and 42 inches in the 120 yard race. Because of the distance, the 120 yard race is an all-out sprint where speed is crucial. It is also a fairly simple race. Once the hurdling skill is perfected, most hurdlers run the race without ever looking at the barriers. The number of steps in the 120 yard race is, therefore, constant—eight steps to the first hurdle, three in between, and then a dash to the finish line. On the other hand, the 440 yard race is one of the most demanding and grueling. It requires the speed of a quartermiler and the skill of a hurdler. The number of steps in this race varies, especially near the end, so the runner must constantly pay attention to and reanalyze the race. The 440 yard race is also more exciting since strategy is involved and every runner's strategy is slightly different. The race can break open at any second. The two races are so different, in fact, that many hurdlers choose to specialize in one rather than try to compete in both.

Some Things to Remember

1. Limit your comparison and contrast to subjects that can be adequately developed in a paragraph or an essay.
2. Make sure that the subjects you are comparing and contrasting have some basic similarities. Make a list of similarities and differences before you begin to write.
3. Decide why the comparison or contrast is important. What does it reveal? Remember to make the reason clear to the reader.

4. Decide what points of comparison or contrast are the most important or the most revealing. In general, omit any points of comparison that would be obvious to anybody.
5. Decide which of the three patterns of comparison and contrast best fits your purpose: subject by subject, point by point, or mixed.
6. Remember to make clear to your reader when you are switching from one subject to another or from one point of comparison to another.

The Transaction: Two Writing Processes

WILLIAM ZINSSER

William Zinsser was born in New York in 1922 and received a B.A. from Princeton in 1940. Zinsser was a columnist for Look, Life, *and* The New York Times *and a contributor to* The New Yorker. *He taught a course in expository writing at Yale from 1970 to 1979 and is now executive editor of the Book of the Month Club. His* On Writing Well: An Informal Guide to Writing Nonfiction *is becoming a textbook classic. His other books include* Any Old Place with You *(1957),* Pop Goes America *(1966),* The Lunacy Boom *(1970),* Writing With a Word Processor *(1983),* Extraordinary Lives: The Art and Craft of American Biography *(1986), and* Inventing the Truth: The Art and Craft of Memoir *(1987). His most recent book,* Writing to Learn *(1988), deals with writing in different disciplines. Ever wonder if other people find writing as hard (or as easy) as you do? Zinsser dramatizes two completely different attitudes toward writing in this selection taken from* On Writing Well.

Several years ago a school in Connecticut held "a day devoted to the arts," and I was asked if I would come and talk about writing as a vocation. When I arrived I found that a second speaker had been invited—Dr. Brock (as I'll call him), a surgeon who had recently begun to write and had sold some stories to national magazines. He was going to talk about writing as an avocation. That made us a panel, and we sat down to face a crowd of student newspaper editors and reporters, English teachers and parents, all eager to learn the secrets of our glamorous work. 1

Dr. Brock was dressed in a bright red jacket, looking vaguely Bohemian, as authors are supposed to look, and the first question went to him. What was it like to be a writer? 2

He said it was tremendous fun. Coming home from an arduous day at the hospital, he would go straight to his yellow pad and write his tensions away. The words just flowed. It was easy. 3

I then said that writing wasn't easy and it wasn't fun. It was hard and lonely, and the words seldom just flowed. 4

Next Dr. Brock was asked if it was important to rewrite. Absolutely not, he said. "Let it all hang out," and whatever form the sentences take will reflect the writer at his most natural. 5

I then said that rewriting is the essence of writing. I pointed out that professional writers rewrite their sentences repeatedly and then rewrite what they have rewritten. I mentioned that E. B. White and James Thurber were known to rewrite their pieces eight or nine times. 6

"What do you do on days when it isn't going well?" Dr. Brock was asked. He said he just stopped writing and put the work aside for a day when it would go better. 7

I then said that the professional writer must establish a daily schedule and stick to it. I said that writing is a craft, not an art, and that the man who runs away from his craft because he lacks inspiration is fooling himself. He is also going broke. 8

"What if you're feeling depressed or unhappy?" a student asked. "Won't that affect your writing?" 9

Probably it will, Dr. Brock replied. Go fishing. Take a walk. 10

Probably it won't, I said. If your job is to write every day, you learn to do it like any other job. 11

A student asked if we found it useful to circulate in the literary world. Dr. Brock said that he was greatly enjoying his new life as a man of letters, and he told several luxurious stories of being taken to lunch by his publisher and his agent at Manhattan restaurants where writers and editors gather. I said that professional writers are solitary drones who seldom see other writers. 12

"Do you put symbolism in your writing?" a student asked me. 13

"Not if I can help it," I replied. I have an unbroken 14

record of missing the deeper meaning in any story, play or movie, and as for dance and mime I have never had even a remote notion of what is being conveyed.

"I *love* symbols!" Dr. Brock exclaimed, and he described 15
with gusto the joys of weaving them through his work.

So the morning went, and it was a revelation to all of us. 16
At the end Dr. Brock told me he was enormously interested in my answers—it had never occurred to him that writing could be hard. I told him I was just as interested in *his* answers—it had never occurred to me that writing could be easy. (Maybe I should take up surgery on the side.)

As for the students, anyone might think that we left 17
them bewildered. But in fact we probably gave them a broader glimpse of the writing process than if only one of us had talked. For of course there isn't any "right" way to do such intensely personal work. There are all kinds of writers and all kinds of methods, and any method that helps somebody to say what he wants to say is the right method for him.

QUESTIONS ON SUBJECT AND PURPOSE

1. Zinsser uses contrast to make a point about how people write. What is that point?
2. How effective is the beginning? Would the effect have been lost if Zinsser had opened with a statement similar to his final sentence?
3. What process do you use when you write? Does it help in any way to know what other people do? Why? Why not?

QUESTIONS ON STRATEGY AND AUDIENCE

1. Which method of development does Zinsser use for his example? How many points of contrast does he make?
2. Would it have made any difference if he had used another pattern of development? Why?
3. How effective are the short paragraphs? Should they be longer?

QUESTIONS ON VOCABULARY AND STYLE

1. What makes Zinsser's story humorous? Try to isolate several aspects of humor.
2. Zinsser uses a number of parallel structures in his narrative. Make a list of them and be prepared to show how they contribute to the narrative's effectiveness.
3. Be able to explain or define the following: *avocation* (paragraph 1), *Bohemian* (2), *arduous* (3), *drone* (12), *mime* (14), *gusto* (15).

WRITING SUGGESTIONS

1. Using the details provided by Zinsser, rewrite the narrative using the subject-by-subject pattern. (Put Dr. Brock's process in one paragraph, Zinsser's advice in another.)
2. Let's be honest—writing instructors and textbooks offer one view of the writing process, but the practice of most writers can differ sharply. Prewriting and revising get squeezed out when a paper is due and only one night is available. In an essay compare and contrast your typical behavior as a writer with the process outlined in this text. Do not be afraid to be truthful.

   Prewriting:

   a. For 15 minutes freewrite on the topic. Do not stop to edit or check spelling. Just write without stopping about how you write your papers—or how you wrote them before you took this course. Take a short break and then write for another 15 minutes.
   b. Based on what you have learned so far in the course, make a list of some steps involved in the writing process. Be sure to include some details or examples under each step.
   c. On a separate sheet of paper, divided into halves, list the stages of the ideal writing process on the left-hand side and the stages of your typical (or former) writing process on the right-hand side.
   d. Before you begin, weigh the three possible structures for your paper—point-by-point, subject-by-subject, or the mixed sequence. Consider all the alternatives.

   Rewriting:

   a. Look carefully at the points of comparison or contrast that you have chosen. Are they the most important? The most revealing?

b. Have you adequately developed each point? Have you included appropriate details and examples? Check to make sure that your body paragraphs are more than two or three sentences in length.

c. Copy your introduction onto a separate sheet of paper. Show it to some friends and ask them to be honest—do they want to keep reading? Or is this just another boring English essay?

3. Compare the creative processes of two or more artists. Your library will have a number of books that feature artists (writers, musicians, painters) talking about how they work. Use those interviews or statements as a source of examples.

Oranges: Florida and California

JOHN McPHEE

John McPhee was born in Princeton, New Jersey, in 1931, educated at Princeton University, and studied at Cambridge University in England. He began his career as a writer for television in the mid-1950's and later worked as a journalist and served as an assistant editor for Time *magazine. In 1964, he was hired as a staff writer for* The New Yorker *magazine. Since 1965, McPhee has published numerous books, including* A Sense of Where You Are *(1965),* Oranges *(1967),* The Pine Barrens *(1968),* The Crofter and the Laird *(1969),* Levels of the Game *(1970),* The Deltoid Pumpkin Seed *(1973), and* The Survival of the Bark Canoe *(1975). Two of his books—*Encounters with the Archdruid *(1972) and* The Curve of Binding Energy *(1974)—were nominated for National Book Awards in science. In 1977, McPhee received an award from the American Academy and Institute of Arts and Letters. His most recent books include two geological studies,* Basin and Range *(1981) and* In Suspect Terrain *(1983);* Table of Contents *(1985), a collection of essays about travel and people;* La Place de la Concorde Suisse *(1985), a profile of the Swiss army; and* Rising from the Plains *(1986), a geology/travel book. In this paragraph from his book* Oranges, *McPhee contrasts Florida and California oranges. On your next trip to the supermarket, compare the two varieties for yourself.*

An orange grown in Florida usually has a thin and tightly fitting skin, and it is also heavy with juice. Californians say that if you want to eat a Florida orange you have to get into a bathtub first. California oranges are light in weight and have thick skins that break easily and come off in hunks. The flesh inside is marvelously sweet, and the segments almost separate themselves. In Florida, it is said that you can run over a California orange with a ten-ton truck and not even wet the pavement. The differences from which these hyperboles arise will prevail in the two states even if the type of orange is the same. In arid climates, like California's, oranges develop a thick albedo, which is the white part of the skin. Florida is one of the two or three most rained-upon states in the United States. California uses the Colorado River and similarly impressive sources to irrigate its oranges, but of course irrigation can only do so much. The annual difference in rainfall between the Florida and California orange-growing areas is one million one hundred and forty thousand gallons per acre. For years, California was the leading orange state, but Florida surpassed California in 1942, and grows three times as many oranges now. California oranges, for their part, can safely be called three times as beautiful.

QUESTIONS ON SUBJECT AND PURPOSE

1. What are the differences between Florida and California oranges?
2. How does McPhee keep his reader's attention in the paragraph? After all, a paragraph on the differences between Florida and California oranges could be very dull.
3. How does humor work in the paragraph? Why would McPhee use it?

QUESTIONS ON STRATEGY AND AUDIENCE

1. Which method of development does McPhee use for his paragraph? How many points of contrast does he use?
2. Would it have made any difference if he had used another pattern of development? Why? Why not?
3. How as a reader do you react to McPhee's paragraph? Do you want to know more? Does he catch your interest?

QUESTIONS ON VOCABULARY AND STYLE

1. How many examples of parallel structure can you find in the paragraph? How do they help the reader?

2. Why does McPhee quantify the difference in the rainfall? Why does he do it in gallons per acre?
3. What is a hyperbole? Where is it used in this selection?

WRITING SUGGESTIONS

1. Take any two subjects that belong to the same class in a paragraph and contrast them. You might consider possibilities such as:
   a. Two varieties of apples
   b. Two types of soft drinks
   c. Two kinds of running shoes
   d. Two types of potato chips
   Remember to keep your choice fairly simple—you are only writing. Do not try to compare them on every point. Select maybe two or three major differences.
2. For a longer essay, take two more complicated subjects and compare and contrast them. Try to select four or five major points. You might choose two subjects, philosophies or ideas that are central to another academic course you are taking or you might consider possibilities such as:
   a. Writing with a pen or typewriter/writing on a word processor
   b. Graded courses/pass-fail courses
   c. Drafted army/volunteer army
   d. Fraternity or sorority life/dorm life
   Remember that there are no bad subjects, just bad approaches to subjects. Be certain that you have a thesis and try to say something interesting and insightful about both subjects.

Prewriting:

a. Try brainstorming for two possible subjects. Remember that the subjects must have some basic similarities. On a sheet of paper, jot down possible pairs of subjects. Try to work on your idea sheet over a two-day period.
b. Once you have a promising pair, divide another sheet of paper in half. Make lists of possible points of comparison/contrast. Remember that your points must be parallel.
c. In the margins, number the points in order of significance. Omit any that are too obvious or irrelevant.
d. Answer the following question: "What does my comparison/contrast reveal?"

Rewriting:

a. Which pattern of organization did you use? Make a copy of your paper, cut it apart (or move blocks of text on your word processor), and try another pattern of order.
b. Look closely at the transitions you have used. Highlight those transitions with a colored pen. Are they adequate?
c. Concluding is never a simple matter. How did you end? Did you just stop? Did you just reword your introduction? Try another strategy.

3. Extend your comparison/contrast of two subjects by doing some research; do not rely just on personal experience or general knowledge.

On Societies as Organisms

LEWIS THOMAS

Lewis Thomas was born in Flushing, New York, in 1913 and after graduating from Princeton and the Harvard Medical School worked as a pathologist and medical administrator at Tulane University, Bellevue Hospital, the University of Minnesota, and Yale University School of Medicine. From 1973 to 1980 he was president of Memorial Sloan-Kettering Cancer Center and is currently its chancellor. Thomas's essays have appeared frequently in scientific journals, and in 1971 he began the column "Notes of a Biology Watcher" for the New England Journal of Medicine. *His first collection of these columns,* The Lives of a Cell *(1974), won the National Book Award and was a best seller probably because of his literacy, optimism, and ability to move from precise scientific observation to philosophic speculation. Later books are* The Medusa and the Snail *(1979);* The Youngest Science *(1983), a memoir of his medical career; and* Late Night Thoughts on Listening to Mahler's Ninth Symphony *(1983). Recently, he contributed to William Zinsser's* Inventing the Truth: The Art and Craft of Memoir *(1987). In 1984 he was inducted into the American Academy of Arts and Letters. In this essay, reprinted from* The Lives of a Cell, *Thomas explores the similarities between the scientific community and insect and animal societies.*

Viewed from a suitable height, the aggregating clusters of medical scientists in the bright sunlight of the boardwalk at Atlantic City, swarmed there from everywhere for the annual meetings, have the look of assemblages of social insects. There is the same vibrating, ionic movement, interrupted by the darting back and forth of jerky individuals to touch antennae and exchange small bits of information; periodically, the mass casts out, like a trout-line, a long single file unerringly toward Childs'. If the boards were not fastened down, it would not be a surprise to see them put together a nest of sorts. 1

It is permissible to say this sort of thing about humans. They do resemble, in their most compulsively social behavior, ants at a distance. It is, however, quite bad form in biological circles to put it the other way round, to imply that the operation of insect societies has any relation at all to human affairs. The writers of books on insect behavior generally take pains, in their prefaces, to caution that insects are like creatures from another planet, that their behavior is absolutely foreign, totally unhuman, unearthly, almost unbiological. They are more like perfectly tooled but crazy little machines, and we violate science when we try to read human meanings in their arrangements. 2

It is hard for a bystander not to do so. Ants are so much like human beings as to be an embarrassment. They farm fungi, raise aphids as livestock, launch armies into wars, use chemical sprays to alarm and confuse enemies, capture slaves. The families of weaver ants engage in child labor, holding their larvae like shuttles to spin out the thread that sews the leaves together for their fungus gardens. They exchange information ceaselessly. They do everything but watch television. 3

What makes us most uncomfortable is that they, and the bees and termites and social wasps, seem to live two kinds of lives: they are individuals, going about the day's business without much evidence of thought for tomorrow, and they are at the same time component parts, cellular elements, in the huge, writhing, ruminating organism of the Hill, the nest, the hive. It is because of this aspect, I think, that we most wish for them to be something foreign. We do not like the notion that there can be collective societies with the capacity to behave like organisms. If such things exist, they can have nothing to do with us. 4

Still, there it is. A solitary ant, afield, cannot be considered to have much of anything on his mind; indeed, with only a few neurons strung together by fibers, he can't be imagined to have a mind at all, much less a thought. He is more like a ganglion on legs. Four ants together, or ten, encircling a dead moth on a path, begin to look more like an idea. They fumble and shove, gradually moving the food 5 toward the Hill, but as though by blind chance. It is only when you watch the dense mass of thousands of ants, crowded together around the Hill, blackening the ground, that you begin to see the whole beast, and now you observe it thinking, planning, calculating. It is an intelligence, a kind of live computer, with crawling bits for its wits.

At a stage in the construction, twigs of a certain size are needed, and all the members forage obsessively for twigs of just this size. Later, when outer walls are to be finished, thatched, the size must change, and as though given new orders by telephone, all the workers shift the search to the new twigs. If you disturb the arrangement of a part of the Hill, hundreds of ants will set it vibrating, shifting, until it is put right again. Distant sources of food are somehow sensed, and long lines, like tentacles, reach out over the ground, up over walls, behind boulders, to fetch it in. 6

Termites are even more extraordinary in the way they seem to accumulate intelligence as they gather together. Two or three termites in a chamber will begin to pick up pellets and move them from place to place, but nothing comes of it; nothing is built. As more join in, they seem to reach a critical mass, a quorum, and the thinking begins. They place pellets atop pellets, then throw up columns and beautiful, curving, symmetrical arches, and the crystalline architecture of vaulted chambers is created. It is not known how they communicate with each other, how the chains of termites building one column know when to turn toward the crew on the adjacent column, or how, when the time comes, they manage the flawless joining of the arches. The stimuli that set them off at the outset, building collectively instead of shifting things about, may be pheromones released when they reach committee size. They react as if alarmed. They become agitated, excited, and then they begin working, like artists. 7

Bees live lives of organisms, tissues, cells, organelles, all at the same time. The single bee, out of the hive retrieving sugar (instructed by the dancer: "south-southeast for seven hundred meters, clover—mind you make corrections for the 8 sundrift") is still as much a part of the hive as if attached by a filament. Building the hive, the workers have the look of embryonic cells organizing a developing tissue; from a distance they are like the viruses inside a cell, running off row after row of symmetrical polygons as though laying down crystals. When the time for swarming comes, and the old queen prepares to leave with her part of the population, it is as though the hive were involved in mitosis. There is an agitated moving of bees back and forth, like granules in cell sap. They distribute themselves in almost precisely equal parts, half to the departing queen, half to the new one. Thus, like an egg, the great, hairy, black and golden creature splits in two, each with an equal share of the family genome.

The phenomenon of separate animals joining up to form 9
an organism is not unique in insects. Slimemold cells do it all the time, of course, in each life cycle. At first they are single amebocytes swimming around, eating bacteria, aloof from each other, untouching, voting straight Republican. Then, a bell sounds, and acrasin is released by special cells toward which the others converge in stellate ranks, touch, fuse together, and construct the slug, solid as a trout. A splendid stalk is raised, with a fruiting body on top, and out of this comes the next generation of amebocytes, ready to swim across the same moist ground, solitary and ambitious.

Herring and other fish in schools are at times so closely 10
integrated, their actions so coordinated, that they seem to be functionally a great multi-fish organism. Flocking birds, especially the seabirds nesting on the slopes of offshore islands in Newfoundland, are similarly attached, connected, synchronized.

Although we are by all odds the most social of all social 11
animals—more interdependent, more attached to each other, more inseparable in our behavior than bees—we do not often feel our conjoined intelligence. Perhaps, however, we are linked in circuits for the storage, processing, and retrieval of information, since this appears to be the most basic and universal of all human enterprises. It may be our biological function to build a certain kind of Hill. We have

access to all the information of the biosphere, arriving as elementary units in the stream of solar photons. When we have learned how these are rearranged against randomness, to make, say, springtails, quantum mechanics, and the late quartets, we may have a clearer notion how to proceed. The circuitry seems to be there, even if the current is not always on.

The system of communications used in science should provide a neat, workable model for studying mechanisms of information-building in human society. Ziman, in a recent *Nature* essay, points out, "the invention of a mechanism for the systematic publication of *fragments* of scientific work may well have been the key event in the history of modern science." He continues: 12

> A regular journal carries from one research worker to another the various . . . observations which are of common interest . . . . A typical scientific paper has never pretended to be more than another little piece in a larger jigsaw—not significant in itself but as an element in a grander scheme. *This technique, of soliciting many modest contributions to the store of human knowledge, has been the secret of Western science since the seventeenth century, for it achieves a corporate, collective power that is far greater than one individual can exert* [italics mine].* 13

With some alternation of terms, some toning down, the passage could describe the building of a termite nest. 14

It is fascinating that the word "explore" does not apply to the searching aspect of the activity, but has its origins in the sounds we make while engaged in it. We like to think of exploring in science as a lonely, meditative business, and so it is in the first stages, but always, sooner or later, before the enterprise reaches completion, as we explore, we call to each other, communicate, publish, send letters to the editor, present papers, cry out on finding. 15

*Ziman, J. M., "Information, Communications, Knowledge," *Nature*, 224:318-24, 1969.

QUESTIONS ON SUBJECT AND PURPOSE

1. What exactly is Thomas comparing? What are the points of comparison?
2. Why bother to develop the analogy at such length? Why not just make the assertion without constructing the analogy?
3. One key to understanding Thomas's essay is to know the origin of the word "explore" (see paragraph 15). Check a dictionary for the etymology of the word. How does that knowledge illuminate the point he is making?

QUESTIONS ON STRATEGY AND AUDIENCE

1. Study the essay's introduction and conclusion. What are the effects of his beginning and ending?
2. How does Thomas structure his comparison? Make a brief outline of the essay.
3. For whom is Thomas writing? What details or techniques in the essay help define that audience?

QUESTIONS ON VOCABULARY AND STYLE

1. How would you characterize the tone of Thomas's essay? Does he sound like a scientist writing a scientific paper? Is he ever humorous?
2. Find six examples of figurative language, especially similes and metaphors. What does each contribute to the essay?
3. Be able to define the following words and phrases: *ionic* (1), *ruminating* (4), *ganglion* (5), *forage* (6), *quorum* (7), *pheromones* (7), *polygons* (8), *mitosis* (8), *genome* (8), *amebocytes* (9), *acrasin* (9), *stellate* (9), *biosphere* (11), *photons* (11), *quantum mechanics* (11).

WRITING SUGGESTIONS

1. Take a single, significant point of contrast between you and your mother or father, brother or sister, roommate or best friend. In a paragraph explore that point of difference.
2. An analogy is an extended comparison, normally used to liken an unfamiliar or complex object to a familiar or simple one.

Analogies make the complex ideas more vivid and more easily understood. For example, computers are frequently likened to the human mind; success in business or government to participation in athletics (being a "team player"). In an essay use an analogy to explain or illuminate a subject. You might consider one of the following possible subjects:

a. Living in a dormitory or an apartment complex
b. Babysitting/raising/giving birth to a child
c. Failing or succeeding beyond your wildest expectations
d. Experiencing pain
e. Explaining a scientific concept to a lay audience. (You might choose something from another academic course you are taking this semester.)

Remember that a good analogy is based on real similarities. Look again at Thomas's analogy as an example.

Prewriting:

a. Brainstorm for some possible analogies. Start by writing this sentence: "[My subject] is like [compared subject]." Try to use simple ideas or concepts to describe more complex ones. See how many analogies spring to mind.
b. Remember that an effective analogy should illuminate. It should not be forced or mechanical. See how many of the analogies on your list meet that test.
c. Once you have at least two promising analogies, make a list of the ways in which each is similar to the subject you want to explain or make vivid. Remember to concentrate only on similarities. You will want to have three points of similarity at the very least.

Rewriting:

a. This assignment can really benefit from the help of honest peer readers. Ask at least two people to read a draft of your essay. Once they are finished, ask them if the analogy seemed appropriate or forced and boring.
b. Look again at your introduction—do you announce your thesis or do you provoke the reader's curiosity? Look back to Thomas's introduction as an example.
c. Part of the success of Thomas's essay comes from his use of specific, concrete examples. Check to make sure that your comparisons are precisely drawn. Exactly how is one subject like another? Be as exact as possible in the comparison.

3. It is quite common for writers of children's books, movies, cartoons, or television shows to personify animals. We buy children stuffed animals; we decorate their rooms and clothing with animal figures. Moreover, the appeal of such things is not limited to children; many adults laugh at animal cartoon characters, such as Snoopy or Opus, and many have saved a favorite childhood stuffed animal. Select a range of examples, and in an essay analyze the use of personification as analogy. Why do such comparisons or analogies seem appropriate for children? Why do we (as adults) find them funny or even consoling?

Grant and Lee: A Study in Contrasts

BRUCE CATTON

Born in Petoskey, Michigan, the son of a Congregationalist minister, Bruce Catton (1899-1978) attended Oberlin College in 1916 but left to serve in World War I. After the war, Catton became a journalist, writing for the Cleveland News, *the* Cleveland Plain Dealer, *and the* Boston American, *as well as editing* American Heritage. *Catton won the Pulitzer Prize and the National Book Award for* A Stillness at Appomattox *(1953). This, along with such works as* Mr. Lincoln's Army *(1951),* This Hallowed Ground *(1956), and* Never Call Retreat *(1965), rank him as one of the major Civil War historians. As this essay demonstrates, Catton's approach to history emphasized the personalities of those who made it. Catton's classic essay was first a radio address in a series of broadcasts made by American historians and then later revised for printed publication.*

When Ulysses S. Grant and Robert E. Lee met in the parlor 1
of a modest house at Appomattox Court House, Virginia, on April 9, 1865, to work out the terms for the surrender of Lee's Army of Northern Virginia, a great chapter in American life came to a close, and a great new chapter began.

These men were bringing the Civil War to its virtual 2
finish. To be sure, other armies had yet to surrender, and for a few days the fugitive Confederate government would struggle desperately and vainly, trying to find some way to go on living now that its chief support was gone. But in effect it was all over when Grant and Lee signed the papers. And the little room where they wrote out the terms was the scene of one of the poignant, dramatic contrasts in American history.

They were two strong men, these oddly different gener- 3

als, and they represented the strengths of two conflicting currents that, through them, had come into final collision.

Back of Robert E. Lee was the notion that the old aristocratic concept might somehow survive and be dominant in American life. 4

Lee was tidewater Virginia, and in his background were family, culture, and tradition . . . the age of chivalry transplanted to a New World which was making its own legends and its own myths. He embodied a way of life that had come down through the age of knighthood and the English country squire. America was a land that was beginning all over again, dedicated to nothing much more complicated than the rather hazy belief that all men had equal rights, and should have an equal chance in the world. In such a land Lee stood for the feeling that it was somehow of advantage to human society to have a pronounced inequality in the social structure. There should be a leisure class, backed by ownership of land; in turn, society itself should be keyed to the land as the chief source of wealth and influence. It would bring forth (according to this ideal) a class of men with a strong sense of obligation to the community; men who lived not to gain advantage for themselves, but to meet the solemn obligations which had been laid on them by the very fact that they were privileged. From them the country would get its leadership; to them it could look for the higher values—of thought, of conduct, of personal deportment—to give it strength and virtue. 5

Lee embodied the noblest elements of this aristocratic ideal. Through him, the landed nobility justified itself. For four years, the Southern states had fought a desperate war to uphold the ideals for which Lee stood. In the end, it almost seemed as if the Confederacy fought for Lee; as if he himself was the Confederacy . . . the best thing that the way of life for which the Confederacy stood could ever have to offer. He had passed into legend before Appomattox. Thousands of tired, underfed, poorly clothed Confederate soldiers, long-since past the simple enthusiasm of the early days of the struggle, somehow considered Lee the symbol of everything for which they had been willing to die. But they could not 6 quite put this feeling into words. If the Lost Cause, sanctified by so much heroism and so many deaths, had a living justification, its justification was General Lee.

Grant, the son of a tanner on the Western frontier, was 7
everything Lee was not. He had come up the hard way, and embodied nothing in particular except the eternal toughness and sinewy fiber of the men who grew up beyond the mountains. He was one of a body of men who owed reverence and obeisance to no one, who were self-reliant to a fault, who cared hardly anything for the past but who had a sharp eye for the future.

These frontier men were the precise opposites of the 8
tidewater aristocrats. Back of them, in the great surge that had taken people over the Alleghenies and into the opening Western country, there was a deep implicit dissatisfaction with a past that had settled into grooves. They stood for democracy, not from any reasoned conclusion about the proper ordering of human society, but simply because they had grown up in the middle of democracy and knew how it worked. Their society might have privileges, but they would be privileges each man had won for himself. Forms and patterns meant nothing. No man was born to anything, except perhaps to a chance to show how far he could rise. Life was competition.

Yet along with this feeling had come a deep sense of 9
belonging to a national community. The Westerner who developed a farm, opened a shop or set up in business as a trader, could hope to prosper only as his own community prospered—and his community ran from the Atlantic to the Pacific and from Canada down to Mexico. If the land was settled, with towns and highways and accessible markets, he could better himself. He saw his fate in terms of the nation's own destiny. As its horizons expanded, so did his. He had, in other words, an acute dollars-and-cents stake in the continued growth and development of his country.

And that, perhaps, is where the contrast between Grant 10
and Lee becomes most striking. The Virginia aristocrat, inevitably, saw himself in relation to his own region. He lived in a static society which could endure almost any-

thing except change. Instinctively, his first loyalty would go to the locality in which that society existed. He would fight to the limit of endurance to defend it, because in defending it he was defending everything that gave his own life its deepest meaning.

The Westerner, on the other hand, would fight with an equal tenacity for the broader concept of society. He fought so because everything he lived by was tied to growth, expansion, and a constantly widening horizon. What he lived by would survive or fall with the nation itself. He could not possibly stand by unmoved in the face of an attempt to destroy the Union. He would combat it with everything he had, because he could only see it as an effort to cut the ground out from under his feet. 11

So Grant and Lee were in complete contrast, representing two diametrically opposed elements in American life. Grant was the modern man emerging; beyond him, ready to come on the stage, was the great age of steel and machinery, of crowded cities and a restless, burgeoning vitality. Lee might have ridden down from the old age of chivalry, lance in hand, silken banner fluttering over his head. Each man was the perfect champion of his cause, drawing both his strengths and his weaknesses from the people he led. 12

Yet it was not all contrast, after all. Different as they were—in background, in personality, in underlying aspiration—these two great soldiers had much in common. Under everything else, they were marvelous fighters. Furthermore, their fighting qualities were really very much alike. 13

Each man had, to begin with, the great virtue of utter tenacity and fidelity. Grant fought his way down the Mississippi Valley in spite of acute personal discouragement and profound military handicaps. Lee hung on in the trenches at Petersburg after hope itself had died. In each man there was an indomitable quality . . . the born fighter's refusal to give up as long as he can still remain on his feet and lift his two fists. 14

Daring and resourcefulness they had, too; the ability to think faster and move faster than the enemy. These were the qualities which gave Lee the dazzling campaigns of Sec- 15 ond Manassas and Chancellorsville and won Vicksburg for Grant.

Lastly, and perhaps greatest of all, there was the ability, at the end, to turn quickly from war to peace once the fighting was over. Out of the way these two men behaved at Appomattox came the possibility of a peace of reconciliation. It was a possibility not wholly realized, in the years to come, but which did, in the end, help the two sections to become one nation again . . . after a war whose bitterness might have seemed to make such a reunion wholly impossible. No part of either man's life became him more than the part he played in their brief meeting in the McLean house at Appomattox. Their behavior there put all succeeding generations of Americans in their debt. Two great Americans, Grant and Lee—very different, yet under everything very much alike. Their encounter at Appomattox was one of the great moments of American history. 16

QUESTIONS ON SUBJECT AND PURPOSE

1. According to Catton what were the differences between Grant and Lee? What were the similarities?
2. How were both men representative of America?
3. Why does Catton use comparison in order to make his main point? What is that point?

QUESTIONS ON STRATEGY AND AUDIENCE

1. How does Catton structure his essay? Does he use the subject-by-subject pattern or the point-by-point pattern?
2. How does the structure of the last four paragraphs differ from that of the first part of the essay?
3. Catton devotes most of the essay to contrasting Grant and Lee. How then does he manage to emphasize finally the similarities between the two? Why does he do so?
4. Catton was a very popular historian of the American Civil War. What would be the range of audiences to whom Catton's essay might appeal? What does Catton expect of his audience?

QUESTIONS ON VOCABULARY AND STYLE

1. How does Catton use paragraphing in his essay to make his argument clearer?
2. Does Catton show any bias in his comparison? Is there any point in the essay when it appears that he favors one man over the other?
3. Be able to define the following words: *poignant* (paragraph 2), *sinewy* (7), *obeisance* (7), *tenacity* (11), *diametrically* (12), *burgeoning* (12), *indomitable* (14).

WRITING SUGGESTIONS

1. You did something wrong. It does not matter what it was; it was just wrong. Pick two people you know—parents, friends, relatives—and compare/contrast how they would react to your bad news.
2. In an essay compare two people you know. Remember that there must be some basis for comparison, that is, some basic similarities as well as differences between your subjects. You should also try to make some interesting main point or points based on your comparison. Assume that your reader does not know either person.

Prewriting:

a. Review the advice about describing people given in Chapter 3. Your paper will be more successful if your comparison involves more than physical qualities.
b. With that advice in mind, jot down a list of possible pairs of subjects. Fold sheets of paper into quarters and write one subject's name in the left margin and one in the right margin. In the top two quarters list differences; in the bottom, similarities. You ought to have three or four points of comparison as a minimum.
c. Number those points in order of significance. Omit any that seem too obvious. You will need to decide whether you want to begin with similarities or with differences and whether you will begin or end with the most significant point.

Rewriting:

a. Look carefully at the structural decisions you made in item c above. Remember that any order is possible; it is just a question of what seems to work most effectively. Try changing the order of your body paragraphs. Make a copy of the paper, cut it into pieces, and paste up a new version. Does it work better?

b. Find two peer readers. Once they have finished reading your draft, ask them to answer each of the following questions: First, what is the paper's thesis, or why is this comparison being made? Second, which points of similarity or difference seem the least important? Compare their answers. Do they agree with your answers to those questions?

c. Be honest—how good is your conclusion? Did you have trouble ending? Try freewriting a new ending. Force it to be different from your original conclusion.

3. Choose two figures from history or two current people of some notoriety (e.g, politicians, entertainers, artists, scientists, public figures). Research your subjects. Then write an essay in which you compare the two. Remember that there must be some basis or reason for making the comparison.

English and American Concepts of Space

EDWARD T. HALL

Edward T. Hall—scholar, author, teacher, and lecturer—was born in Webster Groves, Missouri, in 1914, studied at the University of Denver, and earned his master's degree at the University of Arkansas. He completed his Ph.D. in anthropology at Columbia University and is currently professor of anthropology at Northwestern University. He is author of a number of books including The Silent Language *(1959), a study of nonverbal communication;* The Hidden Dimension *(1966), a study of social and personal space;* The Dance of Life *(1983), a study of time in other cultures; and* Hidden Differences: Doing Business with the Japanese *(1987), coauthored with Mildred Hall. In this selection from* The Hidden Dimension, *Hall contrasts English and American concepts of personal space.*

It has been said that the English and the Americans are two great people separated by one language. The differences for which language gets blamed may not be due so much to words as to communications on other levels beginning with English intonation (which sounds affected to many Americans) and continuing to ego-linked ways of handling time, space, and materials. If there ever were two cultures in which differences of the proxemic details are marked it is in the educated (public school) English and the middle-class Americans. One of the basic reasons for this wide disparity is that in the United States we use space as a way of classifying people and activities, whereas in England it is the social system that determines who you are. In the United States, your address is an important cue to status (this applies not only to one's home but to the business address as well). The Joneses from Brooklyn and Miami are not as "in" as the 1

Joneses from Newport and Palm Beach. Greenwich and Cape Cod are worlds apart from Newark and Miami. Businesses located on Madison and Park avenues have more tone than those on Seventh and Eighth avenues. A corner office is more prestigious than one next to the elevator or at the end of a long hall. The Englishman, however, is born and brought up in a social system. He is still Lord—no matter where you find him, even if it is behind the counter in a fishmonger's stall. In addition to class distinctions, there are differences between the English and ourselves in how space is allotted.

The middle-class American growing up in the United States feels he has a right to have his own room, or at least part of a room. My American subjects, when asked to draw an ideal room or office, invariably drew it for themselves and no one else. When asked to draw their present room or office, they drew only their own part of a shared room and then drew a line down the middle. Both male and female subjects identified the kitchen and the master bedrooom as belonging to the mother or the wife, whereas father's territory was a study or a den, if one was available; otherwise, it was "the shop," "the basement," or sometimes only a workbench or the garage. American women who want to be alone can go to the bedroom and close the door. The closed door is the sign meaning "Do not disturb" or "I'm angry." An American is available if his door is open at home or at his office. He is expected not to shut himself off but to maintain himself in a state of constant readiness to answer the demands of others. Closed doors are for conferences, private conversations, and business, work that requires concentration, study, resting, sleeping, dressing, and sex. 2

The middle- and upper-class Englishman, on the other hand, is brought up in a nursery shared with brothers and sisters. The oldest occupies a room by himself which he vacates when he leaves for boarding school, possibly even at the age of nine or ten. The difference between a room of one's own and early conditioning to shared space, while seeming inconsequential, has an important effect on the Englishman's attitude toward his own space. He may never 3 have a permanent "room of his own" and seldom expects one or feels he is entitled to one. Even Members of Parliament have no offices and often conduct their business on the terrace overlooking the Thames. As a consequence, the English are puzzled by the American need for a secure place in which to work, an office. Americans working in England may become annoyed if they are not provided with what they consider appropriate enclosed work space. In regard to the need for walls as a screen for the ego, this places the Americans somewhere between the Germans and the English.

The contrasting English and American patterns have 4
some remarkable implications, particularly if we assume that man, like other animals, has a built-in need to shut himself off from others from time to time. An English student in one of my seminars typified what happens when hidden patterns clash. He was quite obviously experiencing strain in his relationships with Americans. Nothing seemed to go right and it was quite clear from his remarks that we did not know how to behave. An analysis of his complaints showed that a major source of irritation was that no American seemed to be able to pick up the subtle clues that there were times when he didn't want his thoughts intruded on. As he stated it, "I'm walking around the apartment and it seems that whenever I want to be alone my roommate starts talking to me. Pretty soon he's asking 'What's the matter?' and wants to know if I'm angry. By then I am angry and say something."

It took some time but finally we were able to identify 5
most of the contrasting features of the American and British problems that were in conflict in this case. When the American wants to be alone he goes into a room and shuts the door—he depends on architectural features for screening. For an American to refuse to talk to someone else present in the same room, to give them the "silent treatment," is the ultimate form of rejection and a sure sign of great displeasure. The English, on the other hand, lacking rooms of their own since childhood, never developed the practice of using space as a refuge from others. They have in effect

internalized a set of barriers, which they erect and which others are supposed to recognize. Therefore, the more the Englishman shuts himself off when he is with an American the more likely the American is to break in to assure himself that all is well. Tension lasts until the two get to know each other. The important point is that the spatial and architectural needs of each are not the same at all.

QUESTIONS ON SUBJECT AND PURPOSE

1. What is Hall's thesis? Is this essay an example of comparison or contrast?
2. What is proxemics? Why might it be important to understand such a concept?
3. Do you agree with Hall's observations on American behavior? Can you think of any other relevant examples?

QUESTIONS ON STRATEGY AND AUDIENCE

1. How does Hall structure his essay? Make a brief outline.
2. From where does Hall draw his information and examples? How authoritative does his argument seem?
3. Why might Hall include the example of the English student and his American roommate?

QUESTIONS ON VOCABULARY AND STYLE

1. What are some words or phrases from the essay that specifically denote comparisons?
2. Hall uses some terms, phrases, and passages that sound scientific or psychological. Locate these. What effect(s) do they have?
3. Be able to define the following words: *proxemic* (paragraph 1), *public school* (1), *disparity* (1), *fishmonger* (1).

WRITING SUGGESTIONS

1. Based on your observations of friends or roommates and your experiences, compare and contrast in a paragraph two people's

attitudes toward something. Focus on a single significant point of comparison. You might consider the following as possible subjects:

a. Telephone habits or use
b. Clothes
c. Shared versus private space
d. Shared versus private objects
e. Loudness of conversations or music
f. Public behavior

2. Differences such as Hall writes about are not limited to people from different cultures. People of different ages or people from different parts of the country or people with different values can show substantial disagreement. Compare the attitudes of any two people on a specific subject.

Prewriting:

a. Unless you have been told to use outside sources, it is best to draw upon your own experiences and observations. Begin by thinking about people whose behaviors or values are different from yours. Have you ever been suddenly aware of a fundamental difference between you and someone else? Are there subjects about which you must make conscious compromises with this person?
b. Remember that your points of difference or conflict ought to be interesting to a reader and that there ought to be several of them. Avoid the obvious or the trite. Fundamental differences about common behavior or values probably have the greatest interest. Make a list of possible comparisons and include examples.
c. Try beginning with a striking example of a difference. Have a clear thesis, but avoid writing a thesis introduction for the first draft.

Rewriting:

a. Convert the list of things to remember at the end of this chapter's introduction into a list of questions. After a day or more has passed since you finished the first draft, sit down and answer those questions about your paper. Try to look critically at what you have done.
b. Give the list and your draft to a roommate or classmate and ask for honest answers to the questions. Remember that you need a critical reader's response to improve any piece of writing.

3. As an objective observer, write an essay on cultural differences between two groups. You should have a central theme (Hall's was people's differing needs for space). The two cultures can be foreign, one foreign and the other American, or subcultures within America. Using specific examples to support your statements will help you avoid overgeneralization. And, of course, you should beware of making biased judgments.

Understanding the Difference

PHYLLIS SCHLAFLY

Born in 1924 in St. Louis, Missouri, Phyllis Schlafly received an A.B. from Washington University. She received an M.A. degree from Radcliffe, and later earned a law degree from Washington University. Schlafly is a well-known and highly vocal opponent of the Equal Rights Amendment and is also active in defending the conservative point of view on other issues. In 1957 she began publication of her monthly newsletter The Phyllis Schlafly Report. *In addition, she is the author of* The Power of the Positive Woman *(1977) and* The Power of the Christian Woman *(1981). Involved not only in women's issues, Schlafly has written editorials and essays on timely topics, such as the AIDS epidemic and censorship in the schools. In "Understanding the Difference," an excerpt from* The Power of the Positive Woman, *Schlafly classifies men as logical and women as emotional. She also raises a number of issues and questions that were significant in the battle over the ERA.*

The first requirement for the acquisition of power by the Positive Woman is to understand the differences between men and women. Your outlook on life, your faith, your behavior, your potential for fulfillment, all are determined by the parameters of your original premise. The Positive Woman starts with the assumption that the world is her oyster. She rejoices in the creative capability within her body and the power potential of her mind and spirit. She understands that men and women are different, and that those very differences provide the key to her success as a person and fulfillment as a woman. 1

The women's liberationist, on the other hand, is imprisoned by her own negative view of herself and of her place in the world around her. This view of women was most succinctly expressed in an advertisement designed by 2 the principal women's liberationist organization, the National Organization for Women (NOW), and run in many magazines and newspapers and as spot announcements on many television stations. The advertisement showed a darling curlyheaded girl with the caption: "This healthy, normal baby has a handicap. She was born female."

This is the self-articulated dog-in-the-manger, chip-on-the-shoulder, fundamental dogma of women's liberation movement. Someone—it is not clear who, perhaps God, perhaps the "Establishment," perhaps a conspiracy of male chauvinist pigs—dealt women a foul blow by making them female. It becomes necessary, therefore, for women to agitate and demonstrate and hurl demands on society in order to wrest from an oppressive male-dominated social structure the status that has been wrongfully denied to women through the centuries. 3

By its very nature, therefore, the women's liberation movement precipitates a series of conflict situations—in the legislatures, in the courts, in the schools, in industry—with man targeted as the enemy. Confrontation replaces cooperation as the watchword of all relationships. Women and men become adversaries instead of partners. 4

The second dogma of the women's liberationists is that, of all the injustices perpetrated upon women through the centuries, the most oppressive is the cruel fact that women have babies and men do not. Within the confines of the women's liberationist ideology, therefore, the abolition of this overriding inequality of women becomes the primary goal. This goal must be achieved at any and all costs—to the woman herself, to the baby, to the family, and to society. Women must be made equal to men in their ability *not* to become pregnant and *not* to be expected to care for babies they may bring into the world. 5

This is why women's liberationists are compulsively involved in the drive to make abortion and child-care centers for all women, regardless of religion or income, both socially acceptable and government-financed. Former Congresswoman Bella Abzug has defined the goal: "to enforce 6 the constitutional right of females to terminate pregnancies that they do not wish to continue."

If man is targeted as the enemy, and the ultimate goal of women's liberation is independence from men and the avoidance of pregnancy and its consequences, then lesbianism is logically the highest form in the ritual of women's liberation. Many, such as Kate Millett, come to this conclusion, although many others do not. 7

The Positive Woman will never travel that dead-end road. It is self-evident to the Positive Woman that the female body with its baby-producing organs was not designed by a conspiracy of men but by the Divine Architect of the human race. Those who think it is unfair that women have babies, whereas men cannot, will have to take up their complaint with God because no other power is capable of changing that fundamental fact. On some college campuses, I have been assured that other methods of reproduction will be developed. But most of us must deal with the real world rather than with the imagination of dreamers. 8

Another feature of the woman's natural role is the obvious fact that women can breast-feed babies and men cannot. This functional role was not imposed by conspiratorial males seeking to burden women with confining chores, but must be recognized as part of the plan of the Divine Architect for the survival of the human race through the centuries and in the countries that know no pasteurization of milk or sterilization of bottles. 9

The Positive Woman looks upon her femaleness and her fertility as part of her purpose, her potential, and her power. She rejoices that she has a capability for creativity that men can never have. 10

The third basic dogma of the women's liberation movement is that there is no difference between male and female except the sex organs, and that all those physical, cognitive, and emotional differences you *think* are there, are merely the result of centuries of restraints imposed by a male-dominated society and sex-stereotyped schooling. The role 11 imposed on women is, by definition, inferior, according to the women's liberationists.

The Positive Woman knows that, while there are some physical competitions in which women are better (and can command more money) than men, including those that put a premium on grace and beauty, such as figure skating, the superior physical strength of males over females in competitions of strength, speed, and short-term endurance is beyond rational dispute. 12

In the Olympic Games, women not only cannot win any medals in competition with men, the gulf between them is so great that they cannot even qualify for the contests with men. No amount of training from infancy can enable women to throw the discus as far as men, or to match men in push-ups or in lifting weights. In track and field events, individual male records surpass those of women by 10 to 20 percent. 13

Female swimmers today are beating Johnny Weissmuller's records, but today's male swimmers are better still. Chris Evert can never win a tennis match against Jimmy Connors. If we removed lady's tees from golf courses, women would be out of the game. Putting women in football or wrestling matches can only be an exercise in laughs. 14

The Olympic Games, whose rules require strict verification to ascertain that no male enters a female contest and, with his masculine advantage, unfairly captures a woman's medal, formerly insisted on a visual inspection of the contestants' bodies. Science, however, has discovered that men and women are so innately different physically that their maleness/femaleness can be conclusively established by means of a simple skin test of fully clothed persons. 15

If there is *anyone* who should oppose enforced sex-equality, it is the women athletes. Babe Didrickson, who played and defeated some of the great male athletes of her time, is unique in the history of sports. 16

If sex equality were enforced in professional sports, it would mean that men could enter the women's tournaments and win most of the money. Bobby Riggs has already threatened: "I think that men 55 years and over should be 17 allowed to play women's tournaments—like the Virginia Slims. Everybody ought to know there's no sex after 55 anyway."

The Positive Woman remembers the essential validity of the old prayer: "Lord, give me the strength to change what I can change, the serenity to accept what I cannot change, and the wisdom to discern the difference." The women's liberationists are expending their time and energies erecting a make-believe world in which they hypothesize that *if* schooling were gender-free, and *if* the same money were spent on male and female sports programs, and *if* women were permitted to compete on equal terms, *then* they would prove themselves to be physically equal. Meanwhile, the Positive Woman has put the ineradicable physical differences into her mental computer, programmed her plan of action, and is already on the way to personal achievement. 18

Thus, while some militant women spend their time demanding more money for professional sports, ice skater Janet Lynn, a truly Positive Woman, quietly signed the most profitable financial contract in the history of women's athletics. It was not the strident demands of the women's liberationists that brought high prizes to women's tennis but the discovery by sports promoters that beautiful female legs gracefully moving around the court made women's tennis a highly marketable television production to delight male audiences. 19

Many people thought that the remarkable filly named Ruffian would prove that a female race horse could compete equally with a male. Even with the handicap of extra weights placed on the male horse, the race was a disaster for the female. The gallant Ruffian gave her all in a noble effort to compete, but broke a leg in the race and, despite the immediate attention of top veterinarians, had to be put away. 20

Despite the claims of the women's liberation movement, there are countless physical differences between men and women. The female body is 50 to 60 percent water, the male 60 to 70 percent water, which explains why males can 21 dilute alcohol better than women and delay its effect. The average woman is about 25 percent fatty tissue, while the male is 15 percent, making women more buoyant in water and able to swim with less effort. Males have a tendency to color blindness. Only 5 percent of persons who get gout are female. Boys are born bigger. Women live longer in most countries of the world, not only in the United States where we have a hard-driving competitive pace. Women excel in manual dexterity, verbal skills, and memory recall.

Arianna Stassinopoulos in her book *The Female Woman* has done a good job of spelling out the many specific physical differences that are so innate and so all-pervasive that 22

> even if Women's Lib was given a hundred, a thousand, ten thousand years in which to eradicate *all* the differences between the sexes, it would still be an impossible undertaking . . .
>
> It is inconceivable that millions of years of evolutionary selection during a period of marked sexual division of labor have not left pronounced traces on the innate character of men and women. Aggressiveness, and mechanical and spatial skills, a sense of direction, and physical strength—all masculine characteristics—are the qualities essential for a hunter; even food gatherers need these same qualities for defense and exploration. The prolonged period of dependence of human children, the difficulty of carrying the peculiarly heavy and inert human baby—a much heavier, clumsier burden than the monkey infant and much less able to cling on for safety—meant that women could not both look after their children and be hunters and explorers. Early humans learned to take advantage of this period of dependence to transmit rules, knowledge and skills to their offspring—women needed to develop verbal skills, a talent for personal relationships, and a predilection for nurturing going even beyond the maternal instinct.* 23

Does the physical advantage of men doom women to a life of servility and subservience? The Positive Woman knows that she has a complementary advantage which is at 24

*Arianna Stassinopoulos, *The Female Woman* (New York: Random House, 1973) p. 30-31.

least as great—and, in the hands of a skillful woman, far greater. The Divine Architect who gave men a superior strength to lift weights also gave women a different kind of superior strength.

The women's liberationists and their dupes who try to 25
tell each other that the sexual drive of men and women is really the same, and that it is only societal restraints that inhibit women from an equal desire, an equal enjoyment, and an equal freedom from the consequences, are doomed to frustration forever. It just isn't so, and pretending cannot make it so. The differences are not a woman's weakness but her strength.

Dr. Robert Collins, who has had ten years's experience 26
in listening to and advising young women at a large eastern university, put his finger on the reason why casual "sexual activity" is such a cheat on women:

> A basic flaw in this new morality is the assumption that 27
> males and females are the same sexually. The simplicity of the male anatomy and its operation suggest that to a man, sex can be an activity apart from his whole being, a drive related to the organs themselves.
>
> In a woman, the complex internal organization, correlated 28
> with her other hormonal systems, indicates her sexuality must involve her total self. On the other hand, the man is orgasm-oriented with a drive that ignores most other aspects of the relationship. The woman is almost totally different. She is engulfed in romanticism and tries to find and express her total feelings for her partner.
>
> A study at a midwestern school shows that 80 percent of 29
> the women who had intercourse hoped to marry their partner. Only 12 percent of the men expected the same.
>
> Women say that soft, warm promises and tender touches 30
> are delightful, but that the act itself usually leads to a "Is that all there is to it?" reaction . . .
>
> [A typical reaction is]: "It sure wasn't worth it. It was no 31
> fun at the time. I've been worried ever since. . . ."
>
> The new morality is a fad. It ignores history, it denies the 32
> physical and mental compositions of human beings, it is intolerant, exploitative, and is oriented toward intercourse, not love.*

**Chicago Tribune*, August 17, 1975.

The new generation can brag all it wants about the new liberation of the new morality, but it is still the woman who is hurt most. The new morality isn't just a "fad"—it is a cheat and a thief. It robs the woman of her virtue, her youth, her beauty, and her love—for nothing, just nothing. It has produced a generation of young women searching for their identity, bored with sexual freedom, and despondent from the loneliness of living a life without commitment. They have abandoned the old commandments, but they can't find any new rules that work. 33

The Positive Woman recognizes the fact that, when it comes to sex, women are simply not the equal of men. The sexual drive of men is much stronger than that of women. That is how the human race was designed in order that it might perpetuate itself. The other side of the coin is that it is easier for women to control their sexual appetites. A Positive Woman cannot defeat a man in a wrestling or boxing match, but she can motivate him, inspire him, encourage him, teach him, restrain him, reward him, and have power over him that he can never achieve over her with all his muscle. How or whether a Positive Woman uses her power is determined solely by the way she alone defines her goals and develops her skills. 34

The differences between men and women are also emotional and psychological. Without woman's innate maternal instinct, the human race would have died out centuries ago. There is nothing so helpless in all earthly life as the newborn infant. It will die within hours if not cared for. Even in the most primitive, uneducated societies, women have always cared for their newborn babies. They didn't need any schooling to teach them how. They didn't need any welfare workers to tell them it is their social obligation. Even in societies to whom such concepts as "ought," "social responsibility," and "compassion for the helpless" were unknown, mothers cared for their new babies. 35

Why? Because caring for a baby serves the natural maternal need of a woman. Although not nearly so total as the baby's need, the woman's need is nonetheless real. 36

The overriding psychological need of a woman is to love 37

something alive. A baby fulfills this need in the lives of most women. If a baby is not available to fill that need, women search for a baby-substitute. This is the reason why women have traditionally gone into teaching and nursing careers. They are doing what comes naturally to the female psyche. The schoolchild or the patient of any age provides an outlet for woman to express her natural maternal need.

This maternal need in women is the reason why mothers whose children have grown up and flown from the nest are sometimes cut loose from their psychological moorings. The maternal need in women can show itself in love for grandchildren, nieces, nephews, or even neighbors' children. The maternal need in some women has even manifested itself in an extraordinary affection lavished on a dog, a cat or a parakeet. 38

This is not to say that every woman must have a baby in order to be fulfilled. But it is to say that fulfillment for most women involves expressing their natural maternal urge by loving and caring for someone. 39

The women's liberation movement complains that traditional stereotyped roles assume that women are "passive" and that men are "aggressive." The anomaly is that a women's most fundamental emotional need is not passive at all, but active. A woman naturally seeks to love affirmatively and to show that love in an active way by caring for the object of her affections. 40

The Positive Woman finds somebody on whom she can lavish her maternal love so that it doesn't well up inside her and cause psychological frustrations. Surely no woman is so isolated by geography or insulated by spirit that she cannot find someone worthy of her maternal love. All persons, men and women, gain by sharing something of themselves with their fellow humans, but women profit most of all because it is part of their very nature. 41

One of the strangest quirks of women's liberationists is their complaint that societal restraints prevent men from crying in public or showing their emotions, but permit women to do so, and that therefore we should "liberate" men to enable them, too, to cry in public. The public dis- 42 play of fear, sorrow, anger, and irritation reveals a lack of self-discipline that should be avoided by the Positive Woman just as much as by the Positive Man. Maternal love, however, is not a weakness but a manifestation of strength and service, and it should be nurtured by the Positive Woman.

Most women's organizations, recognizing the preference of most women to avoid hard-driving competition, handle the matter of succession of officers by the device of a nominating committee. This eliminates the unpleasantness and the tension of a competitive confrontation every year or two. Many women's organizations customarily use a prayer attributed to Mary, Queen of Scots, which is an excellent analysis by a woman of women's faults: 43

> Keep us, O God, from pettiness; let us be large in thought, in word, in deed. Let us be done with fault-finding and leave off self-seeking . . . Grant that we may realize it is the little things that create differences, that in the big things of life we are at one. 44

Another silliness of the women's liberationists is their frenetic desire to force all women to accept the title *Ms* in place of *Miss* or *Mrs.* If Gloria Steinem and Betty Friedan want to call themselves *Ms* in order to conceal their marital status, their wishes should be respected. 45

But that doesn't satisfy the women's liberationists. They want all women to be compelled to use *Ms* whether they like it or not. The women's liberation movement has been waging a persistent campaign to browbeat the media into using *Ms* as the standard title for all women. The women's liberationists have already succeeding in getting the Department of Health, Education and Welfare to forbid schools and colleges from identifying women students as *Miss* or *Mrs.** 46

All polls show that the majority of women do not care to be called *Ms.* A Roper poll indicated that 81 percent of 47

*HEW—Regulation on Sex Discrimination in Schools and Colleges, effective July 18, 1975, #86.21(c)(4).

the women questioned said they prefer *Miss* or *Mrs.* to *Ms.* Most married women feel they worked hard for the *r* in their names, and they don't care to be gratuitously deprived of it. Most single women don't care to have their name changed to an unfamiliar title that at best conveys overtones of feminist ideology and is polemical in meaning, and at worst connotes misery instead of joy. Thus, Kate Smith, a very Positive Woman, proudly proclaimed on television that she is "Miss Kate Smith, not Ms." Like other Positive Women, she has been succeeding while negative women have been complaining.

Finally, women are different from men in dealing with 48
the fundamentals of life itself. Men are philosophers, women are practical, and 'twas ever thus. Men may philosophize about how life began and where we are heading; women are concerned about feeding the kids today. No woman would ever, as Karl Marx did, spend years reading political philosophy in the British Museum while her child starved to death. Women don't take naturally to a search for the intangible and the abstract. The Positive Woman knows who she is and where she is going, and she will reach her goal because the longest journey starts with a very practical first step.

Amaury de Riencourt, in his book *Sex and Power in* 49
History, shows that a successful society depends on a delicate balancing of male and female factors, and that the women's liberation movement, which promotes unisexual values and androgyny, contains within it "a social and cultural death wish and the end of the civilization that endorses it."

One of the few scholarly works dealing with woman's 50
role, *Sex and Power in History* synthesizes research from a variety of disciplines—sociology, biology, history, anthropology, religion, philosophy, and psychology. De Riencourt traces distinguishable types of women in different periods in history, from prehistoric to modern times. The "liberated" Roman matron, who is most similar to the present-day feminist, helped bring about the fall of Rome through her unnatural emulation of masculine qualities, which

resulted in a large-scale breakdown of the family and ultimately of the empire.

De Riencourt examines the fundamental, inherent differences between men and women. He argues that man is the more aggressive, rational, mentally creative, analytical-minded sex because of his early biological role as hunter and provider. Woman, on the other hand, represents stability, flexibility, reliance on intuition, and harmony with nature, stemming from her procreative function. 51

Where man is discursive, logical, abstract, or philosophical, woman tends to be emotional, personal, practical, or mystical. Each set of qualities is vital and complements the other. Among the many differences explained in de Riencourt's book are the following: 52

> Women tend more toward conformity than men—which is why they often excel in such disciplines as spelling and punctuation where there is only one correct answer, determined by social authority. Higher intellectual activities, however, require a mental independence and power of abstraction that they usually lack, not to mention a certain form of aggressive boldness of the imagination which can only exist in a sex that is basically aggressive for biological reasons. 53
>
> To sum up: The masculine proclivity in problem solving is analytical and categorical; the feminine, synthetic and contextual . . . Deep down, man tends to focus on the object, on external results and achievements; woman focuses on subjective motives and feelings. If life can be compared to a play, man focuses on the theme and structure of the play, woman on the innermost feelings displayed by the actors.* 54

De Riencourt provides impressive refutation of two of the basic errors of the women's liberation movement: (1) that there are no emotional or cognitive diferences between the sexes, and (2) that women should strive to be like men. 55

A more colloquial way of expressing the de Riencourt conclusion that men are more analytical and women more personal and practical is in the different answers that one is 56

*Amaury de Riencourt, *Sex and Power in History* (New York: David McKay Co., Inc. 1974), p. 56.

likely to get to the question, "Where did you get that steak?" A man will reply, "At the corner market," or wherever he bought it. A woman will usually answer, "Why? What's the matter with it?"

An effort to eliminate the differences by social engineer- 57
ing or legislative or constitutional tinkering cannot succeed, which is fortunate, but social relationships and spiritual values can be ruptured in the attempt. Thus the role reversals being forced upon high school students, under which guidance counselors urge reluctant girls to take "shop" and boys to take "home economics," further confuse a generation already unsure about its identity. They are as wrong as efforts to make a left-handed child right-handed.

SUBJECT AND PURPOSE

1. What is Schlafly comparing and contrasting in this selection?
2. Using just the material included here, define the "Positive Woman." With whom is the "Positive Woman" contrasted?
3. According to Schlafly, what are the differences between men and women?
4. What is Schlafly's purpose in this essay? Is it specific (for example, to denounce women's liberationists), or is it more general?

QUESTIONS ON STRATEGY AND AUDIENCE

1. How does Schlafly structure her argument? Make a brief outline of the selection.
2. What do each of the following add to Schlafly's argument? Why might she include each?
   a. The example of Ruffian (paragraph 20)
   b. The quotations from Stassinopoulos (following paragraph 22), Collins (after 26), and De Riencourt (after 52)
   c. The example of the use of Ms. rather than Mrs. or Miss
3. Reread the opening sentence of the selection. Would anyone disagree with this statement? What is the implication behind this sentence?

QUESTIONS ON VOCABULARY AND STYLE

1. At several points, Schlafly uses clichés. Make a list of those that you recognize. Why does she use them?
2. How would you characterize Schlafly's tone in the selection? How is that tone achieved?
3. Be able to define the following words: *parameters* (paragraph 1), *succinctly* (2), *dogma* (3) *cognitive* (11), *ineradicable* (18), *innate* (22), *anomaly* (40), *quirks* (42), *frenetic* (45), *gratuitously* (47), *polemical* (47), *androgyny* (49), *emulation* (50), *discursive* (52), *proclivity* (54).

WRITING SUGGESTIONS

1. Schlafly sees a number of significant differences between men and women. On the basis of your personal experience, write a paragraph in which you contrast men and women on a single point. Concentrate on a specific attitude or type of behavior. Be sure to use examples to substantiate your contrast.
2. Schlafly uses contrast to define. The "positive woman" is defined through contrasting her both with the "woman's liberationist" and with men. In an essay, use contrast to define something. You might consider the following possibilities:
   a. The ideal mate/relationship/marriage
   b. The ideal career
   c. The ideal college education
   d. The greatest good

   Do not hesitate to substitute a topic of your choice.

   Prewriting:

   a. Make a list of at least six possible topics. Do not rush into making a decision on a single one. Instead, jot down ideas over a two-day period. For each topic, note several ways to develop the contrast.
   b. Look carefully at Schlafly's writing strategy. Whether you agree with her points or not does not matter; you are examining her strategy as a writer. Try to sketch out a working outline for your essay.
   c. Once you have a promising topic and a possible organizational scheme, try freewriting each body paragraph. Write for 15 minutes without stopping. That will allow you to play with ideas and organization without committing yourself to a final, fixed form.

Rewriting:

a. Read each paragraph with a critical eye. Is every sentence relevant? Do you have a clear, controlling focus for each paragraph? If not, do some editing.

b. Are your transitions clearly signaled for the reader? Use a colored pen to mark the transitional devices.

c. Once you have a complete draft, jot down on a separate sheet of paper what troubles you the most about the paper. What could be better? What are you most uneasy about? Allow a day to pass and then try to solve just that particular problem. If your college has a writing center or a peer tutoring program, take your specific problem there.

3. Compare and contrast the modern woman of the late 1980s with the turn-of-the-century woman. Select four to six points of comparison/contrast, and, using secondary sources, document the changes that have occurred or have not occurred. How have the role, position, status, and self-definition of women changed during the twentieth century? You might prepare your paper either as a traditional college research paper or as a feature article for a popular magazine.

C H A P T E R 6

Process

What do a recipe in a cookbook, a discussion of how the body converts food into energy and fat, a description of how igneous rocks are formed, and three sentences from your college's registration office on how to drop or add a course have in common? Each is a process analysis—either a set of directions for how to do something (make lasagna or drop a course) or a description of how something happens or is done (food is converted or rocks are formed). These two different types of process writing have two different purposes. The function of a set of directions is to allow the reader to duplicate the process; the function of process description is to tell the reader how something happens. The selection from *The Amy Vanderbilt Complete Book of Etiquette* outlines how a young executive woman should deal with the business lunch or dinner. Peter Elbow explains how to do a quick revision of your prose. Joan Didion in "On Keeping a Notebook" and Judith Viorst in "How Books Helped Shape My Life" describe processes not meant to be done or imitated by the reader. Even Didion's purpose, for example, is not to offer the reader advice on how to keep a notebook but rather to describe how and why *she* keeps a notebook.

How Do You Choose a Subject to Write About?

Choosing a subject is not a problem if you have been given a specific assignment—to describe how a congressional bill becomes a law, how a chemistry experiment was performed, how to write an A paper for your English course. Often, however, you have to choose your own subject. Several considerations are crucial in making that decision.

First, choose a subject that can be adequately described or analyzed in the space you have available. When Judith Viorst in "How Books Helped Shape My Life" catalogs the heroines with whom she identified on her "journey into young womanhood," she isolates six examples, one from each stage of her own development. She does not try to identify every influential heroine or every possible influence; she confines her analysis to these six examples.

Second, in a process analysis, as in any other writing assignment, identify the audience to whom you are writing. What does that audience already know about your subject? Are you writing to a general audience, an audience of your fellow classmates, or a specialized audience? You do not want to bore your reader with the obvious, nor do you want to lose your reader in a tangle of unfamiliar terms and concepts. Your choice of subject and certainly your approach to it should be determined by your audience. Peter Elbow's advice on "quick revising" appeared in a writing textbook; he knew or could assume that his audience would be interested in the fine points of such a process. Judith Viorst's essay orginally appeared in *Redbook*, a magazine that targets its audience as "women 18–34 years old," obviously a group of readers who would identify with Viorst's experience. Identifying your audience—what they might be interested in, what they already know—will help in both selecting a subject and deciding on how or what to write about it. Subjects can generally be approached from a number of different points of view. A process essay on how to apply eye makeup reaches a large but still limited audience (women who wear eye makeup), but an essay explaining why women wear eye makeup would have, potentially, a much broader audience.

How Do You Structure a Process Paper?

If you have ever tried to assemble something from a set of directions, you know how important it is that each step or stage in the process be clearly defined and properly placed in the sequence. Because process always involves a series of events or steps that must be done or must occur in proper order, the fundamental structure for a process paragraph or essay will be chronological.

Since proper order is essential, begin your planning by making a list of the various steps in the process. Once your list seems complete, arrange the items in the order in which they are performed or in which they occur. Check to make sure that nothing has been omitted or misplaced. If your process is a description of how to do or make something, you should check your arranged list by performing the process according to the directions you have assembled so far. This ordered list will serve as the outline for your process paper.

Converting your list or outline into a paragraph or essay is the next step. Be sure that all of the phrases on your outline have been turned into complete sentences and that any technical terms have been carefully explained for your reader. You will need some way of signaling to your reader each step or stage in the process. On your list, you simply numbered the steps, but in your paragraph or essay you generally cannot use such a device. More commonly, process papers employ various types of step or time markers to indicate order. Step markers like "first," "second," and "third" can be added to the beginnings of either sentences or paragraphs devoted to each individual stage. Time markers like "begin," "next," "in three minutes," or "while this is being done" remind the reader of the proper chronological sequence. Peter Elbow in "Quick Revising" carefully uses time markers to direct his reader ("First," "next," "now," "if after all this").

Writing a Process Analysis: A Student Example

Like many college students, Lyndsey Curtis had had considerable experience waiting on customers. Lyndsey decided to use that experience as the basis for some simple but relevant advice to any salesperson:

Pleasing the Customer

After 2½ years working in an ice cream store and countless times being annoyed by salespeople, I have devised a surefire three-point plan to please your customers.

(1) Always greet the customer with a smile and a friendly "May I help you?" Not only does this make him or her feel good, but it has an added bonus for you: if you are friendly to the customer, he or she will be more friendly to you and less likely to give you a hard time. Sometimes this is difficult to do if you have had a hard day, but just remember that there is nothing more aggravating than an unfriendly salesperson. If you absolutely cannot stand to smile at one more person, ask another employee to cover for you and go to the back of the store and scream. You'll feel much better and will be able to face the shoppers pleasantly.

(2) Give the customer your undivided attention. If another employee or your boss needs to know something or to have you do something immediately, then take care of it. Customers will usually understand if you interrupt them to take care of something related to business. Just don't talk about your plans for the weekend or what happened on "General Hospital" yesterday.

(3) When the customer leaves, smile and tell him or her to have a nice day or to come back soon. Let him or her know that you appreciate his or her business, and make him or her want to continue doing business with you.

The most important thing to remember is that if it weren't for the customer, you wouldn't be getting paid. If you keep this in mind, you shouldn't have any trouble following the guidelines described above.

After Lyndsey had finished a draft of her essay, she went to see her instructor for a conference. Together they discussed what she had written. The obvious strength of her essay was that its central portion—the three-step process—

was logically arranged from greeting the customer to concluding the sale. Some other areas of her paper, however, needed attention. Specifically, her instructor suggested that she look again at her opening and closing paragraphs. In the introductory sentence Lyndsey tries to establish her experience both as a salesperson and as a customer, but linking the two together is confusing. In the final paragraph she could reorder the last two sentences so that the climactic statement ("you wouldn't be getting paid") comes at the end of the paper. After this discussion of rhetorical choices (choices made for reasons of effectiveness rather than correctness), Lyndsey asked about her third paragraph. She noticed that she began with a statement—"Give the customer your undivided attention"—only to qualify it in the sentence that follows. One final trouble spot was the fourth paragraph where, in attempting to be nonsexist in her use of pronouns, she was forced into the awkward "him or her." Lyndsey and her instructor arrived at the obvious way to avoid the situation—make the reference plural ("customers"). When Lyndsey revised her paper, she tried to address each of the problems that had been discussed in the conference.

How to Wait on a Customer

I've been on both sides of the sales counter, so I can sympathize with both parties. I've worked in an ice cream store for 2½ years, and I know that some customers are obnoxious or rude. On the other hand, however, I've been annoyed by ignorant salespeople who seemed to think that helping me was a great chore. As a result of my experiences, I have devised a surefire three-point plan to please your customers.

(1) Always greet your customers with a smile and a friendly "May I help you?" Not only does this make them feel good, but it has an added bonus for you: if you are friendly to them, they will be more friendly to you and less likely to give you a hard time. Sometimes this is difficult to do if you have had a bad day, but just remember that there is nothing more aggravating than an unfriendly salesperson. If you absolutely cannot stand to smile at one more person, ask another employee to cover for you and go to the back of the store and scream! It always worked for me.

(2) Give the customers your undivided attention. They will understand an interruption due to store business, as long as you apologize for it and assure them that you will return to help them as soon as possible. Just don't talk about your plans for the weekend or what happened on "General Hospital" yesterday!

(3) When customers leave, smile and tell them to have a nice day or to come back soon. Let them know that you appreciate their business, and make them want to continue doing business with you.

If you have any trouble following the guidelines described above, just keep this in mind: if it weren't for the customers, you wouldn't be getting paid.

Some Things to Remember

1. Choose a subject that can be analyzed and described within the space you have available.
2. Remember that process takes two forms, reflecting its two possible purposes: first, to tell the reader how to do something; second, to tell the reader how something happens. Make sure that you have a purpose clearly in mind before you start your paper.
3. Identify your audience and write to that audience. Ask yourself, "Will my audience be interested in what I am writing about?" and "How much does my audience know about this subject?"
4. Make a list of the various steps or stages in the process.
5. Order or arrange a list, checking to make sure nothing is omitted or misplaced.
6. Convert the list into paragraphs using complete sentences. Remember to define any unfamiliar terms or concepts.
7. Use step or time markers to indicate the proper sequence in the process.
8. Check your process one final time to make sure that nothing has been omitted. If you are describing how to do something, use your paper as a guide to the process. If you are describing how something happens, ask a friend to read your process analysis to see whether it is clear.

A Woman Picks Up The Tab

AMY VANDERBILT and LETITIA BALDRIGE

Born into a prominent New York family, Amy Vanderbilt (1908-1974) attended New York University from 1926 to 1928. She then worked in a variety of capacities—as an advertising executive, a columnist, the vice-president and president of Publicity Associates, a dress designer, and a wine consultant. With the publication of Amy Vanderbilt's Complete Book of Etiquette *(1932), she came to be considered by many as America's foremost authority on taste and manners, treating etiquette as a flexible expression of kindness rather than a set of formal rules. Her other books include* Amy Vanderbilt's Everyday Etiquette *(1952) and* Amy Vanderbilt's Complete Cookbook *(1961). In addition, she wrote the long-running column "Amy Vanderbilt's Etiquette," contributed to* McCall's *and* Ladies Home Journal, *and hosted the television program "It's Good Taste" and the radio program "The Right Thing to Do."*

Letitia Baldrige was born in Miami Beach, Florida, received a B.A. from Vassar, and did graduate work at the University of Geneva. She has served as social secretary to Ambassador Clare Booth Luce and First Lady Jacqueline Kennedy, and has been an intelligence officer, public relations director for Tiffany & Company, president of her own public relations firm, and director of consumer affairs for Burlington Industries. In 1978, she revised and expanded Amy Vanderbilt's Complete Book of Etiquette *and* Amy Vanderbilt's Everyday Etiquette. *Her own books include* Roman Candle *(1956),* Tiffany Table Settings *(1959), the autobiographic* Of Diamonds and Diplomats *(1968), and* Home *(1970). Here the authors discuss a common problem faced by young executive women: how to pick up the tab when dining with a male business companion.*

One of the things women who are reaching for the executive suite are going to have to accept is the financial responsibilities of their new status. They must learn how to do things gracefully that heretofore they may have regarded as a man's duty—such as paying the bill for meals, taxis, or rented limousines. When a woman lunches or dines with a man on business, they are not on a date. If he begins to act as though they were, she should quickly discourage such attempts. (It is up to her to set the mood of business for such meals.) It is perfectly proper for a man to pick up the check for the first business lunch they have together, but she should pick it up the second time, and they should continue alternating, as men properly do. Sometimes these lunch meetings occur twice a year only, so one should keep a record of who took whom to lunch the last time. 1

Some jobs necessitate the transaction of regular business over the lunch table. It makes the situation easier for a woman if that lunch table is situated in her company's executive dining room or at a club, where, as a member, she can sign the bill without a fuss. She should not, however, invite her male colleague to a women's club for a business lunch if that club is used almost exclusively by women at lunchtime. A woman does not mind being overpowered by the number of men in *his* club (in fact, she usually quite enjoys it), but a man minds being overpowered by the number of women in *her* club. 2

No one likes a man who is known never to pick up a check. In today's world, people are going to feel the same about a woman who is known never to pick up a tab. The woman executive is going to learn how to pay gracefully when it's her turn. 3

In order to save embarrassment all around, who will pay for the next business lunch should be decided without question in advance. If it's a woman's turn, she should make it very clear over the telephone or face to face when the appointment is made that she will be paying. She has only to say with a smile that it really *is* her turn. She should name the time and the place, call the restaurant, and make the reservation in her name. 4

5 At the end of lunch she should unobtrusively ask for the bill, add the waiter's tip to the total without an agonizing exercise in mathematics, and then use her credit card or sign her name and her company's address on the back of the check (if she has a charge account there). If she does this quietly, no one around them need be aware of her actions.

6 If the man she has invited to lunch is really uncomfortable about her paying (and a woman should sense this immediately when she is making arrangements with him beforehand), then it is better to settle the bill with the head waiter away from the table. She should excuse herself at dessert time on the pretext of going to the powder room and make the bill arrangements then.

7 If a head waiter has performed a lot of service at the table, a woman who is paying the bill at an expensive restaurant should tip him just as a man would (from one to three dollars, according to the restaurant and the service). She can include his tip along with the waiter's by writing it on the bill, if she wishes. The woman who is hosting the meal should also tip the hat check person for the coats of her guests, although any guest leaving separately should pay for his or her coat upon leaving.

8 A dilemma confronting men who are the guests of women at business meals is one that has worried women since men began taking them out to restaurants. Many women were taught by their families when they were young (and especially by older brothers) that a girl on a date must always order the least expensive thing on the menu, if she was to be invited out again. I think we should all be careful in our business lives, too, to watch the right-hand column where the prices are. A man who is a guest of a woman should follow his hostess' lead in respect to suggestions she makes from the menu. Particularly if you are the guest of a self-employed person, you should order carefully, because paying for the meal will affect that person financially much more than it would a large corporation. However, corporate expense account or not, it is always better to order moderate-priced items when you are another's guest, keeping a firm check on overly expensive preferences.

QUESTIONS ON SUBJECT AND PURPOSE

1. In what way is this selection a process narrative?
2. Why would an etiquette book treat such a topic? Why would it be important?
3. Where did you learn about proper social behavior? Have you ever consulted an etiquette book? Would you in the future? Why or why not?

QUESTIONS ON STRATEGY AND AUDIENCE

1. How is the selection structured? Is the process always clear?
2. On six occasions, the authors enclose additional information or comments within parentheses. Why use this particular device? Is the information enclosed in this way similar in each instance?
3. What assumptions do the writers make about their audience? Characterize their assumed audience.

QUESTIONS ON VOCABULARY AND STYLE

1. How would you describe the tone used in the selection? How is it achieved? How appropriate is it for the audience or the context?
2. What is the effect of the following sentence: "A woman does not mind being overpowered by the number of men in *his* club (in fact, she usually quite enjoys it), but a man minds being overpowered by the number of women in *her* club" (paragraph 2)?
3. Be able to define the following words: *unobtrusively* (paragraph 5), *pretext* (6).

WRITING SUGGESTIONS

1. The traditional rituals of behavior between men and women have changed in recent years. For example, today a woman can ask a man out on a date, but twenty years ago such an action would have been rare or even unthinkable. Select a single area of etiquette in male/female relationships and in a paragraph

write an etiquette guide for that particular situation. You might consider writing for several different possible audiences such as:

a. young adults
b. middle-aged parents
c. a mature, senior audience

2. Expand what you did in Suggestion 1. Write an essay guide to proper etiquette in several related, common situations.

Prewriting:

a. One way to gather ideas is to consult some etiquette books available in the reference section of your college library. Spend some time thumbing through at least two different guides. Make a list of possible topics.
b. Ask some friends for other possibilities. Did their parents or grandparents provide any etiquette instruction? Did yours? Add these ideas to your list.
c. Look back over your list. Place an asterisk next to those topics/situations that are fairly common. Remember that for your essay you will need probably three to six developed examples.

Rewriting:

a. Jot down a brief list of the examples you used on a separate sheet of paper. Is there a logical principle behind the order you have used? Is there any other way in which the examples might be organized? Try renumbering them.
b. Have you made clear transitions from one paragraph to another? Use a colored pen to mark those transitions on a copy of your paper.
c. Before you began writing, you identified an audience. Now that you have finished, answer this question: "Will my audience be interested in my subject?" Remember, there are no bad or boring subjects, just bad and boring approaches to subjects.

3. Etiquette books and columns in newspapers have always been popular in America. Check the best seller list in a Sunday newspaper. Probably half of the books listed offer advice—on widely differing subjects. Study the list and visit a bookstore or library to examine copies. Then analyze the popularity of such books. Why do Americans buy them in such numbers? What do they say about us as a people?

Maple Recipes for Simpletons

NOEL PERRIN

Noel Perrin, currently a professor of American literature at Dartmouth, was born in 1927 in New York City. He received a B.A. from Williams College, an M.A. from Duke University, and a M.Litt. from Trinity Hall, Cambridge, England. Among his many books are several collections of essays about life in New England, including Amateur Sugar Maker *(1972),* Vermont: In all Weathers *(1973),* First Person Rural: Essays of a Sometime Farmer *(1978),* Second Person Rural: More Essays *(1980), and* Third Person Rural: Further Essays *(1983). He has also been a contributor to* New England Monthly *and* The New Yorker. *In "Maple Recipes for Simpletons," from* Second Person Rural, *Perrin praises the culinary versatility and tastiness of homemade maple syrup and offers a series of recipes that anyone can try.*

There are a lot of maple recipes in existence. Someone once 1
gave me a book that contains at least three hundred—in fact, that's all the book *does* contain. There are recipes for Maple-Cheese Spoon Dessert, and for Modern Maple-Pumpkin Pie. For baked squash covered with crushed pineapple and doused with maple syrup. For peanut-butter cookies. Even directions for a truly revolting salad dressing. (You mix cream and lemon juice, and then add a big slug of maple syrup. Oil and vinegar with a discreet touch of garlic is more my idea of a salad dressing.)

I yield to no one in my admiration for maple syrup. I've 2
been making it for fifteen years; and even with my little rig, total production now comes to many hundred gallons. I have gradually learned to make not only syrup, but tub sugar, maple candy, and finally, just in the last few years, the highest art of all: granulated maple sugar that pours as readily as the white stuff you get in a five-pound bag at the

store. These products taste, if anything, even better as the years go by.

But all the same, I view most maple recipes with dark suspicion. Too many of them put a noble product to unworthy, not to say peculiar, uses. Many also ignore the fact that maple syrup currently costs about eighteen dollars a gallon, and is thus a pretty expensive sweetening agent. 3

Take those peanut-butter cookies. To make one batch requires half a pint of maple syrup, and all you wind up with is something that tastes like sweet peanut butter. Ten cents' worth of cane sugar could handle that job—and it's just the sort of humble task cane sugar was born for. As for mixing syrup with crushed pineapple and plastering it on hunks of squash, I'd as soon mix twelve-year-old Scotch with diet Pepsi. 4

I certainly don't claim all maple recipes are like that. A good maple cake, maybe with some butternuts in the frosting, is one of the joys of life. And I've had a maple charlotte I would walk several miles to have again. These are splendid uses of syrup; the maple flavor comes out, if anything, enhanced. My only problem is that I am not personally competent to make either a cake or a charlotte. 5

However, there are some recipes that I *can* handle and that are maple-enhancing. I propose to share three of them. Two are my own discoveries, the third is a standard rural treat. All three are notably easy to prepare. In fact, they are so simple that any cook is going to regard the word *recipe* as absurdly out of place. So perhaps I should instead say, here are three good uses for maple syrup. 6

The first recipe is for Vermont baklava. Greek baklava (which came first by about five hundred years) is a many-layered pastry soaked in and fairly oozing honey. Vermont baklava is less complex. The ingredients are a loaf of good-quality white bread (homemade, Pepperidge Farm, Arnold, etc.) and a can of maple syrup. To prepare it, you take two slices of bread from the loaf and place them in your toaster. Set the toaster on medium. When the toast pops up, remove and place on a plate. Then cover each piece generously with maple syrup. Wait two or three minutes for it to soak in. 7

The baklava is now ready for consumption.

Two important tips: On no account heat the syrup, and 8
on no account butter the toast. It is essential that the only ingredients be white bread and room-temperature syrup.

I stumbled on the recipe for Vermont baklava about ten 9
years ago, when I first became a commercial-syrup producer. People began to stop by my farm to buy syrup. I would ask them what grade they wanted; and naturally enough a fair number didn't even know there *were* grades. My usual impulse was to give them a sample of each grade. But straight syrup from a spoon is a little overwhelming, and I certainly wasn't going to fire up the stove and make a batch of pancakes for every visitor. One day it occurred to me to try toast. I omitted butter simply because we happened to be out. And I then discovered that toasted white bread is one of the great vehicles for maple syrup. One gets the full brilliance of the flavor—if you'll forgive the arty term—and one gets something else that I have never experienced elsewhere except in tasting partly finished syrup in an evaporator. Poured at room temperature over toast, maple syrup by itself seems to have the qualities of butter, along with its own characteristics. The dish thus recommends itself especially to those who love butter but avoid it on account of their fear of polysaturated fats.

May be made with Fancy, A, or B. Not suggested with 10
Grade C.

The second recipe will be of interest only to those who 11
like to eat sliced bananas and milk. And even within that already limited group, only to those who feel that sliced bananas and milk go much better with brown sugar than with white sugar.

I have felt thus since roughly the age of six. In those 12
early years I was likely to have a base of cornflakes under the bananas and brown sugar; since about sophomore year of college I have omitted the cornflakes. They only get soggy, anyway.

The ingredients called for in the second recipe are one or 13
more ripe bananas, a supply of whole milk, and some dark maple syrup. Slice the bananas in the usual way, add the

normal quantity of milk, and then pour in a couple of tablespoons of maple syrup. (Right in the milk? You feel it might be like adding syrup to crushed pineapples and squash? I assure you it is not.)

The recipe is again one I stumbled on. One night a cou- 14
ple of years ago I happened to be fixing dinner alone. My wife and daughters had gone to a fair, and wouldn't be back until late. I usually figure on a maximum preparation time of ten minutes when I'm fixing dinner alone, so as to waste as little time as possible indoors. The menu this particular evening was a hamburger, to be followed by sliced bananas, milk, and brown sugar. Then I couldn't find the brown sugar. Not only no real brown sugar, but not even any of that light-tan stuff that will do in a pinch.

I already had the bananas sliced. Some kind of sweeten- 15
ing was necessary for the milk. We happened to have an open jar of Grade C in the pantry. I went and got it. At first bite I realized that for over forty years I had been having second-class bananas and milk. With brown sugar it's good. With dark maple syrup it's better.

May be made with Grade C or Grade B. Not recom- 16
mended with Fancy or A.

The third recipe is the New England equivalent of 17
sweet-and-sour pork in a Chinese restaurant, and it is a traditional spring dish. Warning: Anyone on a diet—in fact anyone who is not something of a glutton—should not even read about this dish.

Ingredients: a dozen plain raised doughnuts (two doz- 18
ens, if more than four people will be present), a large jar of dill pickles, a quart or more of maple syrup.

First you boil the syrup down by about one-third, so that 19
it has the consistency of a sugar glaze. Meanwhile, quarter the dill pickles and put them in a dish in the middle of the table, right next to the unsweetened raised doughnuts. Then, while it is still warm, you put some syrup in the bottom of a soup dish for each person.

Everybody then takes a doughnut, dips it in his or her 20
bowl of syrup, and begins to gorge. After every two or three bites—or at a minimum twice per doughnut—you stop and

eat a bite of pickle. With this constant resharpening of the palate, it is possible to eat an astonishingly large number of doughnuts. Stop just before you are comatose, and conclude with a cup of brewed coffee. Then retire to bed.

Should be prepared with Fancy or A. B will do, though not as well. C is not recommended. 21

This by no means exhausts the list of simple maple recipes—a small quantity of B or C does wonders in a pot of baked beans, a little A on popcorn beats Cracker Jack hollow. But it's enough to use as much spare syrup as most people are going to have in the course of a year. 22

QUESTIONS ON SUBJECT AND PURPOSE

1. Why are these "recipes for simpletons"? How do they differ from recipes you might expect to find in a cookbook?
2. What seems to be the most important criterion about these three recipes? What is important (to Perrin) about each?
3. In what ways is this a process narrative?

QUESTIONS ON STRATEGY AND AUDIENCE

1. How does Perrin structure the middle of his essay (paragraphs 7 to 21)?
2. Look again at Perrin's conclusion (paragraph 22). Why end the essay in this way? How else might it end?
3. To whom does Perrin seem to be writing? Characterize his audience.

QUESTIONS ON VOCABULARY AND STYLE

1. What difference would it make to the essay or to its tone if Perrin eliminated all of the first-person pronouns?
2. How would you describe Perrin's word choice in the essay? How does that influence the essay's tone?
3. Be able to define the following words: *charlotte* (paragraph 5), *palate* (20), *comatose* (20).

WRITING SUGGESTIONS

1. Think of a special recipe or food treat that you or your family enjoy. In a paragraph describe for your reader how to make that favorite, unusual indulgence.
2. The thread that links Perrin's recipes is his love of maple syrup: these recipes are three ways to enjoy eating maple syrup, ways that emphasize the "mapleness" of that syrup. Select another type of food for which you have a similar weakness. It could be chocolate, raisins, marshmallows, peanut butter, yogurt, or a more unusual food. In an essay similar to Perrin's, offer a reader some advice on ways in which this food might be prepared. Your essay can be serious or light-hearted, but do not be silly or ridiculous and do **not** title your essay "——— Recipes for Simpletons."

   Prewriting:

   a. Brainstorm for 30 minutes. List your food weaknesses and your favorite ways of indulging in those weaknesses. Avoid complicated recipes that your readers would have trouble visualizing or making.
   b. Outline Perrin's essay in order to see how he structures his process narrative. Do **not** copy that order. Use the essay as a suggested framework that you can modify to fit your subject.
   c. Define and analyze your audience—their interests, their prior knowledge about this food, their possible reactions—before you begin to write. If you are writing about a food that others might find unusual (eggplant, for example), you will have to work a little harder to make the subject accessible to a wide audience.

   Rewriting:

   a. Find a classmate or roommate willing to read your essay. Are the examples clear to your reader? Does the essay hold the reader's interest? If possible, ask your reader to compare your essay to Perrin's. Consider carefully what your reader says; make changes in your essay as necessary.
   b. Look again at your introduction. Do you catch your reader's interest? Try starting with an example that makes your essay vivid. Avoid a traditional English paper introduction.
   c. Look again at your conclusion. Endings to process narratives can get fairly boring. Check the advice on writing conclusions in the Glossary. Then freewrite a new conclusion. Try something different, even if you later discard it.

3. Food plays an important role in many different cultures and religions. Select a particular religious or cultural holiday that has food rituals associated with it. It can be something that is a part of your heritage or something from a completely different culture or religion. Research the traditions behind that meal or ritual. What foods are eaten? Why? How are they prepared? What does the food symbolize? Then in a process essay describe its elements for an audience unfamiliar with this custom. If your instructor approves, write your essay in the form of a feature article that might appear in a Sunday newspaper.

A Manual: Training for Landlords

FRAN LEBOWITZ

Fran Lebowitz was born in Morristown, New Jersey in 1950, and now lives in New York City. Prior to becoming a writer, she worked at a number of what she calls "colorful and picturesque" jobs, such as driving taxis and cleaning apartments. She eventually found a job on the advertising staff of Changes *and convinced the editors to publish her book and film reviews. She later became a columnist for Andy Warhol's* Interview *and for* Mademoiselle. *She is best known for her two best-selling collections of satirical essays,* Metropolitan Life *(1978) and* Social Studies *(1981). One reviewer observed, "The quick-witted, quick-tempered Lebowitz may be the funniest chronic complainer on the scene." In this essay from* Metropolitan Life, *Lebowitz uses process analysis to provide a satiric look at the relationship between landlords and tenants. She writes that a landlord should not be "a slave to convention" and has the option of providing such extras as heat, hot water, and walls.*

Every profession requires of its members certain skills, talents, or training. Dancers must be light on their feet. Brain surgeons must attend medical school. Candlestick makers must have an affinity for wax. These occupations, though, are only the tip of the iceberg. How do others learn their trades? We shall see. 1

How to Be a Landlord: An Introduction

In order to be a landlord, it is first necessary to acquire a building or buildings. This can be accomplished in either of two ways. By far the most pleasant is by means of inheritance—a method favored not only because it is easy on the pocketbook but also because it eliminates the tedious chore of selecting the property. This manual, however, is not 2 really intended for landlords of that stripe, since such an inheritance invariably includes a genetic composition that makes formal instruction quite superfluous.

Less attractive but somewhat more common (how often 3
those traits go hand in hand) is the method of actual purchase. And it is here that our work really begins.

Lesson One: Buying

Buildings can be divided into two main groups: cheap 4
and expensive. It should be remembered, however, that these terms are for professional use only and never to be employed in the presence of tenants, who, almost without exception, prefer the words *very* and *reasonable.* If the price of a building strikes you as excessive, you would do well to consider that wise old slogan "It's not the initial cost—it's the upkeep," for as landlord you are in the enviable position of having entered a profession in which the upkeep is taken care of by the customer. This concept may be somewhat easier to grasp by simply thinking of yourself as a kind of telephone company. You will be further encouraged when you realize that while there may indeed be a wide disparity in building prices, this terrible inequity need not be passed on to the tenant in the degrading form of lower rent. It should now be clear to the attentive student that choosing a building is basically a matter of personal taste and, since it is the rare landlord who is troubled by such a quality, we shall proceed to the next lesson.

Lesson Two: Rooms

The most important factor here is that you understand 5
that a room is a matter of opinion. It is, after all, your building, and if you choose to designate a given amount of space as a room, then indeed it *is* a room. Specifying the function of the room is also your responsibility, and tenants need frequently to be reminded of this as they will all too often display a tendency to call one of your rooms a closet. This is, of course, a laughable pretension, since few tenants have ever seen a closet.

Lesson Three: Walls

A certain numbers of walls are one of the necessary evils of the business. And while some of you will understandably bridle at the expense, the observant student is aware that walls offer a good return on investment by way of providing one of the basic components of rooms. That is not to say that you, as landlord, must be a slave to convention. Plaster and similarly substantial materials are embarrassingly passé to the progressive student. If you are a father, you know that walls can enjoyably be made by children at home or camp with a simple paste of flour and water and some of Daddy's old newspapers. The childless landlord might well be interested in Wallies—a valuable new product that comes on a roll. Wallies tear off easily and *can* be painted, should such a procedure ever be enforced by law. 6

Lesson Four: Heat

The arrival of winter seems invariably to infect the tenant with an almost fanatical lust for warmth. Sweaters and socks he may have galore; yet he refuses to perceive their usefulness and stubbornly and selfishly insists upon obtaining *his* warmth through *your* heat. There are any number of ploys available to the resourceful landlord, but the most effective requires an actual cash outlay. No mind, it's well worth it—fun, too. Purchase a tape recorder. Bring the tape recorder to your suburban home and place it in the vicinity of your heater. Here its sensitive mechanism will pick up the sounds of impending warmth. This recording played at high volume in the basement of the building has been known to stymie tenants for days on end. 7

Lesson Five: Water

It is, of course, difficult for the landlord to understand the tenant's craving for water when the modern supermarket is fairly bursting with juices and soft drinks of every description. The burden is made no easier by the fact that at 8 least some of the time this water must be hot. The difficult situation is only partially alleviated by the knowledge that *hot,* like *room,* is a matter of opinion.

Lesson Six: Roaches

It is the solemn duty of every landlord to maintain an adequate supply of roaches. The minimum acceptable roach to tenant ratio is four thousand to one. Should this arrangement prompt an expression of displeasure on the part of the tenant, ignore him absolutely. The tenant is a notorious complainer. Just why this is so is not certain, though a number of theories abound. The most plausible of these ascribes the tenant's chronic irritability to his widely suspected habit of drinking enormous quantities of heat and hot water—a practice well known to result in the tragically premature demise of hallway light bulbs. 9

QUESTIONS ON SUBJECT AND PURPOSE

1. According to Lebowitz, what is the major goal of a landlord? A tenant?
2. Probably no reader thinks that Lebowitz is being serious. At what point in the essay do you know that she is not writing a serious analysis of the subject?
3. What possible purpose might Lebowitz have in writing such an essay?

QUESTIONS ON STRATEGY AND AUDIENCE

1. How does Lebowitz structure her essay? Does that structure seem effective?
2. What strategy does Lebowitz use to end the essay? Why not write a conventional ending?
3. What expectations does Lebowitz have about her audience? How do you know?

QUESTIONS ON VOCABULARY AND STYLE

1. How would you describe the tone of the essay? How is that tone achieved and maintained?

2. In what ways are the style and tone of the essay appropriate for both the essay's subject and purpose?
3. Be able to define the following words: *stripe* (paragraph 2), *disparity* (4), *pretension* (5), *bridle* (6), *passé* (6), *ploys* (7), *stymie* (7), *demise* (9).

WRITING SUGGESTIONS

1. In a substantial paragraph, write a training guide for a position such as older or younger brother/sister, roommate, parent, child, spouse. Try to capture a tone similar to Lebowitz's.
2. Your college's office of residence life has asked for an article that offers advice on being a good roommate. The article will appear in a guide sent to incoming freshmen and should be written with a serious, helpful tone. Sarcasm such as Lebowitz uses is inappropriate.

   Prewriting:
   a. Make a list of qualities that you would like to see in a potential roommate. You can draw from your own personal experience, or you can just theorize about those qualities that seem ideal to you.
   b. Poll your friends on the subject. Try for a range of contributors who have had differing experiences with roommates.
   c. Once you have a list of qualities, decide on an order or arrangement. Is there anything inherent in the material that suggests which one should come first or last?

   Rewriting:
   a. Reexamine the tone of your paper. Is it serious? Helpful? Ask a peer reader to evaluate that aspect of your essay.
   b. Look back at the assignment. Remember the type of audience you are writing for. Does your essay appeal to that audience? Does it address that audience in an appropriate style and language?
   c. Check your introduction and conclusion. Remember that the college office wants students to read this. Do you make the subject seem interesting and valuable to your reader? Ask a peer reader to evaluate just your introduction.

3. Assume that you live in an apartment owned by a landlord who certainly appears to have read and believed Lebowitz's essay. What rights do you have as a tenant? How can you redress the

wrongs being done to you? Research the rights of a tenant in your community. In a process essay describe how a tenant can go about obtaining satisfaction from a landlord. Be sure to include specific information in your essay. You might assume that your essay will appear in a Sunday newspaper.

Quick Revising

PETER ELBOW

Born in New York in 1935, Peter Elbow received a B.A. from Williams College, a B.A. and an M.A. from Exeter College, Oxford, and a Ph.D. in 1969 from Brandeis University. Elbow has held various teaching positions at the Massachusetts Institute of Technology, Franconia College, and Evergreen State College. He also has served as a consultant to college and university writing programs. Currently, he is director of the writing program for the State University of New York at Stony Brook. An insightful analyst of the writing process, Elbow is author of Thoughts on Writing Essays *(1965),* Writing Without Teachers *(1973),* Oppositions in Chaucer *(1975),* Writing with Power *(1981), and* Embracing Contraries: Explorations in Learning and Teaching *(1986). He has also contributed to numerous education and literature journals. "It is 10:30 P.M. now and you have only ten pages of helter-skelter thinking on paper [and] you need an excellent, polished, full report by tomorrow morning." What do you do? You use Elbow's method of "quick revising."*

The point of quick revising is to turn out a clean, clear, professional final draft without taking as much time as you would need for major rethinking and reorganizing. It is a clean-and-polish operation, not a growing-and-transforming one. You specifically refrain from meddling with any deeper problems of organization or reconceptualization. 1

The best time to use quick revising is when the results don't matter too much. Perhaps you are not preparing a final, finished product but rather a draft for friends. It has to be clear, easy to read—if possible even a pleasure to read. But it needn't be your best work or your final thinking. Perhaps it's a draft for discussion or perhaps just a chance for people to learn your thinking about some matter as though you were writing a letter to them. Or perhaps you 2 are just writing for yourself but you want to clean up your draft so that it will be easier and more productive to read when you come back to it.

But there is another situation when you can use quick revising and unfortunately it is the one when you are most likely to use it: an occasion that is *very* important when the writing *has* to work for an important audience, but you lack time. You can't afford to re-see, re-think, and re-write completely your raw writing in the amount of time you have left. Maybe it was your fault and now you are kicking yourself; maybe it was unavoidable. But either way you are stuck. It is 10:30 P.M. now and you have only ten pages of helter-skelter thinking on paper, you need an excellent, polished, full report by tomorrow morning, and you care very much how the reader reacts to it. In such situations you have to contend with anxiety as well as lack of time. You need the discipline of the quick revising process. I will describe it here as though you are preparing a substantial piece of writing for tomorrow morning for an important audience because I want to stress the experience of battle conditions with live ammunition. (If it is a small job such as writing that memo in thirty minutes, you probably won't go through all the separate steps I describe below. You'll probably just stand up and stretch now after your fifteen minutes of raw writing, and use your remaining time to look with fresh eyes through what you've written, figure out what you really want to say, and just write out your final draft—perhaps using substantial portions of your raw writing unchanged.) 3

Quick revising is simple and minimal. A lot depends on having the right spirit: businesslike and detached. A certain ruthlessness is best of all. Not desperate-ruthless, "Oh God, this is *awful*, I've *got* to change *everything*," but breezy-ruthless, "Yes, this certainly does have some problems. I wish I could start over and get the whole thing right, but not this time. I guess I'll just have to put the best face on things." If you are too worried about what you wrote or too involved with it, you'll have to work overtime to get the 4 right spirit. You need to stand outside yourself and be someone else.

5 First, if this piece is for an audience, think about who that audience is and what your purpose is in writing to it. You had the luxury of putting aside all thoughts of audience and purpose during the producing stage (if that helped you think and write better), but now you must keep them in mind as you make critical decisions in revising. Try to see your audience before you as you revise. It's no good ending up with a piece of writing that's good-in-general—whatever that means. You need something that is good for your purpose with your audience.

6 Next, read through all your raw writing and find the good pieces. When I do it, I just mark them with a line in the margin. Don't worry about the criteria for choosing them. It's fine to be intuitive. If the sentence or passage feels good for this purpose or seems important for this audience, mark it.

7 Next, figure out your single main point and arrange your best bits in the best order. It's easiest if you can figure out your main point first. That gives you leverage for figuring out what order to put things in. But sometimes your main point refuses to reveal itself—the one thing you are really trying to *say* here, the point that sums up everything else. All your writing may be circling around or leading up to a main idea that you can't quite figure out yet. In such a dilemma, move on to the job of working out the best order for your good passages. That ordering process—that search for sequence and priorities—will often flush your main point out of hiding.

8 You can just put numbers in the margin next to the good bits to indicate the right order if your piece is short and comfortable for you. But if it is long or difficult you need to make an outline before you can really work out the best order. It helps most to make an outline consist of complete assertions with verbs—*thoughts*, not just *areas*.

9 And of course as you work out this order or outline you will think of things you left out—ideas or issues that belong

in your final draft that weren't in your raw writing. You can now indicate each of them with a sentence.

If after all this—after getting, as it were, *all* your points 10
and getting them in the right order—you still lack the most important idea or assertion that ties them all together into a unity; if you have connected all this stuff but you cannot find the single thought that pulls it all together, and of course this sometimes happens, you simply have to move on. You have a deadline. There is a good chance that your main idea or center of gravity will emerge later, and even if it doesn't you have other options.

The next step is to write out a clean-but-not-quite-final 11
draft of the whole piece—excluding the very beginning. That is, don't write your first paragraph or section now unless it comes to you easily. Wait till you have a draft of the main body before deciding how to lead up to it—or whether it *needs* leading up to. How can you clearly or comfortably introduce something before you know precisely what it is you are introducing? So just begin this draft with your first definite point. Out of the blue. Start even with your second or third point if the first one raises confusing clouds of "how-do-I-get-started."

Perhaps you can use the good passages almost as they 12
are—copy them or use scissors—and only write transitional elements to get you from one to another. Or perhaps you need to write out most of it fresh. But you can go fast because you have all your points in mind and in order, and probably you have a clearly stated, single main idea holding it all together.

If you don't yet know your single main point, there is a 13
very good chance that it will come to you as you are writing this draft. The process of writing the real thing to the real audience will often drive you to say, "What I'm really trying to make clear to you is . . ." and *there* is your main point. This is especially likely to happen toward the end of your piece as you are trying to sum things up or say why all this is important or makes sense. When your main point emerges late in this way, you may have to go back and fiddle a bit

with your structure. It is very common that the last paragraph you write, when you finally say exactly what you mean in the fewest words, is just what you need (with perhaps a minor adjustment) for your first paragraph.

On rare occasions you still won't be able to find your main point. You know this is a coherent train of thought, and you know you are saying something, but you cannot sum it up in one sentence. You are stuck and you now have to make some choices. You can open or close your piece with a clear admission that you haven't focused it yet. This is usually the most helpful strategy when you are writing for yourself. (Sometimes, in fact, stating your dilemma—as dilemma—as accurately as you can, serves to produce the solution.) Or you can just present your train of thought without any statement at all of a single main idea. Or you can try to trick the reader into a feeling of unity with a vague, waffling pseudo-summary. But this is dangerous. If a reader sees you waffling he is liable to be mad or contemptuous, and even if he is not conscious of what you are doing he is liable to be irritated. If it is important—for this audience and situation—to end up with a piece of writing that is genuinely unified and focused, there is nothing for it but radical surgery. Settle for the best idea you *can* find in your writing and make that your main point. Organize what goes with it and throw away everything else. This usually hurts because it means throwing away some of your best bits. 14

So now you have a draft and a clear statement of your main idea. Finally you can write what you need for an introductory paragaph or section. Almost certainly you need something that gives the reader a clear sense of your main point—where you are going. If you have been writing under the pressure of a tight deadline your final draft will probably have some problems, and so this is no time for tricky strategies or leaving the reader in the dark. Subtlety is for when you can get everything just right. 15

This is also the time to make sure you have a satisfactory conclusion: a final passage that sums up everything 16 you have said with the precision and complexity that is only possible now that the reader has read and understood all the details. For example you have to begin an essay for most readers with a general statement that is easy to understand, such as "I want to explain how atomic bombs work," but at the end you can sum up your point more quickly and precisely: "In short, $E = mc^2$."

Now you have a draft of the whole thing that probably comes close to what you'll end up with. The next step is to change from writer-consciousness to reader-consciousness. For in writing that draft you were, obviously enough, functioning as a writer: a person trying to put down on paper what you had finally gotten clear in your own mind. Now you should read through this draft *as a reader*. The best way to do this is to read your draft *out loud*: you won't have to search for places that are unclear or awkward or lacking in life, you will *hear* them. If you are in an office or a library or some other place unsuitable for declaiming, you can get almost as much benefit by silently mouthing or whispering your draft as though you were speaking. If you put your fingers in your ears at the same time, you will actually hear your words good and loud. It is the *hearing* of your own words that serves to get you out of the writer-consciousness and into the audience-consciousness. 17

Finally, get rid of mistakes in grammar and usage. 18

Certain people on certain occasions can afford to collapse some of these steps together and type out their final, clean copy after they have settled on their main idea and numbered or outlined their best bits. But this means paying attention to spelling, grammar, and usage while you are engaged in trying to write clear language: focusing simultaneously on the pane of glass and on the scene beyond it. It's not a wise or efficient thing to do unless you are an exceptionally fluent and polished writer. Most people—and that includes myself—save time by waiting to the very end before worrying about mistakes in grammar and usage. 19

Even if you are writing informally for friends you must take care to get rid of these mistakes. Your friends may say, "Oh, who cares about trivial details of correctness," but in 20 fact most people are prejudiced, even if unconsciously, against writing flawed in this way. They are more apt to patronize your writing or take it less seriously or hold back from experiencing what you are saying if there are mistakes in mechanics.

In thinking about the whole process of quick revising, you 21
should realize that the essential act is *cutting*. Learn to leave out everything that isn't already good or easily made good. Learn the pleasures of the knife. Learn to retreat, to cut your losses, to be chicken. Learn to say, "Yes, I *care* more about this passage than about any other, I'm involved in it, but for that very reason, I can't make it work right. Out it goes!" Of course you don't need to be so ruthless about cutting if you are writing something to share informally among friends or to save for yourself. You can retain sections that feel important but don't quite work or don't quite fit. You can let your piece be an interesting muddle organizationally or conceptually—*so long as it's not muddled in wording or sentences*. Friends are willing to ponder your not-quite-digested thinking so long as your sentences and paragraphs are clear and easy to understand.

When you have *lots* of time for revising you tend to 22
finish with something longer than you have expected. The thing cooks and grows on its own and you have time to integrate that growth. But quick revising usually produces something shorter than you had expected. The reader should probably finish a bit startled: "Done already? This seems a bit skimpy. Still, everything here is well done. Actually, it's not too bad." Better to give your reader mild disappointment at a certain tight skimpiness than to bog him down in a mess so that he stops paying attention or even stops reading.

In the last analysis, the main thing for quick revising is 23
to get into the right spirit. Be your brisk, kindly, British aunt who is also a nurse: "Yes. Not to worry. I know it's a mess. But we'll clean it up and make it presentable in no time. It won't be a work of art, ducks, but it'll do just fine."

QUESTIONS ON SUBJECT AND PURPOSE

1. How does a "quick revision" differ from a "major rethinking and reorganizing" (paragraph 1)?
2. Why does Elbow caution against trying to write an opening paragraph too soon?
3. What is involved in changing from "writer-consciousness" to "reader-consciousness" (paragraph 17)?

QUESTIONS ON STRATEGY AND AUDIENCE

1. How does Elbow organize his process? Does he use any step or sequence markers?
2. What is the effect of using metaphors and images when describing the process of writing and revising? Consider each of the following:
   a. "Clean-and-polish operation, not a growing-and-tranforming one" (paragraph 1)
   b. "Raw writing" (3)
   c. "Experience of battle conditions with live ammunition" (3)
   d. "Flush your main point out of hiding" (7)
   e. "Radical surgery" (14)
   f. "Focusing simultaneously on the pane of glass and on the scene beyond it" (19)
   g. "The thing cooks and grows on its own" (22)
3. Elbow says: "Try to see your audience before you as you revise." Does Elbow seem to see his audience? Who comprises that audience? How do you know?

QUESTIONS ON VOCABULARY AND STYLE

1. Characterize Elbow's tone in the essay. How does he sound? What techniques does Elbow use to develop that tone?
2. Does Elbow ever use sentence fragments? How many?
3. How appropriate is Elbow's conclusion? Does it coincide with the advice that he gives?
4. Be able to define the following words: *refrain* (paragraph 1), *helter-skelter* (3), *intuitive* (6), *leverage* (7), *waffling* (14), *declaiming* (17), *patronize* (20).

WRITING SUGGESTIONS

1. Go through Elbow's essay and make a list of the steps involved in "quick revising." Then summarize his procedure in a process paragraph. Assume that your summary will be handed out to your classmates as a revision guide.
2. Using the material provided in Elbow's essay, in Chapter 10 of this text, and your own writing experience, write an essay about how to revise a paper.

   Prewriting:
   a. Begin by taking notes on Elbow's essay and on Chapter 10. Add to this material anything else that works for you.
   b. Organize the notes into an outline. Remember, you need to order the notes in an appropriate sequence. For example, are the steps chronological (do this, then that)?
   c. Make sure that you have provided adequate transitional step or sequence markers. Underline those that you already have, and, if necessary, add others.

   Rewriting:
   a. Look back over Elbow's essay, and follow his advice in revising your essay.
   b. Elbow's essay is very "reader friendly." He tries to make the process sound easy; he is very reassuring. Is that an effective strategy to use in a process essay? What about your essay? What is its tone? Does it sound helpful? Interesting? Or does it sound boring? Ask a peer reader to characterize the tone of your paper.

3. Interview twenty students, asking them what revision means and how they revise their papers. Try to get a mix of students, not just the students in your English class. Use your interviews to write an essay titled "Revising and the College Writer."

How Books Helped Shape My Life

JUDITH VIORST

Judith Viorst was born in Newark, New Jersey, and educated at Rutgers University. She is a poet, journalist, and writer of children's books. She has worked as contributing editor and columnist for Redbook *magazine and has contributed many of her poems and essays to* The New York Times, New York, Venture, *and* Washington *magazines. Among her better known works are* It's Hard to Be Hip over Thirty and Other Tragedies of Married Life, *a book of poems (1968);* Yes, Married: A Saga of Love and Complaint, *collected prose (1972);* Free to be . . . You and Me, *children's fiction (1974);* Necessary Losses *(1985); and* When Did I Stop Being 20 and Other Injustices: Selected Poems from Single to Mid-Life *(1987). In 1970, Viorst won an Emmy Award for her poetic monologues written for a television special called* Annie: The Women in the Life of a Man. *"How Books Helped Shape My Life" was first published in* Redbook *magazine, a consideration that obviously influenced her choice of subject and approach. Viorst traces the influence of fictional heroines on her own personality—how they served "as ideals, as models, as possibilities."*

In books I've read since I was young I've searched for heroines who could serve as ideals, as models, as possibilities—some reflecting the secret self that dwelled inside me, others pointing to whole new ways that a woman (if only she dared!) might try to be. The person that I am today was shaped by Nancy Drew; by Jo March, Jane Eyre and Heathcliff's soul mate Cathy; and by other fictional females whose attractiveness or character or audacity for a time were the standards by which I measured myself. 1

I return to some of these books to see if I still under- 2

stand the powerful hold that these heroines once had on me. I still understand.

Consider teen-aged Nancy Drew—beautiful, blond-haired, blue-eyed girl detective—who had the most terrific life that I as a ten-year-old could ever imagine. Motherless (in other words, quite free of maternal controls), she lived with her handsome indulgent lawyer father in a large brick house set back from the street with a winding tree-lined driveway on the outside and a faithful, nonintrusive house-keeper Hannah cooking yummy meals on the inside. She also had a boy friend, a convertible, nice clothes and two close girl friends—not as perfect as she, but then it seemed to me that no one could possibly be as perfect as Nancy Drew, who in dozens and dozens of books (*The Hidden Staircase, The Whispering Statue, The Clue in the Diary, The Clue of the Tapping Heels*) was resourceful and brave and intelligent as she went around solving mysteries left and right, while remaining kind to the elderly and invariably polite and absolutely completely delightfully feminine. 3

I mean, what else *was* there? 4

I soon found out what else when I encountered the four March sisters of *Little Women*, a sentimental, old-fashioned book about girls growing up in Civil War time in New England. About spoiled, vain, pretty Amy. And sickly, saintly Beth. And womanly, decent Meg. And about—most important of all—gawky, bookworm Jo. Dear Jo, who wasn't as flawless as the golden Nancy Drew but who showed me that girls like her—like *us*—could be heroines. Even if we weren't much to look at. Even if we were clumsy and socially gauche. And even if the transition into young womanhood often appeared to our dubious eye to be difficult and scary and even unwelcome. 5

Jo got stains on her dress and laughed when she shouldn't and lost her temper and didn't display tact or patience or restraint. Jo brought a touch of irreverence to the cultural constraints of the world she lived in. And yet her instincts were good and her heart was pure and her headstrong ways led always to virtue. And furthermore Jo—as I yearned to be—was a writer! 6

In the book the years go by, Beth dies, Meg and Amy 7
marry and Jo—her fierce heart somewhat tamed—is alone. "An old maid, that's what I'm to be. A literary spinster, with a pen for a spouse, a family of stories for children, and twenty years hence a morsel of fame, perhaps!' . . . Jo sighed, as if the prospect was not inviting."

This worried young reader concurred—not inviting at 8
all!

And so I was happy to read of Jo's nice suitor, Mr. Bhaer, 9
not handsome or rich or young or important or witty, but possessed of kindness and dignity and enough intelligence to understand that even a girl who wasn't especially pretty, who had no dazzling charms and who wanted to write might make a wonderful wife. And a wonderful mother. And live happily ever after.

What a relief! 10

What Jo and Nancy shared was active participation in 11
life—they went out and *did*; they weren't simply done to—and they taught and promised me (at a time when mommies stayed home and there was no Women's Movement) that a girl could go out and do and still get a man. Jo added the notion that brusque, ungainly girls could go out and do and still get a man. And Jane of *Jane Eyre*, whose author once said, "I will show you a heroine as small and as plain as myself," added the further idea that such women were able to "feel just as men feel" and were capable of being just as passionate.

Orphaned Jane, a governess at stately Thornfield Hall, 12
was a no-nonsense lady, cool and self-contained, whose lonely, painful childhood had ingrained in her an impressive firmness of character, an unwillingness to charm or curry favor and a sense of herself as the equal of any man. Said Jane to Mr. Rochester, the brooding, haughty, haunted master of Thornfield: "Do you think I am an automaton?—a machine without feelings? Do you think, because I am poor, obscure, plain, and little, I am soulless and heartless? You think wrong!—I have as much soul as you, and full as much heart!"

I loved it that such hot fires burned inside so plain a 13

Jane. I loved her for her unabashed intensity. And I loved her for being so pure that when she learned of Mr. Rochester's lunatic wife, she sacrificed romance for honor and left him immediately.

For I think it's important to note that Nancy and Jo and Jane, despite their independence, were basically as good as girls can be: honest, generous, kind, sincere, reliable, respectable, possessed of absolute integrity. They didn't defy convention. They didn't challenge the rules. They did what was right, although it might cause them pain. And their virtue was always rewarded—look at Jane, rich and married at last to her Mr. Rochester. Oh, how I identified with Jane! 14

But then I read *Wuthering Heights*, a novel of soul-consuming love on the Yorkshire moors, and Catherine Earnshaw totally captured me. And she captured me, not in spite of her dangerous, dark and violent spirit, but *because* of it. 15

Cathy was as wild as the moors. She lied and connived and deceived. She was insolent, selfish, manipulative and cruel. And by marrying meek, weak Edgar instead of Heathcliff, her destiny, she betrayed a love she described in throbbing, unforgettable prose as . . . elemental: 16

"My love for Heathcliff resembles the eternal rocks beneath—a source of little visible delight, but necessary. Nelly, I *am* Heathcliff—he's always, always in my mind—not as a pleasure, any more than I am always a pleasure to myself—but as my own being. . . ." 17

Now who, at the age of 16, could resist such quivering intensity? Who would settle for less than elemental? Must we untamed creatures of passion—I'd muse as I lay awake in my red flannel nightie—submit ourselves to conventional morality? Or could I actually choose not to be a good girl? 18

Cathy Earnshaw told me that I could. And so did lost Lady Brett, of *The Sun Also Rises*. 19

Brett Ashley was to me, at 18, free, modern, woman incarnate, and she dangled alluring new concepts before my eyes: 20

The value of style: "She wore a slipover jersey sweater 21

and a tweed skirt, and her hair was brushed back like a boy's. She started all that."

The glamour of having a dark and tortured past: 22
"Finally, when he got really bad, he used to tell her he'd kill her. . . . She hasn't had an absolutely happy life."

The excitement of nonconformity: "I've always done 23
just what I wanted."

The importance of (understated) grace under pressure: 24
"Brett was rather good. She's always rather good."

And the thrill of unrepressed sexuality: "Brett's had 25
affairs with men before. She tells me all about everything."

Brett married lovelessly and drank too much and drifted 26
too much and had an irresponsible fling with a bullfighter. But she also had class—and her own morality. She set her bullfighter free— "I'd have lived with him if I hadn't seen it was bad for him." And even though she was broke, she lied and "told him I had scads of it. . . . I couldn't take his money, you know."

Brett's wasn't the kind of morality that my mother was 27
teaching me in suburban New Jersey. But maybe I wasn't meant for suburban life. Maybe—I would muse as I carefully lined my eyes with blue liner—maybe I'm meant for something more . . . emancipated.

I carried Brett's image with me when, after college, I 28
lived for a while in Greenwich Village, in New York. But I couldn't achieve her desperate gallantry. And it struck me that Brett was too lonely and sad, and that Cathy had died too young (and that Scarlett O'Hara got Tara but lost her Rhett), and that maybe I ought to forget about unconventionality if the price was going to be so painfully high. Although I enjoyed my Village fling, I had no wish to live anguishedly ever after. I needed a heroine who, like me, wanted just a small taste of the wild before settling down into happy domesticity.

I found her in *War and Peace*. Her name was Natasha. 29

Natasha, the leading lady of this epic of Russian society 30
during Napoleon's time, was "poetic . . . charming . . . overflowing with life," an enchanting girl whose sweet eagerness and passionate impulsivity were tempered by historic

and private tragedies. Betrothed to the handsome and excellent Prince Andrew, she fell in love with a heel named Anatole, and when she was warned that this foolish and dangerous passion woud lead to her ruin, "I'll go to my ruin . . .," she said, "as soon as possible."

It ended badly with Anatole. Natasha tried suicide. 31
Prince Andrew died. Natasha turned pale, thin, subdued. But unlike Brett and Cathy, her breach with convention was mended and, at long last, she married Pierre—a decent, substantial, loving man, the kind of man all our mothers want us to marry.

In marriage Natasha grew stouter and "the old fire very 32
rarely kindled in her face now." She became an exemplary mother, an ideal wife. "She felt that her unity with her husband was maintained not by the poetic feelings that had attracted him to her but by something else—indefinite but firm as the bond between her own body and soul."

It sounded—if not elemental and doomed—awfully 33
nice.

I identified with Natasha when, the following year, I 34
married and left Greenwich Village. I too was ready for domesticity. And yet . . . her husband and children became "the subject which wholly engrossed Natasha's attention." She had lost herself—and I didn't want to lose me. What I needed next was a heroine who could reconcile all the warring wants of my nature—for fire and quiet, independence and oneness, ambition and love, and marriage and family.

But such reconciling heroines, in novels and real life, 35
may not yet exist.

Nevertheless Natasha and Jane and Jo, Cathy, Nancy 36
and Brett—each spoke to my heart and stirred me powerfully. On my journey to young womanhood I was fortunate to have them as my companions. They were, they will always remain, a part of me.

QUESTIONS ON SUBJECT AND PURPOSE

1. How many heroines does Viorst treat? What does she see in each? How are those qualities related to her own maturation?

2. When you were a child did any hero or heroine seem a particularly attractive model? Was he or she a character in a novel? Has television or film replaced novels as a source of models?
3. Why would any reader be interested in an essay explaining how something shaped your life? Did you find anything of interest here? If so, why? If not, why not?

QUESTIONS ON STRATEGY AND AUDIENCE

1. How does Viorst structure her essay? What progression is there? What controls the arrangement of the heroines?
2. Viorst switches the way she handles her examples when she reaches Lady Brett in *The Sun Also Rises*. Why the change?
3. For whom is Viorst writing? What expectations does she have of her audience? Can you find specific evidence to support your assumptions?

QUESTIONS ON VOCABULARY AND STYLE

1. Viorst frequently uses dashes in her sentences. What is the effect of their use?
2. Viorst seems to delight in breaking the rules we might expect writing to obey. Consider the following categories of examples and be able to show how and why each works in the essay:
   a. Informal, even casual words ("yummy," "a heel")
   b. Clichés ("solving mysteries left and right," "live happily ever after")
   c. Sentence fragments
   d. Extremely short paragraphs
3. Be able to define the following words: *gawky* (paragraph 5), *gauche* (5), *brusque* (11), *curry favor* (12), *unabashed* (13), *incarnate* (20).

WRITING SUGGESTIONS

1. We have all admired someone—either a real person or a fictional one. Select one such model and in a paragraph explain why that particular model was important to you at that particular moment. Remember to keep your paragraph focused on what the model meant or represented to you.
2. "How ——— Helped Shape My Life." Using Viorst's essay as a

structural model, write a process analysis showing how a series of events, situations, or people helped you grow up.

Prewriting:

a. A workable subject must meet two criteria. First, the items in the series must be parallel in form. (Viorst's are all characters from books.) Second, the items must have played a role in your life over a length of time. (Viorst's reflect her reading from age 10 to her mid-20s.) With those criteria in mind, brainstorm a list of possible subjects.
b. Narrow your list to the two best possibilities. Then decide how many time periods you will represent. Viorst includes six. That is probably too many for your essay, but be sure to have at least three. Under each subject, list in outline form the time periods you will include with an example from each.
c. Develop each example clearly. Ask friends who are the same age what they remember about their growing up. Ask them to evaluate the examples you plan to use. That might help add important details.

Rewriting:

a. For each of the examples that you include, complete the following statement: "What this example meant to me was ———." Write your answers on a separate sheet of paper.
b. Look back at Viorst's essay. Not every reader has read these books, so Viorst is careful to explain exactly what was appealing or influential about each one. Have you made your essay accessible to readers?
c. The appeal of Viorst's essay is its universality. Because we all grow up and because we go through certain common stages in that process, we are interested in her analysis. Can you say the same thing about your essay? Have you made it universal enough? Will the reader want to keep reading? Find a peer reader, and check your essay's appeal. If your reader is bored, ask why.

3. In Viorst's pre-teenage years, girls read Nancy Drew and boys read the Hardy Boys. What do pre-teenagers read today? Anything? Research the popularity of books with 10-to-12-year-olds today. You might want to talk with a brother or sister or interview a fifth or sixth grade teacher or an elementary or middle school librarian. What changes have occurred? What do those changes tell us?

On Keeping a Notebook

JOAN DIDION

Another example of Joan Didion's work ("Marrying Absurd") can be found in Chapter 1, and biographical information is given there. Here Didion reveals a vital part of her writing process—keeping a notebook. Didion's essay is not a "how-to-do something" process analysis, but she does use process to describe how and why she keeps a notebook. Along the way, she establishes some crucial distinctions between a notebook and a diary. "The point of my keeping a notebook," she writes, "has never been, nor is it now, to have an accurate factual record of what I have been doing or thinking."

" 'That woman Estelle,' " the note reads, " 'is partly the reason why George Sharp and I are separated today.' *Dirty crepe-de-Chine wrapper, hotel bar, Wilmington RR, 9:45* A.M. *August Monday morning.*" 1

Since the note is in my notebook, it presumably has some meaning to me. I study it for a long while. At first I have only the most general notion of what I was doing on an August Monday morning in the bar of the hotel across from the Pennsylvania Railroad station in Wilmington, Delaware (waiting for a train? missing one? 1960? 1961? why Wilmington?), but I do remember being there. The woman in the dirty crepe-de-Chine wrapper had come down from her room for a beer, and the bartender had heard before the reason why George Sharp and she were separated today. "Sure," he said, and went on mopping the floor. "You told me." At the other end of the bar is a girl. She is talking, pointedly, not to the man beside her but to a cat lying in the triangle of sunlight cast through the open door. She is wearing a plaid silk dress from Peck & Peck, and the hem is coming down. 2

Here is what it is: the girl has been on the Eastern Shore, and now she is going back to the city, leaving the man beside her, and all she can see ahead are the viscous summer sidewalks and the 3 A.M. long-distance calls that will make her lie awake and then sleep drugged through all the steaming mornings left in August (1960? 1961?). Because she must go directly from the train to lunch in New York, she wishes that she had a safety pin for the hem of the plaid silk dress, and she also wishes that she could forget about the hem and the lunch and stay in the cool bar that smells of disinfectant and malt and make friends with the woman in the crepe-de-Chine wrapper. She is afflicted by a little self-pity, and she wants to compare Estelles. That is what that was all about. 3

Why did I write it down? In order to remember, of course, but exactly what was it I wanted to remember? How much of it actually happened? Did any of it? Why do I keep a notebook at all? It is easy to deceive oneself on all those scores. The impulse to write things down is a peculiarly compulsive one, inexplicable to those who do not share it, useful only accidentally, only secondarily, in the way that any compulsion tries to justify itself. I suppose that it begins or does not begin in the cradle. Although I have felt compelled to write things down since I was five years old, I doubt that my daughter ever will, for she is a singularly blessed and accepting child, delighted with life exactly as life presents itself to her, unafraid to go to sleep and unafraid to wake up. Keepers of private notebooks are a different breed altogether, lonely and resistant rearrangers of things, anxious malcontents, children afflicted apparently at birth with some presentiment of loss. 4

My first notebook was a Big Five tablet, given to me by my mother with the sensible suggestion that I stop whining and learn to amuse myself by writing down my thoughts. She returned the tablet to me a few years ago; the first entry is an account of a woman who believed herself to be freezing to death in the Arctic night, only to find, when day broke, that she had stumbled onto the Sahara Desert, where she would die of the heat before lunch. I have no idea what 5 turn of a five-year-old's mind could have prompted so insistently "ironic" and exotic a story, but it does reveal a certain predilection for the extreme which has dogged me into adult life; perhaps if I were analytically inclined I would find it a truer story than any I might have told about Donald Johnson's birthday party or the day my cousin Brenda put Kitty Litter in the aquarium.

So the point of my keeping a notebook has never been, 6
nor is it now, to have an accurate factual record of what I have been doing or thinking. That would be a different impulse entirely, an instinct for reality which I sometimes envy but do not possess. At no point have I ever been able successfully to keep a diary; my approach to daily life ranges from the grossly negligent to the merely absent, and on those few occasions when I have tried dutifully to record a day's events, boredom has so overcome me that the results are mysterious at best. What is this business about "shopping, typing piece, dinner with E, depressed"? Shopping for what? Typing what piece? Who is E? Was this "E" depressed, or was I depressed? Who cares?

In fact I have abandoned altogether that kind of point- 7
less entry; instead I tell what some would call lies. "That's simply not true," the members of my family frequently tell me when they come up against my memory of a shared event. "The party was not for you, the spider was *not* a black widow, *it wasn't that way at all.*" Very likely they are right, for not only have I always had trouble distinguishing between what happened and what merely might have happened, but I remain unconvinced that the distinction, for my purposes, matters. The cracked crab that I recall having for lunch the day my father came home from Detroit in 1945 must certainly be embroidery, worked into the day's pattern to lend verisimilitude; I was ten years old and would not now remember the cracked crab. The day's events did not turn on cracked crab. And yet it is precisely that fictitious crab that makes me see the afternoon all over again, a home movie run all too often, the father bearing gifts, the child weeping, an exercise in family love and guilt. Or that

is what it was to me. Similarly, perhaps it never did snow that August in Vermont; perhaps there never were flurries in the night wind, and maybe no one else felt the ground hardening and summer already dead even as we pretended to bask in it, but that was how it felt to me, and it might as well have snowed, could have snowed, did snow.

How it felt to me: that is getting closer to the truth about a notebook. I sometimes delude myself about why I keep a notebook, imagine that some thrifty virtue derives from preserving everything observed. See enough and write it down, I tell myself and then some morning when the world seems drained of wonder, some day when I am only going through the motions of doing what I am supposed to do, which is write—on that bankrupt morning I will simply open my notebook and there it will be, a forgotten account with accumulated interest, paid passage back to the world out there: dialogue overheard in hotels and elevators and at the hatcheck counter in Pavillon (one middle-aged man shows his hat check to another and says, "That's my old football number"); impressions of Bettina Aptheker and Benjamin Sonnenberg and Teddy ("Mr. Acapulco") Stauffer; careful *aperçus* about tennis bums and failed fashion models and Greek shipping heiresses, one of whom taught me a significant lesson (a lesson I could have learned from F. Scott Fitzgerald, but perhaps we all must meet the very rich for ourselves) by asking, when I arrived to interview her in her orchid-filled sitting room on the second day of a paralyzing New York blizzard, whether it was snowing outside. 8

I imagine, in other words, that the notebook is about other people. But of course it is not. I have no real business with what one stranger said to another at the hatcheck counter in Pavillon; in fact I suspect that the line "That's my old football number" touched not my own imagination at all, but merely some memory of something once read, probably "The Eighty-Yard Run." Nor is my concern with a woman in a dirty crepe-de-Chine wrapper in a Wilmington bar. My stake is always, of course, in the unmentioned girl in the plaid silk dress. *Remember what it was to be me*: that is always the point. 9

It is a difficult point to admit. We are brought up in the ethic that others, any others, all others, are by definition more interesting than ourselves; taught to be diffident, just this side of self-effacing. ("You're the least important person in the room and don't forget it," Jessica Mitford's governess would hiss in her ear on the advent of any social occasion; I copied that into my notebook because it is only recently that I have been able to enter a room without hearing some such phrase in my inner ear.) Only the very young and the very old may recount their dreams at breakfast, dwell upon self, interrupt with memories of beach picnics and favorite Liberty lawn dresses and the rainbow trout in a creek near Colorado Springs. The rest of us are expected, rightly, to affect absorption in other people's favorite dresses, other people's trout. 10

And so we do. But our notebooks give us away, for however dutifully we record what we see around us, the common denominator of all we see is always, transparently, shamelessly, the implacable "I". We are not talking here about the kind of notebook that is patently for public consumption, a structural conceit for binding together a series of graceful *pensées*; we are talking about something private, about bits of the mind's string too short to use, an indiscriminate and erratic assemblage with meaning only for its maker. 11

And sometimes even the maker has difficulty with the meaning. There does not seem to be, for example, any point in my knowing for the rest of my life that, during 1964, 720 tons of soot fell on every square mile of New York City, yet there it is in my notebook, labeled "FACT." Nor do I really need to remember that Ambrose Bierce liked to spell Leland Stanford's name "£eland $tanford" or that "smart women almost always wear black in Cuba," a fashion hint without much potential for practical application. And does not the relevance of these notes seem marginal at best?: 12

In the basement museum of the Inyo County Courthouse in Independence, California, sign pinned to a mandarin coat: "This MANDARIN COAT was often worn by Mrs. Minnie S. 13

Brooks when giving lectures on her TEAPOT COLLECTION."

Redhead getting out of car in front of Beverly Wilshire Hotel, chinchilla stole, Vuitton bags with tags reading:

MRS LOU FOX
HOTEL SAHARA
VEGAS

Well, perhaps not entirely marginal. As a matter of fact, Mrs. Minnie S. Brooks and her MANDARIN COAT pull me back into my own childhood, for although I never knew Mrs. Brooks and did not visit Inyo County until I was thirty, I grew up in just such a world, in houses cluttered with Indian relics and bits of gold ore and ambergris and the souvenirs my Aunt Mercy Farnsworth brought back from the Orient. It is a long way from that world to Mrs. Lou Fox's world where we all live now, and is it not just as well to remember that? Might not Mrs. Minnie S. Brooks help me to remember what I am? Might not Mrs. Lou Fox help me to remember what I am not? 14

But sometimes the point is harder to discern. What exactly did I have in mind when I noted down that it cost the father of someone I know $650 a month to light the place on the Hudson in which he lived before the Crash? What use was I planning to make of this line by Jimmy Hoffa: "I may have my faults, but being wrong ain't one of them"? And although I think it interesting to know where the girls who travel with the Syndicate have their hair done when they find themselves on the West Coast, will I ever make suitable use of it? Might I not be better off just passing it on to John O'Hara? What is a recipe for sauerkraut doing in my notebook? What kind of magpie keeps this notebook? *"He was born the night the Titanic went down."* That seems a nice enough line, and I even recall who said it, but is it not really a better line in life than it could ever be in fiction? 15

But of course that is exactly it: not that I should ever use the line, but that I should remember the woman who said it 16 and the afternoon I heard it. We were on her terrace by the sea, and we were finishing the wine left from lunch, trying to get what sun there was, a California winter sun. The woman whose husband was born the night the *Titanic* went down wanted to rent her house, wanted to go back to her children in Paris. I remember wishing that I could afford the house, which cost $1,000 a month. "Someday you will," she said lazily. "Someday it all comes." There in the sun on her terrace it seemed easy to believe in someday but later I had a low-grade afternoon hangover and ran over a black snake on the way to the supermarket and was flooded with inexplicable fear when I heard the checkout clerk explaining to the man ahead of me why she was finally divorcing her husband. "He left me no choice," she said over and over as she punched the register. "He has a litle seven-month-old baby by her, he left me no choice." I would like to believe that my dread then was for the human condition, but of course it was for me, because I wanted a baby and did not then have one and because I wanted to own the house that cost $1,000 a month to rent and because I had a hangover.

It all comes back. Perhaps it is difficult to see the value 17
in having one's self back in that kind of mood, but I do see it; I think we are well advised to keep on nodding terms with the people we used to be, whether we find them attractive company or not. Otherwise they turn up unannounced and surprise us, come hammering on the mind's door at 4 A.M. of a bad night and demand to know who deserted them, who betrayed them, who is going to make amends. We forget all too soon the things we thought we could never forget. We forget the loves and the betrayals alike, forget what we whispered and what we screamed, forget who we were. I have already lost touch with a couple of people I used to be; one of them, a seventeen-year-old, presents little threat, although it would be of some interest to me to know again what it feels like to sit on a river levee drinking vodka-and-orange-juice and listening to Les Paul and Mary Ford and their echoes sing "How High the Moon" on the car radio. (You see I still have the scenes, but I no longer perceive myself among those present, no longer could even

improvise the dialogue.) The other one, a twenty-three-year old, bothers me more. She was always a good deal of trouble, and I suspect she will reappear when I least want to see her, skirts too long, shy to the point of aggravation, always the injured party, full of recriminations and little hurts and stories I do not want to hear again, at once saddening me and angering me with her vulnerability and ignorance, an apparition all the more insistent for being so long banished.

It is a good idea, then, to keep in touch and I suppose that keeping in touch is what notebooks are all about. And we are all on our own when it comes to keeping those lines open to ourselves: your notebooks will never help me, nor mine you. *"So what's new in the whiskey business?"* What could that possibly mean to you? To me it means a blonde in a Pucci bathing suit sitting with a couple of fat men by the pool at the Beverly Hills Hotel. Another man approaches, and they all regard one another in silence for a while. "So what's new in the whiskey business?" one of the fat men finally says by way of welcome, and the blonde stands up, arches one foot and dips it in the pool, looking all the while at the cabana where Baby Pignatari is talking on the telephone. That is all there is to that, except that several years later I saw the blonde coming out of Saks Fifth Avenue in New York with her California complexion and a voluminous mink coat. In the harsh wind that day she looked old and irrevocably tired to me, and even the skins in the mink coat were not worked the way they were doing them that year, not the way she would have wanted them done, and there is the point of the story. For a while after that I did not like to look in the mirror, and my eyes would skim the newspapers and pick out only the deaths, the cancer victims, the premature coronaries, the suicides, and I stopped riding the Lexington Avenue IRT because I noticed for the first time that all the strangers I had seen for years—the man with the seeing-eye dog, the spinster who read the classified pages every day, the fat girl who always got off with me at Grand Central—looked older than they once had. 18

It all comes back. Even that recipe for sauerkraut: even 19

that brings it back. I was on Fire Island when I first made that sauerkraut, and it was raining, and we drank a lot of bourbon and ate the sauerkraut and went to bed at ten, and I listened to the rain and the Atlantic and felt safe. I made the sauerkraut again last night and it did not make me feel any safer, but that is, as they say, another story.

QUESTIONS ON SUBJECT AND PURPOSE

1. Why does Didion keep a notebook. What types of things does she record? How does a notebook differ from a diary?
2. In paragraph 7, Didion acknowledges that what she records did not always happen and that, for her purposes, it does not really matter. What does she mean by this? Why would she record "lies"?
3. If the notebook helps Didion remember "what it was to be me" (paragraph 9), why should anyone be interested in her essay? Is the essay as egocentric as the notebook? Is there any purpose to this other than self-discovery—what all this means to *me*, Joan Didion?

QUESTIONS ON STRATEGY AND AUDIENCE

1. The essay follows a pattern of discovery. Didion seems to discover why she keeps a notebook as she writes the essay. But that might also be a lie. She might have known before she wrote the essay. Either way, what does such a pattern add to the essay? Why might Didion have chosen to explain in such a way?
2. How effective is the introduction? The conclusion?
3. What do the examples in her notebook tell Didion? What common thread links all of the examples she uses?
4. What expectations does Didion have of her audience? Are they realized? Use your own reading as a test.

QUESTIONS ON VOCABULARY AND STYLE

1. Why does Didion use typographical devices in the essay (things like the italics or the parentheses or the indented entries in paragraph 13)?

2. At a number of points in the essay Didion will ask a group of questions about a particular entry and then go on to answer them. What is the effect of this stylistic device? How is it related to the structure of the essay?
3. Be able to define the following: *crepe-de-Chine* (paragraph 1), *malcontent* (4), *presentiment* (4), *predilection* (5), *verisimilitude* (7), *aperçus* (8), *implacable* (11), *pensées* (11), *ambergris* (14), *recriminations* (17).

WRITING SUGGESTIONS

1. Using the advice that Didion provides (sometimes indirectly) write a paragraph telling the reader how to keep a notebook. Think of your paragraph as something that could be handed out in your English class. Make your advice clear.
2. Both Didion and Judith Viorst describe by means of process how influences and experiences have shaped their lives. Look back on what has brought you here to this present moment. Then select several important events or influences that helped shape your life. Using those examples, write a process analysis on how you have come to be where you are now.

Prewriting:

a. The events/experiences/influences need to be linked only by the extent to which they helped shape your life. They can be different in form; that is, one can be a person, one an experience, one a book. You will probably need three or four at least. Brainstorm a possible list of subjects by starting with this question: "What has made me what I am?" Try to get more examples than you will eventually use. Work on your list for several days.
b. Use freewriting to develop each of the examples that you plan to use. Write for 15 minutes without stopping on each item. You might not use any of this material in your essay, but freewriting will give you a chance to experiment with what you want to say about each item.
c. Plan an organizational strategy by making an outline. The primary sequence will probably be chronological, but that is not necessary. Didion's examples are not arranged chronologically. Maybe a pattern of discovery is better. Compare the organizational patterns used by Viorst and Didion. Can you use either pattern as a model for your essay?

Rewriting:

a. Viorst and Didion use two different techniques to begin their essays; Viorst's introduction is a clear statement of her thesis. Didion's is a journalistic "hook" designed to provoke the reader's curiosity. Both are effective. Look at your introduction. Which strategy do you use? Freewrite an alternative beginning to your paper.

b. Part of the appeal of Didion's essay—like Viorst's—is its universality. We all feel the need to know who we are and who we were. Does your essay have that same appeal? Ask a peer to read your essay and then respond to the following questions: Are the experiences here common? Do you care about the narrator, or do you feel that the narrator is imposing his or her life story on you? Does the writer explain the significance of these events, experiences, and influences? Use your reader's response in revising your essay.

c. It is always good to rethink your organizational strategy. Make a copy of your essay, cut the body paragraphs apart, and rearrange them in an alternative order. (If you are working on a word processor, you can just move test blocks around.) Force yourself to experiment with this change. Is the new order any better? Even if it isn't, the process will make you look in a new way at the sequence you have used.

3. Didion remarks, "I think we are well advised to keep on nodding terms with the people we used to be" (paragraph 17). Try to remember a person you used to be—maybe you at 7 or 14. A photograph is a good place to start. Who were you then? What were your concerns, your fears, your hopes? What was important? Who were your friends? Use a particular moment, a particular memory, or a photograph to recreate the you you used to be.

CHAPTER 7

Cause and Effect

It is a rainy morning and you are late for class. Driving to campus in an automobile with faulty brakes, you have an accident. Considering the circumstances, the accident might be attributable to a variety of causes:

you were driving too fast
the visibility was poor
the roads were slippery
the brakes did not work properly

The accident, in turn, could produce a series of consequences or effects:

you miss class
you get a ticket
your license might be suspended
you might injure yourself or someone else

As this example suggests, cause and effect analyses frequently can go in either direction—an examination of the reasons why something occurred or of the effects or consequences that follow from a particular event or situation.

Causes and effects can be either immediate or remote with reference to time. The two lists above include only immediate causes and effects, those things which are most directly linked in time to the accident. Another pair of lists of more remote causes and effects could be compiled—for example, your brakes were faulty because you did not have the money to fix them, or, because of your accident, your insurance rates will go up.

Causes and effects can be either primary or secondary with reference to their significance or importance. If you had not been in a hurry and driving too fast, it might not have mattered that the visibility was poor, the roads were slippery, or your brakes were faulty. Similarly, if you or someone else had been injured, the other consequences would have seemed insignificant in comparison.

In some instances, causes and effects are linked in a chain: if you were driving too fast and tried to stop on slippery roads with inadequate brakes, then each of those causes is interlinked in the inevitable accident. Likewise, the accident means that you will get a ticket, that ticket carries points against your license, your license could as a result be suspended, and either way your insurance rates will certainly climb.

Why Do You Write a Cause and Effect Analysis?

Cause and effect analyses are intended to explain why something happened or what the consequences are or will be of a particular occurrence. E. M. Forster in "My Wood" examines the effects of owning property. Cullen Murphy in "Going to the Cats" offers an explanation of why there are now more households in America with cats than with dogs. Carll Tucker in "Fear of Dearth" suggests reasons why jogging is popular. Gloria Steinem in "Why Young Women Are More Conservative" analyzes for herself and her readers why as women grow older they are more likely to become active in the feminist movement. Andrew Revkin in "Hard Facts About Nuclear Winter" summarizes for his readers the complex and devastating chain of events a nuclear war could set off.

Cause and effect analyses can also be used to persuade readers to do or believe something. Steinem's explanation for the conservatism of most young women is not a direct plea for an awakening of feminine consciousness, but after reading her essay, it would be more difficult for any reader simply to ignore the issue. Similarly, although Revkin's essay is not a plea for nuclear disarmament, opponents of nuclear weapons could use his analysis to try to persuade an audience of the folly of the arms race.

How Do You Choose a Subject?

In picking a subject to analyze, first remember the limits of your assignment. The larger the subject, the more difficult it will be to do justice to. Trying to analyze the causes of the Vietnam war or the effects of the national deficit in 500 words is an invitation to disaster. Second, make sure that the relationships you see between causes and effects are genuine. The fact that a particular event preceded another does not necessarily mean that the first caused the second. In logic this error is labeled *post hoc, ergo propter hoc* ("after this, therefore because of this").

How Do You Isolate and Evaluate Causes and Effects?

Before you begin to write, take time to analyze and, if necessary, research your subject thoroughly. It is important that your analysis consider all of the major factors involved in the relationship. Relatively few things are the result of a single cause, and rarely does a cause have a single effect. Gloria Steinem acknowledges that the answer to why young women are conservative is not a simple one—it involves a complex series of reasons.

Depending on your subject, your analysis could be based upon personal experience, thoughtful reflection and examination, or research. E. M. Forster's analysis of the effects of owning property is derived completely from studying his own reactions. Gloria Steinem's explanation comes from a decade's experience as a feminist speaker and organizer, coupled with her own personal experience as a maturing adult. Carll Tucker's playful examination of the phenomenon of jogging is a thoughtful reflection upon American values—one that required no special research but rather an application of general knowledge to a specific subject. Andrew Revkin's subject, however, demanded extensive research—interviewing scientists and reading published studies. As these selections show, sometimes causes and effects are certain and unquestionable. Other times, the relationships are only probable or even speculative. Scientists debate, for example, both the likelihood of a nuclear winter and the nature and extent of the effects it might produce.

Once you have gathered a list of possible causes or effects, the next step is to evaluate each item. Since any phenomenon can have many causes or many effects, you will need to select those explanations which seem most relevant or convincing. Rarely should you list every cause or every effect you can find. Generally, you choose those causes or effects which are immediate and primary, although the choice is always determined by your purpose. Tucker, for example, offers a variety of reasons why people jog, ranging from those which are immediate and personal ("to lower blood pressure," "to escape a filthy household") to those which are remote and philosophical ("modern irreligion," "fear of dearth"). He includes the spectrum because his subject is not why any particular individual jogs, but why a substantial portion of an entire nation jogs.

How Do You Structure a Cause and Effect Analysis?

By definition, causes precede effects, so a cause and effect analysis involves a linear or chronological order. Most commonly, you structure your analysis to reflect that sequence. If you are analyzing causes, typically you begin by identifying the subject that you are trying to explain and then move to analyze its causes. Carll Tucker begins with a phenomenon—jogging—that he feels is an effect or result of a set of values or concerns that are shared in our society. The rest of his essay seeks to explain why that phenomenon occurs, to explain its *causes*. Gloria Steinem begins with an observation that has grown out of of her experience, that women, as they grow older, are more likely to become involved in the feminist movement. Her essay then offers an explanation for why that might be. Steinem begins with an effect and then moves to an analysis of its causes.

If you are analyzing effects, typically you begin by identifying the subject that produced the effects and then move to enumerate or explain what those effects were. E. M. Forster begins by describing how he came to purchase his "wood" and then describes four distinct effects that ownership had upon him.

Within these two structural patterns, you face one other choice: If you are listing multiple causes or effects, how do you decide in what order to treat them? That arrangement depends upon whether or not the reasons or consequences are linked in a chain. If they happen in a definite sequence, then you would arrange them in an order to reflect that sequence—normally a chronological order (this happened, then this, finally this). This linear arrangement is very similar to what you do in a process narrative except that your purpose is to answer the question "why" rather than "how." Andrew Revkin's essay shows this chronological pattern of development: exploding nuclear warheads set forests, fields, and cities ablaze; the fires create smoke; the smoke rises and coalesces in the stratosphere, preventing sunlight from reaching earth; the surface temperature on earth plunges; agriculture and ecosystems are destroyed; and life becomes "a nightmarish mix of cold, dark, and starvation."

But multiple causes and effects are not always linked. Steinem's causes do not occur in any inevitable chronological order, nor do Forster's effects. George Orwell in "Politics and the English Language" asserts that the "decline of a language must ultimately have political and economic causes," but no causal chain is involved. If the causes or effects that you have isolated are not linked in a chain, then you must find another way in which to order them. They could be organized from immediate to remote, for example. When there is a varying degree of significance or importance, the most obvious structural choice would be to arrange from the primary to the secondary or from the secondary to the primary. Before you make any arrangement, study your list of causes or effects to see whether any principle of order is evident—chronological, spatial, immediate to remote, primary to secondary. If you see a logical order, follow it.

Writing a Cause and Effect Analysis: A Student Example

For a cause and effect analysis Cathy Ferguson chose to examine the effects that television's depiction of violence has on young children.

TV Aggression and Children

Let's face it. Television producers are out to make money. Their main concern is with what sells. What does sell? Sensationalism. People like shocking stories. In the effort to sell, the limit of the outrageous on TV has been pushed far beyond what it was, say, ten years ago. Television aggression is one aspect of sensationalism that has been exploited to please a thrill-seeking audience. Television is not showing a greater number of aggressive scenes, but the scenes portray more violent and hostile acts. Psychologists, prompted by concerned parents, have been studying the effects of children viewing increased aggression, since the average program for kids contains 20 acts of violence per hour, while the overall average is only 7 acts of violence per hour. Research reveals three outstanding consequences of viewing greater TV hostility. First of all, TV aggression numbs children to real world violence. One experiment showed that even a brief exposure to a fairly violent show made kids indifferent to the same aggression in real life. Preschoolers are especially affected by TV violence because they are usually unable to distinguish between reality and fantasy. If they see a hostile act, they are liable to believe that it is reality, and accept it as "the norm."

This leads to the second effect of viewing TV aggression: a distorted perception of the world. Most TV shows do not present real world consequences of violence; thus children are getting a false picture of their world. Some kids are led to believe that acts of hostility are normal, common, expected even, and may lead a fearfully restricted life. In general, however, most children learn not how to be afraid of violence, but how to be violent, which is the third and most drastic effect of viewing television aggression. Almost all studies show that kids are more aggressive after they watch an aggressive show, like "Batman" or "Superman," than after watching a pro-social show like "Mr. Rogers," or a neutral show. So, although sensationalism, especially violent sensationalism, is making money for TV producers it is also creating a generation that is numb to real violence, has a distorted picture of the environment, and is itself more hostile. These effects are so palpable, it is now realized that the single best predictor of how aggressive an 18 year old will be is how much aggressive television he watched when he was 8 years old.

After Cathy handed in her first draft, she had a conference with her instructor. The instructor commented on her effective use of examples. Because the essay contains specific evidence, the cause and effect analysis seems much more convincing. Since Cathy's purpose was informational rather than persuasive, it was not essential that she provide specific documentation. However, if she had intended to persuade her reader, it would have been necessary to identify the relevant studies.

Her instructor offered some specific advice about revisions in word choice, sentence structure, and paragraph division. He noted that the essay repeated the phrase "television aggression" or a related variant seven times. Since condensed forms can be confusing, he recommended that she indicate that what she was writing about was aggression, violence, or hostility depicted on television shows. Since her first draft begins with five very short sentences and a single-word sentence fragment, he urged her to combine the sentences in order to reduce the choppy effect. Finally, he recommended that she use paragraph divisions to separate the three effects that she discusses. That division would make it easier for her reader to see the structure of the paper.

Cathy's revision addressed each of the problems that had been discussed in conference. In addition, she made a number of minor changes to tighten the prose and make it clearer.

The Influence of Televised Violence on Children

Let's face it. Television producers are in business to make money. Their main concern is what sells, and nothing sells better than sensationalism. In an effort to gain a larger share of the audience, television producers now treat subject matter that would never have been acceptable ten years ago. The depiction of violence on television is one aspect of that sensationalism, exploited to please a thrill-seeking audience. The number of aggressive scenes shown on television has not increased, but those scenes now portray more violent and hostile acts. This is especially true on shows aimed at children.

Psychologists, prompted by concerned parents, have begun studying the effects on children of viewing this increased aggression. The average program for children contains 20 acts of violence per hour compared to an overall average of 7 acts of violence per hour. Research reveals three significant consequences of viewing violence on television.

First, aggressive acts on television numb children to real world violence. One study showed that even a brief exposure to a fairly violent show made children indifferent to the same aggression in real life. Preschoolers are especially affected by television because they are usually unable to distinguish between reality and fantasy. If they see an aggressive act, they are likely to believe that it is real and so accept it as normal.

This potential confusion leads to the second effect of watching violence on television: a distorted perception of the world. Some children are led to believe that acts of hostility are normal, common, and even expected. As a result, these children may lead a restricted life, afraid of the violence which they imagine lurks everywhere.

In general, however, most children learn not to be afraid of violence but how to be violent—the third and most drastic effect of viewing aggression on television. Almost all studies show that children are more aggressive after they watch a show that includes violence than after watching a show that excludes it.

All three effects are so palpable that is is now realized the single best predictor of how aggressive an 18 year old will be is how much violence he watched on television when he was 8 years old.

Some Things to Remember

1. Choose a topic that can be analyzed thoroughly within the limits of the assignment.

2. Decide upon a purpose: are you trying to explain or to persuade?
3. Determine an audience. For whom are you writing? What does your audience already know about your subject?
4. Analyze and research your subject. Remember to provide factual support wherever necessary. Not every cause and effect analysis can rely on unsupported opinion.
5. Be certain that the relationshps you see between causes and effects are genuine.
6. Concentrate your efforts on immediate and primary causes or effects rather than on remote or secondary ones. Do not try to list every cause or every effect that you can.
7. Begin with the cause and then move to effects or begin with an effect and then move to its causes.
8. Look for a principle of order to organize your list of causes or effects. It might be chronological or spatial, or it might move from immediate to remote or from primary to secondary.
9. Remember that you are explaining why something happens or what will happen. You are not just describing how.

Going to the Cats

CULLEN MURPHY

Born in 1952, Cullen Murphy graduated from Amherst College with a B.A. in medieval history. He was senior editor of the Wilson Quarterly *from 1977 to 1985 and since then has served as managing editor of the* Atlantic. *He is also a cartoonist, and since the early 1970s, he has drawn the comic strip* Prince Valiant. *He has contributed essays and articles to the* Atlantic *and* Harper's. *In "Going to the Cats," which orginially appeared in the* Atlantic, *Murphy explores the significance of a "new demographic reality: the number of cats in American households is rapidly overtaking, if it has not already overtaken, the number of dogs." Murphy finds important connections between the change from dogs to cats and other trends in contemporary American life.*

Every decade or so the United States of America crosses some portentous new threshold that symbolizes the nation's evolution from one kind of society into another. It crossed one after the Second World War, when for the first time in history American men bought more belts than they did suspenders. It crossed another in the mid-1950s, when the number of tractors on American farms for the first time exceeded the number of horses. Now, in the 1980s, the country faces a new demographic reality: the number of cats in American households is rapidly overtaking, if it has not already overtaken, the number of dogs. According to the Pet Food Institute, a Washington-based trade association, there were about 18 million more dogs than cats in the United States as recently as a decade ago, but today there are 56 million cats and only 52 million dogs. Actually, because millions of unregistered dogs and cats—the illegal aliens of the animal kingdom—go uncounted, it may be that dogs still maintain a slight edge. But sales of dog food are holding steady, whereas sales of cat food have been increas- 1 ing in recent years at an annual rate of five to eight percent. The trend is clear.

This is not the place to dredge up all the old arguments on the relative merits of cats and dogs, friend of the mouse though I am. But it does seem to me that the displacement of *Canis familiaris* by *Felis catus* might tell us something larger about the condition of the republic, much as from a single drop of rain (to cite Sherlock Holmes's famous example) one might infer the existence of oceans. Consider an America congenial to the dog: it was a place of nuclear or extended families, of someone always home, of children (or pet) looked after during the day by a parent (or owner), of open spaces and family farms, of sticks and leftovers, of expansiveness and looking outward and being outside: it was the America of Willa Cather and Lassie and Leon Leonwood Bean. Consider an America conducive to the cat: it is a place of working men and women with not much time, of crowded cities, of apartment buildings with restrictive clauses, of day-care and take-out food, of self-absorption and modest horizons; it is the America of Tama Janowitz and *Blade Runner* and The Sharper Image catalogue. 2

These generalizations may, I suppose, be extreme, but they are prompted in part by the new, 1987 edition of the *Statistical Abstract of the United States*, which I recently received in the mail. This may be the best book the government publishes, and I wish I could earmark my taxes every year to pay the salary of its editor. According to the *Abstract*, here is some of what has happened to the country from the time when dogs were an overwhelming majority of household pets (I've chosen the early to middle 1970s) to the present day: the amount of land claimed by cities increased by 191,795 square miles, or 49 percent; the number of people living in cities increased by 33 million; the number of households consisting of only one person doubled, to 21 million, and as a proportion of all households increased by 41 percent; the number of families headed by only one parent more than doubled, to 7 million, and as a proportion of all families increased by 100 percent; the proportion of childless couples with both partners in the labor force 3 increased by 9.5 percent; the proportion of working couples with children under three increased by 56 percent; the proportion of new houses having no more than two bedrooms doubled, and the average size of new housing units shrank by nineteen square feet; the number of people living in a typical rental unit declined by 13 percent, to 2.0, and the number living in the average occupant-owned unit declined by 16 percent, to 2.5; the number of miles Americans traveled (including going to work) increased by 631 billion; the amount of money spent on fast food increased by 153 percent; membership in the Boy Scouts and the Girl Scouts declined by 25 percent. The *Abstract* carries a lot of other suggestive data. It provides a recipe, so to speak, for cats.

I do not propose that we attempt to redress the balance. 4
To be sure, I can imagine certain developments, such as a dramatic worsening of the many social and physical ills with which dogs so nobly help us cope, that might foster a resurgence of the canine population, but this prospect is not, on the whole, very inviting. By the same token, I can imagine expedient ways of reducing the feline population to rough parity with the canine one, although perhaps not without harm to the country's liberal democratic traditions. In the end, I think, there is no turning back the clock. As one who has shaken hands with Rin Tin Tin, I mourn the loss of what was good about dog America. But I accept the inevitability of cat America, and all that this implies about life-styles and public policy. I will be surprised indeed if, after the electorate has spoken in 1988, the next First Pet enters the White House on anything other than little cat feet.

QUESTIONS ON SUBJECT AND PURPOSE

1. What type of society was "dog America"? What type is "cat America"?
2. According to Murphy, why is America "going to the cats"?
3. How does Murphy feel about the change in our society? Point to specific passages that reveal his attitude.

QUESTIONS ON STRATEGY AND AUDIENCE

1. How is this a cause and effect analysis? What is the effect? What are the causes?
2. Why might Murphy include so many statistics in paragraph 3? Is this an effective strategy?
3. Does the essay seem to address any particular audience? Does Murphy seem to have any expectations about his readers?

QUESTIONS ON VOCABULARY AND STYLE

1. Characterize the tone of the essay. How is that tone achieved? Does it seem appropriate for this subject?
2. Identify each item in the following comparison from paragraph 2. Explain what each group of items reveals about the changes in American society:

   "Willa Cather and Lassie and Leon Leonwood Bean"

   as compared to

   "Tama Janowitz and *Blade Runner* and The Sharper Image catalogue"
3. Be able to define the following words and phrases: *demographic* (paragraph 1), *congenial* (2), *nuclear or extended family* (2), *conducive* (2), *parity* (4).

WRITING SUGGESTIONS

1. Select an object that has become particularly popular during the last few years. In a paragraph analyze the popularity of this item with reference to the shifting values and concerns in our society. In what ways does this object reflect American life today?
2. To commemorate the start of a new decade, your college has decided to bury a time capsule containing objects or materials that typify American college life. You have been asked to assemble four to six items and then in an essay explain your choices. Your essay will be published as a feature article in the campus newspaper.

   Prewriting:

   a. Remember that the items reflect college life and that your audience is made up of classmates. Before you begin, spend some time thinking about your audience—their characteristics and their concerns. How will that audience influence both what you say and how you say it?

b. Brainstorm about some possible items to include. The items need to be both popular and indicative of our values and concerns in the last few years. Ask friends for suggestions as well.

c. As your list grows, spend 10 to 15 minutes freewriting about each item. Use these freewriting exercises to help define your subject and to analyze the significance of each item. Keep your freewritings focused on both of these concerns.

Rewriting:

a. On a separate sheet of paper, write a one-sentence explanation of the principle of order you have followed in your essay. Brainstorm for some other possibilities for order. Does any alternative order seem more effective?

b. Check how you made the transitions from one item to another, from one paragraph to another. Have you used transitional devices? Do you provide the reader with a clear set of directions about what comes next?

c. Look again at your introdution and conclusion. Put your essay aside, and, without looking at what you have already written, freewrite a new beginning and a new ending. Do not worry about grammar and spelling; concentrate on a new strategy to get your reader interested.

3. Visit your college's library and examine the *Statistical Abstract of the United States*, found in the reference area. Spend some time analyzing the tables and statistics. Look for evidence of change in American society from one period to another. Pick two dates separated by at least a decade. Look for additional sources if necessary. Using the information you have gathered, write a cause and effect research paper analyzing what these changes signaled about American society and why they occurred.

My Wood

E. M. FORSTER

Edward Morgan Forster (1879–1970) was born in London, England, and graduated from King's College, Cambridge University, with a B.A. in classics (1900) and a B.A. in history (1901). In 1910, he earned an M.A., also from Cambridge. Forster spent several years living in Greece, Italy, Egypt, and India. In addition to teaching at Cambridge, he worked as a journalist and as a civil servant in India. He is best known as a novelist, but he also wrote short stories, literary criticism, biographies, histories, and essays. His novels include Where Angels Fear to Tread *(1905),* The Longest Journey *(1907),* A Room With a View *(1908),* Howards End *(1910), and* A Passage to India *(1924). He also published two collections of essays,* Abinger Harvest *(1936) and* Two Cheers for Democracy *(1951). In this essay from* Abinger Harvest, *Forster explores the consequences of owning property. He writes, "Property produces men of weight, and it is a man of weight who failed to get into the Kingdom of Heaven."*

A few years ago I wrote a book which dealt in part with the difficulties of the English in India. Feeling that they would have had no difficulties in India themselves, the Americans read the book freely. The more they read it the better it made them feel, and a cheque to the author was the result. I bought a wood with the cheque. It is not a large wood—it contains scarcely any trees, and it is intersected, blast it, by a public footpath. Still, it is the first property that I have owned, so it is right that other people should participate in my shame, and should ask themselves, in accents that will vary in horror, this very important question: What is the effect of property upon the character? Don't let's touch economics; the effect of private ownership upon the community as a whole is another question—a more important question, perhaps, but another one. Let's keep to psychology. If you own things, what's their effect on you? What's the effect on me of my wood?

In the first place, it makes me feel heavy. Property does have this effect. Property produces men of weight, and it was a man of weight who failed to get into the Kingdom of Heaven. He was not wicked, that unfortunate millionaire in the parable, he was only stout; he stuck out in front, not to mention behind, and as he wedged himself this way and that in the crystalline entrance and bruised his well-fed flanks, he saw beneath him a comparatively slim camel passing through the eye of a needle and being woven into the robe of God. The Gospels all through couple stoutness and slowness. They point out what is perfectly obvious, yet seldom realized: that if you have a lot of things you cannot move about a lot, that furniture requires dusting, dusters require servants, servants require insurance stamps, and the whole tangle of them makes you think twice before you accept an invitation to dinner or go for a bathe in the Jordan. Sometimes the Gospels proceed further and say with Tolstoy that property is sinful; they approach the difficult ground of asceticism here, where I cannot follow them. But as to the immediate effects of property on people, they just show straightforward logic. It produces men of weight. Men of weight cannot, by definition, move like the lightning from the East unto the West, and the ascent of a fourteen-stone bishop into a pulpit is thus the exact antithesis of the coming of the Son of Man. My wood makes me feel heavy. 2

In the second place, it makes me feel it ought to be larger. 3

The other day I heard a twig snap in it. I was annoyed at first, for I thought that someone was blackberrying, and depreciating the value of the undergrowth. On coming nearer, I saw it was not a man who had trodden on the twig and snapped it, but a bird, and I felt pleased. My bird. The bird was not equally pleased. Ignoring the relation between us, it took fright as soon as it saw the shape of my face, and flew straight over the boundary hedge into a field, the prop- 4 erty of Mrs. Henessy, where it sat down with a loud squawk. It had become Mrs. Henessy's bird. Something seemed grossly amiss here, something that would not have occurred had the wood been larger. I could not afford to buy Mrs. Henessy out, I dared not murder her, and limitations of this sort beset me on every side. Ahab did not want that vineyard—he only needed it to round off his property, preparatory to plotting a new curve—and all the land around my wood has become necessary to me in order to round off the wood. A boundary protects. But—poor little thing—the boundary ought in its turn to be protected. Noises on the edge of it. Children throw stones. A little more, and then a little more, until we reach the sea. Happy Canute! Happier Alexander! And after all, why should even the world be the limit of possession? A rocket containing a Union Jack, will, it is hoped, be shortly fired at the moon. Mars. Sirius. Beyond which . . . But these immensities ended by saddening me. I could not suppose that my wood was the destined nucleus of universal dominion—it is so very small and contains no mineral wealth beyond the blackberries. Nor was I comforted when Mrs. Henessy's bird took alarm for the second time and flew clean away from us all, under the belief that it belonged to itself.

In the third place, property makes its owner feel that he 5
ought to do something to it. Yet he isn't sure what. A restlessness comes over him, a vague sense that he has a personality to express—the same sense which, without any vagueness, leads the artist to an act of creation. Sometimes I think I will cut down such trees as remain in the wood, at other times I want to fill up the gaps between them with new trees. But impulses are pretentious and empty. They are not honest movements towards money-making or beauty. They spring from a foolish desire to express myself and from an inability to enjoy what I have got. Creation, property, enjoyment form a sinister trinity in the human mind. Creation and enjoyment are both very, very good, yet they are often unattainable without a material basis, and at such moments property pushes itself in as a substitute, say-

ing, "Accept me instead—I'm good enough for all three." It is not enough. It is, as Shakespeare said of lust, "the expense of spirit in a waste of shame": it is "Before, a joy proposed; behind, a dream." Yet we don't know how to shun it. It is forced on us by our economic system as the alternative to starvation. It is forced on us by an internal defect in the soul, by the feeling that in property may lie the germs of self-development and of exquisite or heroic deeds. Our life on earth is, and ought to be, material and carnal. But we have not learned to manage our materialism and carnality properly; they are still entangled with the desire for ownership, where (in the words of Dante) "Possession is one with loss."

And this brings us to our fourth and final point: the 6
blackberries.

Blackberries are not plentiful in the meagre grove, but 7
they are easily seen from the public footpath which traverses it, and all too easily gathered. Foxgloves, too—people will pull up the foxgloves, and ladies of an educational tendency even grub for toadstools to show them on the Monday in class. Other ladies, less educated, roll down the bracken in the arms of their gentlemen friends. There is paper, there are tins. Pray, does my wood belong to me or doesn't it? And, if it does, should I not own it best by allowing no one else to walk there? There is a wood near Lyme Regis, also cursed by a public footpath, where the owner has not hesitated on this point. He has built high stone walls each side of the path, and has spanned it by bridges, so that the public circulate like termites while he gorges on the blackberries unseen. He really does own his wood, this able chap. Dives in Hell did pretty well, but the gulf dividing him from Lazarus could be traversed by vision, and nothing traverses it here. And perhaps I shall come to this in time. I shall wall in and fence out until I really taste the sweets of property. Enormously stout, endlessly avaricious, pseudo-creative, intensely selfish, I shall weave upon my forehead the quadruple crown of possession until those nasty Bolshies come and take if off again and thrust me aside into the outer darkness.

QUESTIONS ON SUBJECT AND PURPOSE

1. According to Forster, what are the consequences of owning property?
2. Is there any irony in buying property from the royalties earned from a book about England's problems in India?
3. What purpose(s) might Forster have had in writing the essay?

QUESTIONS ON STRATEGY AND AUDIENCE

1. In what way is this a cause and effect essay?
2. Look at the conclusion of the essay. Why does Forster end in this way? Why not add a more conventional conclusion?
3. What expectations does Forster seem to have about his audience? How do you know?

QUESTIONS ON VOCABULARY AND STYLE

1. Characterize the tone of Forster's essay. Is it formal? Informal? How is that tone achieved?
2. Forster makes extensive use of allusion in the essay. Some of the names are easily recognizable, others less so. Identify the allusions below (all but c are to Biblical stories). How does each fit into the context of the essay?
   a. The wealthy man in the parable (paragraph 2)
   b. Ahab and the vineyard (4)
   c. Canute and Alexander (4)
   d. Dives and Lazarus (7)
3. Be able to define the following words: *asceticism* (paragraph 2), *fourteen-stone* (measure of weight, 2), *depreciating* (4), *pretentious* (5), *carnal* (5), *foxgloves* (7), *bracken* (7), *avaricious* (7) *Bolshies* (Bolsheviks, 7).

WRITING SUGGESTIONS

1. Select something that you own, and in a paragraph describe the consequences of your owning it. Has it changed your behavior?
2. Extend the topic above into an essay. You might choose something such as a house, a car, an expensive stereo, a summer

home, a pet, a boat—whatever seems appropriate given your age and background.

Prewriting:

a. Make a list of possible subjects. For each item try to list at least four possible effects of owning it. Do not commit to a specific subject until you have considered the range of possibilities.

b. Once you have selected an item, try freewriting for 15 minutes on each consequence of ownership. You are still gathering ideas for your essay; this material will not necessarily become part of your first draft.

c. The consequences will surely vary in terms of their significance and order of importance. Plan out an organizational strategy. Which effect should come first? Try writing each paragraph on a separate sheet of paper so that you can shuffle their order easily. Consider the alternatives.

Rewriting:

a. Make a brief outline of Forster's essay. It can be used as a model. Try to consider the author's strategy—that is, how did Forster solve the problems that this type of essay poses? Do not just imitate his form.

b. The biggest problem might come in the conclusion. Look at what you have written. Have you avoided an ending that starts, "In conclusion, there are four consequences that result from owning a ———." See if you can end your essay creatively as Forster does.

c. Do you have an interesting title? Do not title your paper "My ———." Remember that titles figure significantly in arousing a reader's curiosity. Brainstorm for some possibilities. Imagine yourself as a copywriter in an advertising agency trying to sell a product.

3. Property ownership has frequently been used throughout history as a precondition for full participation in the affairs of government (voting, for example). A number of states in this country applied such a restriction until the practice was declared unconstitutional. Using outside sources, write a research essay that explains and analyzes, either the reasons for such practices or the reasons against such practices.

Fear of Dearth

CARLL TUCKER

Carll Tucker was born in New York City in 1951 and received a B.A. from Yale University in 1973. An editor and writer, Tucker began his career as a columnist for the Patent Trader *newspaper. He was theater critic and book columnist for the* Village Voice *from 1974 to 1977 and editor of the* Saturday Review *from 1978 to 1981, for which he wrote a regular column. "The Back Door," from which this selection is drawn. In 1983, Tucker assumed the editorship of the* Patent Trader. *Tucker's subject in "Fear of Dearth" is jogging. In a cause and effect analysis, Tucker sets out to explain why Americans choose to jog. "From a practically infinite array of opportunities," he questions, "we select one that we don't enjoy and can't wait to have done with. Why?"*

I hate jogging. Every dawn, as I thud around New York City's Central Park reservoir, I am reminded of how much I hate it. It's so tedious. Some claim jogging is thought conducive; others insist the scenery relieves the monotony. For me, the pace is wrong for contemplation of either ideas or vistas. While jogging, all I can think about is jogging—or nothing. One advantage of jogging around a reservoir is that there's no dry shortcut home. 1

From the listless looks of some fellow trotters, I gather I am not alone in my unenthusiasm: Bill-paying, it seems, would be about as diverting. Nonetheless, we continue to jog; more, we continue to *choose* to jog. From a practically infinite array of opportunities, we select one that we don't enjoy and can't wait to have done with. Why? 2

For any trend, there are as many reasons as there are participants. This person runs to lower his blood pressure. That person runs to escape the telephone or a cranky spouse or a filthy household. Another person runs to avoid doing anything else, to dodge a decision about how to lead his life 3 or a realization that his life is leading nowhere. Each of us has his carrot and stick. In my case, the stick is my slackening physical condition, which keeps me from beating opponents at tennis whom I overwhelmed two years ago. My carrot is to win.

Beyond these disparate reasons, however, lies a deeper 4
cause. It is no accident that now, in the last third of the twentieth century, personal fitness and health have suddenly become a popular obsession. True, modern man likes to feel good, but that hardly distinguishes him from his predecessors.

With zany myopia, economists like to claim that the 5
deeper cause of everything is economic. Delightfully, there seems no marketplace explanation for jogging. True, jogging is cheap, but then not jogging is cheaper. And the scant and skimpy equipment which jogging demands must make it a marketer's least favored form of recreation.

Some scout-masterish philosophers argue that the 6
appeal of jogging and other body-maintenance programs is the discipline they afford. We live in a world in which individuals have fewer and fewer obligations. The work week has shrunk. Weekend worship is less compulsory. Technology gives us more free time. Satisfactorily filling free time requires imagination and effort. Freedom is a wide and risky river; it can drown the person who does not know how to swim across it. The more obligations one takes on, the more time one occupies, the less threat freedom poses. Jogging can become an instant obligation. For a portion of his day, the jogger is not his own man; he is obedient to a regimen he has accepted.

Theologists may take the argument one step further. It 7
is our modern irreligion, our lack of confidence in any hereafter, that makes us anxious to stretch our mortal stay as long as possible. We run, as the saying goes, for our lives, hounded by the suspicion that these are the only lives we are likely to enjoy.

All of these theorists seem to me more or less right. As 8
the growth of cults and charismatic religions and the resurgence of enthusiasm for the military draft suggest, we

do crave commitment. And who can doubt, watching so many middle-aged and older persons torturing themselves in the name of fitness, that we are unreconciled to death, more so perhaps than any generation in modern memory?

But I have a hunch there's a further explanation of our obsession with exercise. I suspect that what motivates us even more than a fear of death is a fear of dearth. Our era is the first to anticipate the eventual depletion of all natural resources. We see wilderness shrinking; rivers losing their capacity to sustain life; the air, even the stratosphere, being loaded with potentially deadly junk. We see the irreplaceable being squandered, and in the depths of our consciousness we are fearful that we are creating an uninhabitable world. We feel more or less helpless and yet, at the same time, desirous to protect what resources we can. We recycle soda bottles and restore old buildings and protect our nearest natural resource—our physical health—in the almost susperstitious hope that such small gestures will help save an earth that we are blighting. Jogging becomes a sort of penance for our sins of gluttony, greed, and waste. Like a hair shirt or a bed of nails, the more one hates it, the more virtuous it makes one feel. 9

That is why *we* jog. Why *I* jog is to win at tennis. 10

QUESTIONS ON SUBJECT AND PURPOSE

1. If asked why they jog, few people would reply, "Fear of dearth." Tucker's essay does not, in fact, concentrate on the obvious and immediate reason why people jog. Why not analyze those reasons?
2. Characterize America's ideal body types. Why are these characteristics valued? What do they reveal about our society's values and preoccupations?
3. Is Tucker being serious in his analysis? How can you tell?

QUESTIONS ON STRATEGY AND AUDIENCE

1. Tucker offers a series of reasons why people jog. Is there any principle of order underlying his arrangement of those reasons?

2. How effective is Tucker's final paragraph? Does it undercut his causal analysis in the previous paragraphs?
3. What expectations does Tucker seem to have about his audience (readers of the *Saturday Review*)? How do you know?

QUESTIONS ON VOCABULARY AND STYLE

1. How effective is Tucker's title? Why might he have chosen that particular title?
2. Be prepared to discuss how each of the following contributes to Tucker's essay:
   a. the opening sentence
   b. the "carrot and stick" image (paragraph 3)
   c. the paragraph dealing with economic causes (5)
   d. the first-person references
3. Be able to define the following words and phrases: *carrot and stick* (paragraph 3), *myopia* (5), *charismatic religions* (8), *dearth* (9), *hair shirt* (9)

WRITING SUGGESTIONS

1. If you engage in any regular athletic activity, analyze the reasons why you do so. Why that activity? What appeals to you? Why bother? If you avoid any such activity, analyze why you do so. Write a paragraph analyzing the reasons for your activity or inactivity.
2. Select another popular American preoccupation and in an essay analyze the reasons for its popularity. Try to avoid the most obvious reasons and focus instead on what this thing or activity reveals about our society. You might consider one of the following possible topics:
   a. bluejeans
   b. skateboards
   c. 10-12-14-speed bicycles
   d. a particular clothing style
   e. MTV or music videos
   f. athletic shoes
   g. VCR's

   Prewriting:

   a. Whatever you choose, it should reveal something popular. Avoid a scientific or technological development unless it is something that could be considered a national obsession. Make a list of possible subjects. What types of objects do your fellow students own? What is considered an essential possession? What seems distinctively American?

b. If possible, interview some students from another country. How do they answer the questions posed above?

c. Remember that your essay will examine the causes of a particular effect. What are the causes of the popularity of this item? You should have multiple causes. Select your two most promising subjects and brainstorm a list of causes for each.

Rewriting:

a. Look again at your list of causes. Have you analyzed the reasons for the item's popularity? Have you given reasons that illuminate our society or our values?

b. Convert the list of things to remember at the end of the introduction to this chapter into a series of questions. Then answer each question honestly. Try to look at your paper as if someone else wrote it.

c. Presumably your essay, because it is about something that appeals to many people, should be of interest to your readers. With that in mind, try to write an introduction that stimulates reader interest. Assume your essay will appear in a popular magazine. Work to grab your reader's attention. Test your introduction on several peer readers. How do they respond? Do they want to keep reading?

3. The ideal man or woman today is thin, athletic, and suntanned. But what is regarded as perfect at one point in time will change in another. Research the ideal body type for both men and women at three points in the twentieth century—for example, 1900, 1940, and 1980. What did the ideal man or woman look like? How did those ideals reflect the values and concerns of society? Using your research, write an essay in which you first define those types and then analyze what they revealed about America at each point in time.

Hard Facts About Nuclear Winter

ANDREW C. REVKIN

Andrew C. Revkin was born in Rhode Island in 1956 and received a B.A. in biology from Brown University. After a two-year period documenting "man's relationship to the sea" as the first mate on a cutter, he enrolled at Columbia University for an M.S. in journalism. He was contributing editor to Offshore Magazine *and editor and senior writer for* Science Digest. *He is now a staff writer for the* Los Angeles Times. *His work has also appeared in a number of other periodicals, including* Stern *(the German weekly) and the* London Sunday Times. *Revkin wrote "Hard Facts About Nuclear Winter," from which this selection is abridged, for* Science Digest. *Working on it, he notes, "required a healthy dose of skepticism because it is such a highly politicized subject. The science was clear enough, but it had been interpreted, adulterated, and exploited by both the right and the left."*

Early in 1979, the Congressional Office of Technology Assessment (OTA) completed a 151-page report called "The Effects of Nuclear War." The first finding, set off in boldface, was *"The effects of a nuclear war that cannot be calculated are at least as important as those for which calculations are attempted."* That has proved to be an unusually apt caveat. 1

Now, only a few years after the OTA report, and four decades after the invention of nuclear weapons, the scientific and defense communities have suddenly learned of an aspect of nuclear war, overlooked by OTA and almost everyone else who had studied the subject, that could prove to be more devastating than any of the other effects—including the blast and radiation. 2

The forgotten factor? Smoke. Government scientists had been studying the physical effects of nuclear explosions for decades, had produced massive volumes full of detailed 3 observations, had scrutinized accounts of the blasts at Hiroshima and Nagasaki, the firestorms at Dresden, Hamburg, and Tokyo. But no one had calculated the climatological effects of the globe-spanning pall of dark smoke that could rise from the thousands of fires ignited by a nuclear war. Indeed, with the exception of two neglected reports produced for the U.S. government in the 1960s, the word *smoke* is hardly mentioned in the scientific literature.

A paper published in the Swedish journal *Ambio* in 4
1982 thus came as a complete surprise, stunning scientists and defense experts alike with its simple, ominous conclusion. Paul Crutzen, a Dutch atmospheric scientist, and John Birks, an American chemist, calculated in a rudimentary but convincing way that smoke from a nuclear war—several hundred million tons of it—"would strongly restrict the penetration of sunlight to the Earth's surface and change the physical properties of the Earth's atmosphere." And their calculations were based only on smoke from burning forests. When another research team considered smoke from burning *cities*, the forgotten factor took on even more significance.

Richard Turco, an atmospheric scientist at R & D Asso- 5
ciates, in Marina del Rey, California, had been working with three researchers at the NASA Ames Research Center, two of whom were former students of Cornell astronomer Carl Sagan, on the atmospheric effects of dust raised by nuclear explosions. When Turco read an advance copy of the *Ambio* study, he immediately saw that smoke would be far more important than dust.

Turco reworked the *Ambio* calculations, adding in the 6
smoke from burning cities. Along with the NASA group—O. Brian Toon, Thomas Ackerman, and James Pollack—and Carl Sagan, he put together a comprehensive analysis, including computer models, of the "global consequences of multiple nuclear explosions." The group, which soon became known at TTAPS (an acronym based on last names), discovered that the smoke could have a devastating effect on the Earth's climate.

The findings were so dramatic, in fact, that in late April 7

1983, more than 100 scientists were invited to a closed session at the American Academy of Arts and Sciences, in Cambridge, Massachusetts, to review the study. The physical scientists met first, testing the assumptions, dissecting the models, checking the data. Some adjustments and refinements were made, but the basic conclusions held.

Then the biologists took a crack at it. They extrapolated from the climatic effects to the impact on agriculture and ecosystems. The destruction wrought by nuclear war, they concluded, would be much greater and more long-lived than anyone had previously conceived. 8

The results were announced to a capacity crowd at a conference in Washington, D.C., on Halloween 1983 and were published in the December 23 issue of *Science*. The TTAPS group concluded that "a global nuclear war could have a major impact on climate—manifested by significant surface darkening over many weeks, subfreezing land temperatures persisting for up to several months, large perturbations in global circulation patterns, and dramatic changes in local weather and precipitation rates—a harsh 'nuclear winter' in any season." 9

The biologists also presented their findings. Their sweeping, controversial conclusion, later published in the same issue of *Science*, was that such a climatic catastrophe could "cause the extinction of a major fraction of the plant and animal species on the Earth. . . . In that event, the possibility of the extinction of *Homo sapiens* cannot be excluded." 10

To be sure, not everyone agreed. A small but powerful cadre of critics, led by Edward Teller, a chief architect of the hydrogen bomb and an important force at Lawrence Livermore National Laboratory, attacked the reports, arguing that the studies were inconclusive and politically motivated. "The only news," Teller says, "is that Sagan has made a lot of propaganda about a very doubtful effect." 11

Three congressional hearings, dozens of scientific meetings, several international conferences, and at least four books later, *nuclear winter* has taken its place—somewhere 12 between *megaton* and *overkill*—in the burgeoning lexicon of terms spawned by the study of nuclear war.

Spelled out, the theory of nuclear winter is as simple as the chill you feel when a cloud passes in front of the sun, and it is as complex as the ever-changing patterns of wind and weather that swirl daily across the surface of the globe. 13

It is based on phenomena as minute as the behavior of the individual particles within a cloud of smoke and on events as massive as the explosion of a thermonuclear warhead with the force of 2 billion pounds of TNT. 14

In general, the theory holds that the sun-hot fireballs of thousands of exploding warheads would set forests, fields, and, especially important, cities ablaze, lofting plumes of dark smoke near the boundary between the troposphere—the lowest region of the atmosphere, where weather occurs—and the stratosphere, the static, weatherless region that starts six to eight miles up. 15

Cities are important because they are loaded with fuel—plastics and petroleum, wood and paper. Reservoirs of oil and gasoline, dense downtowns, and sprawling neighborhoods of wood-frame houses and tenements give cities their high fuel density. Moreover, petroleum and plastics produce more and darker smoke than wood. 16

The individual clouds of smoke would coalesce after a week or two. Pushed by strong west-to-east winds, the smoke would form a uniform belt of particles girdling the Northern Hemisphere from 30 to 60 degrees latitude, a region that reaches from central Florida to southern Alaska. The weapons blasts would also raise tons of dust into the stratosphere, where it can remain for years. 17

The smoke, and to a much smaller extent the dust, would prevent all but a tiny fraction of sunlight from reaching the surface of the Earth in the Northern Hemisphere for weeks, possibly months. According to the TTAPS study, after a "baseline," or medium-size, nuclear war, in which warheads with a total yield of 5,000 megatons were exploded over a variety of targets, average surface temperatures would drop 60 degrees Fahrenheit—below freez- 18 ing even in summer—destroying agriculture, disrupting ecosystems, and making the postwar world a nightmarish mix of cold, dark, and starvation for those humans who survived the other effects. The study also projects the possibility that the high-altitude smoke cloud, and thus the cold and dark, could spread across the equator, plunging sensitive tropical ecosystems and the nations of the Southern Hemisphere into chilly twilight.

By blocking sunlight, the smoke would disrupt the 19
transfer of radiation from the sun that creates and maintains Earth's equable climate. Most of the sun's energy is transmitted as visible light. Sunlight penetrates the atmosphere and strikes the continents and the oceans, which, to varying extents, absorb the energy and heat up. The Earth radiates this energy back toward space in a different form, as infrared radiation.

Fortunately for humans and other life forms, not all of 20
the radiation escapes into space. If it did, the Earth would have a surface temperature below zero Fahrenheit. The heat is trapped by the so-called greenhouse effect. As TTAPS explains, "The atmosphere generally acts as a window for sunlight but a blanket for heat." Carbon dioxide, water vapor, and the water in clouds all absorb some of the escaping energy. The air nearest the surface absorbs the most heat, giving Earth its 56-degree-Fahrenheit average surface temperature. But the air cools rapidly with increasing altitude, to about −67 degrees at the upper limit of the troposphere. The entire troposphere is stirred up and set into motion when the low, heated air masses rise—a process called convection. This is the main source of weather: clouds, wind, and precipitation.

Smoke has optical properties that make it a better 21
blocker of sunlight than dust or water clouds. If enough cities are burned—and according to one of the TTAPS scenarios, 100 cities will suffice—the atmosphere will be turned on its head. Sunlight will be absorbed not at the surface but by the layer of smoke in the upper troposphere. The smoke and the troposphere will heat up, and the Earth

below, deprived of up to 95 percent of its daily ration of solar energy, will cool.

The TTAPS group calls this the "anti-greenhouse effect." One consequence of such a mass inversion would be a lack of convection. With few rising pockets of heated air, there would be little atmospheric turbulence, fewer storms, and thus less of the natural "scavenging" processes, including rain, that normally remove particles from the air. To make matters worse, as the smoke-laden air in the upper troposphere grew warmer, it would tend to rise even higher, taking it farther from the region of cleansing precipitation, perhaps as high as the stagnant stratosphere. The nuclear-winter effect, in Sagan's opinion, could thus be self-perpetuating. 22

At this point, most of the climate-modeling researchers say one thing is clear: *If* enough smoke gets high enough, and stays there long enough, there will be significant surface cooling. But that is a big *if*. Several questions remain, and they all concern smoke. How much is produced? How high does it go? How long does it stay airborne? 23

The amount of smoke produced depends first on the nature of the war. The range of possibilities is impressive—any number of combinations of "counterforce" strikes, against military targets, and "countervalue" strikes, against industrial assets. The only limit is the total number of weapons available. With the combined nuclear arsenals of the United States and the Soviet Union containing 50,000 strategic and tactical weapons that is not much of a limit. 24

More specifically, smoke production depends on how many cities burn. Officially, they are not targeted, but most defense experts assume that it would be impossible to fight a nuclear war without hitting cities. Admiral Noel Gayler, now retired, has been Commander U.S. Forces Pacific, director of the National Security Agency, and deputy director of the Joint Strategic Target Planning Staff. In testimony last year before the Joint Economic Committee of Congress, he said, "Whatever the declarative policy of either country, the weapons that go after leadership, control, military 25 capability, industrial capability, or economic recovery will hit cities. . . . We must face up to it. Whatever our rhetoric or theirs, in a general nuclear war cities will be struck, and they will burn."

The amount of smoke depends not only on how many cities burn but on how *well* they burn. That cities can burn exceptionally well was amply demonstrated in World War II. The Allies raised burning them to a science with a series of devastating raids on German industry and population centers late in the war. 26

The length of time the smoke stays in the atmosphere depends in part on the chemistry of the individual smoke particles. The nature of the particles affects the scavenging rate: Can they provide nuclei upon which water will condense? If so, rainfall following a nuclear war could rapidly clear the air. Do the particles stick together when they collide? This process, called coagulation, makes them fall to Earth faster. And, according to Bob Cess, there is another factor to consider. "I grew up in western Oregon," he says, "where we saw lots of forest-fire smoke in the summertime; it's very light stuff that looks just like water clouds. But a refinery fire is a totally different thing. And I'm sure a burning New York City would produce a different kind of smoke than a burning Moscow. So there's no single smoke characterization that's going to work in this business." 27

How high will the plumes of smoke rise? According to a computer simulation developed at Colorado State University, the smoke may go even higher than TTAPS predicted. William Cotton, an atmospheric scientist, burned Denver. 28

Fortunately for that mile-high city, Cotton did it on a Cray I supercomputer. He used a three-dimensional model that Colorado State researchers had designed to study the behavior of powerful thunderstorms. As far as the atmosphere is concerned, he says, a nuclear explosion and the resulting fires create a "convective disturbance" that is not that different from a thunderstorm; they produce an immense column of rising hot air. Cotton discovered that almost half of the smoke generated by the computerized 29 firestorm was driven into the stratosphere—where it could reside for years instead of months.

There is one more question, perhaps the biggest one of 30
all, that concerns smoke: How could the significance of smoke, the cornerstone of such an enormous, if putative, environmental cataclysm, stay hidden for so long? At a congressional hearing last summer, Richard Wagner, Jr., Assistant to the Secretary of Defense (Atomic Energy), testified, "Not only the Department of Defense but the scientific community in general ought to be a bit chagrined at not realizing that smoke could produce these effects."

John Birks, one of the authors of the *Ambio* study, offers 31
two answers: "Defense scientists, who are the ones funded to look at this, are not attuned to this sort of thing. Their job is to build weapons to prevent war. Their work has focused on prompt effects of single nuclear explosions. They have had no incentive to look at global effects of multiple nuclear explosions." As for why university researchers didn't catch on to the importance of smoke, he says, "You don't get brownie points in academia for studying something as applied as nuclear war. You don't get promotion and tenure and things like that. So there's no incentive there either."

QUESTIONS ON SUBJECT AND PURPOSE

1. What exactly does the term *nuclear winter* mean? How would such a phenomenon be caused?
2. Why have these particular consequences been overlooked until recently?
3. Does Revkin appear to take a stance in the article? Or is the article a neutral summary of the current state of research on nuclear winter and the controversy that surrounds it?

QUESTIONS ON STRATEGY AND AUDIENCE

1. How does Revkin organize his article? Make a brief outline of how the article is constructed.

2. Find some examples of cause and effect in Revkin's essay.
3. What assumptions does Revkin make of his audience? One clue is the frequency with which he defines technical or scientific terms.

QUESTIONS ON VOCABULARY AND STYLE

1. At several points Revkin quotes researchers. What is the value of these quotations? How do they influence the tone of the essay?
2. Revkin is careful to explain scientific terms to his reader. How does he work the definitions into his text?
3. Be able to define the following words: *caveat* (paragraph 1), *pall* (3), *ominous* (4), *rudimentary* (4), *acronym* (6), *extrapolated* (8), *perturbations* (9), *cadre* (11), *burgeoning* (12), *coalesce* (17), *putative* (30), *cataclysm* (30), *chagrined* (30).

WRITING SUGGESTIONS

1. Using the information provided in Revkin's article, write a paragraph in which you summarize the effects that a nuclear winter would produce. Or summarize the causes that would bring about a nuclear winter.
2. Knowing the possible consequences of a nuclear war, why do nations continue to develop and stockpile nuclear weapons? In a cause and effect essay analyze the thinking that has led to the present world situation. If you and your instructor want to add a persuasive element to the assignment, you can develop your essay either as support for the wisdom of such a position or as an attack on the folly behind such thinking.

   Prewriting:
   a. It is not necessary to research the history of nuclear weapons stockpiling to write on this topic. Think about this issue from the point of view of a nation's self-defense, and consider the inevitable escalation that results from most defense technologies. Develop a list of possible causes for stockpiling nuclear weapons. Try for at least four solid ones.
   b. Freewrite for 15 minutes about each reason. Do not stop; do not worry about editing or correcting mistakes. You are just trying to generate ideas.

c. Decide whether or not to put a persuasive slant on the essay. If you choose to do so, read the introduction to Chapter 9 (Argumentation and Persuasion) before you write the first draft.

Rewriting:

a. Look at how you organized the middle of your essay. What principle of order did you follow? For example, did you trace the stages in a chronological order? Did you move from the most significant reason to the least significant? Consider rearranging the middle of your essay. Remember that you need to have a principle. The order of your analysis should not be random.
b. Look at your analysis. Remember that you are not just describing what happened; you are explaining *why* it happened. Ask yourself the following question about each body paragraph: "Does this explain why?"
c. If you have put a persuasive slant on your essay, convert the list of things to remember at the end of the introduction to Chapter 9 into a series of questions. Answer those questions with reference to your essay. Consider those cautions before forming an opinion.

3. Assume that a nuclear bomb will be detonated directly over your college's campus. Using research, trace the results of that explosion. There is an extensive body of literature that deals with the effects. What you need to do is to relate those effects to the particular geographical, typographical, or structural features of your area. Present your findings in an essay intended for the student body at your college.

Why Young Women Are More Conservative

GLORIA STEINEM

Gloria Steinem was born in 1934 in Toledo, Ohio. She earned her B.A. degree in government from Smith College in 1956. In 1968, Steinem helped to found New York *magazine, for which she is now a contributing editor. She cofounded* Ms. *magazine in 1971 and has since served as its editor. Steinem has earned recognition as one of the preeminent leaders of the women's liberation movement and has been active in civil rights organizations, political campaigning, and peace movements. She has contributed to such publications as* Vogue, Cosmopolitan, Time, *and* Esquire. *Her books include* Outrageous Acts and Everyday Rebellions *(1983), a collection of essays, and* Marilyn *(1986), an analysis of Marilyn Monroe's career in Hollywood.*

Steinem starts with what appears to be a reasonable assumption—college-age youth are more likely to be activists and open to change than their parents. But after a decade of traveling to college campuses, she realized that her assumption was wrong—the active feminists are more likely to be middle-aged. In the essay she explores the reason why women, as they grow older, are more interested in the feminist movement.

If you had asked me a decade or more ago, I certainly would have said the campus was the first place to look for the feminist or any other revolution. I also would have assumed that student-age women, like student-age men, were much more likely to be activist and open to change than their parents. After all, campus revolts have a long and well-publicized tradition, from the students of medieval France, whose "heresy" was suggesting that the university be separate from the church, through the anticolonial student riots of British India; from students who led the cultural revolution of the People's Republic of China, to campus demon- 1 strations against the Shah of Iran. Even in this country, with far less tradition of student activism, the populist movement to end the war in Vietnam was symbolized by campus protests and mistrust of anyone over thirty.

It has taken me many years of traveling as a feminist speaker and organizer to understand that I was wrong about women; at least, about women acting on their own behalf. In activism, as in so many other things, I had been educated to assume that men's cultural pattern was the natural or the only one. If student years were the peak time of rebellion and openness to change for men, then the same must be true for women. In fact, a decade of listening to every kind of women's group—from brown-bag lunchtime lectures organized by office workers to all-night rap sessions at campus women's centers, from housewives' self-help groups to campus rallies—has convinced me that the reverse is more often true. Women may be the one group that grows more radical with age. Though some students are big exceptions to this rule, women in general don't begin to challenge the politics of our own lives until later. 2

Looking back, I realize that this pattern has been true for my life, too. My college years were full of uncertainties and the personal conservatism that comes from trying to win approval and fit into the proper grown-up and womanly role, whether that means finding a well-to-do man to be supported by or a male radical to support. Nonetheless, I went right on assuming that brave exploring youth and cowardly conservative old age were the norms for everybody, and that I must be just an isolated and guilty accident. Though every generalization based on female culture has many exceptions, and should never be used as a crutch or excuse, I think we might be less hard on ourselves and each other as students, feel better about our potential for change as we grow older—and educate reporters who announce feminism's demise because its red-hot center is not on campus—if we figured out that for most of us as women, the traditional college period is an unrealistic and cautious time. Consider a few of the reasons. 3

As students, women are probably treated with more 4

equality than we ever will be again. For one thing, we're consumers. The school is only too glad to get the tuitions we pay, or that our families or government grants pay on our behalf. With population rates declining because of women's increased power over childbearing, that money is even more vital to a school's existence. Yet more than most consumers, we're too transient to have much power as a group. If our families are paying our tuition, we may have even less power.

As young women, whether students or not, we're still in the stage most valued by male-dominant cultures: we have our full potential as workers, wives, sex partners, and child-bearers. 5

That means we haven't yet experienced the life events that are most radicalizing for women: entering the paid-labor force and discovering how women are treated there; marrying and finding out that it is not yet an equal partnership having children and discovering who is responsible for them and who is not; and aging, still a greater penalty for women than for men. 6

Furthermore, new ambitions nourished by the rebirth of feminism may make young women feel and behave a little like a classical immigrant group. We are determined to prove ourselves, to achieve academic excellence, and to prepare for interesting and successful careers. More noses are kept to more grindstones in an effort to demonstrate new-found abilities, and perhaps to allay suspicions that women still have to have more and better credentials than men. This doesn't leave much time for activism. Indeed, we may not yet know that it is necessary. 7

In addition, the very progress into previously all-male careers that may be revolutionary for women is seen as conservative and conformist by outside critics. Assuming male radicalism to be the measure of change, they interpret any concern with careers as evidence of "campus conservatism." In fact, "dropping out" may be a departure for men, but "dropping in" is a new thing for women. Progress lies in the direction we have not been. 8

Like most groups of the newly arrived or awakened, our 9

faith in education and paper degrees also has yet to be shaken. For instance, the percentage of women enrolled in colleges and universities has been increasing at the same time that the percentage of men has been decreasing. Among students entering college in 1978, women *outnumbered* men for the first time. This hope of excelling at the existing game is probably reinforced by the greater cultural pressure on females to be "good girls" and observe somebody else's rules.

Though we may know intellectually that we need to 10
have new games with new rules, we probably haven't quite absorbed such facts as the high unemployment rate among female Ph.D.s; the lower average salary among women college graduates of all races than among counterpart males who graduated from high school or less; the middle-management ceiling against which even those eagerly hired new business-school graduates seem to bump their heads after five or ten years; and the barrier-breaking women in nontraditional fields who become the first fired when recession hits. Sadly enough, we may have to personally experience some of these reality checks before we accept the idea that lawsuits, activism, and group pressure will have to accompany our individual excellence and crisp new degrees.

Then there is the female guilt trip, student edition. 11
If we're not sailing along as planned, it must be our fault. If our mothers didn't "do anything" with their educations, it must have been *their* fault. If we can't study as hard as we think we must (because women still have to be better prepared than men), and have a substantial personal and sexual life at the same time (because women are supposed to care more about relationships than men do), then we feel inadequate, as if each of us were individually at fault for a problem that is actually culture-wide.

I've yet to be on a campus where most women weren't 12
worrying about some aspect of combining marriage, children, and a career. I've yet to find one where many men were worrying about the same thing. Yet women will go right on suffering from the double-role problem and terminal guilt until men are encouraged, pressured, or otherwise

forced, individually and collectively, to integrate themselves into the "women's work" of raising children and homemaking. Until then, and until there are changed job patterns to allow equal parenthood, children will go right on growing up with the belief that only women can be loving and nurturing, and only men can be intellectual or active outside the home. Each half of the world will go on limiting the full range of its human talent.

Finally, there is the intimate political training that hits women in the teens and early twenties: the countless ways we are still brainwashed into assuming that women are dependent on men for our basic identities, both in our work and our personal lives, much more than vice versa. After all, if we're going to enter a marriage system that's still legally designed for a person and a half, submit to an economy in which women still average about fifty-nine cents on the dollar earned by men, and work mainly as support staff and assistants, or *co*-directors and *vice*-presidents at best, then we have to be convinced that we are not whole people on our own. 13

In order to make sure that we will see ourselves as half-people, and thus be addicted to getting our identity from serving others, society tries hard to convert us as young women into "man junkies"; that is, into people who are addicted to regular shots of male-approval and presence, both professionally and personally. We need a man standing next to us, actually and figuratively, whether it's at work, on Saturday night, or throughout life. (If only men realized how little it matters *which* man is standing there, they would understand that this addiction depersonalizes them, too.) Given the danger to a male-dominant system if young women stop internalizing this political message of derived identity, it's no wonder that those who try to kick the addiction—and, worse yet, to help other women do the same—are likely to be regarded as odd or dangerous by everyone from parents to peers. 14

With all that pressure combined with little experience, it's no wonder that younger women are often less able to support each other. Even young women who espouse femi- 15 nist goals as individuals may refrain from identifying themselves as "feminist": it's okay to want equal pay for yourself (just one small reform) but it's not okay to want equal pay for women as a group (an economic revolution). Some retreat into individualized career obsessions as a way of avoiding this dangerous discovery of shared experience with women as a group. Others retreat into the safe middle ground of "I'm not a feminist but. . . ." Still others become politically active, but only on issues that are taken seriously by their male counterparts.

The same lesson about the personal conservatism of 16 younger women is taught by the history of feminism. If I hadn't been conned into believing the masculine stereotype of youth as the "natural" time for freedom and rebellion, a time of "sowing wild oats" that actually is made possible by the assurance of power and security later on, I could have figured out the female pattern of activism by looking at women's movements of the past.

In this country, for instance, the nineteenth-century 17 wave of feminism was started by older women who had been through the radicalizing experience of getting married and becoming the legal chattel of their husbands (or the equally radicalizing experience of not getting married and being treated as spinsters). Most of them had also worked in the antislavery movement and learned from the political parallels between race and sex. In other countries, that wave was also led by women who were past the point of maximum pressure toward marriageability and conservatism.

Looking at the first decade of this second wave, it's clear 18 that the early feminist activist and consciousness-raising groups of the 1960s were organized by women who had experienced the civil rights movement, or homemakers who had discovered that raising kids and cooking didn't occupy all their talents. While most campuses of the late sixties were still circulating the names of illegal abortionists privately (after all, abortion could damage our marriage value), slightly older women were holding press conferences and speak-outs about the reality of abortions (including their own, even though that often meant confessing to an illegal act) and demanding reform or repeal of antichoice laws. Though rape had been a quiet epidemic on campus for generations, younger women victims were still understandably fearful of speaking up, and campuses encouraged silence in order to retain their reputation for safety with tuition-paying parents. It took many off-campus speak-outs, demonstrations against laws of evidence and police procedures, and testimonies in state legislatures before most student groups began to make demands on campus and local cops for greater rape protection. In fact, "date rape"—the common campus phenomenon of a young woman being raped by someone she knows, perhaps even by several students in a fraternity house—is just now being exposed. Marital rape, a more difficult legal issue, was taken up several years ago. As for battered women and the attendant exposé of husbands and lovers as more statistically dangerous than unknown muggers in the street, that issue still seems to be thought of as a largely noncampus concern, yet at many of the colleges and universities where I've spoken, there has been at least one case within current student memory of a young woman beaten or murdered by a jealous lover.

This cultural pattern of youthful conservatism makes 19
the growing number of older women going back to school very important. They are life examples and pragmatic activists who radicalize women young enough to be their daughters. Now that the median female undergraduate age in this country is twenty-seven because so many older women have returned, the campus is becoming a major place for cross-generational connections.

None of this should denigrate the courageous efforts of 20
young women, especially women on campus, and the many changes they've pioneered. On the contrary, they should be seen as even more remarkable for surviving the conservative pressures, recognizing societal problems they haven't yet fully experienced, and organizing successfully in the midst of a transient student population. Every women's history course, rape hot line, or campus newspaper that is finally covering *all* the news; every feminist

professor whose job has been created or tenure saved by student pressure, or male administrator whose consciousness has been permanently changed; every counselor who's stopped guiding women one way and men another; every lawsuit that's been fueled by student energies against unequal athletic funds or graduate school requirements: all those accomplishments are even more impressive when seen against the back-drop of the female pattern of activism.

Finally, it would help to remember that a feminist revo- 21
lution rarely resembles a masculine-style one—just as a young woman's most radical act toward her mother (that is, connecting as women in order to help each other get some power) doesn't look much like a young man's most radical act toward his father (that is, breaking the father-son connection in order to separate identities or take over existing power).

It's those father-son conflicts at a generational, national 22
level that have often provided the conventional definition of revolution; yet they've gone on for centuries without basically changing the role of the female half of the world. They have also failed to reduce the level of violence in society, since both fathers and sons have included some degree of aggressiveness and superiority to women in their definition of masculinity, thus preserving the anthropological model of dominance.

Furthermore, what current leaders and theoreticians 23
define as revolution is usually little more than taking over the army and the radio stations. Women have much more in mind that that. We have to uproot the sexual caste system that is the most pervasive power structure in society, and that means transforming the patriarchal values of those who run the institutions, whether they are politically the "right" or the "left," the fathers or the sons. This cultural part of the change goes very deep, and is often seen as too intimate, and perhaps too threatening, to be considered as either serious or possible. Only conflicts among men are "serious." Only a takeover of existing institutions is "possible."

That's why the definition of "political," on campus as 24

elsewhere, tends to be limited to who's running for president, who's demonstrating against corporate investments in South Africa, or which is the "moral" side of some conventional revolution, preferably one that is thousands of miles away.

As important as such activities are, they are also the most comfortable ones when we're young. They provide a sense of virtue without much disruption in the power structure of our daily lives. Even when the most consistent energies on campus are actually concentrated around feminist issues, they may be treated as apolitical and invisible. Asked "What's happening on campus?" a student may reply, "The antinuke movement," even though that resulted in one demonstration of two hours, while student antirape squads have been patrolling the campus every night for two years and women's studies have begun to transform the very textbooks we read. 25

No wonder reporters and sociologists looking for revolution on campus often miss the depth of feminist change and activity that is really there. Women students themselves may dismiss it as not political and not serious. Certainly, it rarely comes in the masculine sixties style of bombing buildings or burning draft cards. In fact, it goes much deeper than protesting a temporary symptom—say, the draft—and challenges the right of one group to dominate another, which is the disease itself. 26

Young women have a big task of resisting pressures and challenging definitions. Their increasing success is a miracle of foresight and courage that should make us all proud. But they should know that they, too, may grow more radical with age. 27

One day, an army of gray-haired women may quietly take over the earth. 28

QUESTIONS ON SUBJECT AND PURPOSE

1. What does Steinem mean by the word *conservative*? In what ways are young women conservative?

2. According to Steinem what are the causes of this conservatism?
3. In what ways do women's cultural patterns differ from men's?

QUESTIONS ON STRATEGY AND AUDIENCE

1. How does Steinem structure her cause and effect analysis? Is there a particular order to her list of causes?
2. How effective is Steinem's conclusion? Does it seem appropriate? Why or why not?
3. What assumptions does Steinem make about her audience? How are those assumptions revealed in the essay?

QUESTIONS ON VOCABULARY AND STYLE

1. Why does Steinem write in the first person ("I")? How would the essay be different if she had avoided all first-person references? If she had not interwoven her experiences with the social commentary?
2. How would you describe Steinem's tone in the essay? What does that tone come from? How formal or informal is her language? Her sentence structure?
3. Be able to define the following words: *demise* (paragraph 3), *transient* (4), *espouse* (15), *chattel* (17), *denigrate* (20).

WRITING SUGGESTIONS

1. In a paragraph summarize Steinem's analysis. Do not quote her exactly. Focus instead on summarizing her reasons for this phenomenon.
2. The 1980s have been a relatively quiet time on college campuses, with few protests about anything. Why should this be? What accounts for the quiet atmosphere on campuses? In a cause and effect essay aimed at your college classmates, explore this situation. As a variation, you might write for an audience of parents of the average college freshman today.

   Prewriting:

   a. If you accept the premise that college students today are not active in social and political issues, you will need to isolate some possible reasons or causes for that apathy. Start by asking yourself what is particularly important to *you*; what are *you* concerned about? As you list the topics, try to record a reason for each concern. (For example, "I am concerned about getting a high-paying job because by the time I graduate, I will have borrowed $15,000 to finance my education.")

b. Extend your information-gathering by polling friends and classmates. Develop both a list of concerns and a list of possible explanations for those concerns. Ideally you should interview ten people, trying for a wide range of ages and backgrounds.

c. Look over the list that you have gathered. Some reasons for student concerns will be more common and more significant than others. Since you are trying to explain the generalized behavior of a large group of people, concentrate on reasons which seem primary and immediate. Place an asterisk next to those items on your lists that seem most important. Then plan an order for those items. You will need to cite at least three possible causes for the apathy of students.

Rewriting:

a. How have you defined your audience? On a separate sheet of paper, analyze the characteristics of that audience. Now look back at the draft of your essay. Have you written to that audience? List the specific ways in which your essay—in its introduction, its style, its examples—acknowledges that audience.

b. Find at least one peer reader. Ask the reader if your essay seems like an adequate (or insightful) explanation. Does the essay analyze your generation? Is it fair? Does it distort?

c. Although Steinem's essay is long and sophisticated, it can serve as a good structural model. Study it again as a writer looking to see how another writer handled a similar subject. You are not imitating form; you are observing technique.

3. On the average, women today still do not earn as much money as men, although the "fifty-nine cents on the dollar" cited by Steinem has increased slightly. Research the problem. Why do women earn less? Present your evidence in a cause and effect analysis.

Politics and the English Language

GEORGE ORWELL

George Orwell—the pen name of Eric Arthur Blair (1903-1950)—was born in Motihari, India, the son of an English colonial administrator. After studying at Eton, Orwell served for five years as a police official in Rangoon, Burma. In 1928, he embarked on a three-year investigation of poverty in London's East End—experiences recorded in his first book, Down and Out in Paris and London *(1933). Attracted to socialism, in 1936 he joined the Loyalists in Spain and was severely wounded during the Spanish Civil War.* Homage to Catalonia *(1938) is a memoir of his experiences in the war. In addition to his best-known works,* Animal Farm *(1945) and* 1984 *(1949), Orwell produced a vast amount of journalism, essays, and reviews. Though much of his writing is political, Orwell's political beliefs do not fall into any neat ideological category. Though a socialist, he was frequently critical of communism, the intellectual Left, and the socialist tendency toward totalitarianism. His writing is marked by an independence of mind, a hatred of oppression, and a sympathy for the underdog. In the following essay, first published in 1946, Orwell reveals how the debasement of language serves the cause of tyranny.*

Most people who bother with the matter at all would admit 1
that the English language is in a bad way, but it is generally assumed that we cannot by conscious action do anything about it. Our civilization is decadent and our language—so the argument runs—must inevitably share in the general collapse. It follows that any struggle against the abuse of language is a sentimental archaism, like preferring candles to electric light or hansom cabs to airplanes. Underneath this lies the half-conscious belief that language is a natural growth and not an instrument which we shape for our own purposes.

Now, it is clear that the decline of a language must 2
ultimately have political and economic causes: it is not due simply to the bad influence of this or that individual writer. But an effect can become a cause, reinforcing the original cause and producing the same effect in an intensified form, and so on indefinitely. A man may take to drink because he feels himself to be a failure, and then fail all the more completely because he drinks. It is rather the same thing that is happening to the English language. It becomes ugly and inaccurate because our thoughts are foolish, but the slovenliness of our language makes it easier for us to have foolish thoughts. The point is that the process is reversible. Modern English, especially written English, is full of bad habits which spread by imitation and which can be avoided if one is willing to take the necessary trouble. If one gets rid of these habits one can think more clearly, and to think clearly is a necessary first step towards political regeneration: so that the fight against bad English is not frivolous and is not the exclusive concern of professional writers. I will come back to this presently, and I hope that by that time the meaning of what I have said here will have become clearer. Meanwhile, here are five specimens of the English language as it is now habitually written.

These five passages have not been picked out because 3
they are especially bad—I could have quoted far worse if I had chosen—but because they illustrate various of the mental vices from which we now suffer. They are little below the average, but are fairly representative samples. I number them so that I can refer back to them when necessary:

> (1) I am not, indeed, sure whether it is not true to say that the Milton who once seemed not unlike a seventeenth-century Shelley had not become, out of an experience ever more bitter in each year, more alien [*sic*] to the founder of that Jesuit sect which nothing could induce him to tolerate.
>
> Professor Harold Laski (Essay in *Freedom of Expression*).

> (2) Above all, we cannot play ducks and drakes with a native battery of idioms which prescribes such egregious colloca-

tions of vocables as the Basic *put up with* for *tolerate* or *put at a loss* for *bewilder*.

Professor Lancelot Hogben (*Interglossa*).

(3) On the one side we have the free personality: by definition it is not neurotic, for it has neither conflict nor dream. Its desires, such as they are, are transparent, for they are just what institutional approval keeps in the forefront of consciousness; another institutional pattern would alter their number and intensity; there is little in them that is natural, irreducible, or culturally dangerous. But *on the other side*, the social bond itself is nothing but the mutual reflection of these self-secure integrities. Recall the definition of love. Is not this the very picture of a small academic? Where is there a place in this hall of mirrors for either personality or fraternity?

Essay on psychology in *Politics* (New York).

(4) All the "best people" from the gentlemen's clubs, and all the frantic fascist captains, united in common hatred of Socialism and bestial horror of the rising tide of the mass revolutionary movement, have turned to acts of provocation, to foul incendiarism, to medieval legends of poisoned wells, to legalize their own destruction of proletarian organizations, and rouse the agitated petty-bourgeoisie to chauvinistic fervor on behalf of the fight against the revolutionary way out of the crisis.

Communist pamphlet.

(5) If a new spirit *is* to be infused into this old country, there is one thorny and contentious reform which must be tackled, and that is the humanization and galvanization of the BBC. Timidity here will bespeak canker and atrophy of the soul. The heart of Britain may be sound and of strong beat, for instance, but the British lion's roar at present is like that of Bottom in Shakespeare's *Midsummer Night's Dream*—as gentle as any sucking dove. A virile new Britain cannot continue indefinitely to be traduced in the eyes, rather ears, of the world by the effete languors of Langham Place, brazenly masquerading as "standard English." When the Voice of Britain is heard at nine o'clock, better far and infinitely less ludicrous to hear aitches honestly dropped then the present priggish, inflated, inhibited, school-ma'amish arch braying of blameless bashful mewing maidens!

Letter in *Tribune*.

Each of these passages has faults of its own, but quite apart from avoidable ugliness, two qualities are common to all of them. The first is staleness of imagery: the other is lack of precision. The writer either has a meaning and cannot express it, or he inadvertently says something else, or he is almost indifferent as to whether his words mean anything or not. The mixture of vagueness and sheer incompetence is the most marked characteristic of modern English prose, and especially of any kind of political writing. As soon as certain topics are raised, the concrete melts into the abstract and no one seems to think of turns of speech that are not hackneyed: prose consists less and less of *words* chosen for the sake of their meaning, and more and more of *phrases* tacked together like the sections of a prefabricated henhouse. I list below, with notes and examples, various of the tricks by means of which the work of prose construction is habitually dodged: 4

Dying Metaphors. A newly invented metaphor assists thought by evoking a visual image, while on the other hand a metaphor which is technically "dead" (e.g., *iron resolution*) has in effect reverted to being an ordinary word and can generally be used without loss of vividness. But in between these two classes there is a huge dump of worn-out metaphors which have lost all evocative power and are merely used because they save people the trouble of inventing phrases for themselves. Examples are *Ring the changes on, take up the cudgels for, toe the line, ride roughshod over, stand shoulder to shoulder with, play into the hands of, no axe to grind, grist to the mill, fishing in troubled waters, rift within the lute, on the order of the day, Achilles' heel, swan song, hotbed.* Many of these are used without knowledge of their meaning (what is a "rift," for instance?), and incompatible metaphors are frequently mixed, a sure sign that the writer is not interested in what he is saying. Some metaphors now current have been twisted out of their original meaning without those who use them even being aware of the fact. For example, *toe the line* is sometimes written *tow the line.* Another example is 5 the *hammer and the anvil* now always used with the implication that the anvil gets the worst of it. In real life it is always the anvil that breaks the hammer, never the other way about: a writer who stopped to think what he was saying would be aware of this, and would avoid perverting the original phrase.

Operators or Verbal False Limbs. These save the trouble of picking out appropriate verbs and nouns, and at the same time pad each sentence with extra syllables which give it an appearance of symmetry. Characteristic phrases are: *render inoperative, militate against, make contact with, be subjected to, give rise to, give grounds for, have the effect of, play a leading part (role) in, make itself felt, take effect, exhibit a tendency to, serve the purpose of,* etc., etc. The keynote is the elimination of simple verbs. Instead of being a single word, such as *break, stop, spoil, mend, kill,* a verb becomes a *phrase,* made up of a noun or adjective tacked on to some general-purposes verb such as *prove, serve, form, play, render.* In addition, the passive voice is wherever possible used instead of gerunds (*by examination of* instead of *by examining*). The range of verbs is further cut down by means of the *-ize* and *de-* formations, and banal statements are given an appearance of profundity by means of the *not un-* formation. Simple conjunctions and prepositions are replaced by such phrases as *with respect to, having regard to, the fact that, by dint of, in view of, in the interests of, on the hypothesis that;* and the ends of sentences are saved from anticlimax by such resounding commonplaces as *greatly to be desired, cannot be left out of account, a development to be expected in the near future, deserving of serious consideration, brought to a satisfactory conclusion,* and so on and so forth. 6

Pretentious Diction. Words like *phenomenon, element, individual* (as noun), *objective, categorical, effective, virtual, basic, primary, promote, constitute, exhibit, exploit, utilize, eliminate, liquidate,* are used to dress up simple statements and give an air of scientific impartiality 7 to biased judgments. Adjectives like *epoch-making, epic, historic, unforgettable, triumphant, age-old, inevitable, inexorable, veritable,* are used to dignify the sordid processes of international politics, while writing that aims at glorifying war usually takes on an archaic color, its characteristic words being: *realm, throne, chariot, mailed fist, trident, sword, shield, buckler, banner, jackboot, clarion.* Foreign words and expressions such as *cul de sac, ancien régime, deus ex machina, mutatis mutandis, status quo, Gleichschaltung, Weltanschauung,* are used to give an air of culture and elegance. Except for the useful abbreviations *i.e., e.g,* and *etc.,* there is no real need for any of the hundreds of foreign phrases now current in English. Bad writers, and especially scientific, political, and sociological writers, are nearly always haunted by the notion that Latin or Greek words are grander than Saxon ones, and unnecessary words like *expedite, ameliorate, predict, extraneous, deracinated, clandestine, subaqueous,* and hundreds of others constantly gain ground from their Anglo-Saxon opposite numbers.* The jargon peculiar to Marxist writing (*hyena, hangman, cannibal, petty bourgeois, these gentry, lackey, flunkey, mad dog, White Guard,* etc.) consists largely of words and phrases translated from Russian, German, or French; but the normal way of coining a new word is to use a Latin or Greek root with the appropriate affix and, where necessary, the *-ize* formation. It is often easier to make up words of this kind (*deregionalize, impermissible, extramarital, nonfragmentatory* and so forth) than to think up the English words that will cover one's meaning. The result, in general, is an increase in slovenliness and vagueness.

Meaningless Words. In certain kinds of writing, particularly in art criticism and literary criticism, it is normal to come across long passages which are almost completely 8

*An interesting illustration of this is the way in which the English flower names which were in use till very recently are being ousted by Greek ones, *snapdragon* becoming *antirrhinum, forget-me-not* becoming *myosotis,* etc. It is hard to see any practical reason for this change of fashion: it is probably due to an instinctive turning-away from the more homely word and a vague feeling that the Greek word is scientific.

lacking in meaning.* Words like *romantic, plastic, values, human, dead, sentimental, natural, vitality,* as used in art criticism, are strictly meaningless in the sense that they not only do not point to any discoverable object, but are hardly ever expected to do so by the reader. When one critic writes, "The outstanding feature of Mr. X's work is its living quality," while another writes, "The immediately striking thing about Mr. X's work is its peculiar deadness," the reader accepts this as a simple difference of opinion. If words like *black* and *white* were involved, instead of the jargon words *dead* and *living,* he would see at once that language was being used in an improper way. Many political words are similarly abused. The word *Fascism* has now no meaning except in so far as it signifies "something not desirable." The words *democracy, socialism, freedom, patriotic, realistic, justice,* have each of them several different meanings which cannot be reconciled with one another. In the case of a word like *democracy,* not only is there no agreed definition, but the attempt to make one is resisted from all sides. It is almost universally felt that when we call a country democratic we are praising it: consequently the defenders of every kind of regime claim that it is a democracy, and fear that they might have to stop using the word if it were tied down to any one meaning. Words of this kind are often used in a consciously dishonest way. That is, the person who uses them has his own private definition, but allows his hearer to think he means something quite different. Statements like *Marshal Pétain was a true patriot, The Soviet Press is the freest in the world, The Catholic Church is opposed to persecution,* are almost made with intent to deceive. Other words used in variable meanings, in most cases more or less dishonestly, are: *class, totalitarian, science, progressive, reactionary, bourgeois, equality.*

*Example: "Comfort's catholicity of perception and image, strangely Whitmanesque in range, almost the exact opposite in aesthetic compulsion, continues to evoke trembling atmospheric accumulative hinting at a cruel, an inexorably serene timelessness. . . . Wrey Gardiner scores by aiming at simple bull's eyes with precision. Only they are not so simple, and through this contented sadness runs more than the surface bittersweet of resignation." (*Poetry Quarterly.*)

9 Now that I have made this catalogue of swindles and perversions, let me give another example of the kind of writing that they lead to. This time it must of its nature be an imaginary one. I am going to translate a passage of good English into modern English of the worst sort. Here is a well-known verse from *Ecclesiastes*:

> I returned and saw under the sun, that the race is not to the swift, nor the battle to the strong, neither yet bread to the wise, nor yet riches to men of understanding, nor yet favor to men of skill; but time and chance happeneth to them all.

Here it is in modern English:

> Objective consideration of contemporary phenomena compels the conclusion that success or failure in competitive activities exhibits no tendency to be commensurate with innate capacity, but that a considerable element of the unpredictable must invariably be taken into account.

10 This is a parody, but not a very gross one. Exhibit (3), above, for instance, contains several patches of the same kind of English. It will be seen that I have not made a full translation. The beginning and ending of the sentence follow the original meaning fairly closely, but in the middle the concrete illustrations—race, battle, bread—dissolve into the vague phrase "success or failure in competitive activities." This had to be so, because no modern writer of the kind I am discussing—no one capable of using phrases like "objective consideration of contemporary phenomena"—would ever tabulate his thoughts in that precise and detailed way. The whole tendency of modern prose is away from concreteness. Now analyze these two sentences a little more closely. The first contains forty-nine words but only sixty syllables, and all its words are those of everyday life. The second contains thirty-eight words of ninety syllables: eighteen of its words are from Latin roots, and one from Greek. The first sentence contains six vivid images, and only one phrase ("time and chance") that could be called vague. The second contains not a single fresh, arresting phrase, and in spite of its ninety

syllables it gives only a shortened version of the meaning contained in the first. Yet without a doubt it is the second kind of sentence that is gaining ground in modern English. I do not want to exaggerate. This kind of writing is not yet universal, and outcrops of simplicity will occur here and there in the worst-written page. Still, if you or I were told to write a few lines on the uncertainty of human fortunes, we should probably come much nearer to my imaginary sentence than to the one from *Ecclesiastes.*

As I have tried to show, modern writing at its worst does 11
not consist in picking out words for the sake of their meaning and inventing images in order to make the meaning clearer. It consists in gumming together long strips of words which have already been set in order by someone else, and making the results presentable by sheer humbug. The attraction of this way of writing is that it is easy. It is easier—even quicker once you have the habit—to say *In my opinion it is a not unjustifiable assumption that* than to say *I think*. If you use ready-made phrases, you not only don't have to hunt about for words; you also don't have to bother with the rhythms of your sentences, since these phrases are generally so arranged as to be more or less euphonious. When you are composing in a hurry—when you are dictating to a stenographer, for instance, or making a public speech—it is natural to fall into a pretentious, Latinized style. Tags like *a consideration which we should do well to bear in mind* or *a conclusion to which all of us would readily assent* will save many a sentence from coming down with a bump. By using stale metaphors, similes and idioms, you save much mental effort, at the cost of leaving your meaning vague, not only for your reader but for yourself. This is the significance of mixed metaphors. The sole aim of a metaphor is to call up a visual image. When these images clash—as in *The Fascist octopus has sung its swan song, the jackboot is thrown into the melting pot*—it can be taken as certain that the writer is not seeing a mental image of the objects he is naming; in other words he is not really thinking. Look again at the examples I gave at the beginning of this essay. Professor Laski (1) uses five negatives in fifty-

three words. One of these is superfluous, making nonsense of the whole passage, and in addition there is the slip *alien* for *akin*, making a further nonsense, and several avoidable pieces of clumsiness which incease the general vagueness. Professor Hogben (2) plays ducks and drakes with a battery which is able to write prescriptions, and, while disapproving of the everyday phrase *put up with*, is unwilling to look *egregious* up in the dictionary and see what it means. (3), if one takes an uncharitable attitude towards it, is simply meaningless: probably one could work out its intended meaning by reading the whole of the article in which it occurs. In (4), the writer knows more or less what he wants to say, but an accumulation of stale phrases chokes him like tea leaves blocking a sink. In (5), words and meaning have almost parted company. People who write in this manner usually have a general emotional meaning—they dislike one thing and want to express solidarity with another—but they are not interested in the detail of what they are saying. A scrupulous writer, in every sentence that he writes, will ask himself at least four questions, thus: What am I trying to say? What words will express it? What image or idiom will make it clearer? Is this image fresh enough to have an effect? And he will probably ask himself two more: Could I put it more shortly? Have I said anything that is avoidably ugly? But you are not obliged to go to all this trouble. You can shirk it by simply throwing your mind open and letting the ready-made phrases come crowding in. They will construct your sentences for you—even think your thoughts for you, to a certain extent—and at need they will perform the important service of partially concealing your meaning even from yourself. It is at this point that the special connection between politics and the debasement of language becomes clear.

In our time it is broadly true that political writing is bad 12
writing. Where it is not true, it will generally be found that the writer is some kind of rebel, expressing his private opinions and not a "party line." Orthodoxy, of whatever color, seems to demand a lifeless, imitative style. The political dialects to be found in pamphlets, leading articles, man-

ifestos, White Papers and the speeches of under-secretaries do, of course, vary from party to party, but they are all alike in that one almost never finds in them a fresh, vivid, homemade turn of speech. When one watches some tired hack on the platform mechanically repeating the familiar phrases—*bestial atrocities, iron heel, bloodstained tyranny, free peoples of the world, stand shoulder to shoulder*—one often has a curious feeling that one is not watching a live human being but some kind of dummy; a feeling which suddenly becomes stronger at moments when the light catches the speaker's spectacles and turns them into blank discs which seem to have no eyes behind them. And this is not altogether fanciful. A speaker who uses that kind of phraseology has gone some distance towards turning himself into a machine. The appropriate noises are coming out of his larynx, but his brain is not involved as it would be if he were choosing his words for himself. If the speech he is making is one that he is accustomed to make over and over again, he may be almost unconscious of what he is saying, as one is when one utters the responses in church. And this reduced state of consciousness, if not indispensable, is at any rate favorable to political conformity.

In our time, political speech and writing are largely the 13
defense of the indefensible. Things like the continuance of British rule in India, the Russian purges and deportations, the dropping of the atom bombs on Japan, can indeed be defended, but only by arguments which are too brutal for most people to face, and which do not square with the professed aims of political parties. Thus political language has to consist largely of euphemism, question-begging and sheer cloudy vagueness. Defenseless villages are bombarded from the air, the inhabitants driven out into the countryside, the cattle machine-gunned, the huts set on fire with incendiary bullets: this is called *pacification*. Millions of peasants are robbed of their farms and sent trudging along the roads with no more than they can carry: this is called *transfer of population* or *rectification of frontiers*. People are imprisoned for years without trial, or shot in the back of the neck or sent to die of scurvy in Arctic lumber camps:

this is called *elimination of unreliable elements*. Such phraseology is needed if one wants to name things without calling up mental pictures of them. Consider for instance some comfortable English professor defending Russian totalitarianism. He cannot say outright, "I believe in killing off your opponents when you can get good results by doing so." Probably, therefore, he will say something like this:

"While freely conceding that the Soviet régime exhibits 14
certain features which the humanitarian may be inclined to deplore, we must, I think, agree that a certain curtailment of the right to political opposition is an unavoidable concomitant of transitional periods, and that the rigors which the Russian people have been called upon to undergo have been amply justified in the sphere of concrete achievement."

The inflated style is itself a kind of euphemism. A mass 15
of Latin words fall upon the facts like soft snow, blurring the outlines and covering up all the details. The great enemy of clear language is insincerity. When there is a gap between one's real and one's declared aims, one turns as it were instinctively to long words and exhausted idioms, like a cuttlefish squirting out ink. In our age there is no such thing as "keeping out of politics." All issues are political issues, and politics itself is a mass of lies, evasions, folly, hatred and schizophrenia. When the general atmosphere is bad, language must suffer. I should expect to find—this is a guess which I have not sufficient knowledge to verify—that the German, Russian and Italian languages have all deteriorated in the last ten or fifteen years, as a result of dictatorship.

But if thought corrupts language, language can also cor- 16
rupt thought. A bad usage can spread by tradition and imitation, even among people who should and do know better. The debased language that I have been discussing is in some ways very convenient. Phrases like *a not unjustifiable assumption, leaves much to be desired, would serve no good purpose, a consideration which we should do well to bear in mind*, are a continuous temptation, a packet of aspirins always at one's elbow. Look back through this

essay, and for certain you will find that I have again and again committed the very faults I am protesting against. By this morning's post I have received a pamphlet dealing with conditions in Germany. The author tells me that he "felt impelled" to write it. I open it at random, and here is almost the first sentence that I see: "(The Allies) have an opportunity not only of achieving a radical transformation of Germany's social and political structure in such a way as to avoid a nationalistic reaction in Germany itself, but at the same time of laying the foundations of a co-operative and unified Europe." You see, he "feels impelled" to write—feels, presumably, that he has something new to say—and yet his words, like cavalry horses answering the bugle, group themselves automatically into the familiar dreary pattern. This invasion of one's mind by ready-made phrases (*lay the foundations, achieve a radical transformation*) can only be prevented if one is constantly on guard against them, and every such phrase anesthetizes a portion of one's brain.

I said earlier that the decadence of our language is proba- 17
bly curable. Those who deny this would argue, if they produced an argument at all, that language merely reflects existing social conditions, and that we cannot influence its development by any direct tinkering with words and constructions. So far as the general tone or spirit of a language goes, this may be true, but it is not true in detail. Silly words and expressions have often disappeared, not through any evolutionary process but owing to the conscious action of a minority. Two recent examples were *explore every avenue* and *leave no stone unturned,* which were killed by the jeers of a few journalists. There is a long list of flyblown metaphors which could similarly be got rid of if enough people would interest themselves in the job; and it should also be possible to laugh the *not un-* formation out of existence,* to reduce the amount of Latin and Greek in the average sentence, to drive out foreign phrases and strayed scientific

*One can cure oneself of the *not un-* formation by memorizing this sentence: *A not unblack dog was chasing a not unsmall rabbit across a not ungreen field.*

words, and, in general, to make pretentiousness unfashionable. But all these are minor points. The defense of the English language implies more than this, and perhaps it is best to start by saying what it does *not* imply.

To begin with it has nothing to do with archaism, with 18
the salvaging of obsolete words and turns of speech, or with the setting up of a "standard English" which must never be departed from. On the contrary, it is especially concerned with the scrapping of every word or idiom which has outworn its usefulness. It has nothing to do with correct grammar and syntax, which are of no importance so long as one makes one's meaning clear, or with the avoidance of Americanisms, or with having what is called a "good prose style." On the other hand it is not concerned with fake simplicity and the attempt to make written English colloquial. Nor does it even imply in every case preferring the Saxon word to the Latin one, though it does imply using the fewest and shortest words that will cover one's meaning. What is above all needed is to let the meaning choose the word, and not the other way about. In prose, the worst thing one can do with words is to surrender to them. When you think of a concrete object, you think wordlessly, and then, if you want to describe the thing you have been visualizing you probably hunt about till you find the exact words that seem to fit. When you think of something abstract you are more inclined to use words from the start, and unless you make a conscious effort to prevent it, the existing dialect will come rushing in and do the job for you, at the expense of blurring or even changing your meaning. Probably it is better to put off using words as long as possible and get one's meaning as clear as one can through the pictures or sensations. Afterwards one can choose—not simply *accept*—the phrases that will best cover the meaning and then switch round and decide what impression one's words are likely to make on another person. This last effort of the mind cuts out all stale or mixed images, all prefabricated phrases, needless repetitions, and humbug and vagueness generally. But one can often be in doubt about the effect of a word or phrase, and

one needs rules that one can rely on when instinct fails. I think the following rules will cover most cases:

(i) Never use a metaphor, simile or other figure of speech which you are used to seeing in print.
(ii) Never use a long word where a short one will do.
(iii) If it is possible to cut a word out, always cut it out.
(iv) Never use the passive where you can use the active.
(v) Never use a foreign phrase, a scientific word or a jargon word if you can think of an everyday English equivalent.
(vi) Break any of these rules sooner than say anything outright barbarous.

These rules sound elementary, and so they are, but they demand a deep change in attitude in anyone who has grown used to writing in the style now fashionable. One could keep all of them and still write bad English, but one could not write the kind of stuff that I quoted in those five specimens at the beginning of this article.

I have not here been considering the literary use of 19
language, but merely language as an instrument for expressing and not for concealing or preventing thought. Stuart Chase and others have come near to claiming that all abstract words are meaningless, and have used this as a pretext for advocating a kind of political quietism. Since you don't know what Fascism is, how can you struggle against Fascism? One need not swallow such absurdities as this, but one ought to recognize that the present political chaos is connected with the decay of language, and that one can probably bring about some improvement by starting at the verbal end. If you simplify your English, you are freed from the worst follies of orthodoxy. You cannot speak any of the necessary dialects, and when you make a stupid remark its stupidity will be obvious, even to yourself. Political language—and with variations this is true of all political parties, from Conservatives to Anarchists—is designed to make lies sound truthful and murder respectable, and to give an appearance of solidity to pure wind. One cannot

change this all in a moment, but one can at least change one's own habits, and from time to time one can even, if one jeers loudly enough, send some worn-out and useless phrase—some *jackboot, Achilles' heel, hotbed, melting pot, acid test, veritable inferno* or other lump of verbal refuse—into the dustbin where it belongs.

QUESTIONS ON SUBJECT AND PURPOSE

1. From the outset of the essay, Orwell insists: "The decline of a language must ultimately have political and economic causes." What does he mean by that? Similarly, later on he writes: "All issues are political issues." What does that mean?
2. How many types of careless English does Orwell find? How does he subdivide his subject?
3. In paragraph 17, Orwell writes: "The decadence of our language is probably curable." How is it curable? What are we, as readers, to do to combat this "decadence"?

QUESTIONS ON STRATEGY AND AUDIENCE

1. How does cause and effect analysis underlie Orwell's argument? What is the cause of these effects ("slovenliness of our language"?)
2. In addition to cause and effect how many other rhetorical strategies do you see in Orwell's essay? Make a list with the relevant paragraph numbers.
3. How does Orwell structure his argument? Make a brief outline of the essay.

QUESTIONS ON VOCABULARY AND STYLE

1. What is the difference between words derived from Latin and Greek and words derived from Anglo-Saxon? Make a list of a few words pairing up the two types of words. Why does Orwell prefer Anglo-Saxon derived words? The preface of a college dictionary will be a help in establishing the difference.
2. In paragraph 16, Orwell writes: "Look back through this essay, and for certain you will find that I have again and again com-

mitted the very faults I am protesting against." Can you find examples of "faults" in Orwell's prose?

3. Be able to define the following words: *decadent* (paragraph 1), *archaism* (1), *slovenliness* (2), *frivolous* (2), *inadvertently* (4), *hackneyed* (4), *banal* (6), *sordid* (7), *regime* (8), *euphonious* (11), *scrupulous* (11), *shirk* (11), *concomitant* (14).

WRITING SUGGESTIONS

1. Using the material provided by Orwell, write a paragraph in which you summarize his cause and effect argument. Do not quote Orwell directly; summarize his analysis in your own words.
2. Look for examples of the type of prose about which Orwell is writing. Bureaucracies of all types—federal and state governments, big business, and even college and university administrations—tend to be good sources. Language is used to obscure information and to justify action (or the lack of it). Collect a range of examples, and, in a cause and effect analysis, explain how and why such words and phrases are used.

Prewriting:

a. Several days before your essay is due, start gathering examples. Newspapers and magazines are always good places to look. Remember that any subject that is potentially embarrassing is a likely candidate—waste disposal, foreign aid to "freedom fighters," tuition increases, plant closings and employee firings, defense spending.
b. Once you have gathered a list of examples, sort them into categories based on what they have in common. What strategies are the writers of such words and phrases using?
c. For each example, suggest in a sentence the reason(s) why such abuse occurs. Remember that you are explaining and analyzing; you are not just giving examples.

Rewriting:

a. The body of your essay could be arranged in several possible ways—that is, there may be no reason why this cause should come first, that one second. Make a copy of your essay, cut the body paragraphs apart, and rearrange them in an alternate order. Does this make the paper any more effective?
b. Are your examples vivid enough? Appropriate? Ask a peer to read your essay and answer those two questions. Can the

reader think of any examples that you might have overlooked?

c. Look again at the conclusion to your paper. Ending effectively is not always easy. Check the advice about conclusions given in the Glossary, and then freewrite another ending to your essay.

3. Nuclear weaponry and the prospect of thermonuclear war have had their own impact on our language (e.g., MX missiles are now Peacekeepers). Research the language associated with these phenomena. Then, using examples, explain how and why such language is used.

C H A P T E R

8

Definition

On the mid-term examination in your introductory economics class only the essay question remains to be answered: "What is capitalism?" You are tempted to write the one-sentence definition you memorized from the glossary of your textbook and dash from the room. On the other hand, it is unlikely that your professor will react positively or even charitably to such a skimpy (and memorized) response. Instead, you realize that what is needed is an extended definition—one that explains what factors were necessary before capitalism could emerge, what elements are most characteristic of a capitalistic economy, how capitalism differs from other economic systems, how a capitalistic economy works, how capitalism is linked to technology and politics. What you need is a narrative, a division, a comparison and contrast, a process, and a cause and effect analysis all working together to give you a full definition of what is finally a very complex term.

When you are asked to define a word, you generally do two things: first, you provide a dictionary-like definition, normally a single sentence; and second, if the occasion demands, you provide a longer, extended definition, analyzing the subject, giving examples or details. If you use technical or specialized words that may be unfamiliar to your reader, you include a parenthetical definition: "Macroeconomics, the portion of economics concerned with large-scale movements such as inflation and deflation, is particularly interested in changes in the GNP, or gross national product."

Most writing situations, especially those you encounter in college, require extended definitions. The selections in this chapter define a variety of subjects, and they suggest how differently definitions can be handled. E. B. White tackles in a short paragraph the complex term *democracy*; Theodore M. Bernstein defines *cliché*; Marie Winn explains what it means to be a "TV addict"; Judy Syfers tries to define the term *wife*; Susan Brownmiller explores the shifting meaning of the word *femininity* in our society; and Loren Eiseley writes about his search for what is probably undefinable—"the secret of life."

Definitions can be denotative or connotative or a mixture of the two. Dictionary definitions are denotative; that is, they offer a literal and explicit definition of a word. Theodore M. Bernstein provides a denotative definition of a cliché: "an overworked, commonplace expression." But words do not always just have literal meanings; they often carry either positive or negative connotations, and these connotations can vary depending on the situation. The term *democracy*, especially when used during wartime, suggests not just a form of government, but a whole way of life. To capture that significance, E. B. White provides a connotative definition—in this instance a series of examples that reveal metaphorically the meaning of democracy.

How Much Do You Include in a Definition?

Every word, whether it refers to a specific physical object or to the most theoretical concept, has a dictionary definition. Whether that one-sentence definition is sufficient depends upon why you are defining the word. For example, the Writers' War Board could have found a definition of the word *democracy* in any dictionary: "government by the people, exercised either directly or through elected representatives." The board knew what a democracy was, so why did it ask E. B. White? Surely the board wanted something more than a dictionary definition, and considering that its request came during the middle of World War II, when the country was waging war in both Europe and the Pacific, the reason for its letter to White seems understandable: it was a way of asking, "What are we, as a nation, fighting to preserve?" White's answer fits the occasion: he provided fourteen different examples of what democracy means.

Similarly, if you were asked, "What is a wife?" you could reply, "A woman married to a man." While that definition is accurate, it does not convey any sense of what such a relationship might involve. Judy Syfers's "I Want a Wife" defines by showing what men (or some men) expect in a wife. Her essay divides and lists a wife's many responsibilities—things expected of her by an actual or potential husband. Syfers's essay, comically overstated as it is, offers a far more meaningful definition of the term *wife* than any one-sentence dictionary entry. Her intention surely was to reveal inequality in marriage, and she makes her point by listing a stereotypical set of male expectations.

Writing a definition is a fairly common activity in college work. In your literature course you are asked to define the romantic movement; in art history, the baroque period; in psychology, abnormal behavior. Since a single-sentence definition can never do justice to such complicated terms, an extended definition is necessary. In each case, the breadth and depth of your knowledge is being tested; your professor expects you to formulate a definition that accounts for the major subdivisions and characteristics of the subject. Your purpose is to convince your professor that you have read and mastered the assigned materials and can select and organize them, often adding some special insight of your own, into a logical and coherent response.

How Do You Structure a Definition?

Sentence definitions are relatively easy to write. You first place the word in a general class ("A wife is a woman") and then add any distinguishing features that set it apart from other members of the class ("married to a man"). The types of definitions you are asked to write are generally more detailed than dictionary entries. How then do you get from a single sentence to a paragraph or an essay?

Extended definitions do not have a structure peculiar to themselves. That is, when you write a definition you do not have a predetermined structural pattern as you do with comparison and contrast, division and classification, process, or cause and effect. Instead, definitions are constructed by using all of the various strategies discussed in this book. E. B. White and Theodore M. Bernstein use examples to define the terms *democracy* and *cliché*. As the selections progress from these two fairly short and simple definitions to the more complex ones, the types of strategies that the writers employ, in addition to example, increase. Marie Winn uses analogy to liken addiction to television viewing to addiction to alcohol or drugs and through a pattern of cause and effect shows why television experiences do not provide "true nourishment" for a viewer. Judy Syfers's definition of a wife uses division to organize the many types of responsibilities demanded of a wife. Susan Brownmiller begins with a narrative of her own experiences with femininity as she moved from childhood into adulthood and then employs a cause and effect analysis to show how cultural biases help define and condition "feminine" behavior. Narration and description are part of Loren Eiseley's search for the definition of "the secret of life."

Once you have chosen a subject for definition, think first about its essential characteristics, steps, or parts. What examples would best define it? Then plan your organization by seeing how those details can be presented most effectively to your reader. If your definition involves breaking a subject into its parts, use division or possibly even process. If you are defining by comparing your subject to another, use a comparison and contrast structure. If your subject is defined as the result of some causal connection, use a cause and effect structure. Definitions can also involve narration, description, and even persuasion. The longer the extended definition, the greater is the likelihood that your paper will involve a series of structures. E. B. White's definition is just a series of examples, but Loren Eiseley's essay to some extent uses each of the strategies covered in this book.

Writing a Definition: A Student Example

Like many people, Lyndsey Curtis is a cat lover, and that determined her choice of subject. Lyndsey, probably influenced by having read Judy Syfers's essay, decided to define the *essence* of a cat:

Felis Catus

Webster's New Collegiate Dictionary defines *cat* as "a carnivorous mammal (*Felis catus*) long domesticated and kept by man as a pet or for catching rats and mice." That is fine if you are interested in a scientific definition. In my opinion, however, if doesn't even begin to tap into the essence of that phenomenon known as "cat."

Cats perform many practical services. On cold winter nights, they keep your feet as warm as an electric blanket but without using electricity. They act as alarm clocks in the morning; it's time for you to get up when they want to be fed. Wouldn't you rather wake up to the gentle but insistent tap of a soft furry paw on your forehead than to a loud, obnoxious buzzing noise anyway? Cats are very entertaining. They are excellent subjects for photographs, as you can easily determine by setting foot inside any true cat lover's home; the walls are inevitably adorned with pictures of his or her favorite feline. They provide "musical enjoyment" for you and your neighbors when they "sing" to each other on warm summer nights. They can supply topics for hours of conversation between mutual cat lovers, who always enjoy recounting their favorite cat story. More important, however, is the emotional completeness a cat brings to your life.

When you've lived with cats your whole life as I have, you begin to realize that they are really just like people and that they become members of your family very quickly. Cats are very reliable; you can always depend on them to know when it is time to go out, when it is time to play, when it is time to eat, and when it is time to sleep (most of the day). They teach children about responsibility, love, and the importance of caring for another living being. In addition, they provide companionship for many lonely people. They sense when you are feeling upset or depressed and will always try to make you feel better by climbing up onto your lap with a great purr. A cat's love is unconditional as long as you care for him or her properly. They'll love you despite all your faults; they'll love you when it seems that no one else in the world will. They'll greet

> you at the door when you come home after a rough day at the office and will listen to your problems and complaints without interrupting. Cats are always there when you need a friend. B. Kliban, in his 1975 book *Cat,* put it very aptly when he defined a cat as "one Hell of a nice animal, frequently mistaken for a meatloaf."

On the peer editing checksheet for definition essays, one of the questions concerned opening sentences: "Does the essay avoid the standard 'according to Webster. . . '?" When Lyndsey's essay was read in class during a peer editing session, several students asked about the wisdom of beginning in this way. The class agreed, however, that even though it is generally not a good idea to begin a definition with a quotation from a dictionary, the device works fairly well here since Lyndsey is trying to show how inadequate that denotative definition is. The strong point of the essay, everyone felt, was its division into "practical services" and "emotional completeness." The transition between the two halves comes smoothly and naturally. The other area that troubled the peer readers was Lyndsey's ending. As one student observed, "Your final quotation from Kliban's book seems inappropriate. You have been making some lighthearted but still serious points, and to end suddenly on such a cynical quotation introduces an abrupt change in tone." When Lyndsey came to revise her essay, she tried to address the problems that the peer editors had raised.

The Essence of Cat

> The dictionary defines *cat* as "a carnivorous mammal (*Felis catus*) long domesticated and kept by man as a pet or for catching rats and mice." That is fine if you are interested in a scientific definition. In my opinion, however, it does not even begin to tap into the essence of that phenomenon known as "cat."
>
> Cats perform many practical services. On cold winter nights, they keep your feet as warm as an electric blanket would, but they do it without using electricity. They act as alarm clocks in the morning; it is time to get up when they want to be fed. Wouldn't you rather wake up to the gentle but insistent tap of a soft paw on your forehead than to a loud, obnoxious buzzing noise? Cats are very entertaining. They are excellent subjects for photographs, as you can easily see from

the pictures of felines that cover the walls of any true cat lover's home. They provide "musical enjoyment" for you and your neighbors, "singing" to each other on warm summer nights. They can supply topics for hours of conversation between cat lovers, who always enjoy recounting their favorite cat stories. More important, however, is the emotional completeness a cat brings to your life.

When you have lived with cats your whole life as I have, you begin to realize that they are really just like people and that they become members of your family very quickly. Cats are very reliable; you can always depend on them to know when it is time to eat, and when it is time to sleep (most of the day). They teach children about responsibility, love, and the importance of caring for another living being. In addition, they provide companionship for many lonely people. They sense when you are feeling upset or depressed and will always try to make you feel better by climbing onto your lap with a great purr. A cat's love is unconditional as long as you care for him or her properly. Cats will love you despite all your faults; they will love you when it seems that no one else in the world will. They will greet you at the door when you come home after a rough day at the office and will listen to your problems and complaints without interrupting. Cats are always there when you need a friend.

Some Things to Remember

1. Choose a subject that can be reasonably and fully defined within the limits of your paper. That is, make sure it is neither too limited nor too large.
2. Determine a purpose for your definition.
3. Spend time analyzing your subject to see what its essential characteristics, steps, or parts are.
4. Write a dictionary definition for your subject. Do this even if you are writing an extended definition. The features that set your subject apart from others in its general class reveal what must be included in your definition.
5. Choose examples that are clear and appropriate.
6. Decide which of the organizational patterns will best convey the information you have gathered.
7. Be careful about beginning, "According to Webster. . . ." There are usually more effective and interesting ways to announce your subject.

Democracy

E. B. WHITE

E. B. White's essay "Once More to the Lake" is included in Chapter 2, and biographical information can be found there. In this short essay White responds to a request for a definition of democracy. His definition is not one you would find in a dictionary, but for a nation at war on two fronts in 1944, it could not have captured the meaning more effectively.

We received a letter from the Writers' War Board the other day asking for a statement on "The Meaning of Democracy." It presumably is our duty to comply with such a request, and it is certainly our pleasure. 1

Surely the Board knows what democracy is. It is the line that forms on the right. It is the don't in Don't Shove. It is the hole in the stuffed shirt through which the sawdust slowly trickles; it is the dent in the high hat. Democracy is the recurrent suspicion that more than half of the people are right more than half of the time. It is the feeling of privacy in the voting booths, the feeling of communion in the libraries, the feeling of vitality everywhere. Democracy is the score at the beginning of the ninth. It is an idea which hasn't been disproved yet, a song the words of which have not gone bad. It's the mustard on the hot dog and the cream in the rationed coffee. Democracy is a request from a War Board, in the middle of a morning in the middle of a war, wanting to know what democracy is. 2

QUESTIONS ON SUBJECT AND PURPOSE

1. White's little essay was written during World War II—that is obvious from the references to the War Board and the rationed

coffee. What else, though, about the definition reflects the time in which it was written?
2. Are the examples that White cites still relevant today? Or do they seem old-fashioned? What other examples might be substituted to bring White's definition up to date?
3. How good a definition is this? What purpose does it serve?

QUESTIONS ON STRATEGY AND AUDIENCE

1. Why does White define the term in this way? How is this a definition?
2. What does this definition do that a more conventional definition would not do?
3. Why is White's final example especially appropriate?

QUESTIONS ON VOCABULARY AND STYLE

1. How does White use parallel structure in his definition? How does it function?
2. How many of White's examples are clichés? Why would he use them? What effect do they create?
3. What more modern clichés might be more appropriate in a new version of White's definition?

WRITING SUGGESTIONS

1. Using a strategy like White's, define in a paragraph a term such as
   a. love
   b. the American way
   c. communism
   d. a classic
2. In an essay write an extended definition of *democracy* (or a similar term approved by your instructor).

   Prewriting

   a. Make a list of at least six possible subjects. Choose words that are used frequently and have a variety of meanings. Remember to get your instructor's approval of your final choice.

b. Look up each word in a college dictionary. Write down that definition at the top of a sheet of paper, and then in the remaining space brainstorm for associations and examples that help you define each word.
c. Look back over the details that you plan to include in your extended definition. What organizational strategy seems appropriate? Are you dividing the subject into parts? Are you comparing it to another subject? Are you establishing a causal relationship? Sketch out a possible framework that organizes the examples and details you plan to use.

Rewriting:
a. Check your introduction. Have you avoided beginning with a sentence such as "According to Webster . . ."? Copy your introduction onto a separate sheet of paper. Ask a roommate or classmate to read it. Does your reader want to continue reading? Does your introduction stimulate interest?
b. Check each individual paragraph. Is there a unified idea that controls each one? Make a copy of your essay, and highlight the topic sentence or key idea of each paragraph with a colored pen.
c. Evaluate the conclusion you have written. Do you conclude or just stop? Do you just repeat in slightly altered words what you wrote in the introduction? Check the advice about introductions and conclusions offered in the Glossary. If your conclusion seems weak, try freewriting at least one alternative ending.

3. Is America still patriotic? Research the question—do not just rely on your own feelings or experiences. What can be said about the nature and depth of patriotism in America today? Define the term using examples you have gathered from your research.

Clichés

THEODORE M. BERNSTEIN

Theodore M. Bernstein (1904-1979) was born in New York City and educated at Columbia University, receiving a B.A. in 1924 and a B.Litt. in 1925. Immediately after graduation, he joined The New York Times *as a copy editor. Within the Times organization, he held a variety of positions, including assistant managing editor and editor, from 1951 to 1978, of "Winners and Sinners," an in-house bulletin that critiqued the writing and usage of the* Times *staff. His position,* Newsweek *magazine observed, was that of "linguistic policeman." Bernstein was an authority on English usage and served as a consultant to the* Random House Dictionary *and the* American Heritage Dictionary. *Beginning in 1972 he wrote a syndicated column, "Bernstein on Words." His many books include* Headlines and Deadlines: A Manual for Copy Editors *(3rd. ed., 1961),* Watch Your Language *(1958),* More Language That Needs Watching *(1962),* The Careful Writer: A Modern Guide to English Usage *(1965), and* Miss Thistlebottom's Hobgoblins: The Careful Writer's Guide to Taboos, Bugbears, and Outmoded Rules of English Usage *(1971). In this selection from* The Careful Writer, *Bernstein displays his usual wit and ingenuity in defining cliché.*

When Archimedes' bath ran over and he discovered something about specific gravity, he was perhaps justified in sprinting into the street without his clothes and exulting. But that does not mean that every kid who sees his Saturday night bath overflow is justified in dashing outdoors naked shouting, "Eureka!" The distinction here is somewhat akin to that between the coiner of a bright phrase and the mere echoer of that phrase. It is the echoing that turns the phrase into a cliché—that is, an overworked, commonplace expression— and the echoer should realize that he has no claim to originality. 1

This is not to say that all clichés should be avoided like, shall we say, the plague. It is no more possible—or desirable—to do that than it is to abolish gravity. Many of today's clichés are likely to be tomorrow's standard English, just as many of today's standard words were yesterday's metaphors: *thunderstruck, astonish, cuckold, conclave, sanguine,* and thousands of others that form a substantial part of any dictionary. Moreover, the cliché is sometimes the most direct way of expressing a thought. Think of the circumlocution that is avoided by saying that someone has a *dog-in-the-manger attitude.* To attempt to write around a cliché will often lead to pompous obscurity. And for a writer to decide to banish all clichés indiscriminately would be to hamstring—yes, *hamstring*—his efforts. 2

There are many varieties of clichés. Some are foreign phrases (*coup de grâce; et tu, Brute*). Some are homely sayings or are based on proverbs ("You can't make an omelet without breaking eggs," *blissful ignorance*). Some are quotations ("To be or not to be"; "Unwept, unhonored, and unsung"). Some are allusions to myth or history (*Gordian knot, Achilles' heel*). Some are alliterative or rhyming phrases (*first and foremost, high and dry*). Some are paradoxes (*in less than no time, conspicuous by its absence).* Some are legalisms (*null and void, each and every*). Some are playful euphemisms (*a fate worse than death, better half*). Some are figurative phrases (*leave no stone unturned, hit the nail on the head*). And some are almost meaningless small change (*in the last analysis, by the same token*). 3

QUESTIONS ON SUBJECT AND PURPOSE

1. What is a cliché? Why are clichés so common?
2. If clichés are "overworked" and "commonplace" (paragraph 1), why not "banish" them (paragraph 2)? How would a writer know when to avoid clichés and when to use them?
3. For class discussion, list at least six additional clichés that are a part of your everyday speech. Can they be classified using the categories Bernstein mentions in the third paragraph?

QUESTIONS ON STRATEGY AND AUDIENCE

1. Why does Bernstein begin with the reference to Archimedes? Why not just begin with the definition?
2. What structural devices does Bernstein use to order his paragraphs? How are they a part of his attempt at definition?
3. What expectations does Bernstein have of his audience? Find specific evidence to support your conclusion.

QUESTIONS ON VOCABULARY AND STYLE

1. In the second paragraph, Bernstein cites some examples of "yesterday's metaphors" that are "today's standard words." Check each word in a dictionary. How were these words metaphoric?
2. Why does Bernstein use clichés in his second paragraph? How many does he use?
3. Be able to define the following words: *specific gravity* (paragraph 1), *Eureka* (1), *akin* (1), *circumlocution* (2), *pompous* (2), *hamstring* (2), *euphemisms* (3).

WRITING SUGGESTIONS

1. Select one of the following words (or a similar word) and define it in a paragraph. Consult a dictionary before beginning. Remember to use examples to make your definition clear and interesting.
   a. euphemism
   b. spoonerism
   c. malapropism
   d. cant
   e. jargon
2. Select a concept central to another academic subject you are studying this semester. Using your textbook and whatever other sources might be available, define that word or idea for a general audience. Remember to make your definition interesting through the use of appropriate examples.

   Prewriting:

   a. Remember that you will need to choose a subject that is complex enough to require an extended definition. On the other hand, you will probably want to avoid a technical subject that is of little interest to a general reader. With these two cautions in mind, use the textbooks from your other courses as guides, and make a list of possible subjects.

b. List several possibilities down the left-hand side of a sheet of paper. In the space to the right, analyze each subject from the point of view of your potential audience. What might a general audience know about this subject? Is that audience likely to be interested in or to have opinions about the subject? Answer these questions for each topic.

c. Visit the current periodicals section of your library and spend some time looking at magazines such as *Time* and *Newsweek*. If either magazine contained an article on the same subject as yours, how would it be handled? How do they write for a general audience? Study appropriate articles in either magazine. Pay attention to the strategy and style of the articles.

Rewriting:

a. Make a copy of your essay, and ask a peer reader to respond to it. Tell that reader to mark any section or any word in the essay that seems too technical or inadequately explained. Try to get a reader who is relatively unfamiliar with the subject.

b. Return to some sample issues of magazines such as *Time* or *Newsweek*. Study the introductions to articles with related topics. Have you used a similar strategy to begin your essay? If you have not, pretend that your essay will appear in a magazine, and try to write an introduction that your editor would like.

c. Also study the conclusions of some magazine articles. Do you conclude in a similar way? If you have not, try freewriting a new ending for your essay.

3. The reference room of your college's library will have a number of guides to English usage. Consult at least six different reference books on the subject *cliché*. Write a definition of the term with appropriate examples. You should also comment on whether clichés are ever appropriate in writing. Your essay will be used as a handout in the freshman English program at your college or university, so remember your audience.

Television Viewing as an Addiction

MARIE WINN

Marie Winn was born in Czechoslovakia in 1937. A graduate of Radcliffe College, she has done graduate work at Columbia University. Author and compiler of over a dozen books, her works include anthologies of children's songs and games, five books intended for children, and three critical studies: Children without Childhood *(1983);* The Plug-in Drug: Television, Children, and the Family *(1977; revised edition, 1985); and* Unplugging the Plug-In Drug *(1987), which offers advice on how to plan a family television turnoff and discusses the possible effects of such an action. In this selection from* The Plug-In Drug, *Winn defines television viewing as potentially addictive since it has adverse effects on the addicted individual's personality and lifestyle.*

The word "addiction" is often used loosely and wryly in conversation. People will refer to themselves as "mystery book addicts" or "cookie addicts." E. B. White writes of his annual surge of interest in gardening: "We are hooked and are making an attempt to kick the habit." Yet nobody really believes that reading mysteries or ordering seeds by catalogue is serious enough to be compared with addictions to heroin or alcohol. The word "addiction" is here used jokingly to denote a tendency to overindulge in some pleasurable activity. 1

People often refer to being "hooked on TV." Does this, too, fall into the lighthearted category of cookie eating and other pleasures that people pursue with unusual intensity, or is there a kind of television viewing that falls into the more serious category of destructive addiction? 2

When we think about addiction to drugs or alcohol, we frequently focus on negative aspects, ignoring the pleasures 3 that accompany drinking or drug-taking. And yet the essence of any serious addiction is a pursuit of pleasure, a search for a "high" that normal life does not supply. It is only the inability to function without the addictive substance that is dismaying, the dependence of the organism upon a certain experience and an increasing inability to function normally without it. Thus a person will take two or three drinks at the end of the day not merely for the pleasure drinking provides, but also because he "doesn't feel normal" without them.

An addict does not merely pursue a pleasurable experi- 4
ence and need to experience it in order to function normally. He needs to *repeat* it again and again. Something about the particular experience makes life without it less than complete. Other potentially pleasurable experiences are no longer possible, for under the spell of the addictive experience, his life is peculiarly distorted. The addict craves an experience and yet he is never really satisfied. The organism may be temporarily sated, but soon it begins to crave again.

Finally a serious addiction is distinguished from a 5
harmless pursuit of pleasure by its distinctly destructive elements. A heroin addict, for instance, leads a damaged life: his increasing need for heroin in increasing doses prevents him from working, from maintaining relationships, from developing in human ways. Similarly an alcoholic's life is narrowed and dehumanized by his dependence on alcohol.

Let us consider television viewing in the light of the 6
conditions that define serious addictions.

Not unlike drugs or alcohol, the television experience 7
allows the participant to blot out the real world and enter into a pleasurable and passive mental state. The worries and anxieties of reality are as effectively deferred by becoming absorbed in a television program as by going on a "trip" induced by drugs or alcohol. And just as alcoholics are only inchoately aware of their addiction, feeling that they control their drinking more than they really do ("I can cut it out any time I want—I just like to have three or four drinks

before dinner"), people similarly overestimate their control over television watching. Even as they put off other activities to spend hour after hour watching television, they feel they could easily resume living in a different, less passive style. But somehow or other while the television set is present in their homes, the click doesn't sound. With television pleasures available, those other experiences seem less attractive, more difficult somehow.

A heavy viewer (a college English instructor) observes: "I find television almost irresistible. When the set is on, I cannot ignore it. I can't turn it off. I feel sapped, will-less, enervated. As I reach out to turn off the set, the strength goes out of my arms. So I sit there for hours and hours." 8

The self-confessed television addict often feels he "ought" to do other things—but the fact that he doesn't read and doesn't plant his garden or sew or crochet or play games or have conversations means that those activities are no longer as desirable as television viewing. In a way a heavy viewer's life is as imbalanced by his television "habit" as a drug addict's or an alcoholic's. He is living in a holding pattern, as it were, passing up the activities that lead to growth or development or a sense of accomplishment. This is one reason people talk about their television viewing so ruefully, so apologetically. They are aware that it is an unproductive experience, that almost any other endeavor is more worthwhile by any human measure. 9

Finally it is the adverse effect of television viewing on the lives of so many people that defines it as a serious addiction. The television habit distorts the sense of time. It renders other experiences vague and curiously unreal while taking on a greater reality for itself. It weakens relationships by reducing and sometimes eliminating normal opportunities for talking, for communicating. 10

And yet television does not satisfy, else why would the viewer continue to watch hour after hour, day after day? "The measure of health," writes Lawrence Kubie, "is flexibility . . . and especially the freedom to cease when sated." But the television viewer can never be sated with his television experiences—they do not provide the true nourish- 11 ment that satiation requires—and thus he finds that he cannot stop watching.

QUESTIONS ON SUBJECT AND PURPOSE

1. How does Winn define the term *addiction*?
2. How effective is Winn's comparison of a television addict to an alcoholic or a drug abuser?
3. Why, according to Winn, are people apologetic when they talk about their television viewing?

QUESTIONS ON STRATEGY AND AUDIENCE

1. Why might Winn write five paragraphs about addictions in general before introducing her thesis about television addiction?
2. How does the example of the college instructor in paragraph 8 contribute to Winn's argument?
3. What expectations does Winn seem to to have of her audience? Point to specific ideas and techniques in the text that support your conclusion.

QUESTIONS ON VOCABULARY AND STYLE

1. What associations are suggested by words such as "sapped," "will-less," and "enervated" in paragraph 8?
2. At a number of points in the essay, Winn encloses words within quotation marks. Why does she do so?
3. Be able to define the following words: *wryly* (paragraph 1), *sated* (2), *inchoately* (7), *enervated* (8), *ruefully* (9).

WRITING SUGGESTIONS

1. Many people get hooked on something—baseball card collecting, exercising, buying clothes, eating a particular food, performing particular daily rituals, washing and waxing their automobiles. In a paragraph define and illustrate your obsession.
2. In paragraph 9 Winn asserts that "almost any other endeavor is more worthwhile [than television viewing] by any human mea-

sure." In an essay, define and illustrate the possible meaning(s) of the phrase "a worthwhile human endeavor."

Prewriting:

a. What constitutes, for you, "worthwhile" activity? Brainstorm on the topic to generate a range of possibilities. Specifically what is it about this activity that makes it worthwhile? How would you like to spend your time? What makes you feel good about each activity?
b. Interview a group of classmates or fellow students. Try to get a range of ages and backgrounds. Ask each to list worthwhile human endeavors.
c. Remember that your essay will include both generalizations that reflect important human values and specific examples that illustrate those general categories. Once you have a list of examples, make sure that you classify them into broader categories.

Rewriting:

a. Look back over the advice on classifying contained in the introduction to Chapter 4. Check to make sure that you have clearly grouped your examples. Can any examples be organized differently? Consider a new outline for your essay.
b. Check each body paragraph. Does each have a clearly stated or implied topic statement? Make a photocopy of your essay, and underline in colored ink that key idea. Do all of the examples in the paragraph relate to that statement?
c. Coming up with an effective, interesting title is not always an easy matter. Moreover, it does not always seem important when you are worried about finishing the essay. Look back at your title. Does it provoke reader interest? Is this a title that you might find in a magazine? Brainstorm for some new possibilities.

3. How typical are Winn's views? That is, do other researchers agree that television viewing can be addictive? Research the problem. How would the term *addictive* be defined by the scientific community? Is excessive television viewing really dangerous? Your school's reference librarians can help you locate relevant information. You might also look for reviews of Winn's two books on the subject of television. (See the headnote at the start of the selection.)

I Want a Wife

JUDY SYFERS

Judy Syfers was born in 1937 in San Francisco, California, and received a B.F.A. in painting from the University of Iowa. She was married in 1960 and raised two children. Now divorced, she lives in San Francisco. As a free-lancer writer, Syfers has written essays on such topics as union organizing, abortion, and the role of women in society. Syfers's most frequently reprinted essay is "I Want a Wife," which originally appeared in Ms. *magazine in 1971. After examining the stereotypical male demands in marriage, Syfers concludes, "Who* wouldn't *want a wife?"*

I belong to that classification of people known as wives. I am A Wife. And, not altogether incidentally, I am a mother. 1

Not too long ago a male friend of mine appeared on the scene fresh from a recent divorce. He had one child, who is, of course, with his ex-wife. He is obviously looking for another wife. As I thought about him while I was ironing one evening, it suddenly occurred to me that I, too, would like to have a wife. Why do I want a wife? 2

I would like to go back to school so that I can become economically independent, support myself, and, if need be, support those dependent upon me. I want a wife who will work and send me to school. And while I am going to school I want a wife to take care of my children. I want a wife to keep track of the children's doctor and dentist appointments. And to keep track of mine, too. I want a wife to make sure my children eat properly and are kept clean. I want a wife who will wash the children's clothes and keep them mended. I want a wife who is a good nurturant attendant to my children, who arranges for their schooling, makes sure that they have an adequate social life with their peers, takes them to the park, the zoo, etc. I want a wife 3 who takes care of the children when they are sick, a wife who arranges to be around when the children need special care, because, of course, I cannot miss classes at school. My wife must arrange to lose time at work, and not lose the job. It may mean a small cut in my wife's income from time to time, but I guess I can tolerate that. Needless to say, my wife will arrange and pay for the care of the children while my wife is working.

I want a wife who will take care of my physical needs. I 4
want a wife who will keep my house clean. A wife who will pick up after me. I want a wife who will keep my clothes clean, ironed, mended, replaced when need be, and who will see to it that my personal things are kept in their proper place so that I can find what I need the minute I need it. I want a wife who cooks the meals, a wife who is a good cook. I want a wife who will plan the menus, do the necessary grocery shopping, prepare the meals, serve them pleasantly, and then do the cleaning up while I do my studying. I want a wife who will care for me when I am sick and sympathize with my pain and loss of time from school. I want a wife to go along when our family takes a vacation so that someone can continue to care for me and my children when I need a rest and change of scene.

I want a wife who will not bother me with rambling 5
complaints about a wife's duties. But I want a wife who will listen to me when I feel the need to explain a rather difficult point I have come across in my course of studies. And I want a wife who will type my papers for me when I have written them.

I want a wife who will take care of the details of my 6
social life. When my wife and I are invited out by my friends, I want a wife who will take care of the babysitting arrangements. When I meet people at school that I like and want to entertain, I want a wife who will have the house clean, will prepare a special meal, serve it to me and my friends, and not interrupt when I talk about the things that interest me and my friends. I want a wife who will have arranged that the children are fed and ready for bed before my guests arrive so that the children do not bother us. I

want a wife who takes care of the needs of my guests so that they feel comfortable, who makes sure that they have an ashtray, that they are passed the hors d'oeuvres, that they are offered a second helping of the food, that their wine glasses are replenished when necessary, that their coffee is served to them as they like it. And I want a wife who knows that sometimes I need a night out by myself.

I want a wife who is sensitive to my sexual needs, a wife who makes love passionately and eagerly when I feel like it, a wife who makes sure that I am satisfied. And, of course, I want a wife who will not demand sexual attention when I am not in the mood for it. I want a wife who assumes the complete responsibility for birth control, because I do not want more children. I want a wife who will remain sexually faithful to me so that I do not have to clutter up my intellectual life with jealousies. And I want a wife who understands that *my* sexual needs may entail more than strict adherence to monogamy. I must, after all, be able to relate to people as fully as possible. 7

If, by chance, I find another person more suitable as a wife than the wife I already have, I want the liberty to replace my present wife with another one. Naturally I will expect a fresh, new life; my wife will take the children and be solely responsible for them so that I am left free. 8

When I am through with school and have a job, I want my wife to quit working and remain at home so that my wife can more fully and completely take care of a wife's duties. 9

My God, who *wouldn't* want a wife? 10

QUESTIONS ON SUBJECT AND PURPOSE

1. In what way is this a definition of a wife? Why does Syfers avoid a more conventional definition?
2. Is Syfers being fair? Is there anything that she leaves out of her definition that you would have included?
3. What purpose might Syfers have been trying to achieve?

QUESTIONS ON STRATEGY AND AUDIENCE

1. How does Syfers structure her essay? What is the order of the development? Could the essay have been arranged in any other way?
2. Why does Syfers identify herself by her roles—wife and mother—at the beginning of the essay? Is that information relevant in any way?
3. What assumptions does Syfers have about her audience (the readers of Ms. magazine)? How do you know?

QUESTIONS ON VOCABULARY AND STYLE

1. How does Syfers use repetition in the essay? Why? Does it work? What effect does it create?
2. How effective is Syfers's final rhetorical question? Where else in the essay does she use a rhetorical question?
3. Be able to define the following words: *nurturant* (paragraph (3), *hors d'oeuvres* (6), *replenished* (6), *monogamy* (7).

WRITING SUGGESTIONS

1. Using the material provided by Syfers, write a paragraph definition of a wife. Be serious; do not try to paraphrase or to imitate Syfers's style.
2. In an essay define a word such as *husband, lover, friend, mother, father,* or *grandparent.* Define indirectly by showing what such a person does or should do.

Prewriting:

a. Select a word as a possible subject. Then write down a dictionary definition. The inadequacies of such a short definition (for example, *wife*: "a woman married to a man") will be obvious. What expectations do you have about the role or function of the person in this position? Make a list.
b. Try freewriting about the items on the list you have just made. Treat each expectation as the subject for a separate freewriting. You might not use any of the prose that you produce here; you are trying to generate ideas.

c. Plan an organizational strategy. Look carefully at how Syfers puts her essay together. How does she structure the middle of her essay? Can you use a similar structure?

Rewriting:

a. Characterize the tone of what you have written. For example, are you serious or satirical? Is it formal or informal? Does your tone complement your purpose? Look back through your essay, and imagine how it would sound to a reader.
b. Check each paragraph in your essay. Is there a consistent, unified subject for each? That unity might be expressed in an explicit topic sentence, or it might just be implicit.
c. Look again at your introduction and conclusion. Avoid imitating Syfers's strategies—especially her conclusion. Look at the advice on introductions and conclusions in the Glossary. Be honest about what you have written. Could either be stronger, clearer, more interesting?

3. What does it mean to be a wife in another culture? Choose at least two other cultures and research those societies' expectations of a wife. Try to find cultures that show significant differences. Using your research, write an essay offering a comparative definition of *wife*. Assume that your audience is American.

Femininity

SUSAN BROWNMILLER

Born in 1935 in Brooklyn, New York, Susan Brownmiller was educated at Cornell and at the Jefferson School of Social Science. Before beginning her writing and editorial work for publications such as The Village Voice *and* Newsweek, *Brownmiller was an actress for four years. Later she was a television newswriter and now works as a free-lance writer, often contributing to* The New York Times, Esquire, *and* Newsweek. *Brownmiller's concern for women and the women's movement is emphasized in her book* Against Our Will: Men, Women, & Rape *(1975). Her concern for women also motivated her to found Women Against Pornography. Brownmiller's latest book,* Femininity *(1984), explores the origins of femininity using biological, cultural, and sociological evidence and illustrates the modern revival of true femininity. This selection, taken from the Prologue to* Femininity, *attempts to define the term.*

We had a game in our house called "setting the table" and I was Mother's helper. Forks to the left of the plate, knives and spoons to the right. Placing the cutlery neatly, as I recall, was one of my first duties, and the event was alive with meaning. When a knife or a fork dropped to the floor, that meant a man was unexpectedly coming to dinner. A falling spoon announced the surprise arrival of a female guest. No matter that these visitors never arrived on cue, I had learned a rule of gender identification. Men were straight-edged, sharply pronged and formidable, women were softly curved and held the food in a rounded well. It made perfect sense, like the division of pink and blue that I saw in babies, an orderly way of viewing the world. Daddy, who was gone all day at work and who loved to putter at home with his pipe, tobacco and tool chest, was knife and fork. Mommy and Grandma, with their ample proportions 1 and pots and pans, were grownup soup spoons, large and capacious. And I was a teaspoon, small and slender, easy to hold and just right for pudding, my favorite dessert.

Being good at what was expected of me was one of my earliest projects, for not only was I rewarded, as most children are, for doing things right, but excellence gave pride and stability to my childhood existence. Girls were different from boys, and the expression of that difference seemed mine to make clear. Did my loving, anxious mother, who dressed me in white organdy pinafores and Mary Janes and who cried hot tears when I got them dirty, give me my first instruction? Of course. Did my doting aunts and uncles with their gifts of pretty dolls and miniature tea sets add to my education? Of course. But even without the appropriate toys and clothes, lessons in the art of being feminine lay all around me and I absorbed them all: the fairy tales that were read to me at night, the brightly colored advertisements I pored over in magazines before I learned to decipher the words, the movies I saw, the comic books I hoarded, the radio soap operas I happily followed whenever I had to stay in bed with a cold. I loved being a little girl, or rather I loved being a fairy princess, for that was who I thought I was. 2

As I passed through a stormy adolescence to a stormy maturity, femininity increasingly became an exasperation, a brilliant, subtle esthetic that was bafflingly inconsistent at the same time that it was minutely, demandingly concrete, a rigid code of appearance and behavior defined by do's and don't-do's that went against my rebellious grain. Femininity was a challenge thrown down to the female sex, a challenge no proud, self-respecting young woman could afford to ignore, particularly one with enormous ambition that she nursed in secret, alternately feeding or starving its inchoate life in tremendous confusion. 3

"Don't lose your femininity" and "Isn't it remarkable how she manages to retain her femininity?" had terrifying implications. They spoke of a bottom-line failure so irreversible that nothing else mattered. The pinball machine had registered "tilt," the game had been called. Disqualification 4 was marked on the forehead of a woman whose femininity was lost. No records would be entered in her name, for she had destroyed her birthright in her wretched, ungainly effort to imitate a man. She walked in limbo, this hapless creature, and it occurred to me that one day I might see her when I looked in the mirror. If the danger was so palpable that warning notices were freely posted, wasn't it possible that the small bundle of resentments I carried around in secret might spill out and place the mark on my own forehead? Whatever quarrels with femininity I had I kept to myself; whatever handicaps femininity imposed, they were mine to deal with alone, for there was no women's movement to ask the tough questions, or to brazenly disregard the rules.

Femininity, in essence, is a romantic sentiment, a 5
nostalgic tradition of imposed limitations. Even as it hurries forward in the 1980s, putting on lipstick and high heels to appear well dressed, it trips on the ruffled petticoats and hoopskirts of an era gone by. Invariably and necessarily, femininity is something that women had more of in the past, not only in the historic past of prior generations, but in each woman's personal past as well—in the virginal innocence that is replaced by knowledge, in the dewy cheek that is coarsened by age, in the "inherent nature" that a woman seems to misplace so forgetfully whenever she steps out of bounds. Why should this be so? The XX chromosomal message has not been scrambled, the estrogen-dominated hormonal balance is generally as biology intended, the reproductive organs, whatever use one has made of them, are usually in place, the breasts of whatever size are most often where they should be. But clearly, biological femaleness is not enough.

Femininity always demands more. It must constantly 6
reassure its audience by a willing demonstration of difference, even when one does not exist in nature, or it must seize and embrace a natural variation and compose a rhapsodic symphony upon the notes. Suppose one doesn't care to, has other things on her mind, is clumsy or tone-deaf despite the best instruction and training? To fail at the fem-

inine difference is to appear not to care about men, and to risk the loss of their attention and approval. To be insufficiently feminine is viewed as a failure in core sexual identity, or as a failure to care sufficiently about oneself, for a woman found wanting will be appraised (and will appraise herself) as mannish or neutered or simply unattractive, as men have defined these terms.

We are talking, admittedly, about an exquisite esthetic. 7
Enormous pleasure can be extracted from feminine pursuits as a creative outlet or purely as relaxation; indeed, indulgence for the sake of fun, or art, or attention, is among femininity's great joys. But the chief attraction (and the central paradox, as well) is the competitive edge that femininity seems to promise in the unending struggle to survive, and perhaps to triumph. The world smiles favorably on the feminine woman: it extends little courtesies and minor privilege. Yet the nature of this competitive edge is ironic, at best, for one works at femininity by accepting restrictions, by limiting one's sights, by choosing an indirect route, by scattering concentration and not giving one's all as a man would to his own, certifiably masculine, interests. It does not require a great leap of imagination for a woman to understand the feminine principle as a grand collection of compromises, large and small, that she simply must make in order to render herself a successful woman. If she has difficulty in satisfying femininity's demands, if its illusions go against her grain, or if she is criticized for her shortcomings and imperfections, the more she will see femininity as a desperate strategy of appeasement, a strategy she may not have the wish or the courage to abandon, for failure looms in either direction.

It is fashionable in some quarters to describe the femi- 8
nine and masculine principles as polar ends of the human continuum, and to sagely profess that both polarities exist in all people. Sun and moon, yin and yang, soft and hard, active and passive, etcetera, may indeed be opposites, but a linear continuum does not illuminate the problem. (Femininity, in all its contrivances, is a very active endeavor.)

What, then, is the basic distinction? The masculine principle is better understood as a driving ethos of superiority designed to inspire straightforward, confident success, while the feminine principle is composed of vulnerability, the need for protection, the formalities of compliance and the avoidance of conflict—in short, an appeal of dependence and good will that gives the masculine principle its romantic validity and its admiring applause.

Femininity pleases men because it makes them appear more masculine by contrast; and, in truth, conferring an extra portion of unearned gender distinction on men, and unchallenged space in which to breathe freely and feel stronger, wiser, more competent, is femininity's special gift. One could say that masculinity is often an effort to please women, but masculinity is known to please by displays of mastery and competence while femininity pleases by suggesting that these concerns, except in small matters, are beyond its intent. Whimsy, unpredictability and patterns of thinking and behavior that are dominated by emotion, such as tearful expressions of sentiment and fear, are thought to be feminine precisely because they lie outside the established route to success. 9

If in the beginnings of history the feminine woman was defined by her physical dependency, her inability for reasons of reproductive biology to triumph over the forces of nature that were the tests of masculine strength and power, today she reflects both an economic and emotional dependency that is still considered "natural," romantic and attractive. After an unsettling fifteen years in which many basic assumptions about the sexes were challenged, the economic disparity did not disappear. Large numbers of women—those with small children, those left high and dry after a mid-life divorce—need financial support. But even those who earn their own living share a universal need for connectedness (call it love, if you wish). As unprecedented numbers of men abandon their sexual interest in women, others, sensing opportunity, choose to demonstrate their interest through variety and a change in partners. A 10 sociological fact of the 1980s is that female competition for two scarce resources—men and jobs—is especially fierce.

So it is not surprising that we are currently witnessing a renewed interest in femininity and an unabashed indulgence in feminine pursuits. Femininity serves to reassure men that women need them and care about them enormously. By incorporating the decorative and the frivolous into its definition of style, femininity functions as an effective antidote to the unrelieved seriousness, the pressure of making one's way in a harsh, difficult world. In its mandate to avoid direct confrontation and to smooth over the fissures of conflict, femininity operates as a value system of niceness, a code of thoughtfulness and sensitivity that in modern society is sadly in short supply. 11

There is no reason to deny that indulgence in the art of feminine illusion can be reassuring to a woman, if she happens to be good at it. As sexuality undergoes some dizzying revisions, evidence that one is a woman "at heart" (the inquisitor's question) is not without worth. Since an answer of sorts may be furnished by piling on additional documentation, affirmation can arise from such identifiable but trivial feminine activities as buying a new eyeliner, experimenting with the latest shade of nail color, or bursting into tears at the outcome of a popular romance novel. Is there anything destructive in this? Time and cost factors, a deflection of energy and an absorption in fakery spring quickly to mind, and they need to be balanced, as in a ledger book, against the affirming advantage. 12

QUESTIONS ON SUBJECT AND PURPOSE

1. How does Brownmiller define "femininity"?
2. How does femininity change as a woman grows older? How has it changed throughout this century?
3. On the basis of this selection, how does Brownmiller seem to feel about femininity?

QUESTIONS ON STRATEGY AND AUDIENCE

1. In what ways(s) does the table-setting analogy in paragraph 1 serve as an introduction to the distinctions between femininity and masculinity?
2. How does Brownmiller structure the essay? Make a brief outline.
3. Who is Brownmiller's audience? What in the text defines or suggests who that audience is?

QUESTIONS ON VOCABULARY AND STYLE

1. Characterize Brownmiller's tone in the selection. How does she feel about femininity? About the "renewed interest" in femininity?
2. At several points in the essay, Brownmiller encloses material within parentheses. What is the effect of doing that? Why not set it off using commas or dashes?
3. Be able to define the following words: *capacious* (paragraph 1), *esthetic* (3), *inchoate* (3), *appeasement* (7), *ethos* (8)

WRITING SUGGESTIONS

1. What do you think are desirable feminine or masculine traits in the ideal mate? In a paragraph, explore your expectations of an ideal mate by defining either masculinity or femininity.
2. In an essay, define the term "masculinity."

   Prewriting:

   a. Part of your definition, like Brownmiller's, has been shaped by expectations learned from family and culture. How, for example, would your grandparents or parents define the term? How does a man act? What does he do? What does he not do? Consider the term from both perspectives. If possible, ask your parents or grandparents to answer these questions.
   b. Ask a series of friends or classmates to answer the questions posed above. Try to get a range of informants of varying ages and backgrounds. How do their answers differ from the answers of your grandparents or parents?

c. How is masculinity defined in our society? What images are projected by magazines, television, comic book characters, movies? Look around you, take notes, jot down examples to support your generalizations.

Rewriting:

a. Have you provided enough examples to support your generalizations? Go through a photocopy of your essay and underline generalizations in one color and examples in another. Is there a good balance between the two?
b. Look carefully at your conclusion. You want to end forcefully; you do not just want to repeat the same ideas and words used in your introduction. Reread your essay several times, and then try freewriting a new conclusion. Aim for a completely different ending than the one you originally wrote.
c. Once you have a complete draft, jot down on a separate sheet of paper what troubles you the most about the essay. What could be better? Allow a day to pass, then try to solve that problem. If your school has a writing center or peer tutoring program, take your specific problem there.

3. How have society's definitions of masculinity and femininity changed over time? Choose one of the two terms, and research its shifting definitions over the past two hundred years. What did society expect of a man or a woman in 1800? In 1900? What will society expect in the 1990s? What is considered masculine or feminine? Concentrate on the major changes or similarities. Present your findings in an essay that might appear in a popular magazine.

The Secret of Life

LOREN EISELEY

Loren Eiseley (1907-1977) was born in Lincoln, Nebraska, and received a B.A. degree from the University of Nebraska. After receiving a Ph.D. from the University of Pennyslvania, Eiseley taught at the University of Kansas and Oberlin College, finally returning to the University of Pennyslvania as head of the Department of Anthropology. He also lectured at numerous universities and served as president of the American Institute of Paleontology. Eiseley was a scientist gifted with a literary sensibility. Thus he could write for scientific journals such as American Anthropologist *and* Scientific American *as well as for popular magazines like* Harper's, American Scholar, *and* Ladies' Home Journal. *His books include* The Immense Journey *(1957),* Darwin's Century *(1958), and* The Unexpected Universe *(1969). Eiseley's talent as a writer is nowhere better displayed than in this selection from* The Immense Journey. *His subject is the search for the ultimate mystery—the secret of life, the link between living and dead matter.*

I am middle-aged now, but in the autumn I always seek for it again hopefully. On some day when the leaves are red, or fallen, and just after the birds are gone, I put on my hat and an old jacket, and over the protests of my wife that I will catch cold, I start my search. I go carefully down the apartment steps and climb, instead of jump, over the wall. A bit further I reach an unkempt field full of brown stalks and emptied seed pods. 1

By the time I get to the wood I am carrying all manner of seeds hooked in my coat or piercing my socks or sticking by ingenious devices to my shoestrings. I let them ride. After all, who am I to contend against such ingenuity? It is obvious that nature, or some part of it in the shape of these seeds, has intentions beyond this field and has made plans to travel with me. 2

We, the seeds and I, climb another wall together and sit 3
down to rest, while I consider the best way to search for the secret of life. The seeds remain very quiet and some slip off into the crevices of the rock. A woolly-bear caterpillar hurries across a ledge, going late to some tremendous transformation, but about this he knows as little as I.

It is not an auspicious beginning. The things alive do 4
not know the secret, and there may be those who would doubt the wisdom of coming out among discarded husks in the dead year to pursue such questions. They might say the proper time is spring, when one can consult the water rats or listen to little chirps under the stones. Of late years, however, I have come to suspect that the mystery may just as well be solved in a carved and intricate seed case out of which the life has flown, as in the seed itself.

In autumn one is not confused by activity and green 5
leaves. The underlying apparatus, the hooks, needles, stalks, wires, suction cups, thin pipes, and iridescent bladders are all exposed in a gigantic dissection. These are the essentials. Do not be deceived simply because the life has flown out of them. It will return, but in the meantime there is an unparalleled opportunity to examine in sharp and beautiful angularity the shape of life without its disturbing muddle of juices and leaves. As I grow older and conserve my efforts, I shall give this season my final and undivided attention. I shall be found puzzling over the saw teeth on the desiccated leg of a dead grasshopper or standing bemused in a brown sea of rusty stems. Somewhere in this discarded machinery may lie the key to the secret. I shall not let it escape through lack of diligence or through fear of the smiles of people in high windows. I am sure now that life is not what it is purported to be and that nature, in the canny words of a Scotch theologue, "is not as natural as it looks." I have learned this in a small suburban field, after a good many years spent in much wilder places upon far less fantastic quests.

The notion that mice can be generated spontaneously 6
from bundles of old clothes is so delightfully whimsical that

it is easy to see why men were loath to abandon it. One could accept such accidents in a topsy-turvy universe without trying to decide what transformation of buckles into bones and shoe buttons into eyes had taken place. One could take life as a kind of fantastic magic and not blink too obviously when it appeared, beady-eyed and bustling, under the laundry in the back room.

It was only with the rise of modern biology and the discovery that the trail of life led backward toward infinitesimal beginnings in primordial sloughs, that men began the serious dissection and analysis of the cell. Darwin, in one of his less guarded moments, had spoken hopefully of the possibility that life had emerged from inorganic matter in some "warm little pond." From that day to this biologists have poured, analyzed, minced, and shredded recalcitrant protoplasm in a fruitless attempt to create life from nonliving matter. It seemed inevitable, if we could trace life down through simpler stages, that we must finally arrive at the point where, under the proper chemical conditions, the mysterious borderline that bounds the inanimate must be crossed. It seemed clear that life was a material manifestation. Somewhere, somehow, sometime, in the mysterious chemistry of carbon, the long march toward the talking animal had begun. 7

A hundred years ago men spoke optimistically about solving the secret, or at the very least they thought the next generation would be in a position to do so. Periodically there were claims that the emergence of life from matter had been observed, but in every case the observer proved to be self-deluded. It became obvious that the secret of life was not to be had by a little casual experimentation, and that life in today's terms appeared to arise only through the medium of preëxisting life. Yet, if science was not to be embarrassed by some kind of mind–matter dualism and a complete and irrational break between life and the world of inorganic matter, the emergence of life had, in some way, to be accounted for. Nevertheless, as the years passed, the secret remained locked in its living jelly, in spite of larger microscopes and more formidable means of dissection. As a 8 matter of fact the mystery was heightened because all this intensified effort revealed that even the supposedly simple amoeba was a complex, self-operating chemical factory. The notion that he was a simple blob, the discovery of whose chemical composition would enable us instantly to set the life process in operation, turned out to be, at best, a monstrous caricature of the truth.

With the failure of these many efforts science was left in 9
the somewhat embarrassing position of having to postulate theories of living origins which it could not demonstrate. After having chided the theologian for his reliance on myth and miracle, science found itself in the unenviable position of having to create a mythology of its own: namely, the assumption that what, after long effort, could not be proved to take place today had, in truth, taken place in the primeval past.

My use of the term *mythology* is perhaps a little harsh. 10
One does occasionally observe, however, a tendency for the beginning zoological textbook to take the unwary reader by a hop, skip, and jump from the little steaming pond or the beneficent chemical crucible of the sea, into the lower world of life with such sureness and rapidity that it is easy to assume that there is no mystery about this matter at all, or, if there is, that it is a very little one.

This attitude has indeed been sharply criticized by the 11
distinguished British biologist Woodger, who remarked some years ago: "Unstable organic compounds and chlorophyll corpuscles do not persist or come into existence in nature on their own account at the present day, and consequently it is necessary to postulate that conditions were once such that this did happen although and in spite of the fact that our knowledge of nature does not give us any warrant for making such a supposition . . . It is simple dogmatism—asserting that what you want to believe did in fact happen."

Yet, unless we are to turn to supernatural explanations 12
or reinvoke a dualism which is scientifically dubious, we are forced inevitably toward only two possible explanations of life upon earth. One of these, although not entirely dis-

proved, is most certainly out of fashion and surrounded with greater obstacles to its acceptance than at the time it was formulated. I refer, of course, to the suggestion of Lord Kelvin and Svante Arrhenius that life did not arise on this planet, but was wafted here through the depths of space. Microscopic spores, it was contended, have great resistance to extremes of cold and might have come into our atmosphere with meteoric dust, or have been driven across the earth's orbit by light pressure. In this view, once the seed was "planted" in soil congenial to its development, it then proceeded to elaborate, evolve, and adjust until the higher organisms had emerged.

This theory had a certain attraction as a way out of an 13
embarrassing dilemma, but it suffers from the defect of explaining nothing, even if it should prove true. It does not elucidate the nature of life. It simply removes the inconvenient problem of origins to far-off spaces or worlds into which we will never penetrate. Since life makes use of the chemical compounds of this earth, it would seem better to proceed, until incontrovertible evidence to the contrary is obtained, on the assumption that life has actually arisen upon this planet. The now widely accepted view that the entire universe in its present state is limited in time, and the apparently lethal nature of unscreened solar radiation are both obstacles which greatly lessen the likelihood that life has come to us across the infinite wastes of space. Once more, therefore, we are forced to examine our remaining notion that life is not coterminous with matter, but has arisen from it.

If the single-celled protozoans that riot in roadside pools 14
are not the simplest forms of life, if, as we know today, these creatures are already highly adapted and really complex, though minute beings, then where are we to turn in the search for something simple enough to suggest the greatest missing link of all—the link between living and dead matter? It is this problem that keeps me wandering fruitlessly in pastures and weed thickets even though I know this is an old-fashioned naturalist's approach, and that busy men in laboratories have little patience with my

scufflings of autumn leaves, or attempts to question beetles in decaying bark. Besides, many of these men are now fascinated by the crystalline viruses and have turned that remarkable instrument, the electron microscope, upon strange molecular "beings" never previously seen by man. Some are satisfied with this glimpse below the cell and find the virus a halfway station on the road to life. Perhaps it is, but as I wander about in the thin mist that is beginning to filter among these decaying stems and ruined spider webs, a kind of disconsolate uncertainty has taken hold of me.

15 I have come to suspect that this long descent down the ladder of life, beautiful and instructive though it may be, will not lead us to the final secret. In fact I have ceased to believe in the final brew or the ultimate chemical. There is, I know, a kind of heresy, a shocking negation of our confidence in blue-steel microtomes and men in white in making such a statement. I would not be understood to speak ill of scientific effort, for in simple truth I would not be alive today except for the microscopes and the blue steel. It is only that somewhere among these seeds and beetle shells and abandoned grasshopper legs I find something that is not accounted for very clearly in the dissections to the ultimate virus or crystal or protein particle. Even if the secret is contained in these things, in other words, I do not think it will yield to the kind of analysis our science is capable of making.

16 Imagine, for a moment, that you have drunk from a magician's goblet. Reverse the irreversible stream of time. Go down the dark stairwell out of which the race has ascended. Find yourself at last on the bottommost steps of time, slipping, sliding, and wallowing by scale and fin down into the muck and ooze out of which you arose. Pass by grunts and voiceless hissings below the last tree ferns. Eyeless and earless, float in the primal waters, sense sunlight you cannot see and stretch absorbing tentacles toward vague tastes that float in water. Still, in your formless shiftings, the *you* remains: the sliding particles, the juices, the transformations are working in an exquisitely patterned rhythm which has no other purpose than your preserva-

tion—you, the entity, the ameboid being whose substance contains the unfathomable future. Even so does every man come upward from the waters of his birth.

Yet if at any moment the magician bending over you 17
should cry, "Speak! Tell us of that road!" you could not respond. The sensations are yours but not—and this is one of the great mysteries—the power over the body. You cannot describe how the body you inhabit functions, or picture or control the flights and spinnings, the dance of the molecules that compose it, or why they chose to dance into that particular pattern which is you, or, again, why up the long stairway of the eons they dance from one shape to another. It is for this reason that I am no longer interested in final particles. Follow them as you will, pursue them until they become nameless protein crystals replicating on the verge of life. Use all the great powers of the mind and pass backward until you hang with the dire faces of the conquerors in the hydrogen cloud from which the sun was born. You will then have performed the ultimate dissection that our analytic age demands, but the cloud will still veil the secret and, if not the cloud, then the nothingness into which, it now appears, the cloud, in its turn, may be dissolved. The secret, if one may paraphrase a savage vocabulary, lies in the egg of night.

Only along the edges of this field after the frost are there 18
little whispers of it. Once even on a memorable autumn afternoon I discovered a sunning blacksnake brooding among the leaves like the very simulacrum of old night. He slid unhurriedly away, carrying his version of the secret with him in such a glittering menace of scales that I was abashed and could only follow admiringly from a little distance. I observed him well, however, and am sure he carried his share of the common mystery into the stones of my neighbor's wall, and is sleeping endlessly on in the winter darkness with one great coil locked around that glistening head. He is guarding a strange, reptilian darkness which is not night or nothingness, but has, instead, its momentary vision of mouse bones or a bird's egg, in the soft rising and ebbing of the tides of life. The snake has diverted me,

however. It was the dissection of a field that was to occupy us—a dissection in search of secrets—a dissection such as a probing and inquisitive age demands.

Every so often one encounters articles in leading magazines with titles such as "The Spark of Life," "The Secret of Life," "New Hormone Key to Life," or other similar optimistic proclamations. Only yesterday, for example, I discovered in the *New York Times* a headline announcing: "Scientist Predicts Creation of Life in Laboratory." The Moscow-date-lined dispatch announced that Academician Olga Lepeshinskaya had predicted that "in the not too distant future, Soviet scientists would create life." "The time is not far off," warns the formidable Madame Olga, "when we shall be able to obtain the vital substance artificially." She said it with such vigor that I had about the same reaction as I do to announcements about atomic bombs. In fact I half started up to latch the door before an invading tide of Russian protoplasm flowed in upon me. 19

What finally enabled me to regain my shaken confidence was the recollection that these pronouncements have been going on for well over a century. Just now the Russian scientists show a particular tendency to issue such blasts—committed politically, as they are, to an uncompromising materialism and the boastfulness of very young science. Furthermore, Madame Lepeshinskaya's remarks as reported in the press had a curiously old-fashioned flavor about them. The protoplasm she referred to sounded amazingly like the outmoded *Urschleim* or *Autoplasson* of Haeckel—simplified mucoid slimes no longer taken very seriously. American versions—and one must remember they are often journalistic interpretations of scientists' studies rather than direct quotations from the scientists themselves—are more apt to fall into another pattern. Someone has found a new chemical, vitamin, or similar necessary ingredient without which life will not flourish. By the time this reaches the more sensational press, it may have become the "secret of life." The only thing the inexperienced reader may not comprehend is the fact that no 20 one of these items, even the most recently discovered, is *the* secret. Instead, the substance is probably a part, a very small part, of a larger enigma which is well-nigh as inscrutable as it ever was. If anything, the growing list of catalysts, hormones, plasma genes, and other hobgoblins involved in the work of life only serves to underline the enormous complexity of the secret. "To grasp in detail," says the German biologist Von Bertalanffy, "the physico-chemical organization of the simplest cell is far beyond our capacity."

It is not, you understand, disrespect for the laudable and persistent patience of these dedicated scientists happily lost in their maze of pipettes, smells, and gas flames, that has led me into this runaway excursion to the wood. It is rather the loneliness of a man who knows he will not live to see the mystery solved, and who, furthermore, has come to believe that it will not be solved when the first humanly synthesized particle begins—if it ever does—to multiply itself in some unknown solution. 21

It is really a matter, I suppose, of the kind of questions one asks oneself. Some day we may be able to say with assurance, "We came from such and such a protein particle, possessing the powers of organizing in a manner leading under certain circumstances to that complex entity known as the cell, and from the cell by various steps onward, to multiple cell formation." I mean we may be able to say all this with great surety and elaboration of detail, but it is not the answer to the grasshopper's leg, brown and black and saw-toothed here in my hand, nor the answer to the seeds still clinging tenaciously to my coat, nor to this field, nor to the subtle essences of memory, delight, and wistfulness moving among the thin wires of my brain. 22

I suppose that in the forty-five years of my existence every atom, every molecule that composes me has changed its position or danced away and beyond to become part of other things. New molecules have come from the grass and the bodies of animals to be part of me a little while, yet in this spinning, light and airy as a midge swarm in a shaft of sunlight, my memories hold, and a loved face of twenty years ago is before me still. Nor is that face, nor all my 23 years, caught cellularly as in some cold precise photographic pattern, some gross, mechanical reproduction of the past. My memory holds the past and yet paradoxically knows, at the same time, that the past is gone and will never come again. It cherishes dead faces and silenced voices, yes, and lost evenings of childhood. In some odd nonspatial way it contains houses and rooms that have been torn timber from timber and brick from brick. These have a greater permanence in that midge dance which contains them than ever they had in the world of reality. It is for this reason that Academician Olga Lepeshinskaya has not answered the kind of questions one may ask in an open field.

If the day comes when the slime of the laboratory for the 24
first time crawls under man's direction, we shall have great need of humbleness. It will be difficult for us to believe, in our pride of achievement, that the secret of life has slipped through our fingers and eludes us still. We will list all the chemicals and the reactions. The men who have become gods will pose austerely before the popping flashbulbs of news photographers, and there will be few to consider—so deep is the mind-set of an age—whether the desire to link life to matter may not have blinded us to the more remarkable characteristics of both.

As for me, if I am still around on that day, I intend to put 25
on my old hat and climb over the wall as usual. I shall see strange mechanisms lying as they lie here now, in the autumn rain, strange pipes that transported the substance of life, the intricate seedcase out of which the life has flown. I shall observe no thing green, no delicate transpirations of leaves, nor subtle comings and goings of vapor. The little sunlit factories of the chloroplasts will have dissolved away into common earth.

Beautiful, angular, and bare the machinery of life will lie 26
exposed, as it now is, to my view. There will be the thin, blue skeleton of a hare tumbled in a little heap, and crouching over it I will marvel, as I marvel now, at the wonderful correlation of parts, the perfect adaptation to purpose, the individually vanished and yet persisting pattern which is

now hopping on some other hill. I will wonder, as always, in what manner "particles" pursue such devious plans and symmetries. I will ask once more in what way it is managed, that the simple dust takes on a history and begins to weave these unique and never recurring apparitions in the stream of time. I shall wonder what strange forces at the heart of matter regulate the tiny beating of a rabbit's heart or the dim dream that builds a milkweed pod.

It is said by men who know about these things that the 27 smallest living cell probably contains over a quarter of a million protein molecules engaged in the multitudinous coordinated activities which make up the phenomenon of life. At the instant of death, whether of man or microbe, that ordered, incredible spinning passes away in an almost furious haste of those same particles to get themselves back into the chaotic, unplanned earth.

I do not think, if someone finally twists the key suc- 28 cessfully in the tiniest and most humble house of life, that many of these questions will be answered, or that the dark forces which create lights in the deep sea and living batteries in the waters of tropical swamps, or the dread cycles of parasites, or the most noble workings of the human brain, will be much if at all revealed. Rather, I would say that if "dead" matter has reared up this curious landscape of fiddling crickets, song sparrows, and wondering men, it must be plain even to the most devoted materialist that the matter of which he speaks contains amazing, if not dreadful powers, and may not impossibly be, as Hardy has suggested, "but one mask of many worn by the Great Face behind."

QUESTIONS ON SUBJECT AND PURPOSE

1. Can "the secret of life" be defined, according to Eiseley? Why or why not?
2. Where does Eiseley search for the secret of life? Does he expect to find it?
3. What is Eiseley's thesis? Try to put it into a sentence or two at most.

QUESTIONS ON STRATEGY AND AUDIENCE

1. Why does Eiseley delay identifying the "it" until the third paragraph?
2. How does Eiseley structure his essay? Make a topic outline to see how he moves from idea to idea.
3. Why does Eiseley mention his walks into the "unkempt" field (paragraph 1)? Why mix this narrative with his thoughts about attempts of science to find the "answer" to life? What effect does the mixture have on the reader?

QUESTIONS ON VOCABULARY AND STYLE

1. Characterize the tone of Eiseley's essay. Would you characterize the style as formal or informal?
2. In paragraphs 16 and 17, Eiseley reverses "the stream of time." How does this section differ from the rest of the essay? Why does he include such an idea?
3. Be able to define the following words: *unkempt* (paragraph 1), *auspicious* (4), *iridescent* (5), *desiccated* (5), *bemused* (5), *purported* (5), *primordial* (7), *slough* (7), *recalcitrant* (7), *chided* (9), *beneficent* (10), *congenial* (12), *elucidate* (13), *incontrovertible* (13), *coterminous* (13), *microtomes* (15), *ameboid* (16), *eons* (17), *replicating* (17), *simulacrum* (18), *enigma* (20).

WRITING SUGGESTIONS

1. Using only the material provided in either Eiseley's essay or in Annie Dillard's "The Copperhead and the Mosquito" (Chapter 3), write a one-paragraph definition of the "secret of life" from either Eiseley's or Dillard's point of view.
2. Observation of the natural world is central to both Dillard and Eiseley. On the basis of these two selections, define in an essay each author's point of view about nature.

   Prewriting:

   a. Write a group of questions to ask yourself about the meaning of nature and the natural world in each essay. Include these questions: "What does nature reveal?" "What can we learn from studying nature?" "How does Eiseley's view compare with Dillard's?" Then reread each essay and answer the questions.

b. Since your response to the assignment will involve both definition and comparison/contrast, review the advice about writing a comparison/contrast paper in Chapter 5. Plot out a brief outline to structure your essay.
c. Using the material gathered from your questions, expand your outline to include details about each projected paragraph in your essay.

Rewriting:

a. Make sure that you have paraphrased Eiseley and Dillard (that is, expressed their ideas in your own words) or have quoted accurately (using quotation marks to enclose anything directly quoted). Check your paper line by line to be sure you have attributed quotations and paraphrased material for each author.
b. Have you developed the body of your essay using a subject-by-subject or a point-by-point comparison? Try an alternate arrangement. If you are working on a word processor, rearrange the text. Otherwise, make a photocopy of your essay, cut it apart, and paste up a new version. Which is more effective?
c. Ask a classmate or a roommate to read and evaluate your essay in light of the assignment. Have you answered the question? Have you adequately defined each writer's view of nature?

3. Is science any closer to solving the secret of life? Research the state of scientific knowledge, and then in an essay present the definition as it now stands. Use popular essays and books in your search.

C H A P T E R

9

Argument and Persuasion

We live in a world of persuasive messages—billboards, advertisements in newspapers and magazines, commercials on television and radio, signs on stores, bumper stickers, T-shirts with messages, and manufacturers' logos on clothing. Advertisements demonstrate a wide range of persuasive strategies. Sometimes they appeal to logic or reason—they ask you to compare the features available on this automobile and its price with any competitor and judge for yourself. More often they appeal to your emotions or feelings—you will not be stylish unless you wear this particular brand of jeans; you are not a real man unless you drink this brand of beer or smoke this cigarette. Arguments are frequently divided in this way—those that appeal to logic and reason and those that appeal to emotions and prejudices. Legal briefs and scientific proofs are good examples of logical arguments; political and social propaganda, of emotional arguments. Jesse Jackson in "Why Blacks Need Affirmative Action" appeals to reason, citing specific factual evidence to support his claims; Marya Mannes in "Wasteland" appeals to the readers' emotions, describing "the mark of savages, the testament of wasters, the stain of prosperity" that litters our landscape. More typically, argumentation blends the two types of appeal. But no matter what strategy you use, in argumentation your objective is the same: to persuade the reader to believe or act in a certain way.

Whether you realize it or not, you already have had extensive experience in constructing arguments and in persuading an audience. Every time you try to persuade someone to do or to believe something, you have to argue. Consider a hypothetical example: You are concerned about your father's health. He smokes cigarettes, avoids exercise, is overweight, and works long hours in a stressful job. Even though you are worried, he is completely unconcerned and has always resisted your family's efforts to change his ways. Your task is to persuade him to change or modify his life style, and doing so involves making its dangers clear, offering convincing reasons for change, and urging specific action.

Establishing the dangers is the first step, and you have a wide range of medical evidence from which to draw. That evidence involves statistics, testimony or advice from doctors, and case histories of men who have suffered the consequences of years of abusing or ignoring their health. From that body of material, you select those items which are most likely to touch your obstinate father. He might not be moved by cold statistics citing life-expectancy tables for smokers and nonexercisers, but he might be touched by the story of a friend his age who suffered a heart attack or stroke. The evidence you gather and use becomes a part of the convincing reasons for change that you offer in your argument. If your father persists in ignoring his health, he is likely to suffer some consequences. You might at this point include in your argument motivational appeals. If he is not concerned about what will happen to him, what about his family? What will they do if he dies?

Having gotten your father to realize and acknowledge the dangers inherent in his life style and to understand the reasons why he should make changes, it remains to urge specific action. In framing a plan for that action, you again need to consider your audience. If you urge your father to stop smoking immediately, join a daily exercise class at the local YMCA or health club, go on a thousand-calorie-a-day diet, and find a new job, chances are that he will think your proposal too drastic even to try. Instead, you might urge a more moderate plan, phasing in changes over a period of time or offering compromises (e.g., that he work fewer hours).

How Do You Analyze Your Audience?

Argumentation or persuasion, unlike the other forms or types of writing included in this text, has a special purpose—to persuade its audience. Because you want your reader to agree with your position or act as you urge, you need to analyze your audience before you start to write. Try to answer each of the following questions:

Who are my readers?
What do they already know about this subject?
How interested are they likely to be?
How impartial or prejudiced are they going to be?
What values do my readers share?
Is my argument going to challenge any of my readers' beliefs or values?
What types of evidence are most likely to be effective?
Is my plan for requested action reasonable?

Your argumentative strategy should always reflect an awareness of your audience. Even in the hypothetical example concerning your father, it is obvious that some types of evidence would be more effective than others and that some solutions or plans for action would be more reasonable and, therefore, more acceptable than others.

The second important consideration in any argument is to anticipate your audience's objections and be ready to answer them. Debaters study both sides of an argument so that they can effectively counter any opposition. In arguing the abortion issue, the Right-to-Life speaker has to be prepared to deal with subjects such as abnormal fetuses or pregnancy caused by rape or incest. The Pro-Choice speaker must face questions about when life begins and when the rights of the unborn might take precedence over the mother's rights.

What Does It Take to Persuade Your Reader?

In some cases nothing will persuade your reader. For example, if you are arguing for legalized abortion, you will never convince a reader who believes that an embryo is a human being from the moment of conception. Abortion to that reader will always be murder. It is extremely difficult to argue any position that is counter to your audience's moral or ethical values. It is also difficult to argue a position that is counter to your audience's normal patterns of behavior. For example, you could reasonably argue that your readers ought to stop at all red lights and to obey the speed limit. However, the likelihood of persuading your audience to do these two things—even though not doing so breaks the law—is slim.

These cautions are not meant to imply that you should argue only "safe" subjects or that winning is everything. Choose a subject about which you feel strongly; present a fair, logical argument; express honest emotion; but avoid distorted evidence or inflammatory language. Even if no one is finally persuaded, at least you have offered a clear, intelligent explanation of your position.

In most arguments you have two possible types of support—you can supply factual evidence, and you can appeal to your reader's values. Suppose, for example, you are arguing that professional boxing should be prohibited because it is dangerous. The reader may or may not accept your premise but at the very least would expect some support for your assertion. Your first task would be to gather evidence. The strongest evidence is factual—statistics dealing with the number of fighters each year who are fatally injured or mentally impaired. You might quote appropriate authorities—physicians, scientists, former fighters—on the risks connected with professional boxing. You might relate several instances or even a single example of a particular fighter who was killed or permanently injured while boxing. You might describe in detail how blows strike the body or head; you might trace the process by which a series of punches can cause brain damage. You might catalog the effects that years of physical punishment can produce in the human body. In your argument you might use some or all of this factual evidence. You job as a writer is to gather the best—the most accurate and the most effective—evidence and present it in a clear and orderly way for your reader.

You can also appeal to your reader's values. You could argue that a sport in which a participant can be killed or permanently injured is not a "sport" at all. You could argue that the objective of a boxing match—to render one fighter unconscious or unable to continue—is different in kind from any other sport and not one that we, as human beings, should condone, let alone encourage. Appeals to values can be extremely effective. George F. Will, for example, in "Gambling with the Public's Virtue" appeals to the American belief in the value of hard work and the importance of earning success.

One final thing is crucially important in persuading your reader. You must sound (and be) fair, reasonable, and credible in order to win the respect and possibly the approval of your reader. Readers distrust arguments that are loaded with unfair or inflammatory language, faulty logic, and biased or distorted evidence.

Should You Argue Logically or Emotionally?

Effective argumentation generally involves appealing to both reason and emotion. It is often easier to catch your reader's attention by using an emotional appeal. Demonstrators against vivisection, the dissecting of animals for laboratory research, display photographs of the torments suffered by these animals. Oranizations that fight famine throughout the world use photographs of starving children. Advertisers use a wide range of persuasive tactics to touch our fears, our anxieties, our desires. But the types of argumentative writing that you are asked to do in college or in your job rarely allow for only emotional evidence.

Since logic or reason is so crucial to effective argumentation, you will want to avoid logical fallacies or errors.

When you construct your argument, make sure that you have avoided the following common mistakes:

Ad hominem argument (literally to argue "to the person"): criticizing a person's position by criticizing his or her personal character. If an underworld figure asserts that boxing is the manly art of self-defense, you do not counter *argument* by claiming that he makes money by betting on the fights.

Ad populum argument (literally to argue "to the people"): appealing to the prejudices of your audience instead of offering facts or reasons. You do not defend boxing by asserting that it is part of the American way of life and that anyone who criticizes it is a Communist who seeks to undermine our society.

Appeal to an unqualified authority: using testimony from someone who is unqualified to give it. In arguing against boxing, your relevant authorities would be physicians, or scientists, or former fighters—people who have had some direct experience. You do not quote a professional football player or your dermatologist.

Begging the question: assuming as true what you are trying to prove. "Boxing is dangerous and because it is dangerous it ought to be outlawed." The first statement ("boxing is dangerous") is the premise you set out to prove, but the second statement uses that unproved premise as a basis for drawing a conclusion.

Either/or: stating or implying that there are only two possibilities. Do not assert that the two choices are either to ban boxing or to allow this legalized murder to continue. Perhaps other changes might make the sport safer and hence less objectionable.

Faulty analogy: using an inappropriate or superficially similar analogy as evidence. "Allowing a fighter to kill another man with his fists is like giving him a gun and permission to shoot to kill." The analogy might be vivid, but the two acts are far more different than they are similar.

Hasty generalization: basing a conclusion on evidence that is atypical or unrepresentative. Do not assert that *every* boxer has suffered brain damage just because you can cite a few well-known cases.

Non sequitur (literally "it does not follow"): arriving at a conclusion not justified by the premises or evidence. "My father has watched many fights on television; therefore he is an authority on the physical hazards that boxers face."

Oversimplification: suggesting a simple solution to a complex problem. "If professional boxers were made aware of the risks they take, they would stop boxing."

How Do You Structure an Argument?

You construct an argument in either of two ways: you begin with your premise and then provide evidence or support or you begin with your evidence and then move to your conclusion. Jesse Jackson starts with a premise: blacks need affirmative action to achieve "educational and economic equity and parity." He then supports that premise by citing statistics comparing the number of whites in certain professions to the number of blacks. He anticipates and counters the obvious objection to affirmative action—that it is unfair to whites. Lewis Thomas in "On Medicine and the Bomb" structures his essay in the opposite way. He begins by giving examples of what modern medicine can achieve in dealing with patients suffering from lethal radiation injuries, burns, and massive trauma. But these advances, he observes, are achieved at great cost in individual cases. Medicine, given the technology, manpower, and money, can save an individual life, but in the event of a nuclear war, casualties would number in the millions. As a result, Thomas concludes, "modern medicine has nothing whatever to offer, not even a token benefit, in the event of thermonuclear war." Richard Rodriguez in "None of This Is Fair" traces how affirmative action programs have advanced, perhaps unfairly, his own career. That evidence leads him to conclude that such programs often fail to help those who are really the disadvantaged.

If you are constructing an argument based upon a formal, logical progression, you can use either inductive or deductive reasoning. An *inductive* argument begins with specific evidence and then moves to a generalized conclusion to account for that evidence. The detective pieces together the evidence in an investigation and arrives at a conclusion: the butler did it. Lewis Thomas's essay moves basically in an inductive pattern. He starts with particular examples and moves to a general truth: medicine cannot cope with thermonuclear war.

A *deductive* argument moves in the opposite direction: it starts with a general truth and moves to a specific application of that truth. Harry Edwards in "Educating Black Athletes" begins with a general statement: "Student athletes . . . have informally agreed to a contract with the universities they attend: athletic performance in exchange for an education. The athletes have kept their part of the bargain; the universities have not." In the rest of the essay, Edwards provides the evidence that has led him to that conclusion.

The simplest form of a deductive argument is the *syllogism,* a three-step argument involving a major premise, a minor premise, and a conclusion. Few essays—either those you write or those you read—can be reduced to a syllogism. Our thought patterns are rarely so logical, our reasoning rarely so precise. Although few essays state a syllogism explicitly, syllogisms do play a role in shaping an argument. For example, both Jesse Jackson and Martin Luther King, Jr. begin with the same syllogism, even though it is not directly stated in either selection:

Major premise: All people should have equal opportunities.
Minor premise: Blacks are people.
Conclusion: Blacks should have equal opportunities.

Despite the fact that a syllogism is a precise structural form, you should not assume that a written argument will imitate it; that the first paragraph or group of paragraphs will contain a major premise; the next, a minor premise; and the final, a conclusion. Syllogisms can be basic to an argument without being a framework upon which it is constructed.

No matter how you structure your argument, one final consideration is important. Since the purpose of argumentation is to get a reader to agree with your position or to act in a particular way, it is always essential to end your paper decisively. Endings can be used in a variety of ways. You can end with a call to action. Martin Luther King's speech rises to an eloquent, rhythmical exhortation to his people to continue to fight until they are "free at last." You can end with a serious question. Lewis Thomas concludes by questioning "what has gone wrong in the minds of statesmen in this generation" that has allowed the stockpiling of nuclear weapons. You can end by suggesting what steps are necessary. The final section of Edwards's essay outlines some ways in which America must demonstrate "a greater concern for and commitment to educational quality."

Writing an Argument: A Student Example

Beth Jaffe decided to tackle a subject on the minds of many career-minded, dollar-conscious college students: why do you have to take so many courses outside of your major? Beth's argument is sure to arouse the attention of every advocate of a liberal arts education, and you might consider exploring the subject for a paper.

Reducing College Requirements

With the high costs of college still on the rise, it is not fair to make college students pay for courses labeled "requirements" which are not part of their major. Although many students want a well-rounded college education, many cannot afford to pay for one. By eliminating all of the requirements that do not pertain to a student's major, college costs could be cut tremendously. At the University of Delaware, for example, a student in the College of Arts and Science is required to take twelve credits of arts and humanities, twelve of culture and institutions of time, twelve of human beings and their environment, and thirteen of natural phenomena or science which include at least one lab. Although some of their major courses may fit into these categories, many others do not. Frequently students do not like and are not interested in the courses which fit into the four categories and feel they are wasting their money by paying for courses they do not enjoy,

> do not put much work into, and usually do not get much out of. It should be an option to the student to take these extra courses. Why should a humanities or social studies major have to take biology or chemistry? Many of these students thought their struggle with science was over after high school only to come to college and find yet more "requirements" in the sciences. Students are getting degrees in one area of concentration. They should be able to take only courses in their field of study and not have to waste their money on courses they have no desire to take.

Beth's essay, with her permission, was duplicated and discussed in class. Not surprisingly, it provoked a lively reaction. One student asked Beth whether she was serious and exactly what it was that she was proposing. Beth admitted that she did not advocate turning a college education into career training but that she had a number of friends who were deeply in debt because of their four-year education. "Why not just cut some requirements?" Beth asked. Several other students then suggested that since she did not really advocate an extreme position, maybe she could find a compromise proposal. Her instructor added that she might find a way of rewording her remarks about science classes. Few people, after all, are sympathetic to a position that seems to say, "I don't want to do that. It's too hard. It's too boring."

When Beth revised her paper, she tried to follow the advice the class had offered. In addition, she made the problem vivid by using her roommate as an example and by pointing out what specifically might be saved by the Jaffe proposal.

> Lowering the Cost of a College Education
>
> When my roommate graduates in June, she will be $10,000 in debt. The debt did not come from spring breaks in Fort Lauderdale or a new car. It came from four years of college expenses, expenses that were not covered by the money she earned as a part-time waitress or by the small scholarship she was awarded annually. So now in June at age 21, with her first full-time job (assuming she gets one), Alison can start repaying her student loans.

Alison's case is certainly not unusual. In fact, because she attends a state-assisted university, her debt is less than it might be. We cannot expect education to get cheaper. We cannot expect government scholarship programs to get larger. We cannot ask that students go deeper and deeper into debt. We need a new way of combating this cost problem. We need the Jaffe proposal.

If colleges would eliminate some of the general education course requirements, college costs could be substantially lowered. At the University of Delaware, for example, a student in the College of Arts and Science is required to take twelve credits of arts and humanities, twelve of culture and the institutions of time, twelve of human beings and their environment, and thirteen of natural phenomena or science, including at least one laboratory course. Approximately half of these requirements are fulfilled by courses which are required for particular majors. The others are not, and these are likely to be courses that students are not interested in and so get little out of.

If some of these requirements were eliminated, a student would need approximately twenty-five credits less for a bachelor's degree. If a student took a heavier load or went to summer school, he or she could graduate either one or two semesters earlier. The result would cut college costs by anywhere from one-eighth to one-fourth.

The Jaffe proposal does decrease the likelihood that a college graduate will receive a well-rounded education. On the other hand, it allows students to concentrate their efforts in courses which they feel are relevant. Perhaps most important, it helps reduce the burden that escalating college costs have placed on all of us.

Some Things to Remember

1. Choose a subject that allows for the possibility of persuading your reader. Avoid emotionally charged subjects that resist logical examination.
2. Analyze your audience. Who are your readers? What do they already know about your subject? How are they likely to feel about it? How impartial or prejudiced are they going to be?
3. Make a list of the evidence or reasons you will use in

your argument. Analyze each piece of evidence to see how effective it might be in achieving your end.

4. Honest emotion is fair, but avoid anything that is distorted, inaccurate, or inflammatory. Argue with solid, reasonable, fair, and relevant evidence.
5. Avoid the common logical fallacies listed in this introduction.
6. Make a list of all the possible counterarguments or objections your audience might have. Think of ways in which you can respond to those objections.
7. Decide how to structure your essay. You can begin with a position and then provide evidence. You can begin with the evidence and end with a conclusion. Which structure seems to fit your subject and evidence better?
8. End forcibly. Conclusions are what listeners and readers are most likely to remember. Repeat or restate your position. Drive home the importance of your argument.

Why Blacks Need Affirmative Action

JESSE JACKSON

Jesse Jackson was born in Greenville, South Carolina, in 1941. He received a B.A. in sociology in 1964 from the North Carolina Agricultural and Technical State University and later studied at the Chicago Theological Seminary, eventually becoming a Baptist minister in 1968. A follower of Martin Luther King, he participated in several civil rights demonstrations and in 1967 was chosen by King to head Project Breadbasket, an organization to create business opportunities for blacks in Chicago. Jackson was one of the leaders of the 1968 Poor People's Campaign and in 1971 founded People United to Save Humanity (PUSH). A presidential candidate in the elections of 1984 and 1988, Jackson is the foremost black American politician today. A collection of his speeches, sermons, and essays, Straight from the Heart, *was published in 1987.*

In this selection from an essay that appeared in Regulation *(September/October 1978), a publication of the American Enterprise Institute for Public Policy, Jackson argues the need for affirmative action programs. Jackson's remarks were prompted in part by the legal testing of such programs, especially in the Bakke case. In 1973 and 1974 Allan Bakke, a white male, was denied admission to the Davis Medical College of the University of California. In both years, other, less qualified applicants were accepted through a special admissions program that reserved 16 places out of a total class of 100 for nonwhite applicants. Claiming that he was denied equal protection of the law and hence was a victim of reverse discrimination, Bakke sued, and his case was eventually heard by the United States Supreme Court. In 1978, the court ruled that Bakke had been discriminated against and had to be admitted to the school. At the same time, the court held that affirmative action programs could legally continue only if they were not based on a rigid quota system.*

According to a recent publication of the Equal Employment Opportunity Commission, at the present rate of "progress" it will take forty-three years to end job discrimination—hardly a reasonable timetable. 1

If our goal is educational and economic equity and parity—and it is—then we need affirmative action to catch up. We are behind as a result of discrimination and denial of opportunity. There is one white attorney for every 680 whites, but only one black attorney for every 4,000 blacks; one white physician for every 659 whites, but only one black physician for every 5,000 blacks; and one white dentist for every 1,900 whites, but only one black dentist for every 8,400 blacks. Less than 1 percent of all engineers—or of all practicing chemists—is black. Cruel and uncompassionate injustice created gaps like these. We need creative justice and compassion to help us close them. 2

Actually, in the U.S. context, "reverse discrimination" is illogical and a contradiction in terms. Never in the history of mankind has a majority, with power, engaged in programs and written laws that discriminate against itself. The only thing whites are giving up because of affirmative action is unfair advantage—something that was unnecessary in the first place. 3

Blacks are not making progress at the expense of whites, as news accounts make it seem. There are 49 percent more whites in medical school today and 64 percent more whites in law school than there were when affirmative action programs began some eight years ago. 4

In a recent column, William Raspberry raised an interesting question. Commenting on the *Bakke* case, he asked, "What if, instead of setting aside 16 of 100 slots, we added 16 slots to the 100?" That, he suggested, would allow blacks to make progress and would not interfere with what whites already have. He then went on to point out that this, in fact, is exactly what has happened in law and medical schools. In 1968, the year before affirmative action programs began to get under way, 9,571 whites and 282 members of minority groups entered U.S. medical schools. In 1976, the figures were 14,213 and 1,400 respectively. Thus, under affirmative 5 action, the number of "white places" actually rose by 49 percent: white access to medical training was not diminished, but substantially increased. The trend was even more marked in law schools. In 1969, the first year for which reliable figures are available, 2,933 minority-group members were enrolled; in 1976, the number was up to 8,484. But during the same period, law school enrollment for whites rose from 65,453 to 107,064—an increase of 64 percent. In short, it is a myth that blacks are making progress at white expense.

Allan Bakke did not really challenge preferential treatment in general, for he made no challenge to the preferential treatment accorded to the children of the rich, the alumni and the faculty, or to athletes or the very talented—only to minorities. 6

QUESTIONS ON SUBJECT AND PURPOSE

1. What is affirmative action? How does it aid members of minority groups?
2. What is "educational and economic equity and parity"? What would it take to achieve both?
3. What is reverse discrimination? According to Jackson, does it exist?
4. What is Jackson's purpose in this essay? Do you think he achieves that purpose effectively?

QUESTIONS ON STRATEGY AND AUDIENCE

1. How does Jackson's argument differ from Mannes's in "Wasteland" or from Rodriguez's in "None of This is Fair," two other essays in this chapter?
2. How are Jackson's statistics particularly relevant to the argument he is making? Is there any difference between the kind of statistics used in paragraph 2 and those used in paragraph 5?
3. Would Jackson's argument be equally effective with any audience? Why or why not?

QUESTIONS ON VOCABULARY AND STYLE

1. Characterize the tone of Jackson's argument. How does he sound? How do the language, examples, and sentence structures contribute to achieving that tone?
2. How does Jackson use parallel structures in paragraphs 2 and 5 to make his argument clearer?
3. Be able to define the following words or phrases: *equity* (paragraph 2), *parity* (2), *affirmative action* (2), *reverse discrimination* (3), *Bakke case* (5).

WRITING SUGGESTIONS

1. In a paragraph argue for the justice of affirmative action programs. Do not use statistics. Instead appeal to more basic and general human values.
2. Are minorities and women equally represented on the faculty of your college or university? Check the proportions and then in an essay argue for or against the need to achieve "educational and economic equity and parity." Assume that your essay will be published in the student newspaper.

Prewriting:

a. Before you begin writing you will need accurate information. An Affirmation Action Office can provide those statistics. (Check a telephone directory to locate that office.)
b. Statistics about the undergraduate population of your college will also help. The admissions office or the dean of students should be able to provide a breakdown by sex, race, and nationality. That information will also help you to define your audience.
c. On the basis of this evidence and your own feelings, decide upon a position. Make a list of the evidence and the reasons you will use in your paper.
d. Copy that list onto the left-hand side of a separate sheet of paper. On the right-hand side, try to anticipate the objections that your audience might have.

Rewriting:

a. Find a classmate or roommate to read your essay. Ask that reader to evaluate your position. Does your reader agree? Why or why not? Listen carefully to your reader's reactions.
b. Is your essay structured inductively or deductively? Briefly

outline a new strategy. Which of the two arrangements seems more effective? Ask your reader to evaluate both strategies.

c. Look at your conclusion. Arguments—either emotional or logical—need to end forcefully. Freewrite a totally different ending to your essay. Ask your reader to evaluate both.

3. Similar statistical information is available for women, or Hispanics, or Native Americans, or Chinese-Americans, or any other minority in the United States. Choose one such group and research the progress that has been made during the last 10 to 20 years. Have affirmative action programs benefited that minority? Why or why not? Using your research, in an essay argue for the effectiveness (or ineffectiveness) of such programs for this minority.

Wasteland

MARYA MANNES

Marya Mannes, novelist, essayist, and journalist, was born in 1904 in New York City. She worked as a feature editor for Vogue *magazine and later, during World War II, acted as an intelligence analyst for the United States government. She has held a variety of positions such as staff writer for* The Reporter, *feature editor for* Glamour *magazine, and columnist for* The New York Times. *Her publications include* Message from a Stranger, *a novel (1948);* Subverse, *a collection of satirical verse (1959); and* Out of My Time, *an autobiography (1971). She has received many awards for her biting and satiric magazine essays on American arts, education, and morals. Many of those essays have been published in the collections* But Will It Sell? *(1953),* More in Anger *(1958), and* The New York I Know *(1961). In this selection from* More in Anger, *Mannes offers an emotional indictment of our tendency to pollute the environment.*

Cans. Beer cans. Glinting on the verge of a million miles of roadways, lying in scrub, grass, dirt, leaves, sand, mud, but never hidden. Piels, Rheingold, Ballantine, Schaefer, Schlitz, shining in the sun or picked up by moonlight or the beams of headlights at night; washed by rain or flattened by wheels, but never dulled, never buried, never destroyed. Here is the mark of savages, the testament of wasters, the stain of prosperity. 1

Who are these men who defile the grassy borders of our roads and lanes, who pollute our ponds, who spoil the purity of our ocean beaches with the empty vessels of their thirst? Who are the men who make these vessels in millions and then say, "Drink—and discard"? What society is this that can afford to cast away a million tons of metal and to make of wild and fruitful land a garbage heap? 2

What manner of men and women need thirty feet of 3

steel and two hundred horsepower to take them, singly, to their small destinations? Who demand that what they eat is wrapped so that forests are cut down to make the paper that is thrown away, and what they smoke and chew is sealed so that the sealers can be tossed in gutters and caught in twigs and grass?

What kind of men can afford to make the streets of their 4
towns and cities hideous with neon at night, and their roadways hideous with signs by day, wasting beauty; who leave the carcasses of cars to rot in heaps; who spill their trash into ravines and make smoking mountains of refuse for the town's rats? What manner of men choke off the life in rivers, streams, and lakes with the waste of their produce, making poison of water?

Who is as rich as that? Slowly the wasters and despoilers 5
are impoverishing our land, our nature, and our beauty, so that there will not be one beach, one hill, one lane, one meadow, one forest free from the debris of man and the stigma of his improvidence.

Who is so rich that he can squander forever the wealth 6
of earth and water for the trivial needs of vanity or the compulsive demands of greed; or so prosperous in land that he can sacrifice nature for unnatural desires? The earth we abuse and the living things we kill will, in the end, take their revenge; for in exploiting their presence we are diminishing our future.

And what will we leave behind us when we are long 7
dead? Temples? Amphorae? Sunken treasure?

Or mountains of twisted, rusted steel, canyons of plastic 8
containers, and a million miles of shores garlanded, not with the lovely wrack of the sea, but with the cans and bottles and light bulbs and boxes of a people who conserved their convenience at the expense of their heritage; and whose ephemeral prosperity was built on waste.

QUESTIONS ON SUBJECT AND PURPOSE

1. What is Mannes's thesis? Summarize it in a single sentence.
2. How many examples of waste does Mannes cite? What do they have in common?

3. What purpose does Mannes want to achieve? Does it work? How do you as a reader respond to each paragraph?

QUESTIONS ON STRATEGY AND AUDIENCE

1. In what way is Mannes's essay persuasive? How does it differ from a formal argument? What would it take to make it into one?
2. In paragraph 5, Mannes writes: "There will not be one beach, one hill, one lane, one meadow, one forest free from the debris of man and the stigma of his improvidence." Does that seem an accurate statement to make? Is it exaggerated? Why would Mannes make it?
3. Who is Mannes's audience? What assumptions does she make of it? How can you tell from the essay?

QUESTIONS ON VOCABULARY AND STYLE

1. How frequently does Mannes use rhetorical questions? What is the effect of such a device? How is it appropriate for her essay?
2. Why does Mannes use such a short paragraph (7)? Why not merge it with the longer paragraph that follows?
3. Be able to define the following words: *verge* (paragraph 1), *defile* (2), *despoiler* (5), *stigma* (5), *improvidence* (5), *squander* (6), *amphorae* (7), *garlanded* (8), *ephemeral* (8).

WRITING SUGGESTIONS

1. Select a place on campus or in town that shows the effect of what Mannes is saying. In a paragraph describe the place with the intention of persuading your readers to do something about pollution.
2. Select one of the other examples of waste that Mannes finds—or an example of your own—and in an essay persuade your reader to *do* something about the problem. Some possible examples from Mannes's essay include:
   a. large cars and trucks
   b. abandoned cars
   c. excessive packaging

Prewriting:

a. Before you choose a subject, spend a day looking for examples of waste in your environment. As you walk around your campus or your neighborhood, what do you see? Take notes.
b. Once you have a subject, brainstorm a possible outline for your essay. Look at your notes. Where can your examples be placed in your proposed structure?
c. Using your outline as a guide, freewrite for 15 minutes about each point that you wish to make.

Rewriting:

a. Make a copy of your essay, and highlight in one color all emotionally charged words and phrases. Highlight in another color all factual examples. Is your argument based on emotion or factual evidence?
b. Look at all of the emotionally charged words and phrases. How will your audience react to these? Do you avoid distorted or inflammatory statements?
c. What exactly do you want your reader to do about this problem? Do you make that call to action clear in your conclusion? If not, try writing another ending.

3. In many states a deposit is charged on soft-drink and beer bottles and/or cans as an incentive for people not to litter. But have we gone far enough? Research the success of these programs. Argue for or against the extension of such measures in order to clean up America.

Gambling with the Public's Virtue

GEORGE F. WILL

George F. Will was born in Champaign, Illinois, in 1941. He received a B.A. from Trinity College; attended Magdalen College, Oxford; and completed his Ph.D. at Princeton University. A former professor of politics at Michigan State University and the University of Toronto, Will began his career as a journalist when he joined the National Review *as Washington editor in 1972. Since 1975 he has been a contributng editor to* Newsweek. *In 1977 he received the Pulitzer Prize for commentary. His books include* The Pursuit of Happiness, and Other Sobering Thoughts *(1979),* The Pursuit of Virtue and Other Tory Notions *(1982),* Statecraft as Soulcraft: What Government Does *(1982), and* The New Season: A Spectator's Guide to the 1988 Election *(1987). As a political columnist of what he calls "conservative convictions," Will is an articulate advocate of the public good. In "Gambling with the Public's Virtue," written in 1978, Will attacks all forms of "state-sanctioned" gambling as plans that "simultaneously cheat and corrupt . . . citizens."*

On the outskirts of this city of insurance companies,* there is another, less useful, business based on an understanding of probabilities. It is a jai alai fronton, a cavernous court where athletes play a fast game for the entertainment of gamblers and the benefit of, among others, the state treasury. 1

Half the states have legal betting in casinos, at horse or dog tracks, in off-track betting parlors, at jai alai frontons or in state-run lotteries. Only Connecticut has four (the last four) kinds of gambling, and there is talk of promoting the other two. 2

*Hartford, Connecticut.

Not coincidentally, Connecticut is one of just seven 3
still fiercely determined not to have an income tax. Gambling taxes yielded $76.4 million last year—which is not a large slice of Connecticut's $2.1 billion budget, but it would be missed, and is growing.

Last year Americans legally wagered $15 billion, up 8 4
percent over 1976. Lotteries took in 24 percent more than in 1976. Stiffening resistance to taxes is encouraging states to seek revenues from gambling, and thus to encourage gambling. There are three rationalizations for this:

State-run gambling controls illegal gambling. 5

Gambling is a painless way to raise revenues. 6

Gambling is a "victimless" recreation, and thus is a 7
matter of moral indifference.

Actually, there is evidence that legal gambling increases 8
the respectability of gambling and increases public interest in gambling. This creates new gamblers, some of whom move on to illegal gambling, which generally offers better odds. And as a revenue-raising device, gambling is severely regressive.

Gamblers are drawn disproportionately from minority 9
and poor populations that can ill afford to gamble, that are especially susceptible to the lure of gambling and that especially need a government that will not collaborate with gambling entrepreneurs, as in jai alai, and that will not become a gambling entrepreneur through a state lottery.

A depressing number of gamblers have no margin for 10
economic losses and little understanding of the probability of losses. Between 1975 and 1977 there was a 140-percent increase in spending to advertise lotteries—lotteries in which more than 99.9 percent of all players are losers. Such advertising is apt to be especially effective, and cruel, among people whose tribulations make them susceptible to dreams of sudden relief.

Grocery money is risked for such relief. Some grocers in 11
Hartford's poorer neighborhoods report that receipts decline during jai alai season. Aside from the injury gamblers do to

their dependents, there is a subtler but more comprehensive injury done by gambling. It is the injury done to society's sense of elemental equities. Gambling blurs the distinction between well-earned and "ill-gotten" gains.

Gambling is debased speculation, a lust for sudden wealth that is not connected with the process of making society more productive of goods and services. Government support of gambling gives a legitimating imprimatur to the pursuit of wealth without work. 12

"It is," said Jefferson, "the manners and spirit of a people which preserves a republic in vigor." Jefferson believed in the virtue-instilling effects of agricultural labor. Andrew Jackson denounced the Bank of the United States as a "monster" because increased credit creation meant increased speculation. Martin Van Buren warned against "a craving desire . . . for sudden wealth." The early nineteenth-century belief was that citizens could be distinguished by the moral worth of the way they acquired wealth; and physical labor was considered the most ennobling labor. 13

It is perhaps a bit late to worry about all this: the United States is a developed capitalist society of a sort Jefferson would have feared if he had been able to imagine it. But those who cherish capitalism should note that the moral weakness of capitalism derives, in part, from the belief that too much wealth is allocated in "speculative" ways, capriciously, to people who earn their bread neither by the sweat of their brows nor by wrinkling their brows for socially useful purposes. 14

Of course, any economy produces windfalls. As a town grows, some land values soar. And some investors (like many noninvestors) regard stock trading as a form of roulette. 15

But state-sanctioned gambling institutionalizes windfalls, whets the public appetite for them and encourages the delusion that they are more frequent than they really are. Thus do states simultaneously cheat and corrupt their citizens. 16

QUESTIONS ON SUBJECT AND PURPOSE

1. Why does Will object to "state-sanctioned" gambling? Make a list of his objections.
2. How does gambling injure "society's sense of elemental equities" (paragraph 11)? Why types of evidence would prove that? Or will the reader accept that premise without evidence?
3. What is the difference, for Will, between playing the horses (or any other form of gambling) and playing the stock market? Would he object as much to other legalized forms of speculation? Why or why not?

QUESTIONS ON STRATEGY AND AUDIENCE

1. How does Will argue? What types of evidence does he use? Is his argument convincing? Why or why not?
3. What assumptions does Will make about his audience? How does he appeal to that audience? To their sense of values?

QUESTIONS ON VOCABULARY AND STYLE

1. Who is Will's audience? How is that reflected in the essay?
2. Examine how and why Will paragraphs his essay. Do his paragraphs reveal the textbook qualities that you might expect: topic sentences, adequate development, unity, coherence?
3. Be able to define the following words: *jai alai* (paragraph 1), *regressive* (8), *entrepreneurs* (9), *tribulations* (10), *equities* (11), *debased* (12), *imprimatur* (12), *capriciously* (14), *whets* (16).

WRITING SUGGESTIONS

1. In a paragraph or two intended for gamblers, attempt to persuade your audience of the folly of their habit. Remember that the average gambler is looking for a windfall and so you will need to find ways in which to counter such an expectation or hope. You might, for example, show your audience how much money their gambling losses might amount to if more shrewdly invested.

2. Certainly Will has not exhausted the subject. Write an essay in which you support or oppose a particular form of legalized gambling. Remember to anticipate the objections that your opponents will raise.

   Prewriting:

   a. You need to select both a specific subject (a form of gambling) and a position (for or against). Does your state sponsor any gambling activities? If so, investigate how that works.
   b. Interview some friends or relatives. What types of gambling experiences have they had? How do they feel about the subject? Find at least one person who favors it and one who opposes it.
   c. Try freewriting on both sides of the issue. To argue effectively on any subject, you need to anticipate your opponent's position.

   Rewriting:

   a. Check the list of logical fallacies and errors in the introduction to this chapter. Have you avoided each of these in your essay?
   b. Every essay benefits from an interesting, lively introduction. Make a copy of your introduction, and ask some friends to read it. Do they want to read on?
   c. An effective title is also important to an essay. Imagine yourself as a copywriter for an advertising agency. Write some possible titles for your essay.

3. Examine closely the premises that Will uses in his argument (e.g., legalized gambling increases public interest in gambling; gambling is a severely regressive revenue measure; advertisements for gambling are effective and cruel; gambling can produce "ill-gotten" gains; wealth derived from work is better than wealth derived from speculation). Research each premise. Then, in an essay using your evidence, argue either that legalized gambling should be discontinued or that it should be expanded to other states.

On Medicine and the Bomb

LEWIS THOMAS

Another example of Lewis Thomas's work ("On Societies as Organisms") and biographical information can be found in Chapter 5. In "On Medicine and the Bomb," from Thomas's collection Late Night Thoughts on Listening to Mahler's Ninth Symphony *(1983), he explains that medical advances made in treating cancer, burn, and trauma victims have "nothing whatever to offer, not even a token benefit, in the event of thermonuclear war."*

In the complicated but steadily illuminating and linked fields of immunology, genetics, and cancer research, it has become a routine technical maneuver to transplant the bone-marrow cells of one mouse to a mouse of a different line. This can be accomplished by irradiating the recipient mouse with a lethal dose of X rays, enough to destroy all the immune cells and their progenitors, and replacing them with the donor's marrow cells. If the new cells are close enough in their genetic labels to the recipient's own body cells, the marrow will flourish and the mouse will live out a normal life span. Of course, if the donor cells are not closely matched, they will recognize the difference between themselves and the recipient's tissues, and the result, the so-called graft-versus-host reaction, will kill the recipient in the same way that a skin graft from a foreign mouse is destroyed by the lymphocytes of a recipient. 1

It is a neat biological trick, made possible by detailed knowledge of the genetics involved in graft rejection. Any new bone-marrow cells can survive and repopulate the recipient's defense apparatus provided the markers on the cell surfaces are the same as those of the donor, and precise techniques are now available for identifying these markers in advance. 2

Something like this can be done in human beings, and the technique of bone-marrow transplantation is now becoming available for patients whose marrows are deficient for one reason or another. It is especially useful in the treatment of leukemia, where the elimination of leukemic cells by X ray and chemotherapy sometimes causes the simultaneous destruction of the patient's own immune cells, which must then be replaced if the patient is to survive. It is a formidable procedure, requiring the availability of tissue-match donors (usually members of the patient's family), and involving extremely expensive and highly specialized physical facilities—rooms equipped for absolute sterility to prevent infection while the new cells are beginning to propagate. Not many hospitals are outfitted with units for this kind of work, perhaps twenty or twenty-five in the United States, and each of them can take on only a few patients at a time. The doctors and nurses who work in such units are among the most specialized of clinical professionals, and there are not many of them. All in all, it is an enormously costly venture, feasible in only a few places but justifiable by the real prospect of new knowledge from the associated research going on in each unit, and of course by the lifesaving nature of the procedure when it works. 3

This, then, is the scale on which contemporary medicine possesses a technology for the treatment of lethal X-irradiation. 4

The therapy of burns has improved considerably in recent years. Patients with extensively burned skin who would have died ten years ago are now, from time to time, being saved from death. The hospital facilities needed for this accomplishment are comparable, in their technical complexity and cost, to the units used for bone-marrow transplantation. Isolation rooms with special atmospheric controls to eliminate all microbes from the air are needed, plus teams of trained professionals to oversee all the countless details of management. It is still a discouraging undertaking, requiring doctors and nurses of high spirit and determination, but it works often enough to warrant the installation of such units in a limited number of medical 5 centers. Some of these places can handle as many as thirty or forty patients at a time, but no more than that number.

The surgical treatment of overwhelming trauma under- 6
went a technological transformation during the Korean and Vietnam wars, and it is now possible to do all sorts of things to save the lives of injured people—arteries and nerves can be successfully reconnected, severed limbs sewn back in place, blood substitutes infused, shock prevented, massive damage to internal organs repaired. Here also, special units with highly trained people are essential, elaborate facilities for rapid transport to the hospital are crucial, and the number of patients that can be handled by a unit is minimal.

These are genuine advances in medical science. The 7
medical profession can be proud of them, and the public can be confident that work of this kind will steadily improve in the future. The prospects for surviving various kinds of injury that used to be uniformly fatal are better now than at any other time in history.

If there were enough money, these things could be 8
scaled up to meet the country's normal everyday needs with tailormade centers for the treatment of radiation injury, burns, and massive trauma spotted here and there in all major urban centers, linked to outlying areas by helicopter ambulances. It would cost large sums to build and maintain, but the scores, maybe hundreds, of lives saved would warrant the cost.

The Department of Defense ought to have a vested 9
interest in enhancing this array of technologies, and I suppose it does. I take it for granted that substantial sums are being spent from the R & D funds of that agency to improve matters still further. In any conventional war, the capacity to rescue injured personnel from death on the battlefield does more than simply restore manpower to the lines: its effect on troop morale has traditionally been incalculable.

But I wonder if the hearts of the long-range planners in 10
DOD can really be in it.

Military budgets have to be put together with the same 11
analytic scrutiny of potential costs versus benefits that

underlies the construction of civilian budgets, allowing for the necessarily different meanings assigned by the military to the terms "cost" and "benefit." It is at least agreed that money should not be spent on things that will turn out to be of no use at all. The people in the Pentagon offices and their counterparts in the Kremlin where the questions of coping with war injuries are dealt with must be having a hard time of it these days, looking ahead as they must look to the possibility of thermonuclear war. Any sensible analyst in such an office would be tempted to scratch off all the expense items related to surgical care of the irradiated, burned, and blasted, the men, women, and children with empty bone marrows and vaporized skin. What conceivable benefit can come from sinking money in hospitals subject to instant combustion, only capable of salvaging, at their intact best, a few hundred of the victims who will be lying out there in the hundreds of thousands? There exists no medical technology that can cope with the certain outcome of just one small, neat, so-called tactical bomb exploded over a battlefield. As for the problem raised by a single large bomb, say a twenty-megaton missile (equivalent to approximately two thousand Hiroshimas) dropped on New York City or Moscow, with the dead and dying in the millions, what would medical technology be good for? As the saying goes, forget it. Think of something else. Get a computer running somewhere in a cave, to estimate the likely numbers of the lucky dead.

The doctors of the world know about this, of course. 12
They have known about it since the 1945 Hiroshima and Nagasaki "episodes," but it has dawned on them only in the last few years that the public at large may not understand. Some of the physicians in this country and abroad are forming new organizations for the declared purpose of making it plain to everyone that modern medicine has nothing whatever to offer, not even a token benefit, in the event of thermonuclear war. Unlike their response to other conceivable disasters, they do not talk of the need for more research or ask for more money to expand existing facilities. What they say is, in effect, count us out.

It is not a problem that has any real connection to politics. Doctors are not necessarily pacifists, and they come in all sorts of ideological stripes. What they have on their minds and should be trying to tell the world, in the hope that their collective professional opinion will gain public attention and perhaps catch the ears of political and military leaders everywhere, is simply this: if you go ahead with this business, the casualties you will instantly produce are beyond the reach of any health-care system. Since such systems here and abroad are based in urban centers, they will vanish in the first artificial suns, but even if they were miraculously to survive they could make no difference, not even a marginal difference. 13

I wish the psychiatrists and social scientists were further along in their fields than they seem to be. We need, in a hurry, some professionals who can tell us what has gone wrong in the minds of statesmen in this generation. How is it possible for so many people with the outward appearance of steadiness and authority, intelligent and convincing enough to have reached the highest positions in the governments of the world, to have lost so completely their sense of responsibility for the human beings to whom they are accountable? Their obsession with stockpiling nuclear armaments and their urgency in laying out detailed plans for using them have, at the core, aspects of what we would be calling craziness in other people, under other circumstances. Just before they let fly everything at their disposal, and this uniquely intelligent species begins to go down, it would be a small comfort to understand how it happened to happen. Our descendants, if there are any, will surely want to know. 14

QUESTIONS ON SUBJECT AND PURPOSE

1. What is the link between medicine and the bomb? Can medicine cope with the bomb? Why or why not?
2. How does the problem of "cost" and "benefit" apply in this situation?

3. What is the purpose of Thomas's final paragraph? How is this an appropriate conclusion to his essay?

QUESTIONS ON STRATEGY AND AUDIENCE

1. Why does Thomas begin his essay with three examples of medical progress? How does each relate to the larger issue Thomas is discussing?
2. In what way can this be seen as an argument? Does Thomas intend it to be one? How can you tell?
3. What is the effect of paragraph 10? Why is it so short?
4. What assumptions does Thomas make about his audience? How do those assumptions influence or shape his essay?

QUESTIONS ON VOCABULARY AND STYLE

1. Characterize Thomas's tone in the essay. Is he objective, militant, resigned, angry? Can you find specific evidence to support your characterization?
2. What is the effect of short, informal sentences such as those used at the end of paragraphs 11 and 12? Why are such sentences appropriate at these points in the essay?
3. Be able to define the following words: *immunology* (paragraph 1), *progenitor* (1), *lymphocytes* (1), *trauma* (6), *R&D funds* (9), *tactical bomb* (11).

WRITING SUGGESTIONS

1. To a certain extent this is an argument based on fact: medicine cannot cope with thermonuclear war. But what can be done? Write a persuasive paragraph or paragraphs in which you argue for the need for nuclear weapons or for the need to abolish nuclear weapons.
2. Using the material provided in Revkin's "Hard Facts About Nuclear Winter" in Chapter 7, and/or other sources, write a persuasive essay about the potentially fatal dangers of thermonuclear war. Remember that your audience always assumes that such a war will never happen and that such a large issue is out of its hands anyway.

Prewriting:

a. Take notes on Revkin's essay (or on any other source of which your instructor approves). Remember that the facts or the quotations you select must fit into your argument.
b. What action or reaction do you want to elicit in your audience? Write a specific statement.
c. Will you use an inductive or a deductive argument? Make a list of the advantages or disadvantages of both arrangements.

Rewriting:

a. Check each paragraph in your essay to see if it has an explicit or implicit topic sentence. Underline that sentence or write the implicit topic alongside the paragraph.
b. Ask a peer reader to evaluate your essay. Is it persuasive? What does the essay ask the reader to do?
c. What one problem or part of your essay seems the most troubling? Take that specific problem to your instructor or to your writing center.

3. Research the two sides to the nuclear freeze debate. Then in an essay using your research, argue for or against such a freeze. Remember that whichever side you take, you will need to anticipate and counter the arguments of your opponents.

Professions for Women

VIRGINIA WOOLF

Born in London and educated at home, Virginia Woolf (1882–1941) is generally regarded as one of the finest writers of the twentieth century. A novelist, essayist, and critic, she was a member of the Bloomsbury group—a circle of artists and writers, including John Maynard Keynes, Lytton Strachey, Vanessa and Clive Bell, and E. M. Forster, active in London from about 1906 to the early 1930s. She and her husband Leonard Woolf founded the Hogarth Press, which published books by her and other members of the Bloomsbury group. Her novels include The Voyage Out *(1915),* Jacob's Room *(1922),* Mrs. Dalloway *(1925),* To the Lighthouse *(1927),* Orlando *(1928), and* The Waves *(1931). Woolf's essays and reviews have been collected in works such as* The Common Reader *(1925, 1932) and* The Death of the Moth and Other Essays *(1942). In 1967, a four-volume* Collected Essays *was published. Woolf suffered continually from severe depression associated with her sense of failure as an artist, and in 1941 she drowned herself. In "Professions for Women," originally delivered as a speech in 1931, Woolf describes some of the "phantoms and obstacles" that lie in the path of women seeking to practice a profession.*

When your secretary invited me to come here, she told me that your Society is concerned with the employment of women and she suggested that I might tell you something about my own professional experiences. It is true I am a woman, it is true I am employed, but what professional experiences have I had? It is difficult to say. My profession is literature; and in that profession there are fewer experiences for women than in any other, with the exception of the stage—fewer, I mean, that are peculiar to women. For the road was cut many years ago—by Fanny Burney, by Aphra Behn, by Harriet Martineau, by Jane Austen, by George Eliot—many famous women, and many more 1 unknown and forgotten, have been before me, making the path smooth, and regulating my steps. Thus, when I came to write, there were very few material obstacles in my way. Writing was a reputable and harmless occupation. The family peace was not broken by the scratching of a pen. No demand was made upon the family purse. For ten and sixpence one can buy paper enough to write all the plays of Shakespeare—if one has a mind that way. Pianos and models, Paris, Vienna and Berlin, masters and mistresses, are not needed by a writer. The cheapness of writing paper is, of course, the reason why women have succeeded as writers before they have succeeded in the other professions.

But to tell you my story—it is a simple one. You have 2
only got to figure to yourselves a girl in a bedroom with a pen in her hand. She had only to move that pen from left to right—from ten o'clock to one. Then it occurred to her to do what is simple and cheap enough after all—to slip a few of those pages into an envelope, fix a penny stamp in the corner, and drop the envelope into the red box at the corner. It was thus that I became a journalist; and my effort was rewarded on the first day of the following month—a very glorious day it was for me—by a letter from an editor containing a cheque for one pound ten shillings and sixpence. But to show you how little I deserve to be called a professional woman, how little I know of the struggles and difficulties of such lives, I have to admit that instead of spending that sum upon bread and butter, rent, shoes and stockings, or butcher's bills, I went out and bought a cat—a beautiful cat, a Persian cat, which very soon involved me in bitter disputes with my neighbours.

What could be easier than to write articles and to buy 3
Persian cats with the profits? But wait a moment. Articles have to be about something. Mine, I seem to remember, was about a novel by a famous man. And while I was writing this review, I discovered that if I were going to review books I should need to do battle with a certain phantom. And the phantom was a woman, and when I came to know her better I called her after the heroine of a famous poem, The Angel in the House. It was she who used to come between me and

my paper when I was writing reviews. It was she who bothered me and wasted my time and so tormented me that at last I killed her. You who come of a younger and happier generation may not have heard of her—you may not know what I mean by the Angel in the House. I will describe her as shortly as I can. She was intensely sympathetic. She was immensely charming. She was utterly unselfish. She excelled in the difficult arts of family life. She sacrificed herself daily. If there was chicken, she took the leg; if there was a draught she sat in it—in short she was so constituted that she never had a mind or a wish of her own, but preferred to sympathize always with the minds and wishes of others. Above all—I need not say it—she was pure. Her purity was supposed to be her chief beauty—her blushes, her great grace. In those days—the last of Queen Victoria—every house had its Angel. And when I came to write I encountered her with the very first words. The shadow of her wings fell on my page; I heard the rustling of her skirts in the room. Directly, that is to say, I took my pen in hand to review that novel by a famous man, she slipped behind me and whispered: "My dear, you are a young woman. You are writing about a book that has been written by a man. Be sympathetic; be tender; flatter, deceive; use all the arts and wiles of our sex. Never let anybody guess that you have a mind of your own. Above all, be pure." And she made as if to guide my pen. I now record the one act for which I take some credit to myself, though the credit rightly belongs to some excellent ancestors of mine who left me a certain sum of money—shall we say five hundred pounds a year?—so that it was not necessary for me to depend solely on charm for my living. I turned upon her and caught her by the throat. I did my best to kill her. My excuse, if I were to be had up in a court of law, would be that I acted in self-defence. Had I not killed her she would have killed me. She would have plucked the heart out of my writing. For, as I found, directly I put pen to paper, you cannot review even a novel without having a mind of your own, without expressing what you think to be the truth about human relations, morality, sex. And all these questions, according to the

Angel in the House, cannot be dealt with freely and openly by women; they must charm, they must conciliate, they must—to put it bluntly—tell lies if they are to succeed. Thus, whenever I felt the shadow of her wings or the radiance of her halo upon my page, I took up the inkpot and flung it at her. She died hard. Her fictitious nature was of great assistance to her. It is far harder to kill a phantom than a reality. She was always creeping back when I thought I had despatched her. Though I flatter myself that I killed her in the end, the struggle was severe; it took much time that had better have been spent upon learning Greek grammar; or in roaming the world in search of adventures. But it was a real experience; it was an experience that was bound to befall all women writers at that time. Killing the Angel in the House was part of the occupation of a woman writer.

4 But to continue my story. The Angel was dead; what then remained? You may say that what remained was a simple and common object—a young woman in a bedroom with an inkpot. In other words, now that she had rid herself of falsehood, that young woman had only to be herself. Ah, but what is "herself"? I mean, what is a woman? I assure you, I do not know. I do not believe that you know. I do not believe that anybody can know until she has expressed herself in all the arts and professions open to human skill. That indeed is one of the reasons why I have come here—out of respect for you, who are in process of showing us by your experiments what a woman is, who are in process of providing us, by your failures and successes, with that extremely important piece of information.

5 But to continue the story of my professional experiences. I made one pound ten and six by my first review; and I bought a Persian cat with the proceeds. Then I grew ambitious. A Persian cat is all very well, I said; but a Persian cat is not enough. I must have a motor car. And it was thus that I became a novelist—for it is a very strange thing that people will give you a motor car if you will tell them a story. It is a still stranger thing that there is nothing so delightful in the world as telling stories. It is far pleasanter then writing reviews of famous novels. And yet, if I am to obey your

secretary and tell you my professional experiences as a novelist, I must tell you about a very strange experience that befell me as a novelist. And to understand it you must try first to imagine a novelist's state of mind. I hope I am not giving away professional secrets if I say that a novelist's chief desire is to be as unconscious as possible. He has to induce in himself a state of perpetual lethargy. He wants life to proceed with the utmost quiet and regularity. He wants to see the same faces, to read the same books, to do the same things day after day, month after month, while he is writing, so that nothing may disturb or disquiet the mysterious nosings about, feelings round, darts, dashes and sudden discoveries of that very shy and illusive spirit, the imagination. I suspect that this state is the same both for men and women. Be that as it may, I want you to imagine me writing a novel in a state of trance. I want you to figure to yourselves a girl sitting with a pen in her hand, which for minutes, and indeed for hours, she never dips into the inkpot. The image that comes to my mind when I think of this girl is the image of a fisherman lying sunk in dreams on the verge of a deep lake with a rod held out over the water. She was letting her imagination sweep unchecked round every rock and cranny of the world that lies submerged in the depths of our unconscious being. Now came the experience, the experience that I believe to be far commoner with women writers than with men. The line raced through the girl's fingers. Her imagination had rushed away. It had sought the pools, the depths, the dark places where the largest fish slumber. And then there was a smash. There was an explosion. There was foam and confusion. The imagination had dashed itself against something hard. The girl was roused from her dream. She was indeed in a state of the most acute and difficult distress. To speak without figure she had thought of something, something about the body, about the passions which it was unfitting for her as a woman to say. Men, her reason told her, would be shocked. The consciousness of what men will say of a woman who speaks the truth about her passions had roused her from her artist's state of unconsciousness. She could write no more.

The trance was over. Her imagination could work no longer. This I believe to be a very common experience with women writers—they are impeded by the extreme conventionality of the other sex. For though men sensibly allow themselves great freedom in these respects, I doubt that they realize or can control the extreme severity with which they condemn such freedom in women.

These then were two very genuine experiences of my 6
own. These were two of the adventures of my professional life. The first—killing the Angel in the House—I think I solved. She died. But the second, telling the truth about my own experiences as a body, I do not think I solved. I doubt that any woman has solved it yet. The obstacles against her are still immensely powerful—and yet they are very difficult to define. Outwardly, what is simpler than to write books? Outwardly, what obstacles are there for a woman rather than for a man? Inwardly, I think, the case is very different; she has still many ghosts to fight, many prejudices to overcome. Indeed it will be a long time still, I think, before a woman can sit down to write a book without finding a phantom to be slain, a rock to be dashed against. And if this is so in literature, the freest of all professions for women, how is it in the new professions which you are now for the first time entering?

Those are the questions that I should like, had I time, to 7
ask you. And indeed, if I have laid stress upon these professional experiences of mine, it is because I believe that they are, though in different forms, yours also. Even when the path is nominally open—when there is nothing to prevent a woman from being a doctor, a lawyer, a civil servant—there are many phantoms and obstacles, as I believe, looming in her way. To discuss and define them is I think of great value and importance; for thus only can the labour be shared, the difficulties be solved. But besides this, it is necessary also to discuss the ends and the aims for which we are fighting, for which we are doing battle with these formidable obstacles. Thos aims cannot be taken for granted; they must be perpetually questioned and examined. The whole position, as I see it—here in this hall surrounded by women practising for

the first time in history I know not how many different professions—is one of extraordinary interest and importance. You have won rooms of your own in the house hitherto exclusively owned by men. You are able, though not without great labour and effort, to pay the rent. You are earning your five hundred pounds a year. But this freedom is only a beginning; the room is your own, but it is still bare. It has to be furnished; it has to be decorated; it has to be shared. How are you going to furnish it; how are you going to decorate it? With whom are you going to share it, and upon what terms? These, I think, are questions of the utmost importance and interest. For the first time in history you are able to ask them; for the first time you are able to decide for yourself what the answers should be. Willingly would I stay and discuss those questions and answers—but not tonight. My time is up, and I must cease.

QUESTIONS ON SUBJECT AND PURPOSE

1. What were the two problems that Woolf faced as a writer?
2. What did the "Angel in the House" represent?
3. What purpose might Woolf have in using her own experiences as examples?

QUESTIONS ON STRATEGY AND AUDIENCE

1. To what extent is this piece an argument? For what is Woolf arguing?
2. Characterize Woolf's audience. To whom is she writing? How do you know?
3. Do the "phantoms" that Woolf encountered still exist for women today? Do men ever encounter any similar constraints?

QUESTIONS ON VOCABULARY AND STYLE

1. When writing about the novelist (in paragraph 5), Woolf uses a masculine rather than a feminine pronoun. Why might she have done this?

2. Woolf makes use of a number of British expressions and spellings. Make a list of these.
3. Be able to define the following words: *conciliate* (paragraph 3) and *lethargy* (5).

WRITING SUGGESTIONS

1. "Phantoms" such as Woolf described are occasioned by sexual and cultural stereotypes—expectations that we place upon ourselves or that others place upon us. In a paragraph describe a time when you encountered an obstacle because of your age, sex, race, religion, physical appearance, or socioeconomic status. Describe the experience, and then argue against the unfairness of such a phantom.
2. Expand your subject begun in suggestion 1 to essay length.

Prewriting:

a. Make a list of the occasions on which you were pressured by such expectations. Do not initially try to group the experiences; just list them.
b. Look back over your list, and try to group those experiences. For example, Woolf divides the pressures that she felt into two categories—those caused by self-definition (the "Angel in the House") and those caused by a definition imposed by others ("the extreme conventionality of the other sex").
c. Remember that you are using your own experiences to make a particular point—that is, you are trying to persuade an audience to believe something or to act in a certain way. Freewrite about your intention or purpose in the essay. Afterwards, try to formulate a one-sentence statement about your purpose.

Rewriting:

a. Part of the success of your essay will depend upon how effectively you relate your experiences. Look at the introduction to Chapter 2 on narration. Then return to your essay. Have you followed that advice in narrating your experiences?
b. Your argumentative or persuasive purpose ought to be clear, but it need not be blatantly stated in both your introduction and conclusion ("In this essay, I am trying to persuade you to . . ."). Underline, with a colored pen, every explicit statement of intention that you have used.

c. Look at your introduction. Have you begun in an interesting, arresting way? Remember you want to catch your reader's interest. You might start with an example of the pressures that you have felt rather than with a more traditional thesis introduction.

3. What "phantoms and obstacles" will a woman encounter today in a particular profession? Research the problem, perhaps focusing on the career that you intend to pursue (whether you are a woman or not). Present your findings in a essay intended for an audience of young women who plan to enter this profession.

I Have a Dream

MARTIN LUTHER KING, JR.

Martin Luther King, Jr. (1929-1968) was born in Atlanta, the son of a Baptist minister. Ordained in his father's church in 1947, King received a doctorate in theology from Boston University in 1955. In that same year he achieved national prominence by leading the Montgomery, Alabama, bus boycott where he put into practice his ideas of nonviolent resistance derived from Thoreau and Gandhi. King joined the Southern Christian Leadership Conference in 1959 and became a central figure in the civil rights movement, organizing protests and marches, including the August 1963 "March on Washington." King was Time's *1963 Man of the Year and was awarded the Nobel Peace Prize in 1964. He was assassinated in Memphis in 1968. His birthday, January 15, is celebrated as a national holiday.*

King's "I Have a Dream" speech was delivered at the Lincoln Memorial to an audience of 250,000 people who assembled in Washington, D.C., on August 28, 1963. That march, commemorating in part the hundredth anniversary of Lincoln's Emancipation Proclamation, was intended as an act of "creative lobbying" to win the support of Congress and the president for pending civil rights legislation. It was King's most carefully crafted speech, and he spent days worrying over each paragraph, sentence, and mark of punctuation. The final product is one of the most memorable and moving examples of American oratory.

Five score years ago, a great American, in whose symbolic shadow we stand, signed the Emancipation Proclamation. This momentous decree came as a great beacon light of hope to millions of Negro slaves who had been seared in the flames of withering injustice. It came as a joyous daybreak to end the long night of captivity. 1

But one hundred years later, we must face the tragic fact that the Negro is still not free. One hundred years later, the life of the Negro is still sadly crippled by the manacles of 2 segregation and the chains of discrimination. One hundred years later, the Negro lives on a lonely island of poverty in the midst of a vast ocean of material prosperity. One hundred years later, the Negro is still languishing in the corners of American society and finds himself an exile in his own land. So we have come here today to dramatize an appalling condition.

In a sense we have come to our nation's capital to cash a check. When the architects of our republic wrote the magnificent words of the Constitution and the Declaration of Independence, they were signing a promissory note to which every American was to fall heir. This note was a promise that all men would be guaranteed the unalienable rights of life, liberty, and the pursuit of happiness. 3

It is obvious today that America has defaulted on this promissory note insofar as her citizens of color are concerned. Instead of honoring this sacred obligation, America has given the Negro people a bad check; a check which has come back marked "insufficient funds." But we refuse to believe that the bank of justice is bankrupt. We refuse to believe that there are insufficient funds in the great vaults of opportunity of this nation. So we have come to cash this check—a check that will give us upon demand the riches of freedom and the security of justice. We have also come to this hallowed spot to remind America of the fierce urgency of *now*. This is no time to engage in the luxury of cooling off or to take the tranquilizing drugs of gradualism. *Now* is the time to make real the promises of Democracy. *Now* is the time to rise from the dark and desolate valley of segregation to the sunlit path of racial justice. *Now* is the time to open the doors of opportunity to all of God's children. *Now* is the time to lift our nation from the quicksands of racial injustice to the solid rock of brotherhood. 4

It would be fatal for the nation to overlook the urgency of the moment and to underestimate the determination of the Negro. This sweltering summer of the Negro's legitimate discontent will not pass until there is an invigorating autumn of freedom and equality. 1963 is not an end, but a beginning. Those who hope that the Negro needed to blow 5 off steam and will now be content will have a rude awakening if the nation returns to business as usual. There will be neither rest nor tranquillity in America until the Negro is granted his citizenship rights. The whirlwinds of revolt will continue to shake the foundations of our nation until the bright day of justice emerges.

But there is something that I must say to my people who 6
stand on the warm threshold which leads into the palace of justice. In the process of gaining our rightful place we must not be guilty of wrongful deeds. Let us not seek to satisfy our thirst for freedom by drinking from the cup of bitterness and hatred. We must forever conduct our struggle on the high plane of dignity and discipline. We must not allow our creative protest to degenerate into physical violence. Again and again we must rise to the majestic heights of meeting physical force with soul force. The marvelous new militancy which has engulfed the Negro community must not lead us to a distrust of all white people, for many of our white brothers, as evidenced by their presence here today, have come to realize that their destiny is tied up with our destiny and their freedom is inextricably bound to our freedom. We cannot walk alone.

And as we walk, we must make the pledge that we shall 7
march ahead. We cannot turn back. There are those who are asking the devotees of civil rights, "When will you be satisfied?" We can never be satisfied as long as the Negro is the victim of the unspeakable horrors of police brutality. We can never be satisfied as long as our bodies, heavy with the fatigue of travel, cannot gain lodging in the motels of the highways and the hotels of the cities. We cannot be satisfied as long as the Negro's basic mobility is from a smaller ghetto to a larger one. We can never be satisfied as long as a Negro in Mississippi cannot vote and a Negro in New York believes he has nothing for which to vote. No, no, we are not satisfied, and we will not be satisfied until justice rolls down like waters and righteousness like a mighty stream.

I am not unmindful that some of you have come here 8
out of great trials and tribulations. Some of you have come fresh from narrow jail cells. Some of you have come from

areas where your quest for freedom left you battered by the storms of persecution and staggered by the winds of police brutality. You have been the veterans of creative suffering. Continue to work with the faith that unearned suffering is redemptive.

Go back to Mississippi, go back to Alabama, go back to South Carolina, go back to Georgia, go back to Louisiana, go back to the slums and ghettos of our northern cities, knowing that somehow this situation can and will be changed. Let us not wallow in the valley of despair. 9

I say to you today, my friends, that in spite of the difficulties and frustrations of the moment I still have a dream. It is a dream deeply rooted in the American dream. 10

I have a dream that one day this nation will rise up and live out the true meaning of its creed: "We hold these truths to be self-evident: that all men are created equal." 11

I have a dream that one day on the red hills of Georgia the sons of former slaves and the sons of former slaveowners will be able to sit down together at the table of brotherhood. 12

I have a dream that one day even the state of Mississippi, a desert state sweltering with the heat of injustice and oppression, will be transformed into an oasis of freedom and justice. 13

I have a dream that my four little children will one day live in a nation where they will not be judged by the color of their skin but by the content of their character. 14

I have a dream today. 15

I have a dream that one day the state of Alabama, whose governor's lips are presently dripping with the words of interposition and nullification, will be transformed into a situation where little black boys and black girls will be able to join hands with little white boys and white girls and walk together as sisters and brothers. 16

I have a dream today. 17

I have a dream that one day every valley shall be exalted, every hill and mountain shall be made low, the rough places will be made plain, and the crooked places will be made 18 straight, and the glory of the Lord shall be revealed, and all flesh shall see it together.

This is our hope. This is the faith with which I return to 19
the South. With this faith we will be able to hew out of the mountain of despair a stone of hope. With this faith we will be able to transform the jangling discords of our nation into a beautiful symphony of brotherhood. With this faith we will be able to work together, to pray together, to struggle together, to go to jail together, to stand up for freedom together, knowing that we will be free one day.

This will be the day when all of God's children will be 20
able to sing with new meaning

My country, 'tis of thee,
Sweet land of liberty,
Of thee I sing:
Land where my fathers died,
Land of the pilgrims' pride,
From every mountain-side
Let freedom ring.

And if America is to be a great nation this must become 21
true. So let freedom ring from the prodigious hilltops of New Hampshire. Let freedom ring from the mighty mountains of New York. Let freedom ring from the heightening Alleghenies of Pennyslvania!

Let freedom ring from the snowcapped Rockies of Colo- 22
rado!

Let freedom ring from the curvaceous peaks of Cali- 23
fornia!

But not only that; let freedom ring from Stone Moun- 24
tain of Georgia!

Let freedom ring from Lookout Mountain of Tennessee! 25

Let freedom ring from every hill and molehill of Mis- 26
sissippi. From every mountainside, let freedom ring.

When we let freedom ring, when we let it ring from 27
every village and every hamlet, from every state and every city, we will be able to speed up that day when all of God's children, black men and white men, Jews and Gentiles,

Protestants and Catholics, will be able to join hands and sing in the words of the old Negro spiritual, "Free at last! free at last! thank God almighty, we are free at last!"

QUESTIONS ON SUBJECT AND PURPOSE

1. What is King's dream?
2. King's essay was a speech—delivered orally before thousands of marchers and millions of television viewers. How are its oral origins revealed in the written version?
3. In what way is King's speech an attempt at persuasion? Whom was he trying to persuade to do what?

QUESTIONS ON STRATEGY AND AUDIENCE

1. Why does King begin with the words "Five score years ago"? Why does he say at the end of paragraph 6, "We cannot walk alone"? What do such words have to do with the context of King's speech?
2. How does King structure his speech? Is there an inevitable order or movement? How effective is his conclusion?
3. What expectations does King have of his audience? How do you know that?

QUESTIONS ON VOCABULARY AND STYLE

1. How many examples of figurative speech (images, metaphors, similes) can you find in the speech? What effect does such figurative language have?
2. The speech is full of parallel structures. See how many you can find. Why does King use so many?
3. Be able to define the following words: *seared* (paragraph 1), *manacles* (2), *languishing* (2), *promissory note* (3), *unalienable* (3), *invigorating* (5), *inextricably* (6), *tribulations* (8), *nullification* (16), *prodigious* (21).

WRITING SUGGESTIONS

1. In a paragraph argue for equality for a minority on your campus—it should be a serious concern (the handicapped, a sexual, racial, or religious minority, returning adults, commuters).

2. Expand your subject begun in suggestion 1 above to essay length.

   Prewriting:

   a. To write convincingly about such a problem you will need specific information drawn from your own experience and/or the experiences of others. Interview several members of the minority group about whom you are writing. Take notes on index cards.
   b. Organize your cards by sorting them into groups according to topic. Make a list of those topics, and then convert the list into a working outline.
   c. What objections or reservations might your audience have? Try to imagine a critic's objections to your essay.

   Rewriting:

   a. Highlight all the specific evidence in your essay. Remember that details make an argument effective. Have you included enough? Each body paragraph needs details and examples.
   b. Check each paragraph for a unified idea. Is there a single focused idea controlling the paragraph? Jot down a key word or phrase for each paragraph.
   c. Find someone to read your essay. Does your reader find your argument fair? Convincing? If the reader disagrees, ask for specific reasons why.

3. In order to comply with federal guidelines, colleges have had to make extensive structural modifications to grant handicapped people equal access to all facilities. Research the problem on your campus. What has been done? What remains to be done? Argue for the importance of such changes.

None of This Is Fair

RICHARD RODRIGUEZ

Born in 1944 in San Francisco, Richard Rodriguez, the son of Spanish-speaking Mexican-American parents, first learned English in grade school. He received a B.A. in English from Stanford University in 1967, an M.A. from Columbia University, and a Ph.D. from the University of California at Berkeley. He also studied at the Warburg Institute in London. His autobiographic Hunger of Memory: The Education of Richard Rodriguez *(1982) is an important study of the Mexican-American experience, with special attention given to bilingualism. He writes of his regret at losing his Spanish heritage by being assimilated into the English-speaking world; but he disapproves of bilingual education and of the reverse discrimination occasioned by affirmative action programs. Rodriguez's essays have appeared in magazines such as* American Scholar, Saturday Review *and* College English. *He is presently working on a book about migrant workers. In "None of This Is Fair" Rodriguez uses his personal experience to argue the ineffectiveness of affirmative action programs in reaching those people who are seriously disadvantaged.*

My plan to become a professor of English—my ambition during long years in college at Stanford, then in graduate school at Columbia and Berkeley—was complicated by feelings of embarrassment and guilt. So many times I would see other Mexican-Americans and know we were alike only in race. And yet, simply because our race was the same, I was, during the last years of my schooling, the beneficiary of their situation. Affirmative Action programs had made it all possible. The disadvantages of others permitted my promotion; the absence of many Mexican-Americans from academic life allowed my designation as a "minority student." 1

For me opportunities had been extravagant. There were fellowships, summer research grants, and teaching assistantships. After only two years in graduate school, I 2 was offered teaching jobs by several colleges. Invitations to Washington conferences arrived and I had the chance to travel abroad as a "Mexican-American representative." The benefits were often, however, too gaudy to please. In three published essays, in conversations with teachers, in letters to politicians and at conferences, I worried the issue of Affirmative Action. Often I proposed contradictory opinions. Though consistent was the admission that—because of an early, excellent education—I was no longer a principal victim of racism or any other social oppression. I said that but still I continued to indicate on applications for financial aid that I was a Hispanic-American. It didn't really occur to me to say anything else, or to leave the question unanswered.

Thus I complied with and encouraged the odd bureaucratic logic of Affirmative Action. I let government officials treat the disadvantaged condition of many Mexican-Americans with my advancement. Each fall my presence was noted by Health, Education, and Welfare department statisticians. As I pursued advanced literary studies and learned the skill of reading Spenser and Wordsworth and Empson, I would hear myself numbered among the culturally disadvantaged. Still, silent, I didn't object. 3

But the irony cut deep. And guilt would not be evaded by averting my glance when I confronted a face like my own in a crowd. By late 1975, nearing the completion of my graduate studies at Berkeley, I was so wary of the benefits of Affirmative Action that I feared my inevitable success as an applicant for a teaching position. The months of fall—traditionally that time of academic job-searching—passed without my applying to a single school. When one of my professors chanced to learn this in late November, he was astonished, then furious. He yelled at me: Did I think that because I was a minority student jobs would just come looking for me? What was I thinking? Did I realize that he and several other faculty members had already written letters on my behalf? Was I going to start acting like some other minority students he had known? They struggled for success and then when it was almost within reach, grew 4 strangely afraid and let it pass. Was that it? Was I determined to fail?

I did not respond to his questions. I didn't want to admit to him, and thus to myself, the reason I delayed. 5

I merely agreed to write to several schools. (In my letter I wrote: "I cannot claim to represent disadvantaged Mexican-Americans. The very fact that I am in a position to apply for this job should make that clear.") After two or three days, there were telegrams and phone calls, invitations to interviews, then airplane trips. A blur of faces and the murmur of their soft questions. And, over someone's shoulder, the sight of campus buildings shadowing pictures I had seen years before when I leafed through Ivy League catalogues with great expectations. At the end of each visit, interviewers would smile and wonder if I had any questions. A few times I quietly wondered what advantage my race had given me over other applicants. But that was an impossible question for them to answer without embarrassing me. Quickly, several persons insisted that my ethnic identity had given me no more than a "foot inside the door"; at most, I had a "slight edge" over other applicants. "We just looked at your dossier with extra care and we liked what we saw. There was never any question of having to alter our standards. You can be certain of that." 6

In the early part of January, offers arrived on stiffly elegant stationery. Most schools promised terms appropriate for any new assistant professor. A few made matters worse—and almost more tempting—by offering more: the use of university housing; an unusually large starting salary; a reduced teaching schedule. As the stack of letters mounted, my hesitation increased. I started calling department chairmen to ask for another week, then 10 more days—"more time to reach a decision"—to avoid the decision I would need to make. 7

At school, meantime, some students hadn't recieved a single job offer. One man, probably the best student in the department, did not even a get a request for his dossier. He and I met outside a classroom one day and he asked about my opportunities. He seemed happy for me. Faculty mem- 8 bers beamed. They said they had expected it. "After all, not many schools are going to pass up getting a Chicano with a Ph.D. in Renaissance literature," somebody said, laughing. Friends wanted to know which of the offers I was going to accept. But I couldn't make up my mind. February came and I was running out of time and excuses. (One chairman guessed my delay was a bargaining ploy and increased his offer with each of my calls.) I had to promise a decision by the 10th; the 12th at the very latest.

On the 18th of February, late in the afternoon, I was in the office I shared with several other teaching assistants. Another graduate student was sitting across the room at his desk. When I got up to leave, he looked over to say in an uneventful voice that he had some big news. He had finally decided to accept a position at a faraway university. It was not a job he especially wanted, he admitted. But he had to take it because there hadn't been any other offers. He felt trapped, and depressed, since his job would separate him from his young daughter. 9

I tried to encourage him by remarking that he was lucky at least to have found a job. So many others hadn't been able to get anything. But before I finished speaking I realized that I had said the wrong thing. And I anticipated his next question. 10

"What are your plans?" he wanted to know. "Is it true you've gotten an offer from Yale?" 11

I said that it was. "Only, I still haven't made up my mind." 12

He stared at me as I put on my jacket. And smiling, then unsmiling, he asked if I knew that he too had written to Yale. In his case, however, no one had bothered to acknowledge his letter with even a postcard. What did I think of that? 13

He gave me no time to answer. 14

"Damn!" he said sharply and his chair rasped the floor as he pushed himself back. Suddenly, it was to *me* that he was complaining. "It's just not right, Richard. None of this is fair. You've done some good work, but so have I. I'll bet our records are just about equal. But when we look for jobs 15 this year, it's a different story. You get all of the breaks."

To evade his criticism, I wanted to side with him. I was about to admit the injustice of Affirmative Action. But he went on, his voice hard with accusation. "It's all very simple this year. You're a Chicano. And I am a Jew. That's the only real difference between us." 16

His words stung me: there was nothing he was telling me that I didn't know. I had admitted everything already. But to hear someone else say these things, and in such an accusing tone, was suddenly hard to take. In a deceptively calm voice, I responded that he had simplified the whole issue. The phrases came like bubbles to the tip of my tongue: "new blood"; "the importance of cultural diversity"; "the goal of racial integration." These were all the arguments I had proposed several years ago—and had long since abandoned. Of course the offers were unjustifiable. I knew that. All I was saying amounted to a frantic self-defense. I tried to find an end to a sentence. My voice faltered to a stop. 17

"Yeah, sure," he said. "I've heard all that before. Nothing you say really changes the fact that Affirmative Action is unfair. You see that, don't you? There isn't any way for me to compete with you. Once there were quotas to keep my parents out of certain schools; now there are quotas to get you in and the effect on me is the same as it was for them." 18

I listened to every word he spoke. But my mind was really on something else. I knew at that moment that I would reject all of the offers. I stood there silently surprised by what an easy conclusion it was. Having prepared for so many years to teach, having trained myself to do nothing else, I had hesitated out of practical fear. But now that it was made, the decision came with relief. I immediately knew I had made the right choice. 19

My colleague continued talking and I realized that he was simply right. Affirmative action programs *are* unfair to white students. But as I listened to him assert his rights, I thought of the seriously disadvantaged. How different they were from white, middle-class students who come armed 20 with the testimony of their grades and aptitude scores and self-confidence to complain about the unequal treatment they now receive. I listen to them. I do not want to be careless about what they say. Their rights are important to protect. But inevitably when I hear them or their lawyers, I think about the most seriously disadvantaged, not simply Mexican-Americans, but of all those who do not ever imagine themselves going to college or becoming doctors: white, black, brown. Always poor. Silent. They are not plaintiffs before the court or against the misdirection of Affirmative Action. They lack the confidence (my confidence!) to assume their right to a good education. They lack the confidence and skills a good primary and secondary education provides and which are prerequisites for informed public life. They remain silent.

The debate drones on and surrounds them in stillness. 21
They are distant, faraway figures like the boys I have seen peering down from freeway overpasses in some other part of town.

QUESTIONS ON SUBJECT AND PURPOSE

1. In paragraph 4, Rodriguez makes reference to the "irony" of the situation. In what ways was it ironic?
2. Why does Rodriguez decide to reject all of the offers?
3. Is Rodriguez criticizing affirmative action policies? How could such policies reach or change the lives of those who are really seriously disadvantaged?

QUESTIONS ON STRATEGY AND AUDIENCE

1. To what extent does Rodriguez present a formal argument based on an appeal to reason? To what extent does he attempt to persuade through an appeal to emotion? Which element is stronger in the piece?
2. What is the difference between objectively stating an opinion and narrating a personal experience? Do we as readers react any differently to Rodriguez's story as a result?

3. What expectations does Rodriguez have of his audience? How do you know that?

QUESTIONS ON VOCABULARY AND STYLE

1. In paragraphs 11 through 18, Rodriguez dramatizes a scene with a fellow student. He could have just summarized what was said without using dialogue. What advantage is gained by developing the scene?
2. Be prepared to discuss the significance of the following sentences:
   a. "For me opportunities had been extravagant" (paragraph 2).
   b. "The benefits were often, however, too gaudy to please" (paragraph 2).
   c. "The phrases came like bubbles to the tip of my tongue" (paragraph 17).
   d. "Always poor. Silent" (paragraph 20).
3. What is the effect of the simile ("like the boys I have seen . . .) Rodriguez uses in the final line?

WRITING SUGGESTIONS

1. Rodriguez proposes no solutions to the problem of education for disadvantaged minorities. What, though, might be suggested? How could the seriously disadvantaged be reached? In a paragraph argue for a particular change in affirmative action policies.
2. Expand your subject begun in suggestion 1 to essay length.

   Prewriting:
   a. One possible starting point would be to gather some information about education in America. For example, how many Americans are illiterate? What exactly do those statistics indicate? Ask a reference librarian for help.
   b. Realistically, what might be done to help the seriously disadvantaged? Try to list at least ten realistic possibilities.
   c. Investigate local agencies trying to address these problems. The blue pages of your telephone book contain a variety of sources. Contact three such agencies for information.

   Rewriting:
   a. Convert the list of things to remember at the end of the introduction to this chapter into a checklist. Reread your essay, and check to see if you followed the list.

b. Ask a peer reader to critique your essay using that same checklist. Pay attention to the reader's criticisms as well as praise.
c. What gave you the most trouble in this paper? List two things. Then, go back and tackle just those two problems.

3. How successful have affirmative action programs been? Research their history and their success. Have those most seriously disadvantaged really been helped? Using your evidence, take some aspect of these programs, and write an essay persuading your readers that it should be continued, expanded, changed, or dropped.

Educating Black Athletes

HARRY EDWARDS

Born in 1942 in St. Louis, Harry Edwards earned a B.A. at San Jose State University. Despite offers to play professional football, he chose instead to accept a Woodrow Wilson Fellowship to Cornell University, from which he earned an M.A. and Ph.D. in sociology. Currently on the faculty of the University of California at Berkeley, he is the author of The Revolt of the Black Athlete *(1969);* Sociology of Sport *(1973);* The Struggle that Must Be *(1981), his autobiography; and* Playing to Win: A Short Guide to Sensible Black Sports Participation *(1982). In "Educating Black Athletes," Edwards defends the NCAA's controversial Rule 48, which stipulates that athletes at Division I and II colleges must achieve a minimum SAT score of 700 (or a score of 15 on the ACT) and a C average in eleven designated high school courses in order to participate in college athletics during their freshman year. Edwards also raises many doubts about the adequacy of American education.*

For decades, student athletes, usually seventeen-to-nineteen-year-old freshmen, have informally agreed to a contract with the universities they attend: athletic performance in exchange for an education. The athletes have kept their part of the bargain; the universities have not. Universities and athletic departments have gained huge gate receipts, television revenues, national visibility, donors to university programs, and more, as a result of the performances of gifted basketball and football players, of whom a disproportionate number of the most gifted and most exploited have been black. 1

While blacks are not the only student athletes exploited, the abuses usually happen to them first and worst. To understand why, we must understand sports' impact upon black society; how popular beliefs that blacks 2 are innately superior athletes, and that sports are "inherently" beneficial, combine with the life circumstances of young blacks, and with the aspirations of black student athletes, to make those students especially vulnerable to victimization.

Sports at all levels are widely believed to have achieved 3
extraordinary, if not exemplary, advances in the realm of interracial relations since the time when Jackie Robinson became the first black to play major-league baseball. To some extent, this reputation has been deliberately fostered by skilled sports propagandists eager to project "patriotic" views consistent with America's professed ideals of racial justice and equality of opportunity. To a much greater extent, however, this view of sports has been encouraged by observers of the sporting scene who have simply been naive about the dynamics of sports as an institution, about their relationship to society generally, and about the race-related realities of American sports in particular.

Many misconceptions about race and sports can be 4
traced to developments in sports that would appear on the surface to represent significant racial progress. For instance, though blacks constitute only 11.7 percent of the U. S. population, in 1982 more then 55 percent of the players in the National Football League were black, and, in 1981, twenty-four of the twenty-eight first-round NFL draft choices were black. As for the two other major professional team sports, 70 percent of the players making National Basketball Association rosters during the 1982–1983 season, and 80 percent of the starters that same season, were black, while 19 percent of America's major-league baseball players at the beginning of the 1982 season were black.

Black representation on sports honor rolls has been even 5
more disproportionate. For example, the past nine Heisman trophies, awarded each year to the "best" collegiate football player in the land, have gone to blacks. In the final rushing statistics of the 1982 NFL season, thirty-six of the top forty running backs were blacks. In 1982, not a single white athlete was named to the first team of a major Division I All-American basketball roster. Similarly, twenty-one of the

twenty-four athletes selected for the 1982 NBA All-Star game were black. Since 1955, whites have won the NBA's "most valuable player" award only five times as opposed to twenty-three times for blacks. And, of course, boxing championships in the heavier weight divisions have been dominated by black athletes since the 1960s. But a judicious interpretation of these and related figures points toward conclusions quite different from what one might expect.

Patterns of opportunity for blacks in American sports, like those in the society at large, are shaped by racial discrimination, a phenomenon that explains the disproportionately high number of talented black athletes in certain sports and the utter exclusion of blacks from most other American sports, as well as from decision-making and authority positions in virtually all sports. 6

Most educated people today accept the idea that the level of black representation and the quality of black performance in sports have no demonstrable relationship to race-linked genetic characteristics. Every study purporting to demonstrate such a relationship has exhibited critical deficiencies in the methodological, theoretical, or conceptual design. Moreover, the factors determining the caliber of sports performances are so complex and disparate as to render ludicrous any attempt to trace athletic excellence to a single biological feature. 7

Thus, despite a popular view that blacks are "natural" athletes, physically superior to athletes from other groups, the evidence tends to support cultural and social—rather than biological—explanations of their athletic success. 8

Briefly: 9

—Thanks to the mass media and to long-standing traditions of racial discrimination limiting blacks' access to many high-prestige occupational opportunities, the black athlete is much more visible to black youths, than, say, black doctors or black lawyers. Therefore, unlike white children, who see many different potential role models in the media, black children tend to model themselves after, or to admire as symbolically masculine, the black athlete—the one prevalent and positive black success figure they are exposed to regularly, year in and year out, in America's white-dominated mass media.

—The black family and the black community tend to reward athletic achievement much more and earlier than any other activity. This also lures more young blacks into sports-career aspirations than the actual opportunities for sports success would warrant.

—Because most American sports activities are still devoid of any significant black presence, the overwhelming majority of aspiring black athletes emulate established black role models and seek careers in four or five sports—basketball, football, baseball, boxing, and track. The brutally competitive selection process that ensues eliminates all but the most skilled black athletes by the time they reach the collegiate and advanced-amateur ranks. The competition is made all the more intense because even in these sports, some positions (such as quarterback, center, and middle linebacker in football, and catcher in baseball) are relatively closed to blacks.

—Finally, sports are seen by many black male youths as a means of proving their manhood. This tends to be extraordinarily important to blacks, because the black male in American society has been systematically cut off from mainstream routes of masculine expression, such as economic success, authority positions, and so forth.

Despite the great pool of athletic talent generated in 10
black society, black athletes still get fewer than one in ten of the athletic scholarships given out in the United States. And, at least partially as a result of the emphasis placed upon developing their athletic talents from early childhood, an estimated 25 to 35 percent of male black high school athletes qualifying for athletic scholarships cannot accept those scholarships because of accumulated academic deficiencies. Many of these young men eventually end up in what is called, appropriately enough, the "slave trade"—a nationwide phenomenon involving independent scouts who, for a fee (usually paid by a four-year college), search out talented but academically "high-risk" black athletes

and place them in accommodating junior colleges, where their athletic skills are further honed while they earn the grades they need to transfer to the sponsoring four-year schools.

Of those who are eventually awarded collegiate athletic scholarships, studies indicate, as many as 65 to 75 percent may never graduate from college. Of the 25 to 35 percent who do eventually graduate from the schools they play for, an estimated 75 percent graduate either with physical-education degrees or in majors created specifically for athletes and generally held in low repute. The problem with these "jock majors," and increasingly with the physical-education major as well, is that they make poor credentials in the job market. One might assume that ample occupational opportunities would be available to outstanding black former athletes, at least within the sports world. But the reality is quite different. To begin with, the overwhelming majority of black athletes, whether scholarship-holders or professional, have *no* post-career, occupational plans or formal preparation for any type of post-career employment either inside or outside sports. These blacks are unemployed more often, and earn less when they do have jobs, than their non-athletic college peers; they are also likely to switch jobs more often, to hold a wider variety of jobs, and to be less satisfied with the jobs they hold—primarily because the jobs tend to be dull, dead-end, or minimally rewarding. 11

Few Americans appreciate the extent to which the overwhelming majority of young males seeking affluence and stardom through sports are foredoomed to fail. The three major team sports provide approximately 2,663 jobs for professional athletes, regardless of color, in a nation of 226 million people, roughly half of whom are male. This means that only one American male in about 42,000 is a professional football, basketball, or baseball player. 12

While the proportion of blacks in professional basketball is 70 percent, in professional football 55 percent, and in professional baseball 19 percent, only about 1,400 black people (up from about 1,100 since the establishment of the 13

United States Football League) are making a living as professional athletes in these three major sports today. And if one adds to this number all the black professional athletes in all other American sports, all the blacks in minor and semiprofessional sports leagues, and all the black trainers, coaches, and doctors in professional sports, one sees that fewer than 2,400 black Americans can be said to be making a living in professional athletics today.

This situation, considered in combination with the black athlete's educational underdevelopment, helps explain why so many black athletes not only fail to achieve their expectations of life-long affluence but also frequently fall far short of the levels achieved by the non-athletic peers. 14

Despite the fact, then, that American basketball, boxing, football, and baseball competitions have come more and more to look like Ghana playing Nigeria, sport continues to loom like a fog-shrouded minefield for the overwhelming majority of black athletes. It has been a treadmill to oblivion rather than the escalator to wealth and glory it was believed to be. The black athlete who blindly sets out today to fill the shoes of Dr. J., Reggie J., Magic J., Kareem Abdul-J., or O. J. may well end up with "No J."—no job that he is qualified to do in our modern, technologically sophisticated society. At the end of his sports career, the black athlete is not likely to be running or flying through airports like O. J. He is much more likely to be sweeping up airports—if he has the good fortune to land even that job. 15

These are the tragic circumstances that prompted Joe Paterno, 1982 Division I football "Coach of the Year" of the New York Football Writers' Association, to exclaim in January from the floor of the 1983 NCAA convention in San Diego: "For fifteen years we have had a race problem. We have raped a generation and a half of young black athletes. We have taken kids and sold them on bouncing a ball and running with a football and that being able to do certain things athletically was going to be an end in itself. We cannot afford to do that to another generation." With that statement, Coach Paterno gave impetus to the passage of the 16

NCAA's "Rule 48," which set off what is probably the most heated race-related controversy within the NCAA since the onset of widespread racial integration in major-college sports programs during the 1950s and 1960s.

Put most simply, Rule 48 stipulates that, beginning in 1986, freshman athletes who want to participate in sports in any of the nation's 277 Division I colleges and universities must have attained a minimum score of 700 (out of a possible 1,600) on the Scholastic Aptitude Test (SAT) or a score of 15 (out of a possible 36) on the American College Test (ACT), and must have achieved a C average in eleven designated high school courses, including English, mathematics, social sciences, and physical sciences. Further, *The N.C.A.A. News* reported, Rule 48 17

> does not interfere with the admissions policies of any Division I institution. Nonqualifiers under this legislation may be admitted and attend class. Such a student could compete as a sophomore if he or she satisfies the satisfactory-progress rules and would have four varsity seasons starting as a sophomore if he or she continues to make satisfactory progress.
>
> Further, under related Proposal No. 49-B, any student who achieves at least 2.0 in all high school courses but does not meet the new terms of No. 48 can receive athletically related financial aid in his or her first year, but cannot practice or compete in intercollegiate athletics. This student would have three varsity years of participation remaining.

The outcry in response to the passage of Rule 48 was immediate. Ironically, the most heated opposition to the rule came from black civil-rights leaders and black college presidents and educators—the very groups one might have expected to be most supportive of the action. Their concern was over those provisions of Rule 48 specifying minimum test scores as a condition for sports participation, particularly the 700 score on the S.A.T. Leading the black criticism of the NCAA's new academic standards were the National Association For Equal Opportunity in Higher Education (NAFEO), representing 114 traditionally black colleges and universities; the National Alliance of Black 18

School Educators (NABSE); Rev. Jesse Jackson, president of People United To Serve Humanity (Operation PUSH); Rev. Benjamin Hooks, executive director of the National Association for the Advancement of Colored People (NAACP); and Rev. Joseph Lowery, president of the Southern Christian Leadership Conference (SCLC). They argued, first, that blacks were not consulted in the formulation of Rule 48; second, that the mimimum SAT score requirement was arbitrary; and finally, that the SAT and the ACT are racist diagnostic tests, which reflect a cultural bias favoring whites. They believed that the 700 SAT and 15 ACT score requirements would unfairly penalize black student athletes, given that 55 percent of black students generally score lower than 700 on the SAT and 69 percent score lower than 15 on the ACT. And why would the majority of NCAA Division I institutions vote to support a rule that would reduce participation opportunities for black athletes? For NAFEO and its supporters, the answer was clear. The most outspoken among the critics of Rule 48 was Dr. Jesse N. Stone, Jr., the president of the Southern University System of Louisiana, who said:

> The end result of all this is the black athlete has been too good. If it [Rule 48] is followed to its logical conclusion, we say to our youngsters. "Let the white boy win once in a while." This has set the black athlete back twenty-five or thirty years. The message is that white schools no longer want black athletes.

Members of the American Council on Education (ACE) 19
committee charged with developing Rule 48 vehemently denied claims that no blacks were involved in the process. Whatever the truth of the matter, the majority of black NCAA delegates felt that their interests and views had not been represented.

I could not agree more with NAFEO, Jackson, Hooks, 20
Lowery, *et al.* on their contention that the minimum SAT and ACT test scores are arbitrary. Neither the ACE nor the NCAA has yet provided any reasoned or logical basis for

setting the minimum scores. But whereas NAFEO and others say that the scores are arbitrary and too high, I contend that they are arbitrary and so *low* as to constitute virtually no standards at all. I have other, more fundamental disagreements with the NAFEO position.

One need not survey very much literature on the racist abuse of diagnostic testing in this country to appreciate the historical basis of NAFEO's concerns about rigidly applied test standards. But the demand that Rule 48 be repealed on the grounds that its test-score requirements are racist and will unfairly affect blacks is both factually contestable and strategically regrettable. The evidence is overwhelming that the SAT and the ACT discriminate principally on the basis of class, rather than race. The greater discrepancy between black and white scores occurs on the math section of the SAT, where cultural differences between the races logically would have the least impact. Even on the verbal sections of these diagnostic tests, differences in black and white scores are at least partially explained as class-related phenomena. As Dr. Mary Frances Berry, a NAFEO supporter, asserts: 21

> A major differential [among test scores] was *not* between black and white students, but between students from well-off families and students from poor families. The better-off the family, the higher the score—for whites *and* blacks.

Dr. Norman C. Francis, president of the traditionally black Xavier University of Louisiana and immediate past chairman of the College Board, agrees: 22

> The SAT is not merely a measure of potential aptitude, as many believe, but is also an achievement test which accurately measures what students have learned to that point. Most students do poorly on the test simply because they have never been taught the concepts that will help them to understand what testing and test-taking is all about. It is an educational disadvantage, not an inability to learn . . . The plain truth is that students in poorer schools are never taught to

> deal with word problems and . . . critical analysis. The problem therefore is not with the students, nor with the test, but rather with an educational system which fails to teach youngsters what they need to know.

Rule 48, therefore, involves far more than a simple black-white controversy, as 1981 SAT test statistics bear out. While 49 percent of black male students in 1981 failed to achieve at least a 700 on the combined SAT, as compared with 14 percent of the whites and 27 percent of other minorities, far more whites (31,140) and other minorities (27,145) than blacks (15,330) would have been affected under Rule 48. 23

Furthermore, between 1981 and 1982, blacks' verbal scores rose nine points and mathematics scores rose four points, compared with a two-point gain in verbal and a one-point gain in math for the white majority. 24

NAFEO claims that black athletes would have less access to traditionally white Division I institutions in the wake of Rule 48. But even though proportionately more blacks score below Rule 48's minimum-score requirements, it is unlikely that significant numbers of blacks would be deprived of opportunities to attend traditionally white schools on athletic scholarships. Indeed, if the enrollment of black athletes falls off at any Division I schools for this reason, I submit that the schools most likely to suffer will be the traditionally black colleges. NCAA disciplinary records show that traditionally white institutions have led the way in amateur-athletic rules infractions and in exploiting black athletes. Why? Because they have the largest financial investment in their athletic programs, and because they and their athletic personnel stand to reap the greatest rewards from athletic success. With so much at stake, why would schools that for so long have stretched, bent, and broken rules to enroll black athletes no longer want them? 25

The loopholes in Rule 48 are sufficient to allow any school to recruit any athlete it really wants. Junior colleges are not covered under the rule, so schools could still secure and develop athletes not eligible for freshman sports par- 26 ticipation at four-year Division I colleges. Further, Rule 48 allows Division I schools to recruit freshman athletes who are academically ineligible to participate, and even to provide them with financial support. After several meetings with NAFEO representatives, Rev. Jesse Jackson, and others, I am strongly convinced that for many within the ranks of Rule 48's detractors, fiscal rather than educational issues are the priority concern. The overwhelming majority of athletes recruited by traditionally black Division I schools are black, score below Rule 48 minimum-test-score requirements, and tend to need financial support in order to attend college. However, because they have far more modest athletic budgets than traditionally white schools, traditionally black schools are not nearly so able to provide financial support for both a roster of active athletes and a long roster of newly recruited athletes ineligible for athletic participation under Rule 48. Traditionally black Division I schools, already at a recruiting disadvantage owing to smaller budgets and less access to lucrative TV exposure, would be placed at an even more critical recruiting disadvantage, since they would not be able to afford even those athletes they would ordinarily be able to get.

Thus, the core issue in the Rule 48 controversy is not racist academic standards, or alleged efforts by whites to resegregate major-college sports, so much as parity between black and white institutions in the collegiate athletic arms race. 27

Strategically, the position of NAFEO, the NABSE, and the black civil-rights leaders vis-à-vis Rule 48 poses two problems. First, they have missed the greatest opportunity since the *Brown* v. *Board of Education of Topeka* case thirty years ago to make an impressive statement about quality and equality in education. And, since they had the attention of the nation, they also squandered a rare opportunity to direct a national dialogue on restructuring the role and stipulating the rights of athletes in the academy. Second, with no real evidence to support their claims of racist motives on the part of Rule 48's white supporters, or of simple race bias in the rule's stipulations, these black educators and civil- 28 rights leaders left the unfortunate and unintended impression that they were against *all* academic standards because they believed that black students are unable to achieve even the moderate standards established under Rule 48.

Notwithstanding the transparent criticisms leveled by 29
Rule 48's detractors, the measure does contain some real flaws relative to its proposed goal of shoring up the academic integrity of Division I athletic programs. First, the standards stipulated in Rule 48 are *too low*. A score of 700 on the SAT, for example, projects less than a fifty-fifty chance of graduating from most Division I schools.

Second, Rule 48 does not address in any way the educa- 30
tional problems of students once they have matriculated, which is where the real educational rip-off of collegiate student athletes has occurred. Rather, it establishes standards of high school preparation and scholastic achievement necessary for students who wish to participate in college sports as freshman.

Nonetheless, the NCAA action is worthy of support, 31
not as a satisfactory solution to the educational problems of big-time collegiate sports but as a step—a very small and perhaps even inept step—toward dealing with these problems. Rule 48 communicates to young athletes, beginning with those who are sophomores in high school, that we expect them to develop academically as well as athletically. In California, 320,000 students each year participate in California Interscholastic Federation athletic programs and most undoubtedly aspire to win athletic scholarships to Division I institutions. However, only 5 percent of these students will ever participate in college sports at any level (including junior college), and the overwhelming majority will never even enroll at a four-year school. If Rule 48 does indeed encourage greater academic seriousness among high school athletes, the vast majority of high school student athletes who are *not* going on to college may benefit most from the NCAA's action—since they face the realities of life after sports immediately upon graduation from high school.

Further, were I not to support Rule 48, I would risk communicating to black youth in particular that I, a nationally known black educator, do not believe that they have the capacity to achieve a 700 score on the SAT, with three years to prepare for the test, when they are given a total of 400 points simply for answering a single question in each of the two sections of the test, and when they have a significant chance of scoring 460 by a purely random marking of the test. Finally, I support the NCAA's action because I believe that black parents, black educators, and the black community must insist that black children be taught and that they learn whatever subject matter is necessary to excel on diagnostic and all other skills tests. 32

Outcries of "racism," and calls for black boycotts of or exemptions from such tests, seem to me neither rational nor constructive long-term responses to the problem of black students' low test scorees. Culture can be learned and taught. Class-specific values and perspectives can be learned and taught. And this is what we should be about as black educators—preparing our young people to meet the challenges they face on these tests, and, by extension, in this society. 33

I believe that (1) student athletes and non-athletes alike should be given diagnostic tests on a recurrent basis to assure skills achievement; (2) test-score standards should and must be raised, based upon the skill demands and challenges of our contemporary world; and (3) the test standards set should be established as post-enrollment goals and not pre-enrollment obstacles. 34

In the case of scholarship athletes, every institution should have the right to set its own academic enrollment standards. But those same institutions *must* acknowledge a binding corollary obligation and responsibility to develop and implement support programs sufficiently effective to fulfill their implied contracts with the athletes recruited. 35

For all of its divisive impact, the debate over Rule 48 has illuminated a much larger crisis involving the failure of this nation to educate its young, athletes and non-athletes, prop- 36 erly. In 1967, the national average on the SAT was 958; by 1982, it had dropped to 893. Furthermore, even students who score well on diagnostic tests frequently require remedial work to handle college-level course work. From 1975 to 1980, the number of remedial math courses in public four-year colleges increased by 72 percent; they now constitute a quarter of all math courses offered by those institutions. At two-year colleges, 42 percent of math courses are below the level of college algebra.

In high school transcripts, according to a study done for 37
the National Commission on Excellence in Education, credit value for American history has declined by 11 percent over the past fifteen years, for chemistry by 6 percent, for algebra by 7 percent, and for French by 9 percent. In the same period, credit value for remedial English has risen by 39 percent and for driver education by 75 percent. Only 31 percent of recent high school graduates took intermediate algebra, only 16 percent took geography, and only 13 percent took French. High school students have abandoned college-preparatory and vocational-education "tracks" in droves, so that between 1964 and 1979 the number who chose the "general" track rose from 12 to 42 percent. About 25 pecent of all credits earned by general-track graduates were in physical and health education, driver education, home management, food and cooking, training for adulthood and marriage, remedial courses, and for work experience outside school.

Part of the problem is with our teachers: the way they 38
are recruited, their low status, and their even lower rewards. According to a recent article in *U.S. News & World Report,* "A study conducted for the National Institute of Education, which looked at college graduates who entered teaching in the late '70s, found that those with the highest academic ability were much more likely to leave their jobs than those who were lower achievers. Among high-achieving students, only 26 percent intended to teach at age thirty, as compared with approximately 60 percent of those with the lowest academic ability." In yet another study, one third of the nearly 7,000 prospective teachers who took the California

minimum-competency test failed to meet the most basic skills requirements. And in 1982,the average SAT score of students indicating teaching as their intended field of study ranked twenty-six among average scores achieved by students declaring twenty-nine different fields of interest.

Black colleges are not blameless with respect to inadequate teacher preparation. Currently, at least twenty states require teacher candidates to pass a state qualifying exam. In Florida, 79 percent of white teacher-college graduates achieved a passing rate, compared with 35 percent for black test-takers. The two black schools that produce the largest number of black teacher candidates in that same state had the worst passing rates—37 percent and 16 percent. 39

That state's Association of Black Psychologists held a press conference and denounced the tests as "instruments of European cultural imperialism," and urged the black community—as a front—to resist the tests. But there is really only one legitimate concern relative to such tests: Do they measure what should be taught in schools of education if teachers are to be competent? 40

The majority of black students today come from schools in which blacks either predominate or make up the entire student body. And much—if not most—of the failure to educate black youths has occurred under black educators. In the 1960s, from Ocean Hill-Brownsville, in New York, to Watts, in California, blacks quite rightly criticized inner-city schools where white teachers and white superintendents were indifferent to the learning abilities of black students. Many of these school systems now have a majority of black teachers and black superintendents, and many black students still do not learn. Can we afford to be any less critical when white incompetence is replaced by black incompetence? Given what is at stake, the answer must be an emphatic and resounding No. We must let all of our educators know that if they are not competent to do their jobs, they have no business in our schools. 41

But pointing out teachers' inadequacies is not enough. For all of its modernity, education still advances on "four legs." 42

Though formal instruction takes place in the classroom, education is the result of coordinated effort on the part of parents, the school, the community, and the larger society. Parents who do not participate in school activities, who do not attend parent-teacher conferences to review their children's academic progress, who generally show little or no interest in school-related issues—indeed, who do not know, and have never even asked, the name of the teacher charged with instructing their children—over the years communicate to those children the idea that education doesn't matter. The community that undercuts the solvency of its libraries and schools communicates the idea that education doesn't matter. The school that emphasizes and revels in the glories of sports, while fighting efforts to set academic standards for sports participation, communicates the idea that education doesn't matter.

Current national policy, which calls for severe cuts in 43
educational funding, and defense expenditures of $1.6 trillion over the next four years, is both contradictory and shortsighted. Education *is* a national-defense issue. As Jefferson pointed out at this nation's birth, an educated, informed populace is necessary to the operation of a viable democracy. As the world's leading democracy, we simply cannot afford the current burden of 26 million adults who are functionally illiterate and 46 million who are only marginally literate. Since the 1970s, the U. S. military has found that it must print comic-book versions of some of its manuals in order to accommodate the educational deficiencies of troops charged with operating and maintaining some of the most sophisticated weapons in history. Along with greater emphasis upon parental involvement in schools, insistence upon teacher competence, and greater academic expectations of our students, we must put more, not less, money into education.

The National Center for Education Statistics estimates 44
that the average 1980–1981 salary for classroom teachers was $17,602—up from $9,269 in 1971. However, in constant 1981 dollars, teachers have lost money, because their 1971 average salary translates to roughly $20,212. The out-

look for the future is equally bleak. Education cannot attract and hold the best-trained and most competent people without offering competitive salaries. Particularly in the more technologically applicable disciplines, education is suffering a severe "brain-drain." Thus, in 1981, nationwide, half the teachers hired to teach high school math and science were not certified to teach those subjects, while more than forty states reported shortages of qualified teachers in those areas.

Compared with other national school systems, Amer- 45
ican education comes up short. The American school year is 180 days, and the average student misses roughly eighteen of those, but Japan, Germany, and most other industrial nations require at least 220 days a year. In the Soviet Union, students from the first grade on attend school six days a week. About 35 percent of their classwork is in science. They take five years of arithmetic, then are introduced to algebra and geometry, followed by calculus. The national minimum curriculum also calls for one year each of astronomy and mechanical drawing, four years of chemistry, five years of physics, and six years of biology.

In sum, education must be put at the very top of the U.S. 46
domestic agenda. Clearly, we must demonstrate greater concern for and commitment to educational quality for all American youths—athletes as well as non-athletes. I am confident that with adequate support and proper encouragement, they can achieve whatever levels of performance are necessitated by the challenges they face. In today's world, neither they nor we have any other choice.

QUESTIONS ON SUBJECT AND PURPOSE

1. According to Edwards, in what ways are the "patterns of opportunity for blacks in American sports . . . shaped by racial discrimination"?
2. Does Edwards have any objections to Rule 48? If so, what are they?
3. What purpose does Edwards seem to have in this essay? To what extent is he writing about issues larger than Rule 48?

QUESTIONS ON STRATEGY AND AUDIENCE

1. Edwards develops his points through a detailed use of facts and figures. How do these numbers and statistics contribute to his argument? How do they contrast with the arguments that he quotes from his opponents?
2. At one point (paragraph 32), Edwards identifies himself as a "nationally known black educator." What is the effect of such an identification? Why not make it earlier in the essay?
3. How might Edwards define his audience? To whom is he writing? Is he writing, for example, to young black athletes? Point to specific features in the essay that suggest an awareness of audience.

QUESTIONS ON VOCABULARY AND STYLE

1. Characterize the tone of Edwards's essay. Does he ever use emotionally charged language? Or does he just let the statistics speak for themselves?
2. At several points throughout the essay, Edwards quotes other authorities. What do these quotations contribute to his argument? Why use them at all?
3. Be able to define the following words: *judicious* (paragraph 5), *disparate* (7), *ludicrous* (7), *emulate* (9), *honed* (10), *affluence* (12), *impetus* (16), *lucrative* (26), *vis-à-vis* (28), *inept* (31), *corollary* (35), *divisive* (36), *viable* (43).

WRITING SUGGESTIONS

1. Many high schools have implemented minimum grade point averages for participation in any extracurricular activity (for example, athletics, musical organizations, theater, social or academic clubs). In a paragraph, drawing upon your own experiences or the experiences of others you knew in high school, argue for or against such requirements.
2. Colleges and universitites compete for gifted athletes in a variety of sports by offering athletic scholarships. On the other hand, few, if any, colleges offer scholarships for students to work on the campus newspaper or to perform in theatrical productions (or to take part in any other activities that occur on college campuses). In an essay argue for or against offering

scholarships to students to perform or participate in non-athletic activities.

Prewriting:

a. It might be wise to establish first the nature of the scholarships that your school already offers. In how many areas other than athletics are scholarships offered? Your school's admissions office can probably provide a convenient breakdown. The information might also be available in a current undergraduate catalog.
b. Brainstorm a list of activities that might be supported in a way similar to athletics. A listing of campus organizations might provide some suggestions. Choose activities that are currently not supported.
c. Make a list of the advantages and disadvantages that would arise from such a plan. In what ways are these other activities unlike college athletics and, therefore, not entitled to funding?

Rewriting:

a. Remember that a successful argument is generally one that is reasonable and fair. Regardless of the side you took, have you avoided distorted or exaggerated language? Reexamine your essay to make sure.
b. Ask a classmate or roommate to read your essay. Ask your reader if she or he agrees with your position. Ask for specific reasons why or why not. Do not ignore such feedback; a persuasive or argumentative essay works only if it wins the support of its readers.
c. Look again at your conclusion. Did you end forcefully? Did you make it clear what you want your audience to do or believe? If not, try freewriting a new conclusion to your essay.

3. What has been the effect of Rule 48? Research the impact of the ruling on college and high school athletic programs. Then, using that research, write an essay in support of or in opposition to Rule 48.

C H A P T E R

10
Revision

By the time you have finished a paper, typed or recopied it in your most legible handwriting, proofread it carefully, and handed it in on the due date, the last thing you ever want to do is to revise it. "I wrote it; it is finished," you announce. Your instructor, however, counters: "You have only written it once; it is never finished. Besides, the real writing occurs in the rewriting."

Most writers, even professional writers, confess that writing and rewriting are agonizing tasks. It is one thing to look back after everything is over and admire the finished product; it is quite another to live through the process required to get to that end. Nevertheless, most writers do revise their work, often very extensively. You would expect that a poet, a novelist, or a playwright would keep rethinking and rewriting a work, but creative writers are not the only writers who revise, as the examples in this chapter show.

Just as writers use a variety of composing strategies, they also approach the problem of revising in vastly different ways. For some, the process of composition is so painstaking and logical that a single written draft is sufficient. The revision has taken place in small steps as the writing occurred. For other writers, draft follows draft. One famous writer, when asked to contribute to this chapter, remarked, "Usually I take many, many drafts, even with simple-minded prose. But as I am sure you know, one cannot really just turn over the *actual* drafts, not most of the time . . . one would have to edit them and so forth." The extent of the revisions included in this chapter varies widely. In some instances, the prose underwent a single revision; in others, many. For example, Nora Ephron in "Revision and Life" describes her revision process—one which can require 300 to 400 pieces of typing paper for a six-page essay. Some of the revisions in this chapter are relatively minor—changing words, tightening sentences, adding or deleting examples. Some of the revisions are major—substituting new beginnings or endings, reshuffling paragraphs, changing the emphasis. William Ouchi, for example, in "Why We Need to Learn" added a new paragraph to the beginning of his book as he moved from one draft to another.

What Is a Revision?

Literally, the word *revision* means "to see again." You do not revise a paper by just proofreading it for mechanical and grammatical errors; that is an expected final step in the writing process. Instead, a revision takes place after a draft of a whole paper or part of it has been completed, after a period of time has elapsed and you have had a chance to get some advice or criticism on what you wrote, after you can see what you *wrote*, not what you think you wrote. The advice and criticism of others can come in a variety of forms: from peer editing or critiquing that is done in class, from classroom discussions of mimeographed papers or sections of papers, from a conference with your instructor, from a tutorial in your college's writing center. In revising, however, you do not just depend upon others. Revisions should always involve an active, careful scrutiny on your part of every aspect of your paper—your subject, audience, thesis, paragraph structures, sentence constructions, and word choice.

To some people, revising a paper means changing words—a thesaurus approach that substitutes bigger, more unusual words for smaller, more common ones. Probably every writer, certainly each of the writers in this chapter, changes some words from one draft to another. Professional writers, however, rarely look for bigger, more impressive words. Instead, they look for better words—words that are more precise, more vivid, more easily understood. For example, when Joseph Epstein in "Confessions of a Low Roller" revised his description of having an imaginary drink with the "big-time bookie," he changed the phrase "in the cool, wooded bar" to the "cool, wood-paneled bar." "Wooded" is an adjective typically meaning "covered with trees or woods" and is obviously not as precise or as accurate as "wood-paneled." In Susan Toth's first description of her adventures in Boston, she "sampled German cooking," but in her revision the general term *cooking* was replaced by the more precise noun *sausages*.

Writers rework sentences, trying to make them tighter, clearer, more varied, adding, deleting, and substituting details. Nora Ephron in "Revision and Life" remembers her college writing practices. In one draft she wrote: "When I was in college, I revised almost nothing. It seems to me (I know my memory isn't what it used to be but I'm fairly sure about this) I typed papers and pretty much turned them in." She revised those sentences, removing the qualifiers "almost," "pretty much," and the parenthetical comment and adding the phrase "in longhand." The new sentences are sharper, more defininte, and more vivid: "When I was in college, I revised nothing. I wrote out my papers in longhand, typed them up and turned them in." Andrew Ward in "Yumbo" writes about an experience with humanized sandwiches on a children's menu (Ferdinand Burger, Freddie the Fish Stick, and Porky Pig Sandwich). In his first draft he wrote: "Like most children's menus, it made the mistake of reminding Kelly Susan, a devout vegetarian of her own choosing, that Ferdinand had been led off to the meatyards, Freddie the Fish had been caught on a hook, Porky Pig had stuttered his entreaties as the ax descended." In the revision he deleted the evaluative judgment ("made the mistake") and changed the verbs to make the animals' fates even more vivid: "Like most children's menus, it first anthropomorphized the ingredients and then killed them off. As Kelly read it her eyes grew large, and in them I could see gentle Ferdinand being led away to the stockyard, Freddie gasping at the end of a hook, Porky stuttering his entreaties as the ax descended."

In one way, the drafts included in this chapter and even the drafts of the student essays in each previous chapter can be misleading. In each of these cases, the first draft with changes did eventually become the final draft. As many writers will tell you, though, revisions do not always work in that way. Sometimes first drafts are completely discarded and the paper is started anew. That does not mean that the first draft was a waste, for it at least showed you what you did not want to do. It might also have served to suggest a new subject, a new thesis, or a new point of view. Revising can always involve that discovery, and in order to do a good revision you may occasionally need to discard the first draft instead of wasting time trying to save it.

Where Does Revision Begin?

Revision should start not with the smallest unit—the choice of a particular word—but with the largest—the choice of subject, purpose, audience, and organization. A revision in its broadest sense involves a complete rethinking of a paper from idea through execution. Once you have finished a paper, think first about these four groups of questions—if possible, write out answers to each:

1. What is my *subject?* Is it too large? Too small? Is it interesting? Do I have something fresh, original, or informative to say?
2. What is my *purpose?* Why did I write *this* paper? Have I expressed my purpose in a clear thesis statement? Is everything in the paper related to that statement of purpose?
3. Who do I imagine as my *audience?* Who will read this? What do they already know about the subject? Have I written the paper with that audience in mind? Have I used language that is understandable and appropriate?

4. How is my paper *structured?* Have I followed the advice on structure given in the appropriate chapter introductions of this text? Is the organization of my paper clear and inevitable? Can it be easily outlined? Have I provided enough examples and details?

After you have answered these questions you can begin to reexamine the overall structure of your paper as well as individual paragraphs, sentences, and even word choices. Part of the secret in doing an effective revision is to learn to scrutinize your own writing, to look at your prose as if it were written by someone else. For this reason, revision works best when some time passes between drafts. Once you have finished a paper, you are generally either so tired or so blind to its strengths and weaknesses that you cannot be an effective critic of your own prose. If you can, allow at least a day or two to pass before you look again at your paper.

Another great help in revising is to find an editor/critic. If your writing instructor has the time to look at your draft or if your college or university has a writing center or a writing tutor program, you can get the advice of an experienced, trained reader. If your paper or part of it is discussed in class, you can listen to your classmates' comments as a way of gauging how successful your writing has been. If your writing class uses peer editing, you can study the responses of your editors for possible areas for revision. Peer evaluation works best when readers start with a series of specific directions—questions to answer or things for which to look. If you are interested in trying peer evaluation, you and a classmate could start with an editing checksheet adapted from the "Some Things to Remember" section at the end of the introduction to each chapter in this book. Whenever you are responding to someone else's writing, remember that your comments are always more valuable if they are specific and suggest ways in which changes could be made.

It is often difficult to accept criticism, but if you want to improve your writing skills, you need someone to say,

"Why not do this?" After all, you expect that an athletic coach or a music or dance teacher will offer criticism. Your writing instructor plays the same role, and the advice and criiticism he or she offers is meant to make your writing more effective; it is not intended as a personal criticism of you or your abilities. As you will discover, writing instructors are not the only audience—or the only critical audience—that you will face in life. Writing done on the job—whether it is a report, a memorandum, a letter, or an article—will be read by many readers. Even professional writers have colleagues, editors, and occasionally even readers who offer advice and criticism.

Ultimately, though, it is up to you as the writer to decide how valid your readers' criticisms are and how helpful their suggestions might be. Even experienced readers and editors can offer conflicting advice. After listening to or seeing the viewpoints of others, you have the final responsibility for making any revisions.

How Important Is Length?

After you have finished a draft of a paper, count the total number of words you have written. On most writing assignments, your instructor will probably indicate some length guidelines (3 paragraphs, 750 words, 10 pages). Those guidelines are important, for they give you some idea of the amount of space you will need to develop and illustrate your thesis sufficiently. An effective essay—no matter what the length—has a well defined thesis that is adequately explored and illustrated with specific details and examples. Comparing the number of words or pages that you have written to the guidelines provided is often a quick way of checking how thorough you have been. If your papers consistently fall under the guidelines (300 words instead of 750), you probably rely on empty generalizations and do not include enough examples or illustrating details. Writing the designated number of words does not, of course, guarantee a good essay, but writing only half of the suggested number because you fail to develop and illustrate your thesis can result in a lower grade.

Similarly, if your papers consistently exceed the guidelines (20 pages instead of 10), you probably tackled subjects that are too large or you have included too many details and examples. Of the material available to support, develop, and illustrate a thesis, some is more significant and relevant than the rest. Never try to include everything—select the best, the most appropriate, the most convincing.

Some Tests for Sentences

Spend some time looking carefully at each sentence you have written. You are checking for two things: first, that each sentence is mechanically and grammatically correct; and second, that each sentence is clear and effective. Before you begin checking for correctness, review the material on sentences included in the handbook you are using in your writing course. That can serve as a guide to identifying and solving problems within your sentences. Make sure that everything you have punctuated as if it were a sentence is, in fact, a sentence. If you write incomplete sentences—sentence fragments—your instructor will assume that they are errors. Fragments can be intentional: for example, a number of writers included in this text use them, often very effectively. But fragments do mark a piece of writing as informal and so may be inappropriate in college writing assignments. If you want to use a fragment for an intentional purpose, check first to make sure that your instructor is willing to accept intentional fragments.

Effective writing involves both correct sentences and mature, varied sentences. Achieving the first is a matter of diligence; achieving the second involves a careful attention to how sentences interact with each other. Another simple test can possibly provide you with some useful information about the types of sentences you write. Count the number of sentences you have written, including only those that end in a period, an exclamation mark, or a question mark.

Once you have the number of sentences, divide that number into the total number of words in your paper. This gives you the total number of words per sentence, something that can provide a useful check on your writing. One study has shown, for example, that the average number of words per sentence is related to the age and maturity of the writer: fourth-grade students wrote sentences containing an average of 13.5 words; twelfth-grade students averaged 16.9 words, and professional writers publishing in magazines like *Atlantic* and *Harper's* averaged 24.7. Generalizing from such a study can be dangerous. Do not assume that if you write long sentences your prose will necessarily sound professional. The objective is never to keep your number high, but a very low number (10 to 13 words per sentence) does indicate something about the structure of your sentences. If you consistently write sentences that average 10 to 13 words, you are probably writing strings of simple sentences. Writing only short simple sentences will make your prose sound immature and choppy.

If your numbers are low, look at your sentences. Can you use modification, coordination, or subordination to combine sentences, thereby cutting out unnecessary words and increasing the density of your sentences? A good way to improve sentences is through sentence-combining or -generating activities. Again the material provided in your handbook can be a useful resource. Low numbers also indicate that you are probably using a limited range of sentence types. In most of the selections in this text, the writers are careful to vary their sentence constructions. That is not to say that a professional writer consciously plans: "I've just written a simple sentence, I'll follow that with a complex sentence beginning with a long introductory adverbial clause and then end with a compound sentence each half of which will contain a series of three items." But prose writers, like poets and novelists, are very much aware of the variety of sentence types that they write.

Just as you ought to be careful about a low average number of words per sentence, so you ought to be careful about a high number. Long sentences require a strong sense of structure and order, as well as marks of punctuation, to help the reader understand them. Since long sentences can make the reader's job harder, it is important that you do everything you can to make those sentences as clear as possible. You can do so by carefully using modification, subordination, and coordination. Parallelism, having syntactical and grammatical elements in the same form, is another crucial device for making a complicated sentence structure easily understood.

Some Advice About Paragraphs

The qualities of a good paragraph—things like unity, coherence, organization, completeness—have been stressed in every writing course you have taken, with good reason. When you revise your paper, look carefully at each paragraph to see whether or not it exhibits those qualities. For a simple but helpful test, count the total number of paragraphs you have used. As a rough guide, the average 500 to 750 word essay should probably have something between 3 to 7 paragraphs. If you have only one or two paragraphs, you have not clearly indicated the structure of your essay to your reader or your essay does not have a clear, logical organization. On the other hand, if you have 10 to 15 paragraphs, you are overparagraphing, probably shifting ideas too quickly and failing to develop each one adequately. A good paragraph is meaty; it is not a string of undeveloped ideas or bare generalizations. In short, a large number of short paragraphs could be an indication that you have tried to include too many ideas or have not developed or illustrated those ideas sufficiently.

An Error-Free Paper Is an "A" Paper, Right?

Although good, effective writing is mechanically and grammatically correct, you cannot reverse the equation. It is perfectly possible to write a paper that has no "errors" but that is still a poor paper. An effective paper fulfills the requirements of the assignment, has something interesting or meaningful to say, includes specific evidence and examples rather than vague generalizations. Effective writing is a combination of many factors: appropriate content, a focused purpose, a clear organization, effective expression.

Although perfect grammar and mechanics do not make a perfect paper, such things are important. Minor errors are like static in your writing. If there are too many of them or they are obvious, they distract your reader. They focus the reader's attention not on your message, but on your faulty expression. Minor errors can undermine your reader's confidence in you as a qualified authority. If you make careless errors in spelling or punctuation, for example, your reader might assume that you made analogous errors in reporting information. So while a revision is not just a proofreading, proofreading should be a part of the revision process.

Some Things to Remember

1. Put your paper aside for a period of time before you attempt to revise it.
2. Seek the advice of your instructor or a writing center tutor, or the help of classmates.
3. Reconsider your choice of subject. Were you able to treat it adequately in the space you had available?
4. State your thesis in a sentence as a way of checking your content. Is everything in the paper relevant to that thesis?
5. Check to make sure that you have given enough examples to support your argument or to make your thesis clear. Relevant specifics convince and interest a reader.
6. Look back through the advice given in each of the introductions to this text. Have you organized your paper carefully? Is its structure clear?
7. Define your audience. To whom are you writing? What assumptions have you made about your audience? What changes are necessary to make your paper clear and interesting to that audience?

8. Count the number of words in your paper. How close did you come to the guidelines you were given?
9. Examine each sentence to make sure that it is complete and grammatically correct. Try for a variety of sentence structures and lengths.
10. Look carefully at each paragraph. Does it obey the rules for effective paragraph construction? Do your paragraphs clearly indicate the structure of your essay?
11. Check your word choice. Have you avoided slang, jargon, clichés? Have you used specific words? Have you used words appropriate for your intended audience?
12. Proofread one final time.

Yumbo

ANDREW WARD

Andrew Ward, author, humorist, and essayist, was born in Chicago, Illinois, in 1946. He was educated at Oberlin College and the Rhode Island School of Design. Following his graduation, he worked as a photographer for the Ford Foundation in New Delhi, India, from 1968 to 1970. After two years as a free-lance writer and photographer, he took a position as an art teacher at a private school in Connecticut where he taught until 1974. His books include Fits and Starts: The Premature Memoirs of Andrew Ward *(1978), for which he was awarded an Atlantic Grant from the* Atlantic; Bits and Pieces *(1980), a book of essays and parodies; and* The Blood Seed: A Novel of India *(1985). His work has appeared in magazines such as* Redbook, Fantasy and Science Fiction, Horizon, American Heritage, *and* Inquiry. *He is presently a contributing editor for the* Atlantic.

On revising, Ward observes: "I make it a practice to retain just about every scrap of discarded material: partially, no doubt, out of some touching concern for my biographers, but ostensibly, at least, out of my continuing need to reassure myself that I haven't lost my touch. After I've gone over draft after draft of some perfectly simple little paragraph, and find myself still dissatisfied, I pluck out a file on an earlier essay and reassure myself with all the early attempts I had to make to sound fluent, poised, and casual."

The selection reproduced here from the Atlantic *is the first paragraph from the short essay "Yumbo" named after a ham and cheese sandwich once sold by Burger King. The essay reflects on how restaurants have "lately taken to treating us all as if we were children" by turning ordinary food into something "festive."*

FINAL VERSION

I was sitting at an inn with Kelly Susan, my ten-year-old niece, when she was handed the children's menu. It was printed in gay pastels on construction paper and gave her a choice of a Ferdinand Burger, a Freddie the Fish Stick, or a Porky Pig Sandwich. Like most children's menus, it first anthropomorphized the ingredients and then killed them off. As Kelly read it her eyes grew large, and in them I could see gentle Ferdinand being led away to the stockyard, Freddie gasping at the end of a hook, Porky stuttering his entreaties as the ax descended. Kelly Susan, alone in her family, is a resolute vegetarian and has already faced up to the dread that whispers to us as we slice our steaks. She wound up ordering a cheese sandwich, but the children's menu had ruined her appetite, and she spent the meal picking at her food.

QUESTIONS FOR DISCUSSION

1. How effective does this paragraph seem as an introduction? Does it catch your interest? Why or why not?
2. How does Ward seem to feel about children's menus? About vegetarianism? Does anything in the paragraph reveal his attitudes and values?
3. How does Ward use parallel structure in his paragraph?
4. Be able to define the following words: *anthropomorphize, entreaties*, and *resolute*.

EARLIER DRAFT

I was sitting with my ten-year-old niece this weekend when she was handed the children's menu. It gave her the choice of a Ferdinand Burger, a Freddie the Fish Stick, a Porky Pig Sandwich, and something called a College Boy, which was a grilled cheese sandwich. Like most children's menus it made the mistake of reminding Kelly Susan, a devout vegetarian by her own choosing, that Ferdinand had been led off to the meatyards, Freddie the Fish had been caught on a hook, Porky Pig had stuttered his entreaties as the ax descended. Kelly wound up ordering the College Boy, but the children's menu had ruined her appetite and she wound up picking at her food.

QUESTIONS ON THE REVISION

1. In the earlier draft Ward includes the name of the cheese sandwich (College Boy), but in the final draft he omits it. Why?
2. Writers frequently revise to make word choices more precise and vivid. Which changes seem to have been made for that reason?
3. In the earlier draft, Ward observes, "it made the mistake of reminding," but he deletes that remark in the final version. Why? What replaces that evaluative comment?
4. What is the difference between a "devout" vegetarian and a "resolute" one? Why change the word?

WRITING SUGGESTIONS

1. The tendency for restaurants to use special names for items on their menus is not limited to those intended for children. Visit one or more local restaurants and notice the menus. What special terms are used? In a paragraph report your findings. Focus your paragraph around either a particular restaurant or a particular pattern that you see occurring in several restaurants.
2. Later in his essay Ward remarks that restaurants give names to sandwiches (e.g., Whopper, Big Mac, Triple-R Burger) to "convert an essentially bleak industry, mass-marketed fast foods, into something festive." The idea of assigning names to products is not unique to the fast-food industry. Choose another industry that uses special names, and in an essay analyze those names and the reasons why they might have been chosen. Some possibilities include:
   a. Automobiles
   b. Breakfast cereals
   c. Musical groups (for example, heavy metal, country, reggae bands)
   d. Cosmetics
   e. Candy bars

   Prewriting:
   a. Once you have chosen a possible subject, make a list of the names currently in use. Do not rely on just your memory; try to locate advertisements in magazines.
   b. Look for characteristics that the names have in common. What associations do those names have? In what way are

those associations appropriate? Make a list of the characteristics. Then try to construct a classification scheme.

c. Remember that your essay will not be just a collection of examples. You need to analyze the information that you have gathered. Make a brief outline of your paper, and be sure to include some analysis under each subsection.

Rewriting:

a. Your essay needs to have a clear, explicit thesis and a clear, explicit structure. Using a colored pen, underline your thesis statement and the topic sentence (or the subject) of each paragraph.
b. Have you included enough examples? Do not generalize based on just one or two examples. Remember that readers need specific, relevant information.
c. Carefully examine each sentence in your essay. Is each a complete sentence? Have you used a variety of sentence structures and lengths?

3. Companies spend large amounts of money trying to find the "right" name for a particular product. Expand your topic from suggestion 2 to include library research. Business, marketing, and advertising magazines are good sources for information.

Revision and Life: Take It from the Top—Again

NORA EPHRON

Nora Ephron was born in 1941 in New York City. After she received her B.A. from Wellesley College in 1962, Ephron worked as a journalist and columnist for the New York Post, New York *magazine, and* Esquire. *Her books include* Wallflower at the Orgy *(1970),* Scribble, Scribble: Notes on the Media *(1979), and the novel* Heartburn *(1983), which was made into a film. She also wrote the screenplay for* Silkwood *(1983).*

"Revision and Life," written in response to an invitation to participate in this chapter, was originally published in The New York Times Book Review. *As the title suggests, for Ephron revision and life are closely linked. When she was a college student, with the limitless potential of youth, her goal was "to get to the end"—to finish the piece, to get on with life. As she has grown older, however, revision has come to mean that more lies ahead. "By the time you reach middle age," she observes, "you want more than anything for things not to come to an end; and as long as you are revising, they don't."*

FINAL VERSION

I have been asked to write something for a textbook that is 1
meant to teach college students something about writing and revision. I am happy to do this because I believe in revision. I have also been asked to save the early drafts of whatever I write, presumably to show these students the actual process of revision. This too I am happy to do. On the other hand, I suspect that there is just so much you can teach college students about revision; a gift for revision may be a developmental stage—like a 2-year-old's sudden ability to place one block on top of another—that comes along

somewhat later, in one's mid-20s, say; most people may not be particularly good at it, or even interested in it, until then.

When I was in college, I revised nothing. I wrote out my papers in longhand, typed them up and turned them in. It would never have crossed my mind that what I had produced was only a first draft and that I had more work to do; the idea was to get to the end, and once you had got to the end you were finished. The same thinking, I might add, applied in life: I went pell-mell through my four years in college without a thought about whether I ought to do anything differently; the idea was to get to the end—to get out of school and become a journalist. 2

Which I became, in fairly short order. I learned as a journalist to revise on deadline. I learned to write an article a paragraph at a time—and I arrived at the kind of writing and revising I do, which is basically a kind of typing and retyping. I am a great believer in this technique for the simple reason that I type faster than the wind. What I generally do is to start an article and get as far as I can—sometimes no farther in than a sentence or two—before running out of steam, ripping the piece of paper from the typewriter and starting all over again. I type over and over until I have got the beginning of the piece to the point where I am happy with it. I then am ready to plunge into the body of the article itself. This plunge usually requires something known as a transition. I approach a transition by completely retyping the opening of the article leading up to it in the hope that the ferocious speed of my typing will somehow catapult me into the next section of the piece. This does not work—what in fact catapults me into the next section is a concrete thought about what the next section ought to be about—but until I have the thought the typing keeps me busy, and keeps me from feeling something known as blocked. 3

Typing and retyping as if you know where you're going is a version of what therapists tell you to do when they suggest that you try changing from the outside in—that if you can't master the total commitment to whatever change 4 you want to make, you can at least do all the extraneous things connected with it, which make it that much easier to get there. I was 25 years old the first time a therapist suggested that I try changing from the outside in. In those days, I used to spend quite a lot of time lying awake at night wondering what I should have said earlier in the evening and revising my lines. I mention this not just because it's a way of illustrating that a gift for revision is practically instinctive, but also (once again) because it's possible that a genuine ability at it doesn't really come into play until one is older—or at least older than 25, when it seemed to me that all that was required in my life and my work was the chance to change a few lines.

5 In my 30's, I began to write essays, one a month for *Esquire* magazine, and I am not exaggerating when I say that in the course of writing a short essay—1,500 words, that's only six double-spaced typewritten pages—I often used 300 or 400 pieces of typing paper, so often did I type and retype and catapult and recatapult myself, sometimes on each retyping moving not even a sentence farther from the spot I had reached the last time through. At the same time, though, I was polishing what I had already written: as I struggled with the middle of the article, I kept putting the beginning through the typewriter; as I approached the ending, the middle got its turn. (This is a kind of polishing that the word processor all but eliminates, which is why I don't use one. Word processors make it possible for a writer to change the sentences that clearly need changing without having to retype the rest, but I believe that you can't always tell whether a sentence needs work until it rises up in revolt against your fingers as you retype it.) By the time I had produced what you might call a first draft—an entire article with a beginning, middle and end—the beginning was in more like 45th draft, the middle in 20th, and the end was almost newborn. For this reason, the beginnings of my essays are considerably better written than the ends, although I like to think no one ever notices this but me.

As I learned the essay form, writing became harder for me. I was finding a personal style, a voice if you will, a way of writing that looked chatty and informal. That wasn't the hard part—the hard part was that having found a voice, I had to work hard month to month not to seem as if I were repeating myself. At this point in this essay it will not surprise you to learn that the same sort of thing was operating in my life. I don't mean that my life had become harder—but that it was becoming clear that I had many more choices than had occurred to me when I was marching through my 20's. I no longer lost sleep over what I should have said. Not that I didn't care—it was just that I had moved to a new plane of late-night anxiety: I now wondered what I should have done. Whole areas of possible revision opened before me. What should I have done instead? What could I have done? What if I hadn't done it the way I did? What if I had a chance to do it over? What if I had a chance to do it over as a different person? These were the sorts of questions that kept me awake and led me into fiction, which at the very least (the level at which I practice it) is a chance to rework the events of your life so that you give the illusion of being the intelligence at the center of it, simultaneously managing to slip in all the lines that occurred to you later. Fiction, I suppose, is the ultimate shot at revision. 6

Now I am in my 40's and I write screenplays. Screenplays—if they are made into movies—are essentially collaborations, and movies are not a writer's medium, we all know this, and I don't want to dwell on the craft of screenwriting except insofar as it relates to revision. Because the moment you stop work on a script seems to be determined not by whether you think the draft is good but simply by whether shooting is about to begin: if it is, you get to call your script a final draft; and if it's not, you can always write another revision. This might seem to be a hateful way to live, but the odd thing is that it's somehow comforting; as long as you're revising, the project isn't dead. And by the same token, neither are you. 7

It was, as it happens, while thinking about all this one recent sleepless night that I figured out how to write this particular essay. I say "recent" in order to give a sense of immediacy and energy to the preceding sentence, but the truth is that I am finishing this article four months after the sleepless night in question, and the letter asking me to write it, from George Miller of the University of Delaware, arrived almost two years ago, so for all I know Mr. Miller has managed to assemble his textbook on revision without me. 8

Oh, well. That's how it goes when you start thinking about revision. That's the danger of it, in fact. You can spend so much time thinking about how to switch things around that the main event has passed you by. But it doesn't matter. Because by the time you reach middle age, you want more than anything for things not to come to an end; and as long as you're still revising, they don't. 9

I'm sorry to end so morbidly—dancing as I am around the subject of death—but there are advantages to it. For one thing, I have managed to move fairly effortlessly and logically from the beginning of this piece through the middle and to the end. And for another, I am able to close with an exhortation, something I rarely manage, which is this: Revise now, before it's too late. 10

QUESTIONS FOR DISCUSSION

1. What links does Ephron see between revision and life?
2. How does Ephron structure her essay? What principle of order does she follow?
3. It would have been a simple matter for Ephron to omit the references to this textbook (paragraphs 1 and 8). The *New York Times* audience, for example, would not be interested in knowing these details. Why might she have chosen to include these references in her essay?
4. Why is fiction the "ultimate shot at revision"?
5. What might Ephron mean by her final sentence ("Revise now, before it's too late")?
6. Be able to define the following words: *pell-mell* (paragraph 2), *extraneous* (4), *exhortation* (10).

EARLIER DRAFT

Corresponds to paragraphs 1 and 2

I have been asked to write something that will show college students something about writing and revision. I am happy to do this because I believe in revision. I have been asked to write something and save all the early drafts, which I am also happy to do. On the other hand, I believe there is just so much you can teach college students about revision, that an ability for revision is something (a Piaget stage, like a 2½ year old's sudden ability to put one block on top of another) that is acquired slightly later, and that most people aren't particularly good at it or even interested in it until then.

When I was in college, I revised almost nothing. It seems to me (I know my memory isn't what it used to be but I'm fairly sure about this) I typed papers and pretty much turned them in. The same thing I might add applied in life: I pretty much went pell mell through my four years of higher education without a thought about whether I ought to have done anything differently. The things I wrote were a means to an end—to turn in the assignment, I suppose—and so was the way I lived my life—to get out of school and become a journalist.

QUESTIONS ON THE REVISION

1. In the final version, Ephron omits the reference to Piaget (paragraph 1). Who was Piaget? Why eliminate the reference?
2. In the final version Ephron suggests when it might be that people acquire an interest in revising ("in one's mid-20's, say"). Why add that detail?
3. What changes occur in the following passage from one draft to another? What is the effect of those changes?

Draft

> When I was in college, I revised almost nothing. It seems to me (I know my memory isn't what it used to be but I'm fairly sure about this) I typed papers and pretty much turned them in.

Final

> When I was in college, I revised nothing. I wrote out my papers in longhand, typed them up and turned them in. It would never have crossed my mind that what I had produced was only a first draft and that I had more work to do; the idea was to get to the end, and once you had got to the end you were finished.

4. What is the effect of changing "four years of higher education" to "four years in college"?

WRITING SUGGESTIONS

1. Study the two versions of the opening of Ephron's essay. Formulate a thesis about her revision strategy. In a paragraph assert your thesis and support it with appropriate evidence.
2. On the basis of your own experience as a writer and as a student in this course, argue for or against *requiring* revision in a college writing course. Should a student be forced to do it? Does revision always produce a better paper?

   Prewriting:
   a. Remember that regardless of your stand, your argument should be based on solid, meaningful reasons. For example, you should not argue that revision is too much trouble or that it will please your instructor and get you a higher grade. Make a list of reasons.
   b. Interview classmates and friends for their experiences and opinions. Remember to take notes.
   c. Plan a possible organization for your essay. Does an inductive or a deductive approach seem better? In what order will you arrange your reasons? Will you start or end with the strongest reason?

   Rewriting:
   a. Check your tone in the essay. Do you sound convincing? Reasonable? Ask a friend or classmate to read your essay and to characterize its tone.
   b. Have you avoided emotionally charged language? Examine your word choice carefully. Underline any words that might seem distorted, inaccurate, or too emotional.

c. Titles are an important part of any essay. An effective title should clearly signal the essay's subject and should also arouse the reader's interest. Look carefully at your original title. Does it meet those tests? Try writing some alternative titles.

3. What role does revision play in the writing process of faculty and staff at your college or university? Interview a range of people—faculty (especially professors in disciplines other than English) and other professional staff members who write as a regular part of their job (for example, librarians, information officers, and admissions officers). Using notes from your interviews, write an essay about the revision practices of these writers. Your essay could be a feature article in the campus newspaper.

Should Teen-Agers Have Free Speech?

CHUCK STONE

Chuck Stone was born in St. Louis, Missouri, in 1924. After serving in the Air Force during World War II, he earned an A.B. in political science and economics from Wesleyan University in 1948 and an M.A. in sociology from the University of Chicago in 1951. Presently Stone is a professor of English at the University of Delaware, where he teaches a course on opinion writing, and a senior editor and columnist for the Philadelphia Daily News. *Stone's books include* Tell It Like It Is, *a collection of essays;* Black Political Power in America *(1968); and* King Strut *(1970), a novel. Stone has been involved in journalism for nearly thirty years, has taught and lectured at a number of colleges and universities, and has hosted several different television programs.*

About revision, Stone comments: "Any writer who doesn't revise just really isn't a writer. It's impossible to write without revising. I never feel that I am completely done with a piece; I always want to make more changes."

Stone's revision process is particularly evident in the two versions of the column reprinted here. Both were published. The first version was written for the United Media syndicate and appeared in about 125 newspapers. The revised version was published three days later in the Philadelphia Daily News.

The case of Hazelwood School District vs. Kulhmeier, Smart, and Tippett-Wise was filed in 1983, when Robert Reynolds, principal of Hazelwood East High School in Hazelwood, Missouri, excised two pages from the student publication, The Spectrum. *Reynolds deleted articles addressing the problems of divorce of parents and teen-age pregnancy within the school district. In January 1988, in a 5-to-3 decision, the Supreme Court upheld the principal's right to censor the student newspaper. This decision contradicts the 1969 Tinker decision, which permitted students rights of expression. The Hazelwood case will form the basis of future decisions on the part of school administrators to suppress what they consider controversial, poorly written, biased, vulgar, or unsuitable stories.*

FINAL DRAFT

On the basis of a preference for pedagogical tyranny over 1
dislogical freedom, the Supreme Court took a giant step backwards.

Affirming a Hazelwood, Mo., high school administra- 2
tion's right to censor its newspaper, the court was as contradictory as it was despotic:

"A school need not tolerate student speech that is 3
inconsistent with its basic educational mission *even though the government could not censor similar speech outside the school* [My emphasis].

"Educators do not offend the First Amendment by exer- 4
cising control over the style and content of student speech in school-sponsored expressive activities so long as their actions are reasonably related to legitimate pedagogical concerns."

That jargonistic flirtation with the First Amendment is 5
almost too silly to refute. Are "legitimate pedagogical concerns" the same in a high school in Harlem and Hattiesburg as they are in Hazelwood?

Most parents of elementary school children would 6
endorse last week's court ruling.

But at the high school level, I see no difference between 7
the censorship of textbooks and the censorship of school newspapers.

Obviously, the reasonable and prudent limits to free 8
speech would not permit a high school newspaper to publish scatology, child pornography, or social paroxysms of racial hate.

Yet, after preventing someone from crying "Fire" in a 9
crowded theater, where do we draw the line?

If presidential candidates discuss abortion or the break- 10
down in family values due to a spiraling divorce rate, could their discussions be published in a high school newspaper?

Not in Hazelwood, Mo. 11

The Supreme Court upheld the right of the high school 12
principal in this Rip Van Winkle community of 12,000 to censor the school newspaper's articles on divorce and teenage pregnancy.

Such high button shoes censorship obscures a modern reality. Most of today's kids already know all about sex. They watch soap operas, listen to suggestive song lyrics, go to X-rated movies, and read steamy novels. 13

But in today's information explosion, many teen-agers also are intellectual sophisticates. 14

Rather than serving as receptacles into which Mother Goose rhymes are deposited, teen-agers should be encouraged to grapple with truth and falsehood. 15

John Stuart Mill did. 16

By the age of 10, he had gone through all of the Latin and Greek authors, some of whom discussed incest and adultery. By 14, he had mastered history, logic, and political economy. 17

Perhaps, this early exposure to the clash of divergent ideas impelled Mill to be such an unrelenting defender of free speech. As he wrote: 18

Truth gains more even by the errors of one who, with due study and preparation, thinks for himself than by the true opinions of those who only hold them because they do not suffer themselves to think. 19

In 1988, five Supreme Court justices and a Hazelwood principal read to "suffer themselves to think" that teenagers must think more responsibly about why so many babies are being born out of wedlock and why so many parents are getting divorced. 20

Censoring their right to inquire into ideas only stunts democracy's growth. 21

QUESTIONS FOR DISCUSSION

1. In what ways does Stone's column (an expression of opinion) differ from a newspaper story about the same event? Why does Stone include only limited information about the Supreme Court case?
2. Can you find examples of word choice that make Stone's opinion obvious to the reader? What is the effect of these words and phrases? How does Stone's subjective style of writing differ from the style of other selections in this text?

3. Because Stone's column was written for a newspaper, it is paragraphed differently from most of the other essays in this collection. Does the need for frequent paragraphs affect the structure of the editorial? Could it be easily reparagraphed? Which paragraphs might be grouped together and why?
4. In reparagraphing the essay, would you change the two short one-sentence paragraphs (11 and 16)? What effect do they have?
5. Why does Stone use the example of John Stuart Mill? How does that fit into the argument he is making?
6. Be able to define the following words: *despotic* (paragraph 2), *jargonistic* (5), *scatology* (8), *paroxysms* (8), *divergent* (13).

FIRST DRAFT

Last week, the Supreme Court ruled that the First Amendment existed *only* after high school graduation. 1

The Court set an arbitrary cut-off point that denied the constitutional right of free speech to high school students who want to write about abortion, teen-age pregnancy or divorce. 2

Does free speech, like the court's ruling on abortion, require a cut-off point which doesn't begin until after high school? 3

By the Court's interpretation, yes. 4

But free speech is not a function of biological growth. It flowers with the freest exchange of ideas. 5

The following two paragraphs from the Court's despotic decision confirmed the Hazelwood, Mo., principal's right to be a Torquemada of ideas: 6

"A school need not tolerate student speech that is inconsistent with its basic educational mission *even though the government could not censor similar speech outside the school . . .* [My emphasis]. 7

"Educators do not offend the First Amendment by exercising control over the style and content of student speech in school-sponsored expressive activities so long as their actions are reasonably related to legitimate pedagogical concerns." 8

Hitler's brilliant propaganda chief, Paul Joseph Goebbels, couldn't have said it better. 9

But the Rehnquist court majority knew it was on shaky 10
ground. That's why it took such pains to differentiate *Hazelwood* from *Tinker, Des Moines School District 969.*

In the *Tinker* landmark case, the Warren Court ruled 11
that students' right to free speech included the right to wear black armbands on school grounds to protest the Vietnam war.

"Whenever a student is at school no matter what the 12
hour or activity that student is free to express his or her views as long as they do not materially and substantially interfere with the operation of the school."

That sentence forced Justice White to tapdance in trying 13
to show a constitutional distinction where none existed.

Apparently, he had forgotten that the *Tinker* ruling had 14
been applied to two similar high school students' free speech cases (*Eisner,* 1971 and *Fujishama,* 1972).

But Justice William J. Brennan, the high court's 15
patriarchal liberal and judicial genius, gently reminded his colleagues that *Tinker* did indeed apply to *Hazelwood.* It "struck the balance" between school instruction, students learning and their exercise of sometimes contentious free speech.

I realize that most of today's high school students are 16
not John Stuart Mills.

By 10, Mill had mastered political economy, geometry, 17
Latin and Greek authors, and logic.

But today's high school kids are still wordly wise 18
sophisticates. They watch sexy soap operas, read technical stories about space explorations, buy X-rated videos, and operate computers.

They're finding ways to cope with the drug and AIDS 19
crises.

But the *Hazelwood* ruling declares them too immature 20
to listen to 13 presidential candidates discuss abortion, teen-age pregnancy, and divorce in a Missouri forum, and then write about it in their high school newspaper.

And that is the biggest disservice the Rehnquist court 21
has done to free speech for our young citizens.

QUESTIONS ON THE REVISION

1. Which introduction seems more effective? Why?
2. Both versions contain examples of word choice that make Stone's opinion obvious to the reader. Remember that each version was published. Most of these examples were changed from the first to the final version. Why did Stone make these changes? Is the changed material more effective? Does it show a greater awareness of audience?
3. In rethinking the tone of his argument, Stone deleted references in paragraphs 6 and 9. Do these changes make his argument more persuasive to his audience?
4. Initially, Stone cited several other related Supreme Court decisions and quoted from the Tinker decision. In the final version, however, he omitted these references. Why did he choose to do so?
5. The section on John Stuart Mill was greatly expanded in the final version. How does the additional information contribute to Stone's argument?

WRITING SUGGESTIONS

1. Compare both versions of Stone's column. How does Stone's awareness of audience influence the final version? In a paragraph assert your thesis, and support it with appropriate evidence.
2. "Why not? Because you aren't old enough!" It is an answer that every child has heard and every parent has used. In an essay explore some aspect(s) of the problems of freedom and responsibility for teen-agers. Imagine that your audience is made up of parents of teen-age children.

   Prewriting:
   a. Try to focus your essay on a particular issue or experience. Make a list of conflicts you remember having with your parents or with your children.
   b. Ask classmates, friends, or perhaps your own children for their experiences. Add these to your list.
   c. Remember that you are arguing to a group of parents. Choose a topic, keeping that audience in mind. Your language and choice of examples should help persuade that audience. You are more likely to succeed if you offer logical reasons in

support of a realistic request (no parent, for example, is likely to think that a thirteen-year-old should be allowed to stay out all night).

Rewriting:

a. Look again at how you structured your essay. Have you started or ended with your strongest point? If you reversed the order, would your argument be any stronger?
b. Check through your essay line by line. Mark any words or phrases that might be ineffective or might detract from your argument. Ask a classmate or friend to evaluate each marked example.
c. What troubles you the most about your paper? Take that single problem to your writing center, writing tutor, or instructor.

3. Research the background for the Hazelwood decision. Exactly what happened? Was the event reported in the national news media? How long did it take the case to reach the Supreme Court? What was the reaction to the Supreme Court decision? Write a research paper in which you objectively report the facts of the case and the public and legal reaction to the Court's decision. Be factual and impartial in your presentation of the evidence.

E Pluribus Onion

JAMES VILLAS

James Villas was born in Charlotte, North Carolina, in 1938. He left college teaching of comparative literature and Romance languages to become a food writer, and is now food and wine editor of Town and Country *magazine. His essays have appeared in a variety of magazines including* Esquire, Cuisine, Bon Appetit, *and* Gourmet. *He is the author of* American Taste: A Celebration of Gastronomy Coast to Coast *(1982), a selection of essays celebrating the best of native American cooking, and* James Villas's The Town and Country Cookbook *(1985).*

On revising, Villas writes: "I think I did four different drafts of the piece, and this specimen shows as well as any what hell I go through getting a story into shape. Not just the language and style but the never-ending research."

This selection reproduces the introductory paragraphs from an essay that appeared in the January 1985 issue of Town and Country, *a magazine that characterizes itself as appealing to "upper-income Americans." In that issue, Villas's essay was accompanied by a color photograph of a roasted onion and twelve recipes for dishes using other members of the* Allium *genus.*

FINAL VERSION

When the most sagacious of Victorian culinarians, Mrs, Beeton, spoke rather cryptically of "the alliaceous tribe," she was referring to none other than the ancient and noble members of the lily family known in kitchens round the world as the onion, scallion, leek, shallot, chive, and garlic. I don't suppose it really matters that many cooks today are hardly aware of the close affinity the common bulb onion we take so much for granted has with these other vegetables of the *Allium* genus, but it does bother me how Americans underestimate the versatility of the onion and how so few give a second thought to exploiting the potential of its aromatic relatives. More often than not, the onion itself is 1 considered no more than a flavoring agent to soups, stews, stocks, sauces, salads, and sandwiches. Though I'd be the last to deny that nothing awakens the gustatory senses or inspires the soul like the aroma of onions simmering in a lusty stew or the crunch of a few sweet, odoriferous slices on a juicy hamburger, it would be nice to see the onion highlighted in ways other than the all-too-familiar fried rings and creamed preparations.

As for scallions, about the only time you encounter 2
these peppery "green onions" is when they are mixed into Oriental food, added to a plate of *nouvelle cuisine* for garnish, or added raw to salads for zest. And how many cooks can taste the delicate but distinctive difference between genuine shallots and tiny yellow onions? The only people who've learned about the many uses of fresh chives are those who grow them, and the social status of leeks is still so dubious in this country that the likelihood of finding an ample fresh supply in the supermarket is about as remote in most areas as spotting a bunch of fresh sorrel. Fortunately, garlic as a seasoning has gained wider acceptance in our cookery over the past few decades (there's even an annual garlic festival every June near San Francisco), but only now are adventurous chefs learning about the gustatory advantages of baking, roasting, and braising whole cloves of this deceptively sweet member of the onion family.

The bulb onion predates recorded history but was most 3
likely first cultivated in central Asia. We know it was a favorite vegetable in Mesopotamia around 2400 B.C., and various works of art and temple decorations testify to its popularity in ancient Egypt. Whether Alexander the Great introduced the onion to Europe is debatable, but it's certain that by 500 B.C. the Greeks had incorporated the bulb in their sophisticated style of cooking (Hippocrates believed the onion to be good for sight) and that during the Roman Empire its abundance was such that onions (all except the highly prized sweet specimens from Pompeii) were distributed widely as food for the poor. The lofty role of the onion in Chinese cookery can be traced at least back to the time of Marco Polo, while the earliest medieval tomes of

Britain and western Europe illustrate its importance both as a seasoning for many dishes and as a medicament for all ills. Cortés found many types of onions in Mexico, and it is said that Père Marquette, while exploring Michigan in 1624, was literally saved from starvation by nourishing himself on the vegetable whose odor the Indians of the region called *chicago!* Ironically, it does seem that the onion commanded more creative attention in Colonial America and throughout the nineteenth century than in present-day kitchens, but, with the exception of such enlightened early volumes as *The Joy of Cooking* (which originally included recipes for onion pie, glazed onions, onion shortcake, and onion soufflé), it can hardly be said that this fragrant globe has enjoyed much glory in this country throughout the twentieth century.

QUESTIONS FOR DISCUSSION

1. What is Villas's thesis in this selection? Put it into a sentence of your own.
2. What is the function of each of the three paragraphs? Why does Villas survey the history of the onion in the third paragraph?
3. What does the title "E Pluribus Onion" mean? Where else does part of that phrase occur? Does that seem like an appropriate title?
4. What expectations does Villas seem to have about his audience? How can you tell?
5. Be able to define the following words: *sagacious* (paragraph 1), *culinarians* (1), *cryptically* (1), *affinity* (1), *gustatory* (1), *odoriferous* (1), *nouvelle cuisine* (2), *dubious* (2), *sorrel* (2), *tomes* (3), *medicament* (3), *soufflé* (3).

EARLY DRAFT

The Fragrant Family of Gastronomy

When that most sagacious of British food writers, Mrs. Beeton, spoke of "the alliaceous tribe," she was referring to none other than the ancient and noble members of the lily family known in serious kitchens round the world as the 1 onion, scallion, leek, shallot, chive, and garlic. Of course most cooks today are still unaware of the close affinity the common bulb onion has with these other vegetables of the *Allium* genus, and it does bother me considerably that people take the onion so much for granted and that few give so much as a second thought to exploiting the potential of its aromatic relatives. More often than not the odoriferous onion is considered no more than a flavoring agent to soups, stews, stocks, sauces, salads, and sandwiches, and, with the exceptions of fried onion rings and creamed onions, is rarely allowed to stand on its own merit. When do you ever see scallions (or green onions) except chopped up and added to salads for zest, and who but the most knowledgeable chef ever goes to the trouble to track down fresh chives or genuine shallots? In this country the only people who've learned about the many uses of fresh chives are those who grow them, and even our most respected cookbook writers treat leeks as if they were as rare as fresh sorrel. Garlic has gained wider acceptance in our cookery over the past few decades, but only now are adventurous chefs learning about the gustatory advantages of baking, roasting, and braising whole cloves of this deceptively sweet member of the onion family.

The onion itself predates recorded history but was most 2
likely first cultivated in Central Asia. We know it was a favorite vegetable in Mesopotamia around 2400 B.C., and its popularity in ancient Egypt is attested to in various works of art and temple decorations. Whether Alexander the Great introduced the onion to Europe is debatable, but it's certain that by 500 B.C. the Greeks had incorporated the bulb in their sophisticated style of cooking and that it was later distributed widely as food for the poor during the Roman Empire. By the time of Marco Polo, numerous varieties of onions were being cultivated in China, while the earliest western European tomes testify to its importance in medieval and Elizabethan kitchens. Cortés found all types of onions in Mexico, and it is said that Père Marquette, while exploring Michigan in 1624, was literally saved from starvation by nourishing himself on a vegetable the odor of which

the Indians of the region called *chicago*! Ironically, the onion figures much more importantly in Colonial American kitchens than in our present-day cookery, and even in the early 1900s, classic volumes like *The Joy of Cooking* were including recipes for onion pie, glazed onions, onion shortcake, and onion soufflé.

QUESTIONS ON THE REVISION

1. Villas expanded the first paragraph of the earlier draft, making it into two separate paragraphs. What does he add? Does the division into two seem more effective?
2. Which title do you like better? Why?
3. Villas expanded the final sentence considerably. What did he add? Are the changes appropriate?
4. What is the effect of each of the following minor changes:
   a. "British food writers" changed to "Victorian culinarians"
   b. The addition of the first-person ("I") references in the first paragraph
   c. The addition of the parenthetical references to Hippocrates and the "sweet specimens from Pompeii" in the last paragraph
   d. "Cortés found all types of onions" changed to "Cortés found many types of onions"
5. Does there seem to be any general principle behind the revisions? Do they have anything in common?

WRITING SUGGESTIONS

1. Condense Villas's paragraphs into a single one. Try to preserve his ideas, but paraphrase them in your own words and write for a more general audience. The point is to encourage the reader to experiment with onions.
2. In an essay celebrate the virtues of your favorite fruit, vegetable, or starch. Like Villas, mix personal experience with some research.

   Prewriting:
   a. Remember that the assignment specifies fruit, vegetable, or starch. It should be something that could be served in a

variety of ways. Do not choose a particular dish (sundaes, pizza, french fries). Make a list of possible subjects, drawing upon your own favorite foods.

b. What does your audience already know about the subject? You must present more information than just the obvious. Find an encyclopedia article on your subject. You might be able to include details about its history, its varieties, and its popularity.

c. Remember that you are not writing an encyclopedia article. An encyclopedia merely gives information. Your essay should celebrate the virtues of your subject. On a separate sheet of paper, list the objectives that the two different types of writing might have.

Rewriting:

a. Find a peer reader. Ask that reader if he or she finds your essay interesting and informative. Encourage an honest response, and then act on that response.

b. Check your word choice. You are writing to a general audience—one that may have only some familiarity with your subject and with cooking. Be careful though to avoid technical terms or jargon that might not be understood by your reader.

c. What one part of your essay gave you the most trouble? Go back and work only on that area.

Up, Up, and Away

SUSAN ALLEN TOTH

Toth's "Cinematypes" is included in Chapter 4, and biographical information can be found there.

Of revising, Toth notes: "I do like to revise. I do a great deal of pre-writing in my head—when gardening, putting away the dishes, taking a walk. I let the ideas slosh around. When I sit down to write, my first draft is usually very close to my final draft. The real difficulty for me takes place in my head before I write that first draft. After that is finished I try to wait at least a day before coming back in cold blood to revise. I spend a lot of time revising sentence rhythms and trying to find the right word."

The selection reprinted here is from the "Up, Up and Away" chapter in Ivy Days: Making My Way Out East *(1984), an autobiographical account of Toth's undergraduate years at Smith College. In this passage a small-town girl explores the "Big City"—Boston.*

FINAL VERSION

But when I finally got to Boston, I arrived on a bus. From the time I came to Smith, I was headed for Boston. When I read in high school about America's literary heritage, I focused on New England: Hawthorne, not Willa Cather; Thoreau, not Sinclair Lewis; Millay, not Edgar Lee Masters. In high-school history, I learned that Boston was where America had started; I had once waded across the springs of the Mississippi at Lake Itasca, and now I wanted to see the beginning of the Revolution at Boston Harbor. 1

As I debated my selection of a college, my mother urged Radcliffe and I leaned toward Smith. Although I wanted to be close to Boston—and on the map, Northampton seemed 2 close—I was afraid of leaping right into it. I did not want to live in a big city. I was not even comfortable in Des Moines. So I settled on Smith, thinking that I could of course get to know Boston on weekends, day trips, vacations.

Once rooted in Northampton, however, I found Boston impossibly far away. I seldom had a weekend free from the pressures of tests and papers, or the subtler pressures of social life. When did I first see Boston? Was it my freshman year when I went to visit a friend at Radcliffe, stayed in her dorm, and ventured down a few of the streets around Harvard Square? Was it my sophomore year when Sophie and I took a two-hour, bumpy bus ride, spent a night in the Y.W.C.A., and window-shopped among the expensive shoe stores and dress shops on Boylston Street? On one of my two or three trips in those freshman and sophomore years, I rode the M.T.A., sampled German sausages in a dark beer-washed cellar, and walked in awe through the Museum of Fine Arts. I loved it all. 3

Most of all, I reveled in Filene's basement. My freshman roommate, Alice, from Framingham, had told me about Filene's, a landmark as notable as the Old North Church. Already an obsessive bargain-hunter from my early days of allowance-stretching, I had practiced my skills only in the relatively small confines of Des Moines' Younkers. Once I walked down the steep basement stairs into Filene's acres of bargains, my horizons suddenly expanded. As I wandered from bin to bin, tantalized by torn-out labels I couldn't quite decipher, I felt as if the inexhaustible wealth and resources of a glamorous city had been called here for my personal advantage. If I didn't feel at home on the streets of Boston, here I was an experienced hand. I snatched a crumpled blouse from another shopper's reach, and jostled my way to the mirror. Identifying it with Boston, I took Filene's to my heart. 4

These brief excursions into the Big City whetted my appetite for more. During my sophomore year, I began to think about the possibility of spending a summer there. Shouldn't I get some job experience besides my internship at the *Ames Daily Tribune*? Could I justify the expense of a 5 shared apartment in Boston by some kind of work in publishing? Miss Bailey, Head of Scholarships and Student Aid, agreed that I could; she would waive the requirement that I earn at least $300 during the summer toward my college expenses. Soon my friend Molly O'Brien and I began talking about living together in Boston. When Molly's best friend, Katie Hill, heard about it, she immediately decided she wanted to join us. With uncertain expectations, we all began sending out job applications, I in publishing, Molly in art-related fields, Katie in summer teaching. To our surprise, we all succeeded. Smith, Katie said, sometimes paid off. Although *The Atlantic*, Houghton Mifflin, Little, Brown, and the Boston *Globe* decided they didn't want me, the *Harvard Business Review* invited me for an interview. Would I like to serve as a vacation replacement, partly in subscriptions and circulation, partly in editorial, wherever they were shorthanded? I would indeed. Did I like Smith? I did. Did I know Art Simpkins, the college business manager, who had been the editor's best man? Sort of. Had I ever met the editor's son, Jack, who was a freshman at Amherst? I hadn't. But I was eager and anxious to please. I mentioned the thrill of learning about publishing by working on a Harvard magazine. I was hired.

QUESTIONS FOR DISCUSSION

1. What do Boston and New England mean to Toth? Why do they remind her of Hawthorne, Thoreau, and Millay rather than Cather, Lewis, and Masters?
2. Why would anyone write an autobiography? Why would anyone read one?
3. How does Toth seem to select details? Study the visits to Boston (paragraph 3), or Filene's (paragraph 4), or the job interview (paragraph 5). Out of everything that might have been included, why select these details?
4. In the final version, Toth split one paragraph into two (see Question 3 on the draft, below). Could she also have split paragraph 5 into two? Where would the split have come? What does that change suggest about paragraphing?

5. How many examples of parallel structure can you find in this selection? How does it help to organize paragraphs?
6. Be able to define the following words: *reveled* (paragraph 4), *tantalized* (4), *decipher* (4), *jostled* (4), *whetted* (5).

FIRST DRAFT

But when I finally got to Boston, I took the bus. From the time I arrived at Smith, I knew Boston hovered at the edge of my dreams. When I read about America's literary heritage in high school, I focused on New England: Hawthorne, not Mark Twain; Thoreau, not Sinclair Lewis; Millay, not Edgar Lee Masters, seemed hallowed by time and tradition. Even my child's pack of "Authors" cards had bearded and imposing Bostonian faces. In American history, I learned that Boston was where it had all started; I had once waded across the springs of the Mississippi at Lake Itasca, and now I wanted to see where democracy had poured from the waters of Boston Harbor. 1

As I debated my selection of a college, my mother urged Radcliffe and I leaned towards Smith. Although I wanted to be close to Boston—and somehow on the map, Northampton seemed close—I was afraid of leaping right into it. I did not want to live in the heart of a big city. I was not even comfortable in Des Moines. So I settled on Smith, thinking that I could of course get to know Boston on weekends, day trips, perhaps some vacations. Once rooted in Northampton, however, Boston seemed impossibly far away. I do not remember when I first saw Boston. My memories are still in a romantic tangle. I seldom had a weekend free from the pressures of looming tests and papers, or the subtler pressures of my erratic social life. Was it my freshman year when I went to visit my Ames friend at Radcliffe, stayed in her dorm, and first ventured down a few of the side streets around Harvard Square, admiring not only the coffeeshops but the lean, tweedy look of the Harvard men? Was it my sophomore year when Sophie and I took that two-hour, bumpy bus ride to Boston, spent a night in the Y.W.C.A., and wistfully peered all morning into the windows of 2

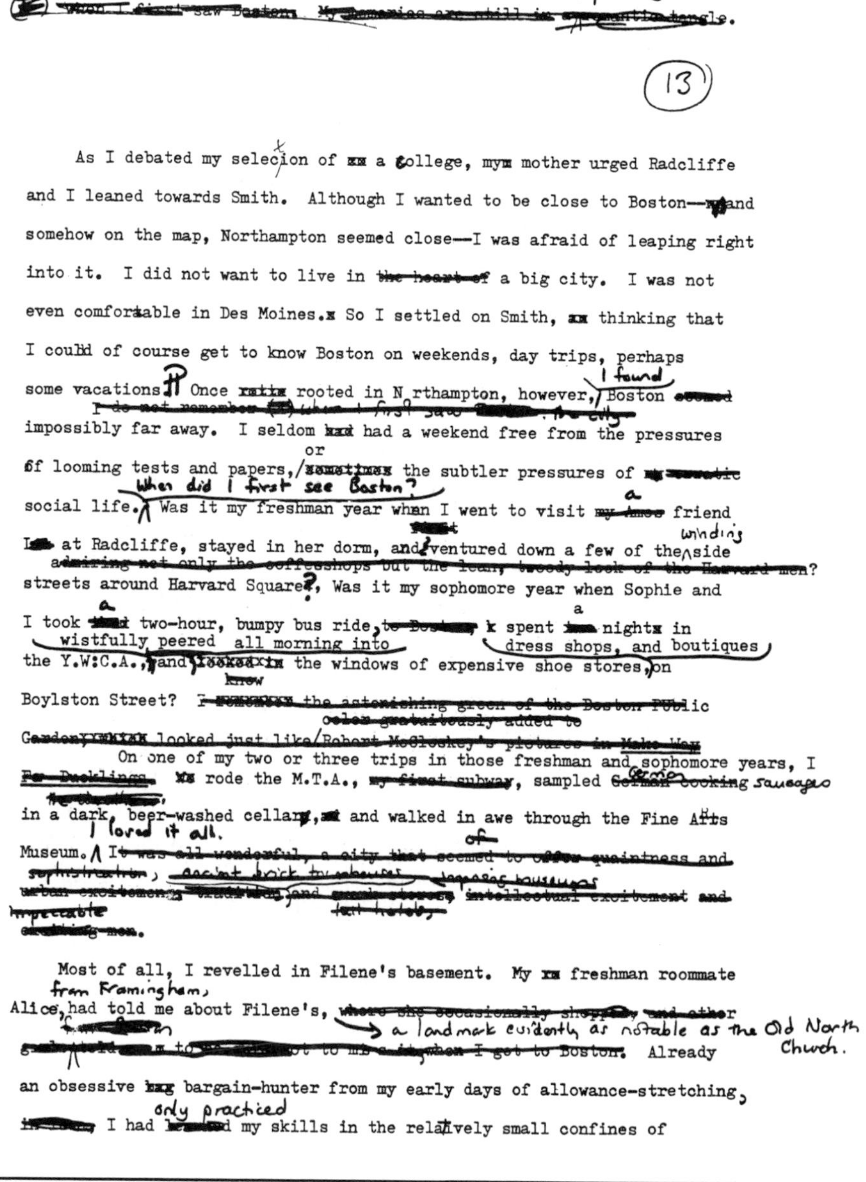

(13)

As I debated my selection of a college, my mother urged Radcliffe and I leaned towards Smith. Although I wanted to be close to Boston—and somehow on the map, Northampton seemed close—I was afraid of leaping right into it. I did not want to live in a big city. I was not even comfortable in Des Moines. So I settled on Smith, thinking that I could of course get to know Boston on weekends, day trips, perhaps some vacations. Once rooted in Northampton, however, I found Boston impossibly far away. I seldom had a weekend free from the pressures of looming tests and papers, or the subtler pressures of social life. When did I first see Boston? Was it my freshman year when I went to visit a friend at Radcliffe, stayed in her dorm, and ventured down a few of the winding side streets around Harvard Square? Was it my sophomore year when Sophie and I took a two-hour, bumpy bus ride, spent a night in the Y.W.C.A., and wistfully peered all morning into the windows of expensive shoe stores, dress shops, and boutiques on Boylston Street? On one of my two or three trips in those freshman and sophomore years, I rode the M.T.A., sampled German sausages in a dark, beer-washed cellar, and walked in awe through the Fine Arts Museum. I loved it all.

Most of all, I revelled in Filene's basement. My freshman roommate from Framingham, Alice, had told me about Filene's, a landmark evidently as notable as the Old North Church. Already an obsessive bargain-hunter from my early days of allowance-stretching, I had only practiced my skills in the relatively small confines of

First draft of a page of Susan Allen Toth's "Up, Up, and Away" expensive shoe stores, dress shops, and boutiques on Boylston Street? I know the astonishing green of the Boston Public Garden looked just like color gratuitously added to Robert McCloskey's pictures in *Make Way for Ducklings*. On one of my two or three trips in those freshman and sophomore years, I rode the M.T.A., my first subway, sampled German cooking in a dark, beer-washed cellar, and walked in awe through the Fine Arts Museum. It was all wonderful, a city that seemed to offer quaintness and urban excitement, tradition and real stores, intellectual excitement and exciting men.

Most of all, I revelled in Filene's basement. My freshman roommate Alice had told me about Filene's, where she occasionally shopped, and other girls told me to be sure not to miss it when I got to Boston. Already an obsessive bargain-hunter from my early days of allowance-stretching, in fact, I had learned my skills in the relatively small confines of Des Moines' Younkers' after-Christmas clearances. Once Sophie guided me down the steep basement stairs into Filene's acres of bargains, my horizons suddenly expanded. As I excitedly wandered from bin to bin, tantalized by torn-out labels I couldn't quite decipher, I felt as if the inexhaustible wealth and resources of a glamorous city had been culled for my personal advantage right here in a tousled heap of lacy underpants, or a rack of imperfect cashmere sweaters, or even a pile of Filene's unbelievably cheap "discontinued" hair-brushes. The smartly dressed women I had seen on Boylston Street wore clothes just like this; if I shopped long enough in Filene's, I would look like them too. After years of ferreting out bargains in odd corners of Younkers, I was offered nothing but bargains with everything "regular priced" already discounted. If I couldn't quite feel at home on the streets of Boston, here I was an experienced hand, grabbing for a crumpled blouse just as another shopper reached for it too, clutching my pile of acquisitions, jostling my way to the mirror. Somehow identifying it with Boston, I took Filene's to my heart. 3

These brief excursions into The Big City whetted my appetite for more. Sometime during my sophomore year, I 4 began to think about the possibility of spending a summer there. Shouldn't I get some job experience besides the *Ames Daily Tribune?* Could I justify the expense of a shared apartment in Boston by the prestige of some kind of work in publishing? Miss Bailey, head of Scholarships, agreed that I could; she would waive the requirement that I earn at least $300 during the summer towards my college expenses. Soon Molly O'Brien, my friend down the hall, who was a year ahead of me, and I began talking seriously about living together in Boston. When Molly's best friend, Katie Hill, heard about it, she immediately decided she wanted to join us. With high expectations, we all began sending out job applications, me in publishing, Molly in art-related fields, Katie in summer teaching. Astonishingly, we all succeeded. Although the *Atlantic,* Houghton Mifflin, Little Brown, and the Boston *Globe* politely decided they didn't need me, the Harvard *Business Review* invited me for an interview. Would I like to serve as a vacation replacement, partly in subscriptions and circulation, partly in editorial, wherever they were shorthanded? I would indeed. Did I like Smith? Had I ever met the editor's son, Jack, who was a freshman at Amherst? I hadn't. But I was eager and anxious to please. I mentioned the unimagined thrill of working on a Harvard magazine, one whose circulation, as the editor had told me, included the highest-placed executives in the country. I was hired.

QUESTIONS ON THE REVISION

1. A large number of changes in descriptive detail are made in what became paragraph 3 in the final version. Make a list of what Toth added and what she deleted. Do you see any general principle that accounts for those changes?
2. Toth also makes changes in the description of the basement at Filene's (paragraph 4) and in the account of the interview at the *Harvard Business Review* (paragraph 5). Make a list of the changes made in both passages.
3. Toth splits the second paragraph in the first draft into two paragraphs (numbered 2 and 3 in the final version). Why? How can one paragraph be split into two without making a change in the opening sentences?

4. Why might Toth have made the following changes from one draft to another?
   a. Deletion of the sentence referring to the game of "Authors."
   b. Deletion of the reference to the Boston Public Garden.

WRITING SUGGESTIONS

1. Formulate a thesis about one strategy Toth used in her revision. In a paragraph support your thesis with evidence from the two versions.
2. Coming to college, whether you are eighteen or thirty-eight, can have its scary moments. Focus on one particular moment in your few first days as a college student—your first night in the dorm, your first college class, your first meal in the dining hall, your first walk through a sea of unfamiliar faces. In an essay make that experience vivid to your reader.

   Prewriting:
   a. Try brainstorming about your memories of those first few days. Jot down notes on everything that you can remember.
   b. Look back over your notes. Do you see a particular experience that seems more vivid or significant than the others? Try freewriting about that experience. Do not worry about developing a story or pattern.
   c. Remember that you will have to re-create that experience for your reader. You cannot just tell your reader what happened and what you felt; you will have to show it. Review the introduction to Chapter 2 on writing narratives.

   Rewriting:
   a. Complete the following sentence: "My purpose in this essay is to ———." Then look through your essay again. Is everything in your essay consistent with that statement?
   b. Check to make sure that you have used vivid verbs and concrete nouns. Do not overuse adjectives and adverbs.
   c. Did you use any dialogue? Using dialogue is a good way of showing rather than telling.

3. What types of support services are available to help freshmen adjust to college life—either as new students or as returning adults? Using research, write a paper intended for incoming students, detailing where they can turn for help.

Why We Need to Learn

WILLIAM OUCHI

William George Ouchi was born in Hawaii in 1943 and received his B.A. from Williams College in 1965. He completed an M.B.A. at Stanford in 1967 and a Ph.D. at the University of Chicago in 1972. A specialist in organizational behavior, he is now a professor of management in the graduate school at the University of California, Los Angeles.

Reprinted here are two versions of the opening chapter of his best-selling Theory Z: How American Business Can Meet the Japanese Challenge. *On his writing and revising, Ouchi has observed: "My writing almost always represents the expression of several years of data gathering, data analysis, field interviews, and other original work. The great majority of* Theory Z *is a description of that work. The introduction you reproduce represents my attempt to capture the essence of my research, couched in terms which will directly communicate to a large number of readers. My practice is to type my first draft, usually at the rate of approximately 20 pages per day, writing in roughly 12-hour days. My draft went to my editor at Addison-Wesley, who read it through several times, attempting to grasp the underlying structure of my argument. She then suggested to me ways that I might delete, add, and reorganize material. The revision you reproduce is a consequence of my attempt to respond to her suggestions. In my books, my editor has never rewritten a word, but has passed along suggestions and criticisms to me, leaving it to me to incorporate as much advice as I can."*

Theory Z gets its name as a contrast to Theories X and Y advanced by Douglas McGregor in The Human Side of Enterprise *(1960). Those theories represent two different assumptions about what motivates people to work. Theory X assumes that people dislike work and must be coerced and directed to do it; Theory Y assumes that people want to work, derive satisfaction from it, and are self-directed. Ouchi's subject in* Theory Z *is the art of Japanese management and how it can be adapted to American business. "While many Japanese admire the American automobile," he observes, "they would never accept the low quality with which they are put together."*

FINAL VERSION

Not long ago, I arranged a luncheon for two of my Ph.D. students with the vice-president of one of the most respected and largest firms in the United States—a company that regularly appears on lists of the "ten best-managed companies." The luncheon provided an opportunity for these educators of the future to ask our guest questions for which his position and experience had given him a unique perspective. After a discussion ranging over many issues, the students summarized their interests in a single question: "What, in your opinion, is the key issue facing American business over the next decade?" His answer: "The key issue will not be technology or investment, not regulation or inflation. The key issue will be the way in which we respond to one fact—the Japanese know how to manage better than we do." 1

A case in point: A team of engineers and managers from the Buick Division of General Motors Corporation recently visited their dealer in Tokyo, who imports Buick automobiles and sells them to the Japanese. The operation appeared to be a massive repair facility, so they asked how he had built up such a large service business. He explained with some embarrassment that this was *not* a repair facility at all but rather a re-assembly operation where newly delivered cars were disassembled and rebuilt to Japanese standards. While many Japanese admire the American automobile, he noted, they would never accept the low quality with which they are put together. 2

Stories like this one abound. We know that productivity in Japan has increased at 400 percent the rate in the United States over the postwar years. More seriously, we know that productivity in the United States is now improving more slowly than in any European nation, including the much-maligned United Kingdom. While many observers have marvelled at the success of the Japanese, they have concluded that Japan is one country from which we cannot learn much. They feel Japanese techniques simply are not applicable to our situation. 3

But our story has a different sequel. The engineers and managers at Buick didn't assume that the Japanese success would work in Flint, Michigan, and they set out to invent their own version of it. They took the Buick Final Assembly Plant, which had dropped to one of the lowest levels of efficiency and quality in the whole corporation, and with the cooperation of workers and their union redesigned the management of that plant in ways that resemble the Japanese approach to management. Within two years, Buick Final Assembly had risen to rank number one among all General Motors assembly plants in quality and efficiency. The ideas that shaped the remaking of General Motors' troubled Buick plant are the basis of what I call the Theory Z approach to management. Quite simply, it suggests that involved workers are the key to increased productivity. 4

As a nation, we have developed a sense of the value of technology and of a scientific approach to it, but we have meanwhile taken people for granted. Our government appropriates hundreds of millions of dollars for research on new techniques in electrical engineering, physics, and astronomy. It supports the development of complex economic ideas. But almost no funds go to develop our understanding of how to manage and organize people at work, and that is what we have to learn by studying the Japanese. The problem of productivity in the United States will not be solved with monetary policy nor through more investment in research and development. It will only be remedied when we learn how to manage people in such a way that they can work together more effectively. Theory Z offers several such ways. American workers perform just as hard as their Japanese counterparts. American managers want high performance just as much as the Japanese. Increased productivity will not come through harder work. Most employees work as hard as they can, and many work too hard for their own good in trying to catch up. Productivity, I believe, is a problem of social organization or, in business terms, managerial organization. Productivity is a problem that can be worked out through coordinating individual efforts in a pro- 5 ductive manner and giving employees the incentives to do so by taking a cooperative, long-range view.

The first lesson of Theory Z is trust. Productivity and trust go hand in hand, strange as it may seem. To understand that assertion, observe the development of the British economy during this century. It is a history of mutual distrust between union, government, and management, a distrust that has paralyzed the economy and lowered the English standard of living to a dismal level. Karl Marx foresaw this distrust as the inevitable product of capitalism and the force that, in his view, would bring about the ultimate failure of capitalism. 6

But capitalism and trust need not be mutually exclusive. 7 Thomas Lifson, a young scholar at the Harvard Business School, has studied in detail the Japanese general trading firms, those firms like Mitsui, Mitsubishi, and Sumitomo that maintain offices worldwide and have traditionally served as the sales force for Japanese-produced goods. Undoubtedly these trading companies have played a central role in the successful export strategy of Japanese industry. They have the capacity to move quickly into new markets, to strike deals where no American company can, and to coordinate far-flung operations. According to Lifson, the central feature of the trading firm is an extensive management system that maintains a sense of trust between employees in the trading company. Japanese employees, just like their American counterparts, want to get ahead. They want to make deals beneficial to both their departments and themselves. They work in an environment of tremendous uncertainty, buying and selling copper ore, crude oil, wheat, and televisions. On a typical day, the central office of one of the major trading firms will receive 35,000 telex messages, each one with an offer to buy or sell. Often, the firm's overall profitability will be maximized if an office takes a loss, which will be more than made up in another office so that the company benefits overall. The success of the trading company depends critically upon the willingness of individual offices and employees to make these sacrifices. That willingness exists because the Japanese trading firm uses managerial practices that foster trust through the knowledge that such sacrifices will always be repaid in the future. Equity will, in the end, be restored.

DISCUSSION QUESTIONS

1. What is the Theory Z approach to management? Why do the Japanese know how to manage better than Americans?
2. How does Ouchi use examples to develop his argument?
3. What is the effect of Ouchi's almost casual beginning—the story about the Buick dealer in Tokyo, the first person pronoun ("I")? Why not begin with a more formal statement of thesis introduction?
4. What assumptions does Ouchi seem to make about his audience? Is there anything in his word choice or writing style that offers clues to those assumptions?
5. Be able to define the following words: *maligned* (paragraph 3), *sequel* (4), *monetary policy* (5), *telex message* (7), *equity* (7).

FIRST DRAFT

A team of engineers and managers from the Buick Division of General Motors Corporation recently visited their dealer in Tokyo, who imports Buick automobiles and sells them to the Japanese. As they toured his operation, they saw what appeared to be a massive repair facility and asked how he had built up such a large service business. He replied, with some embarrassment, that this was not a repair facility at all but rather a re-assembly operation in which he tore down newly delivered cars and rebuilt them to Japanese standards. While many Japanese admire the American automobile, they would never accept the low quality with which they are put together, he explained. 1

Stories like this one abound. We know that productivity in Japan has increased at 400% the rate in the U.S. over the postwar years. More seriously, we know that productivity in the U.S. is improving now more slowly than in any European nation, including the often-maligned U.K. While many observers have marvelled at the success of the Japanese, 2 they have sadly concluded that it is one from which we cannot learn much. The success of the Japanese, it is often said, stems from Japan's relatively recent industrialization, so that they still draw upon a large stock of hard-working farm boys and farm girls who will put in long hours at low pay. It is due to the fact that Japan is still technologically behind the U.S. and thus can make great gains at low cost by borrowing technology, whereas we must invent our own. It is also due, we hear, to the fact that the Japanese have somehow managed to maintain a work ethic, whereas the U.S. has become soft and lazy. The conclusion: the Japanese success is intriguing but not applicable to us.

But our story has a different sequel. The engineers and 3
managers at Buick didn't know that the Japanese success wouldn't work in Flint, Michigan, and they set out to invent their version of it. They took the Buick Final Assembly Plant, which had dropped to one of the lowest levels of efficiency and quality in the whole corporation and, with the cooperation of workers and their union, redesigned the management of that plant in ways that resemble the Japanese approach to management. Within two years, Buick Final Assembly has risen to rank number one among all General Motors assembly plants in quality and efficiency.

It seems that we, as a nation, have developed a fine 4
sense of the value of technology and of a scientific approach to technology, but we have meanwhile taken people for granted. Our government readily appropriates hundreds of millions of dollars for research on new techniques in electrical engineering, it supports the development of complex economic ideas, but almost nothing goes to develop our understanding of how to manage and organize people at work, and that is what we have to learn from the Japanese. The problem of productivity in the U.S. will not be solved with monetary policy, it will not be solved through more investment in research and development, it will only be solved when we learn how to manage people in such a way that they can work together more effectively.

There is a second issue: trust. Productivity and trust go 5
hand in hand, strange as it may seem. To understand that

assertion, we need only observe the development of the British economy over the past thirty years. It is a history of mutual distrust between union, government, and management, a distrust that has paralyzed the economy and lowered the standard of living of all Englishmen to a dismal level. It is the kind of distrust that Karl Marx foresaw as the inevitable product of capitalism and the force that, in this view, will bring about the ultimate failure of capitalism. But capitalism and trust need not be mutually exclusive. Thomas Lifson, a young scholar at the Harvard Business School, has studied in detail the Japanese General Trading Firm, those firms like Mitsui, Mitsubishi, and Sumitomo that maintain offices world-wide and serve as the sales force for Japanese-produced goods. There is no question that these trading companies have played a central role in the successful export strategy of Japanese industry. They have the capacity to move quickly into new markets, to strike deals where no American company can, and to coordinate far-flung operations. According to Lifson, the central feature of the trading firm is an extensive management system that maintains a sense of trust between employees in the trading company. A Japanese employee, just like his American counterpart, is interested in getting ahead. He is interested in making deals that will benefit his department and make him look good. He works in an environment of tremendous uncertainty, buying and selling copper ore, crude oil, wheat, and televisions. On a typical day, the central office of one of the major trading firms will receive 35,000 telex messages, each one with an offer to buy or to sell. Often, the overall profitability of the firm will be maximized if an office takes a loss—that loss will be more than made up in a different office by such an amount that the company benefits overall. In fact, the success of the trading company dependes critically upon the willingness of individual offices and employees to make these sacrifices. That willingness exists because the Japanese trading firm has in place a large number of managerial practices that foster trust through the knowledge that such sacrifices will always be repaid in the future. Equity will, in the end, be restored.

QUESTIONS ON THE REVISION

1. The most obvious change is the added opening paragraph. How does that introduce or prepare the reader for what follows? Does the change seem to be effective?
2. In the third paragraph Ouchi had originally included three sentences citing often-quoted reasons why the Japanese were successful. In the final draft he omitted those sentences. Why?
3. At the end of the fourth paragraph and again in the fifth, Ouchi added sentences dealing with Theory Z. Why might he have done that? Do these additions seem necessary? Are they helpful?
4. Can you find a single strategy that seems to account for most of the large-scale revisions?
5. Ouchi made a number of minor changes in word choice and in sentence structure. Find an example of each, and be ready to comment on the effect of these changes.

WRITING SUGGESTIONS

1. After you have analyzed the two versions, formulate a thesis about one strategy Ouchi used in revising his work. In a paragraph support your thesis by citing appropriate evidence from the two versions.
2. If Theory Z can be used to build better automobiles, could it also be used to produce better educated students? Using just Ouchi's essay and no outside sources, in an essay show how Theory Z might be applied to high school or college education.

   Prewriting:
   a. Start with a definition of Theory Z. What is the Theory Z approach to management?
   b. Brainstorm some possible applications of that theory to American education.
   c. Anticipate your audience's reactions. Make a list of objections that your readers might raise about your proposals. How can each be countered?

   Rewriting:
   a. Have you defined Theory Z for your reader? Remember that your reader will not necessarily be familiar with Ouchi's argument.

b. Have you made explicit proposals for improving education? Look back through your argument. Do not rely just on generalizations. Be specific.
c. Every essay benefits from an interesting, lively introduction. Make a copy of your introduction, and ask a friend to read it. Does your reader want to keep reading?

3. The comparison between Japanese and American industries, products, and workers is a common one. Research one aspect of the problem, and present your conclusions. You might consider the following topics:
   a. A comparison of worker efficiency
   b. A comparison of product quality
   c. An analysis of why Japanese manufactured goods are so popular with Americans
   d. An argument for "buying American"
   e. An analysis of the effects of Japanese imports upon the American economy

Confessions of a Low Roller

JOSEPH EPSTEIN

Joseph Epstein, author, teacher, and humorist, was born in Chicago in 1937 and educated at the University of Chicago, where he received his B.A. in 1959. He is presently teaching at Northwestern University. Since 1975 he has been the editor of The American Scholar. *His books include* Divorced in America: Marriage in an Age of Possibility *(1974),* Familiar Territory: Observations on American Life *(1979),* Ambition: The Secret Passion *(1980),* Masters: Portraits of Great Teachers *(1981),* The Middle of My Tether *(1983), and* Plausible Prejudices *(1985).*

"Revising," says Epstein, "simply is part of the writing act, and anyone who thinks otherwise isn't a serious writer. I usually put things down first in longhand and then type a draft."

In "Confessions of a Low Roller," originally published in the Spring 1988 issue of The American Scholar, *Epstein notes, "No activity has been more rationalized than gambling—odds figured, probabilities worked out, point spreads meticulously established—and no activity, surely, is finally more irrational."*

FINAL DRAFT

Ours has long been a distinguished publishing family, if you take the adjective "distinguished" in a loose sense and if you allow a definition of "publishing" broad enough to include bookmaking. I don't mean to brag about family lineage, but I had an uncle, dead some years now, who had fully two sobriquets: in some quarters he was known as Lefty and in others as Square Sam. All gamblers, it is often enough said, die broke, but my uncle, whom I scarcely knew, is reported to have left the planet with something on the order of twenty-five Ultrasuede jackets hanging in the closet of his home in Los Angeles. Beginning life as a 1 professional gambler, he soon went into publishing (or bookmaking) and eventually owned a small piece of a large casino-hotel in Las Vegas. To place him for you socially, he was a man at whose granddaughter's wedding a guest was Frank Sinatra. Need I say more?

Although the uncle did not carry my family name, there 2
was a prominent gambler who did. Some years ago I read a lengthy obituary in a Chicago newspaper about a man who carried my exact name, first and last, and who was described in the obit headline as "Gentleman Big-Time Bookie, Dies at 75." My namesake—or am I his?—turns out to have run, in the words of the obituarist, "a large betting layoff operation from offices [that covered] wagers that bookies across the nation could not handle." The obituarist continued: "Although his associates were more often coarse, devious, violent men, [he] had the reputation of a bookmaker who kept his word and was mild-mannered in the extreme. He was well-read, fancied himself as a Talmudic scholar and was clearly the intellectual bookie of his time." It gets better. It seems that this man bearing my name also served as a Professor Henry Higgins to a gangland moll named Virginia Hill, who came to Chicago from Alabama at seventeen, whose great and good friend, as *Time* magazine used to put it, he was, though she finally left him for Benjamin (Bugsy) Siegel. "A non-smoker," the obituary notes, "he remained in robust health almost until his death by taking long, daily walks through the city [of Chicago] from his hotel on Ohio St."

The gentleman big-time bookie bearing my name died 3
in Chicago in 1976, a fact that fills me with double regret, first for his death, for he appeared to have been a decent sort, and second because I wish I had had the chance to meet and talk with him. It is not about the Talmud that I wish I could have talked with "the intellectual bookie of his time," but about shop—specifically, about gambling. No photograph appeared with his obituary, but I imagine him to be a smallish man, silverhaired, expensively yet not gaudily dressed, good shoes well shined, nails manicured. We might have walked along Michigan Boulevard together on a late, lightly

breezy afternoon in May, past Tiffany and Cartier and Saks Fifth Avenue and Neiman Marcus, stopping off for an aperitif in the cool, wood-paneled Coq d'Or bar in the Drake Hotel. Seated at one of the small tables in the dark room where sound tends to be gently muffled, I would have encouraged him to recount anecdotes about noble behavior on the part of crooks, in exchange for which I would have supplied him with anecdotes about what crooks academics can be. We should, I do not doubt, have addressed each other as "Mister," with the charm of adding to it our self-same last name.

If the mood were right, perhaps our talk might have 4
ascended to philosophy, always within the confines of shop, of course. Why do men gamble? I might have asked him. Is gambling in the end always a ruinous diversion? Is there something masochistic about it? Was Malraux right when he called it, in connection with his character Clappique in *Man's Fate*, "suicide without death"? Is gambling not a metaphor but a metaphorical activity, since, as has been noted, life itself goes off at something like 6–5 against, though some think these odds unduly generous? Why does gambling excite, exhilarate, and depress some people while not arousing the least interest in others? What does gambling do for those people who go in for it in a big way? For those who enjoy it only occasionally? And, while I am at it, I might just have lowered the tone of the conversation and inquired if I was a chump to agree to an arrangement whereby I would have to pay 10 percent juice, or vigorish, on a $300 bet on this past year's World Series.

Consider, please, that figure $300, or $330 if I lost. 5
Something rather hopeless about those numbers, if you ask me, something neither here nor there. I had originally intended to bet $1,000 ("a grand," in the grand old term), which is a good deal more than I have ever bet on anything, and then I decided that $500 was sufficient. But when I reached an old friend who has a bookie—I bet much too infrequently to have my own publisher—I heard myself say $300. I don't mean to suggest that $300 is a negligible sum; if one is down and out, it is a most impressive sum. I am

sure that someone reading this is ready to inform me, in a properly moral tone, that a family of four could eat for a month on $300. Nowadays, though, there are restaurants in New York where one has to cut corners—go for the California wine instead of the French—to get a full dinner for two for less than $300. I myself consider it immoral to dine in such places. "It is all," as Albert Einstein must at some time have said to Max Planck, "relative."

If all this sounds a little goofy, it is merely because it is. 6
No activity has been more rationalized than gambling—odds figured, probabilities worked out, point spreads meticulously established—and no activity, surely, is finally more irrational. In this essentially irrational activity, the first item that must be fixed, and with some precision, is the stake. Above all, it cannot be too little; it must be enough to stimulate whatever those spiritual glands are that gambling calls into action. The punishment must fit the crime; the agony of losing must be roughly equivalent to the ecstasy of winning. In this sense, it becomes clear that no bet can ever be too large; and herein lies the madness inherent in gambling, for the more you have, the more you need to risk.

"Important money" is what professional gamblers used 7
to call big bets, and such fabled gamblers as Pittsburgh Phil (a horse-player), Nick the Greek (cards and dice), and Ray Ryan (gin rummy) never played for unimportant money. Nick the Greek, whose last name was Dandolos, claimed once to have bet $280,000 on a five coming up before a seven in a crap game. The same Mr. Dandolos is said to have lost $900,000 in a single night in New York on the eve of a holiday trip to Europe, which—surprise! surprise!— had to be canceled. Winning a bet, Nick Dandolos used to say, is man's greatest pleasure; the second greatest pleasure, he claimed, is losing a bet. In more than fifty years of serious gambling, something on the order of $50,000,000 is supposed to have trafficked in and out of his hands. Yet Nick the Greek was no money snob. The late Jimmy Cannon, the sportswriter, told the story of the Greek's playing twenty-four hours straight at Arnold Rothstein's crap table and, after the crap game broke up, sitting down to play casino for

twenty-five cents a hand with one of Rothstein's stickmen. "Action is all he wants," Cannon concluded, "and he has lasted longer than any of them and held on to his dignity."

Some gamblers get a thrill out of the action itself, while 8
others need to be in action at high prices. The greater the stakes, the greater the pressure, the greater the cool (or courage) required. Damon Runyon, a gambler all his life and a student of gamblers, maintained he knew "men who will beat far better card players at gin [rummy] if the stakes are high enough just on simple courage." A gambler is like an airplane in that at a certain altitude—for the gambler, at certain high sums—the controls start to shake. I earlier mentioned certain "spiritual glands" that needed to be stimulated by gambling, but anatomical ones are often also called into play, producing sweaty hands, dry mouth, inconvenient loss of the control of facial muscles. No, nothing quite relaxes a fella like an evening of gambling.

Growing up in Chicago, I had a friend whose father was 9
reputed to have bet $100,000 on a baseball game—and lost. This was during the early 1940s, when $100,000 was extremely important money and not the annual salary of a utility infielder or a Marxist professor of English at Duke University. Inconveniently, my friend's father didn't have the money; conveniently, there was a war on. As the story goes, he showed up the next afternoon at the bookie's with a smile and in a set of U.S. Navy bell-bottoms, having enlisted that morning. The uniform, supposedly, saved his life, for no one was about to kill a man in uniform during wartime, and he was able to arrange terms to pay off his debt.

What made him bet such a sum? He was living in Los 10
Angeles at the time—always a hot gambling town, according to Damon Runyon—and must have waked one sunny weekday morning (I always imagine it to be a Tuesday) in an impatient mood. A voice within must have whispered, "Let 'er rip!" He did, and it nearly tore him in two. Almost all baseball games were played during the day at that time, so he must have known not much later than 2:30 P.M. Los Angeles time that he had made a serious mistake. I am

pleased not to have been the one to serve him that evening's dinner, or to have to ask him if the lamb was properly underdone.

He died before I knew him, whether of heart attack, cancer, or stroke I cannot recall, but he couldn't have been more than in his early fifties. His wife and only son lived on after him in what I think of not as shabby gentility but elegant shabbility. They lived in a small one-bedroom apartment in a building with a doorman on a once posh but now fading Chicago street. Wife and son spoke of him with affection and awe, and in one corner of the small apartment were framed glossy signed photographs taken of him in the company of famous Jewish comedians and Italian singers—or was it Italian comedians and Jewish singers? Not a marathon man, he lived life at a sprint, going fast and dying young. Why is it that we look with wonder upon a man who one day bets a hundred thousand dollars on the outcome of a game and loses yet feel no wonder whatsoever looking upon a man who works a lifetime to stow away a few million? 11

My own interest in gambling—and now we return to someone never likely to have the mad courage to bet $100,000 or the powers of concentration to earn a million—initially derived from the social atmosphere in which I came of age. By this I certainly don't mean my home. My father had not the least interest in cards, sports, or gambling generally, preferring situations, such as the one he had inserted himself into as the owner of a small business, in which as far as possible he could control his own destiny. Most of the men in the rising middle-class Jewish milieu that I grew up in felt much the same. They were physicians and lawyers and businessmen and worked hard so that their children could have an easier life than they, as the sons of immigrants, had had. Some among them gambled—played a little gin rummy or in a small-stakes poker game, bet fifty dollars on a prizefight—but clearly work was at the center of their lives. They believed in personal industry, in thrift, in saving for the future. Entrepreneurial in spirit, they also believed that only a fool works for someone else. 12

On the periphery, though, were a small number of men who lived and believed otherwise. Two boys among my school friends and acquaintances had fathers who were bookies, and rather big-time ones, judging by the scale on which they lived. Nothing back of the candy store or Broadway cigar stand about them; they were rather like the rest of our fathers, but home more often and with better tans and more telephones in the house. They lived on the edge of the criminal world. So, too, I gather did the father of a girl I knew in high school; he played golf from April until October and from October until April played high-stakes gin rummy at a place atop the Sheraton Hotel called The Town Club; the younger brother of a Capone lieutenant, he was rumored to collect a dollar a month on every jukebox installed in Chicago. The brother of a man I once worked for when I was in high school was said to be a full-time gambler, making his living (he was a bachelor) betting on sports events. In his forties then, he carried the nickname "Acey"; if he is still alive, he would now be in his seventies, which is a bit old to carry around such a nickname. I would often see him at baseball games on weekday afternoons, where, well-groomed and well-rested, he looked as if his personal motto, an edited version of my father's and my friends' fathers', might read: "Only a fool works." 13

When young, I felt a strong attraction to such men. The attraction was to their seemingly effortless access to what I then took to be the higher and finer things of life. Their connection to corruption also excited me. Corruption was endemic to Chicago, a city that prided itself on its gangsters the way that other cities were proud of their artists, and one had to be brought up in a glass bubble—make that an isinglass bubble—not to come in contact with it. Dickens, Dostoyevsky, Dreiser, and many a novelist since knew that corruption is more alluring, and more convincingly described, than goodness. Goodness, on first acquaintance, is a bit boring—and, when young, the only thing duller than goodness is common sense. 14

I had an acquaintance whose father became a very rich man in a very brief time through selling very ugly alumi- 15 num awnings. One Saturday afternoon I went with him to his father's small factory, where, among his father and his father's salesmen, each with a high stack of bills in front of him, a serious poker game was in progress. My own father often used the phrase "place of business" with something of the same reverence that some reserve for the phrase "place of worship," and the idea of a poker game on the site of his business would have appalled him. At the time, it rather thrilled me. But then it would be many years until I came round to my father's view, which was essentially the view set out by Henry James in a youthful letter to his friend Charles Eliot Norton: "I have in my own fashion learned the lesson that life is effort, unremittingly repeated. . . . I feel somehow as if the real pity was for those who had been beguiled into the perilous delusion that it isn't."

So beguiled, I spent much of my adolescence in imitation of what I took to be the model of the gambler. During our last year of grammar school, my friends and I met for penny poker games on Saturday afternoons before ballroom dancing lessons. There we sat, at thirteen years old, neckties loosened, jackets draped over the backs of chairs, cigarettes depending unsteadily from the sides of our mouths, smoke causing our eyes to water and squint, playing seven-card stud, deuces usually wild. Quite a scene. Each of us must have thought himself some variant of George Raft, James Cagney, Humphrey Bogart, or John Garfield, when Leo Gorcey and the Dead End Kids gone middle-class was much more like it. "My pair of jacks see your three cents, Ronald, and I bump you a nickel." 16

A misspent youth? I suppose it was, though I never thought of it as such. Perhaps this was owing to its being so immensely enjoyable. In high school, gambling went from an occasional to an almost incessant activity. Although we never shot dice, my friends and I played every variation of poker, blackjack, and gin rummy. From city newsstand vendors we acquired and bet football parlay cards. Every so often, on weekend nights, we would travel out of the city to the sulky races, or "the trotters" as we called them, at Maywood Park. Some unrecognized genius invented a game 17 called "pot-luck," a combination of blackjack and in-between, which guaranteed that, no matter how minimal the stakes to begin with, one would soon be playing for more than one could afford. With its built-in escalation element, pot-luck was a game that produced high excitement, for it was not unusual for someone to walk away from these games a two-hundred-dollar winner. I won my share, but more vividly than any win do I remember one gray wintry afternoon when, between four and six o'clock, I lost $125—this at a time when that figure might pay a month's rent on a two-bedroom apartment in a respectable middle-class neighborhood. If the end of the world had been announced on that evening's news, I, at seventeen, shouldn't in the least have minded. In fact, as I recall, I felt it already had.

Gambling, though scarcely a valuable education in 18
itself, did teach a thing or two about one's own nature. I learned about the limits of my courage with money, for one thing; for another, I learned that, in gambling, as in life, you could figure the odds, the probabilities, the little and large likelihoods, and still, when lightning struck in the form of ill luck, logic was no help. I learned I had to put a good, and insofar as possible stylish, face on defeat, even though losing was very far from my idea of a nice time. If you were even mildly attentive, gambling revealed your character to you, showed it in operation under pressure, often taught you the worst about yourself. Some people wanted to win too sorely; they whined and moaned, banged the table and cursed the gods when they lost and seemed smug and self-justified in victory. Others sat grim and humorless over their cards, gloomy in defeat and always ready to settle for a small win. Still others exhibited, even at sixteen or seventeen, a certain largeness of spirit; they were ready to trust their luck; they had a feeling for the game, which I took to be a feeling for life itself, and were delighted to be in action.

"In action" is an old gambler's phrase; and "the action" 19
used to refer to gambling generally. Yet, for all its insistence on action, gambling can be excruciatingly boring. During one stretch in the army, I played poker at Fort Chaffee, in Arkansas, almost nightly for roughly six weeks; I played

less for the excitement of gambling than to combat the boredom of army life when one is confined to a post. It turned out to be boredom pitted against boredom. In a rather low-stakes game over this period I emerged roughly a four-hundred-dollar winner. Some of this money I sent to a friend to buy me books in Chicago. The rest I spent on a steak and champagne dinner in the town of Fort Smith, Arkansas, for eight or nine barracks mates. Doing this seemed to me at the time a gesture of magnificence befitting a gambling man.

I remember this especially because it is the only use to which I can ever remember putting any money that I have won gambling. I cannot otherwise recall buying with gambling winnings a sweater, a shirt, a sock, a Q-tip. Such money has had a way of disappearing from me. Poof: not very easily come, altogether mysteriously gone. Which reminds me that gambling has never, for me, been primarily about money. I was fortunate, of course, in never having to gamble with money intended for rent or food, thereby, as a character in Pushkin's gambling story "Queen of Spades" puts it, risking "the necessary to win the superfluous." When the money wasn't there—when I was a young husband and father with no extra "tease," as the old horseplayers used to call money—I was easily enough able to refrain from gambling, which strengthens me in my cherished belief that as a gambler I am merely a dreamer and a fool and not an addict. 20

Gambling addicts are not on the whole an elegant sight. The crowds one encounters at a Nevada casino or at a sulky track on a wintry Wednesday night are quite as depressing as those at a national meeting of the Modern Language Association. Many years ago, in an effort to turn up a bit of tease without actually having to gamble for it, I wrote a piece of journalism on an outfit known as Gamblers Anonymous, which operates on the same principles—confession and comradeship in crisis—as Alcoholics Anonymous. At these meetings one hears an *Iliad* of woe, with enough material left over for an *Odyssey* of misery and an *Aeneid* of heartbreak: story after story of disappointed children, weep- 21 ing wives, broken bones accompanying unpaid debts, busted-up homes destroyed by busted-out gamblers. On view here is the other side of gambling, the creepy and crummy side, where one hears a man recount how one morning, when his wife is out at the beauty shop, he sells off all the family furniture to get the money to support his hot hunches at the track that afternoon ("I figured I'd buy all new furniture with my winnings," he reports, "a nice surprise for the wife"), hunches that of course didn't work out; another man recounts how he broke into his son's silver dollar piggy bank for action money, then says nothing when his wife accuses his young son's best friend of taking the money; a man . . . but you get the general idea.

A more particular idea that attendance at these 22
Gamblers Anonymous meetings conveys is the power that gambling can exert over those hooked on it. In its thrall, all other appetites tend to diminish. While one is gambling, food is of no interest, nor is alcohol. Gambling can also throw off one's interior clock, and while at it one is capable of prodigious wakefulness, so that, within limits, gambling can be said to triumph over time and fatigue. When serious gambling is going on, sex seems quite beside the point. At the compulsive level, gambling is all-consuming, and while it doesn't, like drugs or alcohol, fog the mind, it generally monopolizes it. When winning at gambling, one is in the country of the blue; when losing, the world seems mean and red and utterly hopeless. Gambling, one is either flying or crawling, elated or degraded. If any gambler was ever able to find the golden mean, he would probably bet it on the six horse in the fourth race at Pimlico.

As an activity that issues only in extreme states, gam- 23
bling is of course a great Russian subject. Russians have gone in for gambling in a big way, both actually and literarily. Pushkin turned a card or two in his time, and his story "Queen of Spades" gives ample evidence of his knowing at firsthand the desolation of a resounding defeat at the tables. The dissipated young Count Leo Tolstoy was passionate about cards, though not very good at them, even though he devised a system that he set down on paper under the title

"Rules for Card-Playing"; like many another such system, it plunged its creator into great debt. A three-thousand-ruble loss forced Tolstoy to put himself on a ten-ruble-a-month budget. After suffering gambling losses, the young count would proceed to flog himself—in his diary, of course. When his debts grew too great, he could always sell off a meadow or forest or horses from his estate. This is the stuff out of which nineteenth-century Russian novels are made. Tolstoy didn't simply make it all up.

Nor did Dostoyevsky, whose gambling problem ran 24
deeper than Tolstoy's if only because he, not being an aristocrat, had no estate to sell off to clear his debts. Unlike Tolstoy, too, Dostoyevksy's gambling was not a form of dissipation. He gambled for the most commonsensical of reasons: he needed the money. The problem is that gambling—especially roulette, which was Dostoyevsky's game—may be the quickest but is clearly not the most efficient way of obtaining it. According to Joseph Frank, in his splendid biography of Dostoyevsky, the novelist was unfortunate in winning 11,000 francs in his first attempt at gambling. The hook was in. Yet Dostoyevsky, again according to Professor Frank, was not a pathological gambler but a fitful and sporadic one. He did suffer the inability that gamblers share with gluttons—that of not knowing when to leave the table. After each of his inevitably disastrous gambling episodes, Joseph Frank reports, "Dostoyevsky always returned to his writing desk with renewed vigor and a strong sense of deliverance." Dostoyevsky's losses, then, turned out to be world literature's gain. Fate sometimes uses a strange accounting system.

A highly superstitious man, ever on the lookout for 25
omens and portents, Dostoyevsky had a theory about how to win at gambling that was utterly opposed to his own nature. Dostoyevsky's theory, or system, or secret called for mastery of the emotions while in action. "This secret," Dostoyevsky writes in a letter, "I really know it; it's terribly stupid and simple and consists in holding oneself in at every moment and not to get excited, no matter what the play. And that's all; it's then absolutely impossible to lose, and

one is sure of winning." Tolstoy's system, too, called for control of the emotions and moderation—precisely the two things Tolstoy himself was incapable of achieving. "Those who are indifferent are those who are rewarded," wrote Jack Richardson, formulating this view in a single, short, well-made sentence in *Memoir of a Gambler,* his elegant, amusing, and profound book that itself sadly came up snake-eyes, double-zero, and busto in the casino of American publishing when it first appeared in 1979. Richardson's view, like those of Dostoyevsky and Tolstoy, assumes that the gods who watch over gambling are themselves not indifferent or are likely to be fooled by men pretending to a coolness it is not theirs to control. That either assumption is correct is, at best, 9–2 against.

If gambling seems an activity well suited to the Russian 26
temperament with its taste for provoking fate, it is, even though illegal in forty-eight of America's fifty states, very far from un-American. To have come to America in the first place was to take a serious gamble. To advance with the country's frontier was another gamble. When one says that Americans like to gamble, one is of course really saying that the people who have come to America like to gamble. Whenever I have been in a casino, I have noted what seemed to me a high percentage of Asians, most of them Chinese. Jimmy Cannon recalls the older Irishmen in Greenwich Village, where he grew up, disapproving of gambling unless a man was single. Blacks were big for the numbers game and are now, I observe, heavy players in state lotteries. Jews and Italians grow up in gambling cultures—or at least they did when I was a boy—and some among them cross to the other side of the table, becoming bookies or casino owners, donning the expressionless face and the Ultrasuede jacket, like my deceased uncle, squarest of Sams. Texans, to touch on what is almost another ethnic group, have been known to be most earnest about poker played for heart-attack stakes. All of these are what are known as risky generalizations, subject to vehement exceptions: a friend who grew up in a Jewish working-class neighborhood, for example, informs me that in his youth a gambler was considered lower even

If gambling seems an activity well suited to the Russian temperament with its taste for provoking fate, it is, even though illegal in forty-eight of ~~our~~ America's fifty states, very far from un-American. ~~Tocqueville (whom did you expect) noted that, "Those who live in the midst of democratic fluctuations have always had before their eyes the image of chance, and they end by liking all undertakings in which chance plays a part."~~ To have come to America in the first place was to take a serious gamble. To advance with the country's frontier was another gamble. ~~Professional gamblers hung out on riverboats, were found in mining and other boom towns; in towns that considered themselves more refined — New Orleans, say, or San Francisco — gambling provided a note of decadent elegance. With the advent of Las Vegas decadent elegance turned quickly to garish decadence. Of course~~ when one says that Americans like to gamble, one is of course really saying that the people who have come to America like to gamble. Whenever I have been in a casino, I have noted what seemed to me a high percentage of Asians, most of them Chinese. ~~The late sportswriter~~ Jimmy Cannon recalls the older Irishmen in Greenwich Village, where he grew up, disapproving of gambling unless a man was single. Blacks were big for the numbers game and are now, I observe, ~~are~~ heavy players in state lotteries. Jews and Italians grow up in gambling cultures — or at least did when I was a boy — ~~though~~ and some among them cross to the other side of the table, becoming bookies or casino owners, donning the expressionless face and the ultra-suede jacket, like my deceased uncle, squarest of Sams. Texans, to touch on what is almost another ethnic group, have been known to be most earnest about ~~the game of~~ poker played for heart-attack stakes. All of these are what are known as risky generalizations, subject to vehement exceptions: a friend who grew up in a Jewish working-class neighborhood, for example, informs me that in his youth a gambler was considered lower even than a Rumanian. Various anti-defamation leagues — Chinese, Black, Jewish, Italian, Irish, Texan, Rumanian — wishing to protest this paragraph may reach me at my office, ~~write~~ care of the director, Center for Advanced Ethnic Insensitivity. ~~the Highly Insensitive and the Extremely Uncaring.~~

First draft of a page of Joseph Epstein's "Confessions of a Low Roller" than a Rumanian. Various anti-defamation leagues—Chinese, Black, Jewish, Italian, Irish, Texan, Rumanian—wishing to protest this paragraph may reach me at my office, care of the director, Center for Advanced Ethnic Insensitivity.

Men seem to go in for gambling more than women 27
because, as boys, they often play games and thus early acquire the habits of competition. (Competition among women, even as young girls, is subtler, having to do with refinement, sophistication, beauty, and generally less blatant things than strength, agility, and speed.) Games that absorb one's energies in the playing of them do not require gambling for enjoyment. This is true of football, basketball, and baseball—on which men do often bet to get their competitive juices flowing after they are no longer able to play the games themselves—as well as tennis, running, and gymnastics. It isn't true of golf, which needs the stimulus of little side-bets to get one round the course, or billiards, every shot of which seems to cry out for a bet. Chess and bridge are games of sufficient intellectual intricacy to be played without gambling, even though I realize many people—Somerset Maugham among them—have played bridge for high stakes. Poker, blackjack, and gin rummy without money riding on the outcome are games suitable only for some knotty-pined recreation room in hell.

In bringing up boyhood with regard to gambling, I am, I 28
fear, playing into the strong hand of the Freudians. This is a dangerous thing to do, for those guys will sandbag you and whipsaw you. They endlessly raise the stakes. If you open by allowing that gambling is connected with youth, they will call and raise you by saying that it is a neurosis. Bid that gambling can give you pleasure, they return by saying—I quote Dr. Otto Fenichel in *The Psychoanalytic Theory of Neurosis*—that the passion for gambling "is a displaced expression of conflicts around infantile sexuality, aroused by the fear of losing necessary reassurance regarding anxiety or guilt feelings." Aver that gambling issues in excitement, they—I quote Dr. Fenichel again—will counter by asserting that "the unconscious 'masturbatory fantasies' of gambling often center around patricide." I realize that W.

H. Auden once remarked that "the attitude of psychology should always be, 'Have you heard this one?'" but "masturbatory fantasies" and "patricide"? Is this what is truly going on when one gambles? I wouldn't bet on it.

Freud claimed that much of what he knew he learned 29
from the poets, and I, for one, would rather consult the poets than the Freudians on the subject of gambling. Unfortunately, the poets—and writers generally—do not seem to have had all that much to say about it. Pushkin's story "Queen of Spades" is about a young officer who commits murder in the attempt to obtain a secret system for winning at cards, a murder that is revenged when the system betrays him and causes him to live out his days in madness. Pushkin's is a morality tale and is not quite up to the mark either in explaining or depicting the passion for gambling. Dostoyevsky's *The Gambler* is much more like it. The novella's scenes set in the casino are absolutely convincing, not only in detail but in the understanding behind them of the wild roller coaster the gambler travels from exhilaration ("I was only aware of an immense enjoyment—success, victory, power—I don't know how to describe it") to damnable despair expressed in "calm fury" at realizing that one is not "above all these stupid ups and downs of fate" but finally, like everyone else, their victim. *The Gambler* is not among Dostoyevsky's great works; with its characters' propensity for bizarre behavior and the many loose ends that never quite get tied up at the story's conclusion, it is perhaps rather too Dostoyevskian, but it does have the immense authority of a work written by a man who knew his subject from the inside.

For my money, though, the best literary work on the 30
subject of gambling was written by an outsider. That story is "James Pethel" in the collection *Seven Men* by Max Beerbohm, who, so far as I know, had no interest whatsoever in gambling. The James Pethel of Beerbohm's story is known as an active taker of big risks and one who has had tremendous good luck: in stock market speculation, at the baccarat tables at the casino at Dieppe, on wildly venturesome foreign investments. Beerbohm makes plain that the mere

sight of habitual gamblers "always filled me with a depression bordering on disgust." Pethel, however, is no ordinary gambler. On the night that he and Beerbohm meet, after Beerbohm warns him that the water isn't safe to drink, Pethel is encouraged to order not one but two glasses of it, the risk of typhoid only making it more enticing. Casino gambling, one learns, is really only Pethel's way of keeping in trim for such ventures as swimming in dangerous water, driving at maniacal speed (with his wife and daughter, whom he dearly loves, and Beerbohm in the car), and stunt flying. Pethel is, in short, a risk freak, the ultimate gambler who can finally be stimulated only by the ultimate gambles—those in which his own life and the lives of those he loves are on the line. The story is made all the more chilling when at the end we learn that Pethel has died of a heart attack after a flying session, with his daughter and her infant son aboard, and that he had been suffering from a bad heart condition for many years. Beerbohm, with consummate artistry, concludes: "Let not our hearts be vexed that his great luck was with him to the end."

Max Beerbohm despises James Pethel; adore Max Beerbohm though I do, I cannot come down so strongly on his creation, even though I recognize him for the monster he is. The reason I cannot is that through my veins run a few stray bacilli of the virulent virus that has him firmly in its grip. To the vast majority of people it never occurs to gamble—on anything. To others the possibility of gambling is scratched at the painful prospect of losing; Montaigne, interestingly, was among this group, for, though a cardplayer and crapshooter in his youth, he gave up gambling for the reason that "however good a face I put upon my losses, I did not fail to feel stung by them within." A small group of us feel the same sting Montaigne did—with, I suspect, quite the same intensity—but persist. Why? 31

Why, I ask myself, do I, who am surely among the world's luckiest men (I touch wood as I write out that last clause), need to risk $330 on a series of baseball games, the outcome of which is otherwise of less than negligible interest to me? I think it has to do with the need I from time to 32 time feel for venturing forth, for striking out against what has become the general quietude and orderliness of my life. As a boy, I never expected to live so calmly as I now do, with the risk of sending up my cholesterol count from eating an occasional steak being perhaps the biggest risk I take. I live, by a choice I do not quite recall having made, a quiet life, for the most part contemplating the world's foolishness instead of partaking in it directly. But when the quiet life grows too quiet, when it threatens to lapse into the most dread disease I know, which is fear of living, then I call on the antidote of gambling.

Perhaps there are quicker antidotes than a World Series 33
bet on which the tension can be drawn out over more than a week's time. But this was the medicine nearest to hand, and I availed myself of it. Observing myself in action over the course of what turned out to be an extended gamble provided its own slightly tortured amusement. As the Series unfolded, I went from mild depression to measured hopefulness to dignified optimism to serene confidence. I passed a local jeweler's window and noted that he was running a sale of 40 percent off on Movado wristwatches. I already own a Movado watch, but I thought I might use my winnings to buy another. Then it occurred to me to begin a small gambling account, out of which I would begin betting more regularly than I do now. Grand plans were abuilding when—*wham!*—the St. Louis Cardinals, the team I had bet on, lost the last two games of the World Series, and I was seated at my desk writing out a check for $330.

The gods, it is pleasing to learn, are still watching 34
over me.

QUESTIONS FOR DISCUSSION

1. What is Epstein's essay about? Is it just a personal narrative, relating his own experiences with and attitudes toward gambling? Or is he exploring a more general issue?
2. Why is Epstein attracted to gambling?
3. How long is the introduction to the essay? Where does the

introduction end and the body of the essay begin? How do you know?

4. How does Epstein link his introduction to his conclusion?
5. Epstein makes extensive use of metaphor in the essay. Locate some examples, and be prepared to discuss what the metaphor adds to the essay.
6. The essay also contains many allusions—names of people and references to stories and novels. Why might Epstein use such devices? What does their use suggest about Epstein's view of his audience?
7. Be able to define the following words: *sobriquets* (paragraph 1), *moll* (2), *gaudily* (3), *aperitif* (3), *entrepreneurial* (12), *periphery* (13), *endemic* (14), *isinglass* (14), *beguiled* (15), *thrall* (22), *dissipation* (24), *blatant* (27), *propensity* (29).

FIRST DRAFT

What is now paragraph 22

A more particular idea that attendance at these Gamblers Anonymous meetings gives is the power that gambling can exert over those hooked on it. In its thrall, all other appetites tend to diminish. While gambling food is of no interest, nor is alcohol. (Poor Buster Keaton, after his career fell apart, is the only man I have ever heard about who suffered the double addiction to alcohol and to gambling). Gambling can also throw off one's interior clock, and while at it one is capable of prodigious wakefulness, so that even, within limits, can gambling be said to triumph over time and fatigue. When serious gambling is going on, sex seems quite beside the point, and I have heard busted out gamblers tell that they were rather pleased when they learned that, while they were off on extended gambling jags, their wives suspected them of having love affairs, for this gave them more freedom to pursue their more serious passion for gambling. At the compulsive level, gambling is all-consuming, and while it doesn't, like drugs or alcohol, fog the mind, it generally monopolizes it. When winning at gambling, one is in the country of the blue; when losing, the world seems mean and red and utterly hopeless. Gambling, one is either flying or crawling, elated or degraded. If any gambler was ever able to find the golden mean, he would probably bet it on the six horse in the fourth race at Arlington.

QUESTIONS ON THE REVISION

1. Why might Epstein have eliminated the reference to Buster Keaton?
2. The sentence beginning "when serious gambling is going on" is drastically shortened in the final version. Why?
3. At the end of the paragraph the name of the racetrack is changed from Arlington to Pimlico. Can you think of any reason for making such a minor change?

What is now paragraph 26

If gambling seems an activity well suited to the Russian temperament with its taste for provoking fate, it is, even though illegal in forty-eight of our fifty states, very far from un-American. Tocqueville (whom did you expect) noted that, "Those who live in the midst of democratic fluctuations have always had before their eyes the image of chance, and they end by liking all undertakings in which chance plays a part." To have come to America in the first place was to take a serious gamble. To advance with the country's frontier was another gamble. Professional gamblers hung out on riverboats, were found in mining and other boom towns; in towns that consider themselves more refined—New Orleans, say, or San Francisco—gambling provided a note of decadent elegance. With the advent of Las Vegas, decadent elegance turned quickly to garish decadence.

Of course when one says that Americans like to gamble, one is really saying that the people who have come to America like to gamble. Whenever I have been in a casino, I have noted what seemed to me a high percentage of Asians, most of them Chinese. The late sportswriter Jimmy Cannon recalls the older Irishmen in Greenwich Village, where he grew up, disapproving of gambling unless a man was single. Blacks were big for the numbers game and now are heavy players in state lotteries. Jews and Italians grow up in gambling cultures—or at least did when I was a boy—though some among them cross to the other side of the table, becoming bookies or casino owners, donning the expressionless face and the ultra-suede jacket, like my deceased uncle, squarest of Sams. Texans, to touch on another ethnic group, have been known to be most earnest about the game of poker played for heart-attack stakes. All of these are what are known as risky generalizations, subject to vehement exceptions: a friend who grew up in a Jewish working-class neighborhood, for example, informs me that in his youth a gambler was considered lower even than a Rumanian. Various anti-defamation leagues—Chinese, Black, Jewish, Italian, Irish, Texan, Rumanian—wishing to protest this paragraph may reach me at my office; write care of the director, Center for the Highly Insensitive and the Extremely Uncaring.

One would think that the appetite for gambling is among women statistically as great as that among men, yet the tradition isn't there. If there be female counterparts to Pittsburgh Phil, Arnold Rothstein, and Nick Dandolos, I have never heard of them. One thinks of gamblers as youngish men with strong nerves and a taste for the low life; the notion of young women shooting crap, or poring over *The Racing Form*, or sitting up through all-night poker games is, somehow, faintly repulsive. I never saw a woman at Gamblers Anonymous, though I have no doubt that women are as subject to the gambling fever sliding into full addiction as are men. Gambling casinos are loaded with older women, mostly playing blackjack and the slot machines, and church bingo games, too, are chiefly populated by women in search of a small thrill to break up a long night.

QUESTIONS ON THE REVISION

1. The quotation from Tocqueville is appropriate to the point that Epstein is making. Why then remove it?
2. What was originally three paragraphs are condensed into a sin-

gle paragraph. What else did Epstein omit? Can you suggest any reasons for these omissions?

3. Why might Epstein have changed the name of his fictitious center?

WRITING SUGGESTIONS

1. When Epstein discusses his own gambling, he writes, "Gambling has never, for me, been primarily about money." Why then does Epstein gamble? Using the material provided in the essay, write a paragraph explaining the reasons why Epstein gambles.
2. Although gambling might be illegal in nearly all the states, few Americans have not "gambled" in one way or another—bought a state lottery ticket, bet with a friend on the outcome of an event, bought a ticket for a raffle, or even taken chances like James Pethel (paragraphs 30 and 31). In an essay explore our need for such risks. Like Epstein, you might wish to draw from your own personal experience.

   Prewriting:

   a. If you have ever had such experiences, make a list of them. If not, try to imagine why so many people are fascinated by such experiences, and keep a list of possible reasons.
   b. Ask relatives, friends, and classmates about their similar experiences. Do they know why they are attracted to such "chances"?
   c. Remember that you will need to blend examples with analysis. As you begin to draft your essay, look carefully at the proportions between the two.

   Rewriting:

   a. Go back to the list of things to remember at the end of the introduction to this chapter. Use that list to check your draft.
   b. Find a classmate or friend to read your essay. Ask your reader for advice and criticism. Is there any section of the paper that seems particularly awkward? What one thing might be changed?
   c. Every paper benefits from a good title. What about yours? Does it accurately represent your paper? Is it interesting? Catchy? Provocative? Does it arouse your reader's curiosity? If not, try brainstorming a series of alternative titles.

3. State-run lotteries have become increasingly popular in the United States. Typically their revenues are used to fund social or educational programs. Research such lotteries, their history, their effects, their implications. In a research essay, present your findings to a general audience. You might wish to put a persuasive slant to your essay, arguing for or against state lotteries.

A P P E N D I X

How to Read an Essay

Reading an essay like those found in the second edition of *The Prentice Hall Reader* involves the same types of critical activities that you use when reading a poem, a short story, or a play. It is true that an essay is easier to read. Typically, it does not contain the same ambiguities of language as these other forms. Moreover, it is written in prose, not verse. Nevertheless, an essay demands your attention, your active involvement as a reader. Writing and reading are, after all, social acts, and as such they involve an implied contract between a writer and an audience. A writer's job is to communicate clearly and effectively, but a reader's job is to read attentively and critically.

For that reason it is never enough to read an essay just once. Instead, you must study it. You must examine how the author communicates meaning or purpose through prose. You must seek answers to a variety of questions—How does the author structure the essay? How does the author select, organize, and present information? To whom is the author writing? How does that audience influence the essay?

You can increase your effectiveness as an active and critical reader by following the same three-stage model that you use as a writer: divide your time into prereading, reading, and rereading activities.

Prereading

Before you begin reading the essay, look first at the apparatus that accompanies it. Each essay is preceded by a biographical headnote describing the author and her or his work. The headnote and the credits also identify where and when the essay was originally published, including any special conditions or circumstances that surrounded or influenced its publication. A careful reading of this material can help prepare you to read the essay.

Look next at the text of the essay itself. What does the title tell you about the subject or the tone? A serious, dignified title such as "The Value of Children: A Taxonomical Essay" (p. 186) sets up a very different set of expectations than does a playful title such as "Going to the Cats" (p. 312). Page through the essay. Are there any obvious subdivisions in the text (extra spaces, sequence markers, subheadings) that signal an organizational pattern? Does the paragraphing suggest a particular structure?

Finally, look at the series of questions that follow each selection. Those questions focus on subject and purpose, structure and audience, and vocabulary and style. Read through them so that you know what to look for when you read the essay. Before you begin to read, make sure that you have a pen or pencil, some paper for taking notes, and a dictionary to check the meanings of unfamiliar words.

Reading

When you begin to read a selection in the second edition of *The Prentice Hall Reader*, you already have an important piece of information about its structure. Each selection was chosen to demonstrate a particular type of writing (narration, description, exposition, or argumentation) and a particular pattern of organization (chronological, spatial, division and classification, comparison and contrast, process, cause and effect, definition, induction or deduction). As you read, think about how the author organized the essay. On a separate sheet of paper, construct a brief outline. This will help you focus your attention on how the whole essay is put together.

Remember that an essay, like any work of literature, will typically express a particular idea or assertion (*thesis*) about a *subject* for a particular reason (*purpose*). Probably one reading of an essay will be enough for you to answer questions about *subject*, but you may have to reread the essay several times in order to identify the author's *thesis* and *purpose.* Keep these three elements separate and clear in your mind. It will help to answer each of the following questions as you read:

1. *Subject*: What is this essay about?
2. *Thesis*: What particular point is the author trying to make about this subject?
3. *Purpose*: Why is the author writing this? Is the intention to entertain? To inform? To persuade?

Effective writing contains specific, relevant details and examples. Look carefully at the writer's choice of examples. Remember that the author made a conscious decision to include each of these details. Ideally, each is appropriate to the subject, and each contributes to the thesis and purpose.

Rereading

Rereading, like rewriting, is not always a discrete stage in a linear process. Just as you might pause after writing several sentences and then go back and make some immediate changes, so as a reader you might stop at the end of a paragraph and then go back and reread what you have just read. Depending upon the difficulty of the essay, it might take several readings for you to be able to answer the questions posed above about the writer's thesis and purpose. Even if you feel certain about your understanding of the essay, a final rereading is important.

In the final rereading, focus on the essay as an example of a writer's craft. Consider the following questions:

How effective is the essay's introduction and conclusion? How do they reflect the writer's purpose and audience? Have you ever used a similar strategy?

Does the author employ a variety of sentence types and lengths? Do the lengths of paragraphs vary? How do these sentences and paragraphs differ from the ones you typically write?

Is there anything unusual about the author's word choices? Do you use a similar range of vocabulary when you write?

Remember that the writer of essays is just as conscious of craft as the poet, the novelist, or the playwright.

A Sample Reading

Before you begin reading in the second edition of *The Prentice Hall Reader,* you can see how to use these techniques of prereading, reading, and rereading in the following analyzed essay.

To Noble Companions

GAIL GODWIN

Born in 1937 in Birmingham, Alabama, Gail Godwin graduated with a B.A. from the University of North Carolina and then earned an M.A. and a Ph.D. from the University of Iowa. She has held a number of teaching positions in colleges and universities but now devotes her full time to writing. Her books include seven novels—The Perfectionists *(1970),* Glass People *(1972),* The Odd Woman *(1974),* Violet Clay *(1978),* A Mother and Two Daughters *(1982),* The Finishing School *(1985), and* A Southern Family *(1987)—and several collections of short stories. She has contributed essays, stories, and reviews to a wide range of periodicals. "To Noble Companions" was originally published in* Harper's *in a special section devoted to friendship. In this five-paragraph essay, Godwin explores the meaning of the word* friend.

Essay begins with a conventional definition of friendship.

Rejection of that definition

The dutiful first answer seems programmed into us by our meager expectations: "A friend is one who will be there in times of trouble." But I believe this is a skin-deep answer to describe skin-deep friends. There is something irresistible about misfortune to human nature, and standbys for setbacks and sicknesses (as long as they are not too lengthy, or contagious) can usually be found. They can be *hired*. What I value is not the "friend" 1

Godwin develops her own definition, using the extended metaphor of flying.

who, looming sympathetically above me when I have been dashed to the ground, appears gigantically generous in the hour of my reversal; more and more I desire friends who will endure my ecstasies with me, who possess wings of their own and who will fly with me. I don't mean this as arrogance (I am too superstitious to indulge long in that trait), and I don't fly all that often. What I mean is that I seek (and occasionally find) friends with whom it is possible to drag out all those beautiful, old, outrageously *aspiring* costumes and rehearse together for the Great Roles; persons whose qualities groom me and train me up for love. It is for those people that I reserve the glowing hours, too good not to share. It is the existence of these people that reminds me that the words "friend" and "free" grew out of each other. (OE *freo,* not in bondage, noble, glad; OE *freon,* to love; OE *freond,* friend.)

Thesis: friends are "persons whose qualities groom me and train me up for love."

Origins of the word *friend*

Body of paper begins here. Author includes three examples of friendship.

First example: a childhood experience

2 When I was in the eighth grade, I had a friend. We were shy and "too serious" about our studies when it was becoming fashionable with our classmates to acquire the social graces. We said little at school, but she would come to my house and we would sit down with pencils and paper, and one of us would say: "Let's start with a train whistle today." We would sit quietly together and write separate poems or stories that grew out of a train whistle. Then we would read them aloud. At the end of that school year, we, too, were transformed into social creatures and the stories and poems stopped.

3 When I lived for a time in London, I

Second example: an adult relationship

had a friend. He was in despair and I was in despair, but our friendship was based on the small flicker of foresight in each of us that told us we would be sorry later if we did not explore this great city because we had felt bad at the time. We met every Sunday for five weeks and found many marvelous things. We walked until our despairs resolved themselves and then we parted. We gave London to each other.

Third example: an ideal or model friendship

For almost four years I have had a 4
remarkable friend whose imagination illumines mine. We write long letters in which we often discover our strangest selves. Each of us appears, sometimes prophetically, sometimes comically, in the other's dreams. She and I agree that, at certain times, we seem to be parts of the same mind. In my most sacred and interesting moments, I often think: "Yes, I must tell ———." We have never met.

It is such exceptional (in a sense 5
divine) companions I wish to salute. I have seen the glories of the world reflected briefly through our encounters. One bright hour with their kind is worth more to me than a lifetime guarantee of the services of a Job's comforter whose "helpful" lamentations will only clutter the healing silence necessary to those darkest moments in which I would rather be my own best friend.

Restatement of thesis: A friend is more than a "Job's comforter."

Prereading Godwin's Essay

The headnote to Godwin's essay gives you several important pieces of information. The essay originally appeared in a special section of *Harper's* focusing on friendship. Presumably Godwin was asked to contribute, in the form of a short essay, her thoughts on the subject. The context in which the essay originally appeared probably helped shape or influence its form—for example, its brevity and the quickness with which it jumps into the subject. Godwin's educational background might account for some of the details in the essay. That is, while many writers make a reference to "Job's comforter," only someone with a more specialized knowledge might choose to include the references to the Old English (OE) origins for the words *friend* and *free*. The title of the essay indicates the subject, but it also suggests that what follows is not so much a definition as a "toast" to friendship. "To Noble Companions" occasions in the reader different expectations than "A Definition of a Friend."

Reading Godwin's Essay

If Godwin's essay were in the main portion of this book, it would be found in Chapter 8: Definition. Although a definition essay does not have a specific, predetermined structure, you would expect that it will extend a conventional dictionary definition through a series of examples. With a word such as "friend," you know that a simple definition such as "a person whom one knows well and is fond of" is hardly adequate. You expect that Godwin will include examples to illustrate her understanding of the word *friend*.

Godwin begins by rejecting one definition of the term—"a friend is one who will be there in times of trouble." A friend, she suggests, is someone with whom to endure "ecstasies," not "misfortunes." In paragraphs 2, 3, and 4, Godwin offers examples of friendships that she has experienced. Each example is developed in a single paragraph. The first two examples took place in an earler time, and she links the two together by repeating the same structure for the first sentence of the paragraph:

> When I was in the eighth grade, I had a friend.
> When I lived for a time in London, I had a friend.

The third example—set in the present—is introduced in

a slightly different, but clearly related, way: "For almost four years I have had a remarkable friend. . . ." The final paragraph returns to the distinction that Godwin had established in the first paragraph—a friend is someone who helps you grow, develop, and love.

The subject of Godwin's essay is, obviously, friendship. Her thesis is that a friend is someone with whom and through whom human potential and aspirations are realized. Presumably, her purpose is to illuminate for her readers other, less conventional, meanings to be found in the word *friend*.

As you read, always watch for words, phrases, or allusions that you might not recognize and always try to find a definition or explanation for each. A good college dictionary is an essential piece of equipment for any active reader, and it can often answer a range of different questions. In this case, for example, even the allusion to "Job's comforter" in paragraph 5 can be identified by using a dictionary ("a person who aggravates one's misery while attempting or pretending to comfort; see Job 16:1–5").

Rereading Godwin's Essay

Godwin's essay is both conventional and unconventional at the same time. At first, this five-paragraph essay on the topic "define a friend" probably recalls some of the writing that you did in high school. The similarity, though, ends with this superficial observation. From the opening sentence, Godwin's response is uniquely her own and cleverly crafted. You or I might open with a sentence such as "A friend is typically defined as 'one who will be there in times of trouble.' However, this definition does not do justice to a word that can mean many things." Godwin's sentence says much more in a distinctive way: "The dutiful first answer seems programmed into us by our meager expectations. . . ." The sentence is a response to the implied question, "What is a friend?"

Godwin's paragraphs and sentences depend heavily on parallelism. As you reread the essay, you probably noticed the repetitions that hold together paragraphs 2 and 3:

When I was . . .
We were shy . . .
We said little . . .
We would sit . . .
Then we would read . . .

When I lived . . .
He was in despair and I was in despair . . .
We met . . .
We walked . . . and then we parted . . .
We gave London . . .

Defining a complex term is never a simple matter, for words have not only denotations (explicit definitions) but also connotations (associations or suggestions). In this sense, defining can be a reductive act; it cannot always do justice to the complexities and subtleties that are inherent in a word. Godwin's strategy as a writer is to avoid a simple answer. She illustrates her definition with three experiences—arranged chronologically, with each contained within its own paragraph. In the end, though, she resists providing a one-sentence definition of the term, choosing instead to suggest through example and analogy what a friend really means to her.

Each of the essays in the second edition of *The Prentice Hall Reader* will repay you for the time and effort you put into reading it carefully and critically. Each essay shows an artful craftsperson at work, solving the problems inherent in communicating experiences, feelings, ideas, and opinions to an audience. Each writer is someone from whom you, as a reader and as a thinker, can learn. So when your instructor assigns a selection from the text, remember that as a reader you must assume an active role. Don't assume that reading an essay once—to see what it is "about"—will mean that you are prepared to write about it or that you have learned all that you can learn from the essay. Ask questions, seek answers to those questions, analyze, and reread.

Glossary

Abstract words refer to ideas or generalities—words such as "truth," "beauty," and "justice." The opposite of an abstract word is a *concrete* one. In Susan Allen Toth's first description of her Boston adventures in "Up, Up, and Away" (p. 525), she sampled "German cooking," but in the revision the abstract word "cooking" is replaced with the concrete and precise noun "sausages." E. B. White's little essay on "Democracy" (p. 374) defines an abstract word through a series of concrete examples. See *Concrete*.

Allusion is a reference to an actual or fictional person, object, or event. The assumption is that the reference will be understood or recognized by the reader. For that reason, allusions work best when they draw upon a shared experience or heritage. Allusions to famous literary works or to historically prominent people or events are likely to have meaning for many readers for an extended period of time. Martin Luther King, Jr. in "I Have a Dream" (p. 455) alludes to biblical verses, spirituals, and patriotic songs. If an allusion is no longer recognized by an audience, it loses its effectiveness in conjuring up a series of significant associations.

Analogy is an extended comparison in which an unfamiliar or complex object or event is likened to a familiar or simple one in order to make the former more vivid and more easily understood. Inappropriate or superficially similar analogies should not be used, especially as evidence in an argument. See *Faulty analogy* in the list of logical fallacies on pp. 418–19.

Argumentation or **persuasion** seeks to move a reader, to gain support, to advocate a particular type of action. Traditionally, argumentation appeals to logic and reason, while persuasion appeals to emotion and sometimes prejudice. See the introduction to Chapter 9.

Cause and effect analyses explain why something happened or what the consequences are or will be from a particular occurrence. See the introduction to Chapter 7.

Classification is a form of division, but instead of starting with a single subject as a *division* does, classification starts with many items, and groups or classifies them in categories. See the introduction to Chapter 4.

Cliché is an overused common expression. The term is derived from a French word for a stereotype printing block. Just as many identical copies can be made from such a block, so clichés are typically words and phrases used so frequently that they become stale and ineffective. Everyone uses clichés in speech: "in less than no time" they "spring to mind" but "in the last analysis" a writer ought to "avoid them like the plague," even though they always seem "to hit the nail on the head." Theodore Bernstein offers a good definition and many examples in "Clichés" (p. 377).

Coherence is achieved when all parts of a piece of writing work together as a harmonious whole. If a paper has a well-defined thesis that controls its structure, coherence will follow. In addition, relationships between sentences, paragraphs, and ideas can be made clearer for the reader by using pronoun references, parallel structures (see *Parallelism*), and transitional words and phrases (see *Transitions*).

Colloquial expressions are informal words and phrases used in conversation, but inappropriate for more formal writing situations. Occasionally, professional writers use colloquial expressions in order to create an intentional informality. Adam Smith in "Everyday Drugs" (p. 155) begins with a formal, scientific description of xanthines but shifts in the final two paragraphs to a more informal diction using colloquial expressions such as "stuff," "perkin' in the pot," and "okay and non-okay" drugs.

Comparison involves finding similarities between two or more things, people, or ideas. See the introduction to Chapter 5.

Conclusions should always leave the reader feeling that a paper has come to a logical and inevitable end, that the communication is now complete. As a result, an essay that simply stops, or weakly trails off, or moves into a previously unexplored area, or raises new or distracting problems lacks that necessary sense of closure. Endings often cause problems because they are written last and, therefore, often rushed. With proper planning, you can always write an effective and appropriate ending. Keep the following points and strategies in mind:

1. An effective conclusion grows out of a paper—it needs to be logically related to what has been said. It might restate the thesis, summarize the exposition or argument, apply or reflect upon the subject under discussion, tell a related story, call for a course of action, or state the significance of the subject.

2. The extent to which a conclusion can repeat or summarize is determined in large part by the length of the paper. A short paper should not have a conclusion that repeats, in slightly varied words, the introduction. A long essay, however, often needs a conclusion that conveniently summarizes the significant facts or points discussed in the paper.
3. The appropriateness of a particular type of ending is related to a paper's purpose. An argumentative or persuasive essay—one that asks the reader to do or believe something—can always conclude with a statement of the desired action—vote for, do this, do not support. A narrative essay can end at the climactic moment in the action, such as E. B. White's recognition of mortality in "Once More to the Lake" (p. 90). An expository essay in which points are arranged according to significance can end with the major point.
4. The introduction and conclusion can be used as a related pair to frame the body of an essay. Frequently in a conclusion you can return to allude to an idea, an expression, or an illustration used at the beginning of the paper and so enclose the body.

Concrete words describe things that exist and can be experienced through the senses. Abstractions are rendered understandable and specific through concrete examples. See *Abstract*.

Connotation and **denotation** refer to two different types of definition of words. A dictionary definition is denotative—it offers a literal and explicit definition of a word. But words often have more than just literal meanings, for they can carry positive or negative associations or connotations. The denotative definition of "wife" is "a woman married to a man," but as Judy Syfers shows in "I Want a Wife" (p. 386), the word *wife* carries a series of connotative associations as well.

Contrast involves finding differences between two or more things, people, or ideas. See the introduction to Chapter 5.

Deduction is the form of argument that starts with a general truth and then moves to a specific application of that truth. See the introduction to Chapter 9.

Definition involves placing a word first in a general class and then adding distinguishing features that set it apart from other members of that class: "A wife is a woman (general class) married to a man (distinguishing feature)." Most college writing assignments in definition require extended definitions in which a subject is analyzed with appropriate examples and details. See the introduction to Chapter 8.

Denotation. See *Connotation and denotation.*

Description is the re-creation of sense impressions in words. See the introduction to Chapter 3.

Dialect. See *Diction.*

Diction is the choice of words used in speaking or writing. It is frequently divided into four levels: formal, informal, colloquial, and slang. Formal diction is found in traditional academic writing, such as books and scholarly articles; informal diction, generally characterized by words common in conversation contexts, by contractions, and by the use of the first person ("I"), is found in articles in popular magazines. Laurence Perrine's "Escape and Interpretive Literature" (p. 159) exhibits formal diction; Noel Perrin's "Maple Recipes for Simpletons" (p. 262), informal. See *Colloquial expressions* and *Slang.*

Two other commonly used labels are also applied to diction:

Nonstandard. Words or expressions not normally used by educated speakers. An example would be *ain't.*

Dialect. Regional or social differences in a language exhibited in word choice, grammatical usage, and pronunciation. Dialects are primarily spoken rather than written, but are often reproduced or imitated in narratives. William Least Heat Moon in "Nameless, Tennessee" (p. 120) captures the dialect of his speakers.

Division breaks a subject into parts. It starts with a single subject and then subdivides that whole into smaller units. See the introduction to Chapter 4.

Essay literally means an attempt, and in writing courses the word is used to refer to brief papers, generally between 500 to 1000 words, on restricted subjects. Essays can be formal and academic, like Bernard Berelson's "The Value of Children" (p. 186), or informal and humorous, like Russell Baker's "Computer Fallout" (p. 22).

Example is a specific instance used to illustrate a general idea or statement. Effective writing requires examples to make generalizations clear and vivid to a reader. E. B. White in "Democracy" (p. 374) uses fourteen different examples to define the word *democracy.* See the introduction to Chapter 1.

Exposition comes from a Latin word meaning "to expound or explain." It is one of the four modes into which writing is subdivided—the other three being *narration, description,* and *argumentation.* Expository writing is information-conveying; its purpose is to inform its reader. This purpose is achieved through a variety of organizational patterns including *division and classification, comparison and contrast, process analysis, cause and effect,* and *definition.*

Figures of speech are deliberate departures from the ordinary and literal meanings of words in order to provide fresh, insightful perspectives or emphasis. The figures are most commonly used in descriptive passages and include the following:

Simile. A comparison of two dissimilar things generally introduced by the words "as" or "like." Annie Dillard in the "The Copperhead and the Mosquito" (p.139) describes the snake's head as "blunt as a stone ax." When the mosquito bites the copperhead, Dillard describes the action with another simile: "I could make out its lowered head that seemed to bore like a well drill through surface rock to fluid."

Metaphor. An analogy that directly identifies one thing with another. When Dillard refers to the snake as a "nerved rope of matter" she creates in that compressed identification a metaphor: the snake *is* (rather than just being like) a "nerved rope of matter."

Personification. An attribution of human qualities to an animal, idea, abstraction, or inanimate object. Loren Eiseley in "The Secret of Life" (p. 399) personifies a caterpillar he encounters on his walk: "A woolly bear caterpillar hurries across a ledge, going late to some tremendous transformation."

Hyperbole. A deliberate exaggeration, often done to provide emphasis or humor. John McPhee in comparing Florida and California oranges (p. 210) resorts to hyperbole: "Californians say that if you want to eat a Florida orange you have to get into a bathtub first. . . . In Florida it is said that you can run over a California orange with a ten-ton truck and not even wet the pavement."

Understatement. The opposite of hyperbole, or a deliberate minimizing done to provide emphasis or humor. In William Least Heat Moon's "Nameless, Tennessee," (p. 120), Miss Ginny Watts explains how she asked her husband to call the doctor unless he wanted to be "shut of" (rid of) her. Her husband, Thurmond, humorously uses understatement in his reply: "I studied on it."

Rhetorical Questions. Questions not meant to be answered, but instead to provoke thought. Marya Mannes in "Wasteland" (p. 430) poses strings of rhetorical questions.

Paradox. A seeming contradiction used to catch a reader's attention. An element of truth or rightness often lurks beneath the contradiction. Laurence Perrine in "Escape and Interpretive Literature" (p. 159) quotes a writer who uses paradox to point to the shifting line between a "true" history and a "fictional" romance: "The truest history is full of falsehoods and . . . romance is full of truths."

Generalizations are assertions or conclusions based upon some specific instances. The value of a generalization is determined by the quality and quantity of examples upon which it is based. Bob Greene in "Cut" (p. 28) formulates a generalization—being cut from an athletic team makes men superachievers later in life—on the basis of five examples. For such a generalization to have validity, however, a proper statistical sample would be essential.

Hyperbole. See *Figures of speech.*

Illustration is providing specific examples for general words or ideas. A writer illustrates by using *examples.*

Induction is the form of argument that begins with specific evidence and then moves to a generalized conclusion that accounts for the evidence. See the introduction to Chapter 9.

Introductions need to do two essential things: first, catch or arouse a reader's interest, and second, state the thesis of the paper. In achieving both objectives, an introduction can occupy a single paragraph or several. The length of an introduction should always be proportional to the length of the essay—short papers should not have long introductions. Because an introduction introduces what follows, it is always easier to write after a draft of the body of the paper has been completed. When writing an introduction, keep the following strategies in mind:

1. Look for an interesting aspect of the subject that might arouse the reader's curiosity. It could be a quotation, an unusual statistic, a narrative, a provocative question or statement. It should be something that will make the reader want to continue reading, and it should be appropriate to the subject at hand.
2. Provide a clear statement of purpose and thesis, explaining what you are writing about and why.
3. Remember that an introduction establishes a tone or point of view for what follows, so be consistent—an informal personal essay can have a casual, anecdotal beginning, but a serious academic essay needs a serious, formal introduction.
4. Suggest to the reader the structure of the essay that follows. Knowing what to expect makes it easier for the audience to read actively.

Irony occurs when a writer says one thing but means another. Fran Lebowitz in "A Manual: Training for Landlords" (p. 269) offers advice to would-be landlords on how to trick and abuse tenants. Lebowitz's suggestions are ironic; she is not advocating such a plan of action, but instead is dramatizing the tenant-landlord relationship from the tenant's point of view.

Metaphor. See *Figures of speech.*

Narration involves telling a story, and all stories—whether they are personal experience essays, imaginative fiction, or historical narratives—have the same essential ingredients: a series of events arranged in an order and told by a narrator for some particular purpose. See the introduction to Chapter 2.

Nonstandard diction. See *Diction.*

Objective writing is an impersonal, factual approach to a particular subject. Bernard Berelson's "The Value of Children" (p. 186) and Andrew C. Revkin's "Hard Facts About Nuclear Winter" (p. 328) are primarily objective in their approach. Writing frequently blends the objective and subjective together. See *Subjective.*

Paradox. See *Figures of speech.*

Parallelism places words, phrases, clauses, sentences, or even paragraphs equal in importance in equivalent grammatical form. The similar forms make it easier for the reader to see the relationships that exist among the parts; they add force to the expression. Martin Luther King, Jr.'s "I Have a Dream" speech (p. 455) exhibits each level of parallelism: words ("When all God's children, black and white men, Jews and Gentiles, Protestants and Catholics"), phrases ("With this faith, we will be able to work together, to pray together, to struggle together, to go to jail together, to stand up for freedom together"), clauses ("Go back to Mississippi, go back to Alabama, go back to South Carolina, go back to Georgia, go back to Louisiana, go back to the slums and ghettoes of our northern cities"), sentences ("the one hundred years later" pattern in paragraph 2), and paragraphs (the "I have a dream" pattern in paragraphs 11 to 18).

Person is a grammatical term used to refer to a speaker, the individual being addressed, or the individual being referred to. English has three persons: first (I or we), second (you), and third (he, she, it, or they).

Personification. See *Figures of speech.*

Persuasion. See *Argumentation and persuasion.*

Point of view is the perspective or angle the writer adopts toward a subject. In narratives, point of view is either first person (I) or third person (he, she, it). First-person narration implies a *subjective* approach to a subject; third-person narration promotes an *objective* approach. Point of view can be limited (revealing only what the narrator knows) or omniscient (revealing what anyone else in the narrative thinks or feels). Sometimes the phrase "point of view" is used simply to describe the writer's attitude toward the subject.

Premise is logic in a proposition—a statement of a truth—that is used to support or help support a conclusion. For an illustration, see p. 420.

Process analysis takes two forms: a set of directions intended to allow a reader to duplicate a particular action, or a description intended to tell a reader how something happens. See the introduction to Chapter 6.

Proofreading is a systematic check of a piece of writing to make sure that it contains no grammatical or mechanical errors. A proofreading is something quite different from a revision. See *Revision.*

Purpose is intention or the reason why a writer writes. Three purposes are fundamental: to entertain, to inform, or to persuade. Purposes are not necessarily separate or discrete; all can be combined together. An effective piece of writing has a well-defined purpose.

Revision means "to see again." A revision involves a careful, active scrutiny of every aspect of a paper—subject, audience, thesis, paragraph structures, sentence constructions, and word choice. See the introduction to Chapter 10. Revising a piece of writing involves something more complicated and more wide-ranging than proofreading. See *Proofreading.*

Rhetorical questions. See *Figures of speech.*

Satire pokes fun at human behavior or institutions in order to correct them. Judy Syfers in "I Want a Wife" (p. 386) satirizes the stereotypical male demands of a wife, implying that marriage should be a more understanding partnership. Fran Lebowitz in "A Manual: Training for Landlords" (p. 269) satirizes both the materialism and the indifference of landlords.

Simile. See *Figures of speech.*

Slang is common, casual, conversational language that is inappropriate in formal speaking or writing. Slang is frequently used to make or define social groups—a private, shared language not understood by outsiders. William Safire's "Words for Nerds" (p. 37) lists examples of campus slang. As Safire's essay demonstrates, slang changes constantly and is, therefore, always dated. For that reason alone, it is always best to avoid using slang in writing.

Style is the arrangement of words that a writer uses to express meaning. The study of an author's style would include an examination of diction or word choice, figures of speech, sentence constructions, and paragraph divisions.

Subject is what a piece of writing is about. See also *Thesis*. Bruce Catton's subject in "Grant and Lee" (p. 222) is the two generals; his thesis is that the two represented or symbolized "two diametrically opposed elements in American life."

Subjective writing expresses an author's feelings or opinions about a particular subject. Editorials or columns in newspapers and personal essays tend to rely on subjective judgments. George F. Will's "Gambling with the Public's Virtue" (p. 434) or Chuck Stone's "Should Teen-agers Have Free Speech?" (p. 512) are examples of subjective journalism. Writing frequently blends the subjective and objective together. See *Objective*.

Syllogism is a three-step deductive argument including a major premise, a minor premise, and a conclusion. For an illustration, see p. 420.

Thesis is a particular idea or assertion about a subject. Effective writing will always have an explicit or implicit statement of thesis; it is the central and controlling idea, the thread that holds the essay together. Frequently a thesis is stated in a thesis or *topic sentence*. See *Subject*.

Tone refers to a writer's or speaker's attitude toward a subject and audience. Tone reflects human emotions and so can be characterized or described in a wide variety of ways, including serious, sincere, concerned, humorous, sympathetic, ironic, indignant, sarcastic.

Topic sentence is a single sentence in a paragraph that contains a statement of *subject* or *thesis*. The topic sentence is to the paragraph what the thesis statement is to an essay—the thread that holds the whole together, a device to provide clarity and unity. Because paragraphs have various purposes, not every paragraph will have a topic sentence. When they do, topic sentences are frequently found at the beginnings or ends of paragraphs.

Transitions are links or connections made between sentences, paragraphs, or groups of paragraphs. By using transitions, a writer achieves *coherence* and *unity*. Transitional devices include the following:

1. Repeated words, phrases, or clauses.
2. Transitional sentences or paragraphs that act as bridges from one section or idea to the next.
3. Transition-making words and phrases such as those of
   - ADDITION—again, next, furthermore, last
   - TIME—soon, after, then, later, meanwhile
   - COMPARISON—but, still, nonetheless, on the other hand
   - EXAMPLE—for instance, for example
   - CONCLUSION—in conclusion, finally, as a result
   - CONCESSION—granted, of course

Understatement. See *Figures of speech.*

Unity is a oneness in which all of the individual parts of a piece of writing work together to form a cohesive and complete whole. It is best achieved by having a clearly stated *purpose* and *thesis* against which every sentence and paragraph can be tested for relevance.

Thematic Table of Contents

Autobiography and Biography

Children and Family

Contemporary Issues

Culture and Customs

History and Law

Humor and Satire

Men and Women

Minority Experience

Nature and the Environment

Psychology and Behavior

Reading, Writing, and Language

School and College

Science and Technology

Self-Discovery

Sports and Leisure

Women

Work and Business

Credits

ROGER ANGELL, "A Baseball," from *Five Seasons*, by Roger Angell. Copyright © 1972, 1973, 1974, 1975, 1976 by Roger Angell. Reprinted by permission of Simon & Schuster, Inc.

MAYA ANGELOU, "Sister Monroe," from *I Know Why the Caged Bird Sings* by Maya Angelou. Copyright © 1969 by Maya Angelou. Reprinted by permission of Random House, Inc.

RUSSELL BAKER, "Computer Fallout." Copyright © 1987 by The New York Times Company. Reprinted by permission.

BERNARD BERELSON, "The Value of Children: A Taxonomical Essay," reprinted with the permission of the Population Council from *The Population Council Annual Report 1972*, pp. 19–25.

THEODORE M. BERNSTEIN, "Clichés," from *The Careful Writer: A Modern Guide to English Usage*. Copyright © 1965 by Theodore M. Bernstein. Reprinted with the permission of Atheneum Publishers, an imprint of Macmillan Publishing Company.

SUSAN BROWNMILLER, "Femininity," from *Femininity*, copyright © 1984 by Susan Brownmiller. Reprinted by permission of Linden Press, a division of Simon & Schuster, Inc.

BRUCE CATTON, "Grant and Lee: A Study in Contrasts," from *The American Story*, edited by Earl Schenck Miers. By permission of U.S. Capital Historical Society.

JOAN DIDION, "Marrying Absurd" and "On Keeping a Notebook," from *Slouching Towards Bethlehem* by Joan Didion. Copyright © 1966, 1967, 1968 by Joan Didion. Reprinted by permission of Farrar, Straus and Giroux, Inc.

ANNIE DILLARD, "The Copperhead and the Mosquito," copyright © 1974 by *Harper's* Magazine. All rights reserved.

HARRY EDWARDS, "Educating Black Athletes," as originally published in the August, 1983 issue of *The Atlantic Monthly*. By permission of Harry Edwards, Ph.D., Dept. of Sociology, University of California, Berkeley.

LOREN EISELEY, "The Secret of Life." Copyright © 1953 by Loren Eiseley. Reprinted from *The Immense Journey* by Loren Eiseley, by permission of Random House, Inc.

PETER ELBOW, "Quick Revising," from *Writing with Power: Techniques for Mastering the Writing Process* by Peter Elbow. Copyright © 1981 by Oxford University Press, Inc. Reprinted by permission.

NORA EPHRON, "Revision and Life: Take It From the Top—Again," from *The New York Times Book Review*, Nov. 9, 1986. Copyright © 1986 by The New York Times Company. Reprinted by permission.

JOSEPH EPSTEIN, "Confessions of a Low Roller," reprinted from *The American Scholar*, Volume 57, Number 1, Winter, 1988. Copyright © 1988 by the author. By permission of the publisher.

M. F. K. FISHER, "Young Hunger," from *As They Were* by M. F. K. Fisher. Copyright © 1982 by M. F. K. Fisher. Reprinted by permission of Alfred A. Knopf, Inc.

E. M. FORSTER, abridged as "My Wood" in *Abinger Harvest*, copyright © 1936, 1964 by Edward Morgan Forster. Reprinted by permission of Harcourt Brace Jovanovich, Inc.

GAIL GODWIN, "To Noble Companions." Copyright © 1973 by *Harper's* Magazine. All rights reserved. Reprinted from the August 1973 issue by special permission.

BOB GREENE, "Cut." Reprinted by permission of Sterling Lord Literistic, Inc. Copyright © 1984.

EDWARD T. HALL, "English and American Concepts of Space," excerpted from chapter XI of *The Hidden Dimension* by Edward T. Hall. Copyright © 1966 by Edward T. Hall. Reprinted by permission of Doubleday & Company, Inc.

WILLIAM LEAST HEAT MOON, "Nameless, Tennessee," from *Blue Highways: A Journey into America* by William Least Heat Moon. Copyright © 1982 by William Least Heat Moon. Reprinted by permission of Little, Brown and Company in association with the Atlantic Monthly Press.

LANGSTON HUGHES, "Salvation," from *The Big Sea* by Langston Hughes. Copyright 1940 by Langston Hughes. Copyright renewed © 1968 by Arna Bontemps and George Houston Bass. Reprinted by permission of Hill and Wang, a division of Farrar, Straus and Giroux, Inc.

JESSE JACKSON, "Why Blacks Need Affirmative Action." From *Regulation*, September/October 1978, pp. 28–29. By permission of American Enterprise Institute for Public Policy Research.

MARTIN LUTHER KING, JR., "I Have a Dream." Reprinted by permission of Joan Daves. Copyright © 1963 by Martin Luther King, Jr.

ROBIN LAKOFF, "You Are What You Say," *Ms* Magazine, July 1974. Reprinted by permission.

FRAN LEBOWITZ, "A Manual: Training for Landlords." From *Metropolitan Life* by Fran Lebowitz. Copyright © 1974, 1975, 1976, 1977, 1978 by Fran Lebowitz. Reprinted by permission of the publisher, E. P. Dutton, a division of NAL Penguin Inc.

ALISON LURIE, "American Regional Costume," from *The Language of Clothes* by Alison Lurie. Copyright © 1981 by Alison Lurie. Reprinted by permission of Random House, Inc.

JOHN MCPHEE, excerpt from *Oranges* by John McPhee. Copyright © 1966, 1967 by John McPhee. Reprinted by permission of Farrar, Straus and Giroux, Inc.

MARYA MANNES, "Wasteland," from *More in Anger* by Marya Mannes. Copyright 1958 by Marya Mannes. Reprinted by permission of Lippincott.

MARY MEBANE, "Shades of Black," from *Mary* by Mary Mebane. Copyright © 1981 by Mary Elizabeth Mebane. Reprinted by permission of Viking Penguin Inc.

SAMUEL ELIOT MORISON, "Victory in the Pacific," from *Oxford History of the American People*. Reprinted by permission of Curtis Brown, Ltd. Copyright © 1965 by Gilbert Highet.

CULLEN MURPHY, "Going to the Cats." © 1987, Cullen Murphy, as originally published in the August, 1987 issue of *The Atlantic Monthly*.

GEORGE ORWELL, "Politics and the English Language" by George Orwell, copyright 1946 by Sonia Brownell Orwell, renewed 1974 by Sonia Orwell, reprinted from *Shooting an Elephant and Other Essays* by George Orwell. By permission of Harcourt Brace Jovanovich, Inc.

WILLIAM OUCHI, "Why We Need to Learn," from *Theory Z* by William Ouchi. © 1981, Addison-Wesley, Reading, Massachusetts. Pgs. 3, 4, 5 & 6. Reprinted with permission.

NOEL PERRIN, "Maple Recipes for Simpletons," from *Second Person Rural*. Copyright © 1980 by Noel Perrin. Reprinted by permission of David R. Godine, Publisher, Inc.

LAURENCE PERRINE, "Escape and Interpretive Literature." Excerpt from "Escape and Interpretation" in *Literature: Structure, Sound and Sense*, 4th Edition, edited by

Laurence Perrine, copyright © 1967 by Harcourt Brace Jovanovich, Inc., reprinted by permission of the publisher.

ANDREW C. REVKIN, "Hard Facts About Nuclear Winter." Reprinted by permission of *Science Digest*. © 1985 by The Hearst Corporation. All rights reserved.

RICHARD RODRIGUEZ, "None of This Is Fair," copyright © 1977 by Richard Rodriguez. Reprinted by permission of the author.

WILLIAM SAFIRE, "Words for Nerds." Copyright © 1968 by The New York Times Company. Reprinted by permission.

SCOTT RUSSELL SANDERS, "The Inheritance of Tools," reprinted from *The Paradise of Bombs*, published by The University of Georgia Press. © 1987 by Scott Russell Sanders. Reprinted by permission of the author.

PHYLLIS SCHLAFLY, "Understanding the Difference," reprinted from *The Power of the Positive Woman* by Phyllis Schlafly. © 1977 by Phyllis Schlafly. Used by permission of Arlington Press, Inc.

ADAM SMITH, "Everyday Drugs." From *Powers of Mind* by Adam Smith. Copyright © 1975 by Adam Smith. Reprinted by permission of Random House, Inc.

GLORIA STEINEM, "Why Young Women Are More Conservative." From *Outrageous Acts and Everyday Rebellions* by Gloria Steinem. Copyright © 1983 by Gloria Steinem. Reprinted by permission of Henry Holt and Company, Inc.

CHUCK STONE, "Should Teen-agers Have Free Speech?" From the *Philadelphia Daily News*. Copyright © by the *Philadelphia Daily News*. Reprinted by permission.

JUDY SYFERS, "I Want a Wife" from "Why I Want a Wife," by Judy Syfers, *Ms.* Magazine, December 31, 1971.

LEWIS THOMAS, "On Medicine and the Bomb," from *Late Night Thoughts on Listening to Mahler's Ninth Symphony* by Lewis Thomas. Copyright © 1981 by Lewis Thomas. Reprinted by permission of Viking Penguin Inc.

LEWIS THOMAS, "On Societies as Organisms." From *The Lives of a Cell* by Lewis Thomas. Copyright © 1974 by Lewis Thomas. All rights reserved. Reprinted by permission of Viking Penguin Inc.

SUSAN ALLEN TOTH, "Cinematypes." Copyright © 1980 by *Harper's* Magazine. All rights reserved. Reprinted from the May 1980 issue with special permission.

SUSAN ALLEN TOTH, "Up, Up and Away," from *Ivy Days: Making My Way Out East* by Susan Allen Toth. Copyright © 1984 by Susan Allen Toth. By permission of Little, Brown and Company.

CARLL TUCKER, "Fear of Dearth," © 1979 *Saturday Review* Magazine. Reprinted by permission.

AMY VANDERBILT AND LETITIA BALDRIGE, "A Woman Picks Up the Tab" from *The Amy Vanderbilt Complete Book of Etiquette, Revised and Expanded by Letitia Baldrige*. Copyright © 1978 by Curtis B. Kellar and Lincoln G. Clark, Executors of the Estate of Amy Vanderbilt Kellar, and Doubleday & Company, Inc. Copyright © 1952, 1954, 1955, 1956, 1958, 1963, 1967, 1972 by Curtis B. Kellar and Lincoln G. Clark, Executors of the Estate of Amy Vanderbilt Kellar. Reprinted by permission of Doubleday & Company, Inc.

JAMES VILLAS, "E Pluribus Onion." Copyright © 1985 by James Villas. This article first appeared in *Town & Country* Magazine. Reprinted by permission of Robin Straus Agency, Inc.

JUDITH VIORST, "How Books Helped Shape My Life." Copyright © 1980 by Judith Viorst. Originally appeared in *Redbook*.

ANDREW WARD, "Yumbo" (excerpt). Copyright © 1977 by Andrew Ward. First published in *The Atlantic Monthly*, May, 1977. Excerpted by permission.

E. B. WHITE, "Democracy," from *The Wild Flag*, editorials from *The New Yorker* by E. B. White. © 1943, 1971 by E. B. White. Reprinted by permission of Houghton Mifflin.

E. B. WHITE, "Once More to the Lake," from *Essays of E. B. White.* Reprinted by permission of Harper & Row, Publishers, Inc.

WILLIAM ALLEN WHITE, "Mary White," in *America Is West,* edited by John Flannagan. © 1945 University of Minnesota Press, St. Paul.

GEORGE WILL, "Gambling with the Public's Virtue," from *The Pursuit of Virtue and Other Tory Notions* by George Will. Copyright © 1982 by The Washington Post Company. Reprinted by permission of Simon & Schuster, Inc.

MARIE WINN, "Television Viewing as an Addiction," from *The Plug-in Drug* by Marie Winn. Copyright © 1977 by Marie Winn Miller. All rights reserved. Reprinted by permission of Viking Penguin Inc.

TOM WOLFE, "A Sunday Kind of Love" (excerpt) from *The Kandy-Kolored Tangerine-Flake Streamline Baby* by Tom Wolfe. Copyright © 1964 by Thomas K. Wolfe, Jr. Copyright © 1964 by New York Herald Tribune, Inc.

VIRGINIA WOOLF, "Professions for Women," from *The Death of the Moth and Other Essays*; copyright 1942 by Harcourt Brace Jovanovich, Inc., renewed 1970 by Marjorie T. Parsons, Executrix; reprinted by permission of Harcourt Brace Jovanovich, Inc.

WILLIAM ZINSSER, "The Transaction," from *On Writing Well,* 2d ed., published by Harper & Row. Copyright © 1980 by William K. Zinsser. Reprinted by permission of the author.